SAGE was founded in 1965 by Sara Miller McCune to support the dissemination of usable knowledge by publishing innovative and high-quality research and teaching content. Today, we publish over 900 journals, including those of more than 400 learned societies, more than 800 new books per year, and a growing range of library products including archives, data, case studies, reports, and video. SAGE remains majority-owned by our founder, and after Sara's lifetime will become owned by a charitable trust that secures our continued independence.

Los Angeles | London | New Delhi | Singapore | Washington DC | Melbourne

Advance Praise

Devaki Jain has been a pioneer in bringing to light gender inequalities and injustices in India for the past several decades. She was one of the first to highlight through her Time Use Study (included in this volume), women's significant contributions to not just reproductive and care work in India, but to production as well. She has also worked closely with the UN system to ensure women's rights are taken on board in policy and practice.

The first volume *The Journey of a Southern Feminist* contains the speeches and writings of Devaki on various occasions. The present second volume contains papers of more recent origin. She broadly deals with the gender dimensions of poverty and political and social power. The papers have a Gandhian touch with as much attention to ethics and equity as to economics. The final essay in this book titled 'The New World Re-order' is an appropriate term to indicate the potential for creating order from disorder. In short, Devaki's writings and speeches have dominated public and political thinking on gender issues during this century. I commend Volume II and recommend that everyone interested in gender dimensions of our life should read both Volumes I and II.

Professor M.S. Swaminathan
Founder Chairman and Chief Mentor
UNESCO Chair in Ecotechnology
M.S. Swaminathan Research Foundation

Close Encounters
of Another Kind

Close Encounters of Another Kind

Women and Development Economics

Devaki Jain

Los Angeles | London | New Delhi
Singapore | Washington DC | Melbourne

First published in 2018 by

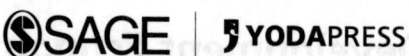

SAGE Publications India Pvt Ltd
B1/I-1 Mohan Cooperative Industrial Area
Mathura Road, New Delhi 110 044, India
www.sagepub.in

SAGE Publications Inc
2455 Teller Road
Thousand Oaks, California 91320, USA

SAGE Publications Ltd
1 Oliver's Yard, 55 City Road
London EC1Y 1SP, United Kingdom

SAGE Publications Asia-Pacific Pte Ltd
3 Church Street
#10-04 Samsung Hub
Singapore 049483

Published by Vivek Mehra for SAGE Publications India Pvt Ltd, typeset in 10.5/13 pts Bembo by Zaza Eunice, Hosur, Tamil Nadu, India and printed at Chaman Enterprises, New Delhi.

Library of Congress Cataloging-in-Publication Data Available

ISBN: 978-93-528-0771-0 (HB)

SAGE Yoda Team: Amrita Dutta, Guneet Kaur Gulati, Ishita Gupta, Arpita Das and Tanya Singh

Fatema Mernissi—the most brilliant and courageous feminist from the South

(27 September 1940–30 November 2015)

Thank you for choosing a SAGE product!
If you have any comment, observation or feedback,
I would like to personally hear from you.

Please write to me at **contactceo@sagepub.in**

Vivek Mehra, Managing Director and CEO, SAGE India.

Bulk Sales

SAGE India offers special discounts
for purchase of books in bulk.
We also make available special imprints
and excerpts from our books on demand.

For orders and enquiries, write to us at

Marketing Department
SAGE Publications India Pvt Ltd
B1/I-1, Mohan Cooperative Industrial Area
Mathura Road, Post Bag 7
New Delhi 110044, India

E-mail us at **marketing@sagepub.in**

Get to know more about SAGE

Be invited to SAGE events, get on our mailing list.
Write today to **marketing@sagepub.in**

This book is also available as an e-book.

Contents

List of Tables

List of Figures

List of Abbreviations

ASEAN	Association of Southeast Asian Nations
BRICS	Brazil, Russia, India, China and South Africa
CIS	Commonwealth of Independent States
DAWN	Development Alternatives with Women for a New Era
ESCAP	Economic and Social Commission for Asia and the Pacific
FAO	Food and Agriculture Organization
FDI	Foreign Direct Investment
FWPR	Female Work Participation Rate
GDI	Gender Development Index
GDP	Gross Domestic Product
GEM	Gender Empowerment Measure
HDI	Human Development Index
HDR	Human Development Report
IBSA	India, Brazil, South Africa
ICSSR	Indian Council of Social Science Research
ILO	International Labour Organization
ISST	Institute of Social Studies Trust
IT	Information Technology
IMF	International Monetary Fund
KVIC	Khadi and Village Industries Commission
LDCs	Less Developed Countries
MNC	Multinational Corporation
NAM	Non-Aligned Movement

NBA	Narmada Bachao Andolan
NFHS	National Family Health Survey
NGO	Non-Governmental Organisation
NREGA	National Rural Employment Guarantee Act
NRI	Non-Resident Indian
NSS	National Sample Survey
NSSO	National Sample Survey Organisation
OECD	Organisation for Economic Co-operation and Development
PDS	Public Distribution System
SADC	South African Development Community
SEWA	Self-Employed Women's Association
SHG	Self-Help Group
SNA	System of National Accounts
SPWD	Society for Promotion of Wasteland Development
TFR	Total Fertility Rate
UN	United Nations
UNCTAD	United Nations Conference on Trade and Development
UNDP	United Nations Development Programme
UNESCO	United Nations Educational, Scientific and Cultural Organization
UNFPA	United Nations Population Fund
UNICEF	United Nations Children's Fund
UNRISD	United Nations Research Institute for Social Development
UNU-WIDER	United Nations University, World Institute for Development Economics Research
WDR	World Development Report
WTO	World Trade Organization

Acknowledgements

My first expression of gratitude for the work that is expressed as chapters in this volume is to the Institute of Social Studies Trust, where we started our engagement with women and development as far back as 1979. The field-based uncovering we undertook of women's roles in the economy was the knowledge base that led me to many of my papers and reflections after I retired in 1993. Four out of the 15 essays in this volume were prepared prior to my retirement.[1]

These volumes of some of my work could not have appeared in this form if it were not for Arpita Das of Yoda Press. Since many of the articles had already been published and were available in one form or the other, it never occurred to me to pull them all together in a volume.

Secondly, knowing how much publishers demand from the author in terms of preparatory work before publication, I baulked at the idea of going back and doing all that digging and pruning. But Arpita not only visited me and went through papers but also exclaimed that the papers were good! This was encouraging and she nurtured me by providing every kind of support, including an outstanding editor. So to Arpita Das, Ishita Gupta (her colleague at Yoda Press), and to my editor, Aruna Ramachandran, my first *namaskaram*.

But while Arpita's encouragement was critical, another critical support was provided by my colleague of the last three years, Neha S Chaudhry, an MPhil in Women and Gender Studies from Ambedkar University, Delhi. She was willing to do what my generation used to do, that is, tighten their saree/pull up their pants and work diligently and do multitasking. This work of digging out and sorting these old papers, of which almost 50 per cent were never typed, took us nearly a year, and half of the previous year when we shifted the office from one apartment to another. During this time she boxed them carefully in categories so that when we opened them in the new office, to bring out this book, there was a certain time advantage. So to Neha S Chaudhry, a rock, standing by me throughout, my second *namaskaram*.

But we realised that it was not enough to have only one person, because there was not only typing to be done but sorting and finding references and so on. So we got on board Smit Gadhia, an MA in Philosophy and also trained in English Literature. She had earlier helped us with the exhibition that was organised on Kamaladevi's life. She worked with us for a year and a half and gave the preparation of these volumes a big push. So to Smit Gadhia, my *namaskaram*.

But of course, all the support of people like Neha S Chaudhry, Smit Gadhia, Purushottam Sharma and Jasleen Arora could not have happened without the extraordinary support of my son Gopal Jain and his partner, Smriti Mishra. They not only gave me an absolutely lovely office attached to Gopal's chambers, but also the financial support for employing my support staff. My *namaskaram*s to them.

NOTE

1 Reproduced as chapters 1, 2, 3 and 4 in this volume.

Publisher's Acknowledgements

Chapter 1, 'Letting the Worm Turn: A Comment on Innovative Poverty Alleviation', earlier published in William P. Lineberry (ed.), *Assessing Participatory Development: Rhetoric versus Reality* (Boulder, CO: Westview Press, 1989).[1]

Chapter 2, 'Development Theory and Practice: Insights Emerging from Women's Experience', *Economic & Political Weekly*, vol. 25, no. 27 (1990), pp. 1454–55.

Chapter 3, 'Gender and Poverty in India: Comment on a World Bank Country Study', A Paper read out at a discussion on Lyn Bennett's paper on poverty, Institute of Social Studies Trust, December 1991.

Chapter 4, 'Healing the Wounds of Development', in Jill Ker Conway and Susan C. Bourque (eds), *The Politics of Women's Education: Perspectives from Asia, Africa, and Latin America* (Ann Arbor: University of Michigan Press, 1993), pp. 45–58.

Chapter 5, 'Valuing Work: Time as a Measure', (with Malini Chand Seth), *Economic & Political Weekly*, vol. 31, no. 43 (1996), pp. WS46–WS57.

Chapter 6, 'Nuancing Globalisation, or Mainstreaming the Downstream, or Reforming Reform', Nita Barrow Memorial Lecture,

---

[1] This chapter was first published in the volume *Assessing Participatory Development: Rhetoric versus Reality* (Boulder, CO: Westview Press, 1989). Despite best efforts to contact the editor of the volume, William P. Lineberry, the author has been unable to reach him. The chapter is being reproduced here in good faith.

Centre for Gender and Development Studies, University of the West Indies, Barbados, November 1999.

Chapter 7, 'Food Battles, or Battling for Food', United Nations Human Rights Council, Session 16, Geneva, 9 March 2011.

Chapter 8, 'Are We Knowledge-Proof? Development as Waste', Lovraj Kumar Memorial Lecture, Society for Promotion of Wastelands Development, New Delhi, 26 September 2003, published in *Wastelands News*, vol. 19, no. 1 (2003), pp. 19–30.

Chapter 9, 'A View from the South: A Story of Intersections', in by Arvonne S. Fraser and Irene Tinker (eds), *Developing Power: How Women Transformed International Development* (New York: The Feminist Press at the City University of New York, 2004), pp. 128–37.

Chapter 10, 'Women, Public Policy and the New World Order', Lecture delivered at Jagori and Sangat, India Habitat Centre, 2 May 2006.

Chapter 11, 'Growth, Poverty and Inequality: The Linkages and Relevance of Macro-economic Policies', Paper presented at the UNDP Gender Equality, Economic Growth and Poverty Reduction Expert Group Meeting, Essex University, 21–22 June 2007.

Chapter 12, 'Walking Together: The Journey of the Non-Aligned Movement and the Women's Movement' (with Shubha Chacko), *Development in Practice*, vol. 19, no. 7 (2009), pp. 895–905. Available at: https://www.tandfonline.com/doi/full/10.1080/09614520903122337

Chapter 13, 'Morals in Politics: The Gandhian Touch', *Man in India*, vol. 89, no. 4 (2010), pp. 543–55.

Chapter 14, 'Exploring Economic Inequality: From Piketty through Adiga to Gandhi', Lecture delivered at Azim Premji University, Bangalore.

Chapter 15, 'The New World Re-order: An Opportunity to Build a Feminist Political Economy', Paper presented at IAFFE Conference held in Hangzhou, China, 24–26 June 2011.

Introduction
Development Is Not Benign

The term 'development'—in my view, one of the legacies of empire—undermined if not destroyed the road to progress for the former colonies. 'Underdevelopment' (most ex-colonies were called 'underdeveloped countries') really meant that their resources, including land, minerals, water and forests, were not being used fully. It was argued by leading economists that developing these resources, mainly natural resources, and putting them to use would generate opportunities for citizens through growth in employment and gross domestic product (GDP). This exploitation of unused resources, however, did not lead to a transformation in the lives of the majority of the population. In fact, it could be argued with hindsight that it led to the destruction of many natural resources.

When I look back at the lectures and papers that I prepared during the 1980s and 1990s, I can see that I was taking an anti-development stance. I had taken the position that the idea and substance of 'development' were not necessarily enabling of economic and social progress. However, whatever evaluations were emerging from the ground, 'development', like a robot, like an exterminator, was marching over the people. Knowledge that was being generated from the ground level was not being translated into development design.

My argument was that the situation confronting what can be called the 'last woman'—those at the ground level, the excluded—was due to the logic of economics, or the economic policies that were being designed, and the measures used to indicate progress, such as GDP, not only at the national but even the international level. Development was being seen basically as an economic issue, but was being designed usually far away from the beneficiaries. And, when India implemented the 74th Amendment to its Constitution and set up elected councils at the village level and other tiers of government, I argued that it was only such political councils, and women's participation in them, that could ensure that the design and substance of development at the local level bore their footprint.

In my opinion, globally accepted ideas on how to generate economic prosperity, namely GDP growth, have been responsible for the persistence of poverty and inequality. The logic of 'progress', and the idea that progress can only be capital- and profit-led, were deeply affecting the masses. We were constantly reminding ourselves, be it at gatherings of grassroots women's organisations or at the level of the United Nations Development Programme (UNDP) and the universities, that it was these theories of economic growth, ideas on how to build the GDP, that were responsible for poverty and inequality. While I referred to Thomas Piketty's analysis of the extraordinary phenomenon of self-perpetuating inequality, my argument was directed towards the women's movement to emphasise that what was required was to attack mainstream macro-economic reasoning and rebuild this reasoning from the facts, from the ground as studied and understood by the women's movement.

In 1985, India hosted the first Non-Aligned Movement (NAM) World Conference on Women. An idea developed by the former colonies, NAM was a way of getting out of the East–West locking of horns. It was founded by some of the greatest freedom fighters of the former colonies—Jawaharlal Nehru from India, Gamal Abdel Nasser from Egypt, Josip Broz Tito from Yugoslavia, Sukarno from Indonesia and Kwame Nkrumah from Ghana. It offered a space for the former colonies to develop their own political economy agenda, and also to have an opinion on various international manoeuvres.

By and large, women were not engaged in the political processes, but a remarkable Yugoslavian woman politician, Vida Tomsic, opened a window to mobilising the women of NAM countries to develop their own view and to present it during world conferences and debates.[1] Through participating in the NAM Conference on Women, women's movements learned to understand and to have a sense of belonging to the political umbrella under which they worked. Even though by

1995 the NAM movement had gradually withered away, it was my belief that NAM had offered a platform for the women's movements of the South.

While inequality, poverty, and their continued existence were a preoccupation, along with the inaccurate measures for the work of poor women, it was necessary also to look at macro-economic programmes, especially the projects that were designed to remove poverty. In the early days of India's post-independence development design, some of the principal ideas and practices for removing poverty that were being considered involved a focus on work and wage. It could be argued that this was the legacy of Gandhi who, with his khadi programme, had insisted that every household should be able to earn its bread through its labour. Thus, broad-based employment programmes were one of the first goals of the policy and programmes undertaken by the Government of India in the 1950s.

While currently the National Rural Employment Guarantee Act (NREGA) is seen as the strong arm of support to remove poverty, as far back as the 1970s, the state of Maharashtra had implemented a programme to give anyone who wished to earn a wage the right to demand work—the Maharashtra Employment Guarantee Programme. But as we found in many such well-meaning programmes, women were not counted correctly, nor was their labour valued fairly. What is now coming to light through NREGA had been uncovered as early as 1979 by a study of the Maharashtra programme. There had been doubt regarding whether women would be able to leave their homes and children and come out to engage in what can be called a public works programme. But the reality was that not only did the women come out in large numbers, sometimes as high as 40 per cent, they often came out to complete jobs that men had left undone in order to earn the wage that was paid. Yet the fact that it was women who were participating did not lead to any change in the design of the programme, especially in the infrastructure provided, such as crèches or the provision of water on the site.

These challenges continue even today—the gaps within programmes that enable women, the question of wage parity, and the question of providing supportive social infrastructure. Any programme—micro or macro, national or international—addressed to the poor needs to be looked at through a gender lens, since not only are women the poorest amongst the poor, they are also the main breadwinners in poor households, the ones who could sacrifice anything in order to bring bread to their families. Therefore, I often argued that focusing on women as the genome that activates success in programme and policy could be the nucleus that would turn around the economy, from one overwhelmed by poverty and unemployment despite attractive GDP growth figures, to one that could sustain itself.

My involvement in the North–South conflict, as I saw it, led me to the view that the South needed to affirm itself and challenge the overwhelming intellectual as well as financial pressure of the North. This led to a great number of speaking engagements all over the world. Whether it was in Manila at the Asian Development Bank or at the World Women's Congress held in Uganda, I could not stop appealing for South–South co-operation, South–South interaction, to redesign economics as well as the content of development.

Another abiding theme was calling attention to the importance of engaging with poverty, especially as experienced by women, but without perceiving it as an issue which required patronising—in other words, viewing the poor not as clients but as agents of change. I often quoted Amartya Sen's classic advice:

> We need a vision of mankind not as patients whose interests have to be looked after, but as agents who can do effective things—both individually and jointly. We also have to go beyond the role of human beings as 'consumers' or as 'people with needs', and consider, more broadly, their general role as agents of change who can—given the opportunity—think, assess, evaluate, resolve, reshape the world.[2]

At the ISST, a small research institute in India, we had undertaken a multitude of studies and surveys, and held many dialogues with women in poverty at the ground level. Simultaneously, the World Bank and other major international agencies were obsessed with poverty and its removal. I suggested that poverty could not be removed in the way one would pick flowers. If we could look not only at women's experience of poverty, but at the ideas with which they were trying to overcome it, we might find a better way out of that terrible experience.

Constantly upturning theories and propositions not only became my practice, but it also seemed the only way to move ahead. The notion that the poor needed to be enabled out of poverty through ideas that were being constructed by the benefactors haunted me. It invariably turned out to be an oppressive arrangement.

The women's movement was struggling to open the eyes of policy makers and practitioners to gender differences in all areas of life—health, education, well-being, work spaces, the entire gamut of life. But not surprisingly, the macro-economic system, the set of ideas that triggered policy, was not a part of their consideration in the goal of removing poverty and realising a moral and equitable political economy. The women's movement was active on the ground, making changes, designing innovative ways in which poverty and inequality could be removed. It seems necessary for the women's movement to take stock of the ideas and theories behind macro-economic policy and to mobilise their voice and their creativity to change that, i.e., change the reasoning, the theory that informs the policy.

Whether it was at ESCAP, the United Nations (UN) regional office in Bangkok, or in New Delhi, my theme became alerting the grassroots women's movement to what I call 'the sky'. That the sky was falling down on them, and our effort now should be to use our creativity not only for grassroots change but also to develop theoretical ideas and formulate an alternative economics which would ensure a more equitable and sustainable economic path. This became a central theme with me, namely the importance of reconstructing economic theory, shedding the preoccupation with the GDP, showing in fact that the GDP was an erroneous measure and that its rate of growth was not an enabling measure of a better life.

Economic growth and inequality became the focus of some attention from feminist movements, particularly through dismantling existing ideas and rebuilding new ones based on the learning from grounded surveys and grassroots connections. While the work of Thomas Piketty exploded onto the scene and obsessed the minds of policy makers and

practitioners, these were not new findings. That inequality is perpetuated by the unequal distribution of power, and that the nexus between
political power and economic power makes for an unbeatable adversary,
had been pointed out by feminist economists. Ways in which this could
be attacked had also been pointed out by several thought leaders. On
this issue, I always find a source of inspiration in Gandhi. Economic
growth and the salesmanship around it by most of the world's leading
economic thinkers, I felt, had to be challenged.

It seemed that even though there were many suggestions from the
field of economics itself on how to handle inequality, the particular
phenomenon as it appeared in poor countries could not be contained
or overpowered without reference to the moral sense of individuals,
of citizens. Tangible inequality, a growing monster in the world, is
rendering all spaces conflict-ridden. The speed and starkness with
which it is exhibiting itself is the outcome of a particular form of
economic globalisation where political economies are driven by the
purely hedonistic basis of economic progress, namely the growth of the
monetised domestic product. In this context, Gandhi offers a doable
political economy where the ethical underpinnings of progress drive
the economy on a non-violent road to well-being.

There has always been concern about how to elicit recognition of
what is happening in the economies of the South, as well as the kinds
of responses that partners and policy makers in the South countries are
putting forward. While the focus on feminist economics arrived on
the international stage with the International Association for Feminist
Economics, the preoccupation of the larger majority of feminist economists in these associations has been with gender issues, with particular
reference to the economies of the North.

Dramatic changes in the distribution of global economic power were
vividly displayed by the outcome of the 2008 global economic crisis.
While the GDP growth rates of the majority of Northern economies
were at an abysmal low, India and China blazed forward at GDP growth
rates of 8 per cent, calling attention to the changing global economic
order. These economies were named 'emerging economies'. Their
arrival on the world economic stage has huge implications for the rest
of the world, especially for women. It is necessary for international

networks of feminist economists to engage with this new phenomenon, which offers a great opportunity to understand the gender dimension in the fast-growing countries. This becomes particularly interesting as China is a clearly socialist economy, whereas India is still acutely a democratic polity where the playing fields are dominated by the private sector apart from the state. What are the gender implications of this difference? It seems worthwhile not only to examine this, but also to use this analysis to critique the current economic growth model.

The essays in this volume are focused more on macro policies and the overall ideas behind development design. In the process of using a gender lens to critique or reformulate or even reconstruct what ideas might be more benign than those currently in use, certain signals emerge. The importance of data becomes evident—not only how it is collected and therefore what it conceals, but which data are used for which purposes. So much design and policy and even ideology are built on data; yet if data are not only incorrect but are not inclusive of phenomena that go unrecognised, then the effect is highly misleading. Yet since data determine rational choice, the struggle to rectify the errors becomes that much more challenging.

NOTES

1. Devaki Jain, *Women, Development and the UN: A Sixty-Year Quest for Equality and Justice* (Bloomington: Indiana University Press, 2005), p. 121.
2. Amartya Sen, 'The Ends and Means of Sustainability', Keynote Address, International Conference on 'Transition to Sustainability in the 21st Century', Inter Academy Panel on International Issues, Tokyo, May 2000.

Chapter 1

Letting the Worm Turn
A Comment on Innovative Poverty Alleviation*

With increasing knowledge on development projects in developing countries, there were many reflections on the 'how to' of removing poverty. Case studies were prepared by agencies from the World Bank down to state governments on what were called 'successful models of poverty alleviation'. Usually these were initiatives or ground-level projects that had been implemented by non-governmental agencies. These projects were called 'innovative poverty alleviation projects'.

However, the overarching focus on these successful projects was such that they were made into models, and an attempt was made to replicate them everywhere. My argument was that if we saw this as the worm turning the soil, it was better to allow it to turn that soil and spread for a while before intervening in the process. Hasty imitation and rubber-stamping of these innovative attempts would actually lead to their demise.

The growth in the number of poor has not only been analysed, theorised and acted upon with varying degrees of commitment, but is a living witness to the overall failure of these efforts. That the problem is still confronting us shows that the cause lies somewhere else. Perhaps

---

* This chapter was first published in the volume *Assessing Participatory Development: Rhetoric versus Reality* (Boulder, CO: Westview Press, 1989). Despite best efforts to contact the editor of the volume, William P. Lineberry, the author has been unable to reach him. The chapter is being reproduced here in good faith.

it is a reflection on human beings themselves, that we can tolerate our own existence side by side with human misery.

When I further reflect on the situation of women—how across cultures and even classes and over history, women do not receive recognition for the value that they so openly provide to society—I am baffled. It is a kind of colour blindness or tone deafness.

But having found that the hard fist of insensitivity to women's worth is impossible to open, I can better understand our failure to remove poverty from the human condition. Unless humans change—become more sensitive to personal ethics—perhaps the kind of transformation we need today both locally and globally will never happen. We need to bring issues of personal ethics, lifestyle, religion and culture to the centre of approaches to poverty alleviation. We must look to our inner spaces—a far more difficult task than rearranging the outer. I used to say that women are the missing link in development. Now I would say that the ethic of the individual, or personal ethics, is the missing factor.

In this paper, I propose to examine the following issues:

1. While non-governmental organisations (NGOs), especially those working with poor women, have demonstrated cost-and-achievement-effective approaches to poverty alleviation, the ultimate responsibility for removing poverty remains with the state. The approach must be generalised if we are serious about the elimination of poverty.
2. Lively initiatives taken on behalf of poor women illuminate sustainable ways and means of improving their status and reducing poverty, but also pose a challenge to accepted theory. In this respect, specific concerns need to take a back seat to process and methodology.
3. Barriers to the paradigms we all suggest and want—local, participatory, self-strengthening, durable paradigms—are not only erected by the so-called vested interests, or by the rich, but by development theory itself—by the values buried in development theory and expressed not only in International Monetary Fund (IMF)–World Bank restructuring packages, but even in seemingly innocuous interventions such as monitoring and evaluation.

Some illustrations from India's experience will help to throw light on these views.

WOMEN AND ANTI-POVERTY PROGRAMMES

In 1984, the Institute of Social Studies Trust (ISST), Bangalore, undertook a study[1] to assess how far the government's anti-poverty schemes, especially designed for the poor, had reached poor women. There was an ongoing debate over whether some reserved quota, either in finance or in 'jobs' in the recipient community, whether some positive form of discrimination, would be necessary to raise the socio-economic level of women.

Twenty schemes targeted at households below the poverty line (approximately US$300 per household per annum) were selected. An 'advanced' locale and a 'backward' locale[2] were chosen for field studies within the state of Karnataka, to see if a general condition of growth and social advancement offered a better field for women's advancement. Conventional indices for advancement/backwardness were used. These included six broad categories—demographics, occupational patterns, land utilisation, agricultural, industrial and infrastructural development.

The study used data from a household survey based on purposive sampling, and from secondary official sources as well as group discussions. The broad pictures were provided by official data, both macro and local, as well as official and academic studies. The analysis revealed that whether it was a poor or a rich area, the benefits of development presumably targeted at the poor had not yet reached these people, irrespective of gender. Apart from the fact that the poor were not made aware of the development schemes reserved for them, the schemes themselves were often unsuited to their needs. It was a world of buzzing functionaries, involving a minute 6–7 per cent of the government's development expenditure.[3]

Among the schemes studied, an attempt was made to provide intensive, earmarked support for tribal populations (also, like women, identified as disadvantaged) by designing and executing tribal sub-plans. These were area-specific programmes. But reviews of the impact of this quota system after 10–15 years revealed that they had failed to reduce the immiserisation of the tribals. The same reasons applied—the gap between the intention and the action, the distance between their aspirations and the design of the official poverty package.

This part of the review led to an interesting question. When 'sub-planning', i.e., reserved budgets for tribal belts, had failed to reduce the immiserisation of tribals, what was the prospect that women would not be led into the same cul-de-sac? This question led the study into an examination of the process of planning and delivery of these programmes. It was found that these indigestible pills were fabricated partly in state capitals, but predominantly in the national capital. They were handed down from above to functionaries to swallow—or to feed to the poor. Issues of gender, therefore, had *ipso facto* to take a back seat to implementation, in terms of both the conceptual framework and the mechanisms of implementation.[4]

In short, the method (top-down) by which the development scheme was designed and implemented prevailed over the aims and objectives. This had little to do with who in government or the non-government sector was doing the implementing, or for whom (i.e., men or women), or with the package or bundle of items being delivered. So much, then, for the attempt to provide earmarked support for tribal populations or anybody else.

WOMEN AGAINST DEVELOPMENT

Another aspect of the study carried out by the ISST focused on poor women, in particular, innovative approaches to poverty alleviation for rural women per se. The study indicated that women tended to organise mainly in resistance against the government's development policy. Women have indeed formed an interesting vanguard in this area. A typical example is provided by the women of the Keithel market in Imphal, who were struggling to prevent the dismantling of their market by the government. Women operate the largest wholesale market in Manipur. It is basically a large platform open on all sides, with a roof, and dominates central Imphal. Urban development experts in New Delhi made a plan for Imphal which included dismantling the market and offering an alternative space to the women. They resisted the dismantling by taking a united stand—including an all-night vigil in cold, wet weather. They won the struggle.

This is not the first time the women of Manipur have been engaged in collective self-defence. The Nupi-Lan was a factor in colonial days, agitating on taxes in the rice trade. During the state of emergency in India, when processions were banned, they marched into Imphal in the thousands demanding the passage of a prohibition bill.[5] These collective resistance actions of Manipuri women are no different from the actions of the Chipko or Khirakhote women, living in Himalayan hamlets, who saved their environment from potential devastation under a development scheme.[6] There are other such examples, and they are not limited to India.

Groups such as the Self-Employed Women's Association (SEWA)[7] and the Working Women's Forum[8] have revealed the strength and viability of poor women's choices when it comes to their economic activity. Strengthening their roles through organisation and the provision of credit has shown not only that their productivity and income can increase, but that women are more creditworthy and more thrifty than men, as well as more easily organised into self-interest groups.[9]

Leaving sex stereotyping aside, the difference in choice of occupations between men and women is essentially due to their domestic responsibilities and the differences in their access to support. This difference reveals innovative survival strategies, some of which can be composed into programmes for sustainable development, through existing documentation on such knowledge and its appropriateness.[10] Water and food storage, kitchen gardening, home-based work, use of trees and their various outputs, disease prevention knowledge and responses to organised management of economic change are some of the areas in which women have shown conserving, viable adaptation.

ASSESSING THE IMPACT OF WOMEN'S STUDIES

Numerous women's studies projects have probed gender differentiation issues, not only in terms of the impact of credit or sectoral development projects, but also in terms of the responses of women to external development impulses (rejection and absorption responses). These studies have exposed inadequacies in concepts and in definitions in the social sciences, and have offered new tools of analysis.[11] Examples, include survey methodology for identifying gainfully active populations on a seasonal basis in agriculture and methods for measuring the energy inputs and outputs of women.[12]

What these studies mainly reveal is that poverty alleviation is a time-consuming process, in which durable success depends on both external support and internal motivation, on both absorption of effective development services as well as resistance to offers of inappropriate development. Success must be evaluated against the backdrop of the degrees of choice offered to the poor, while at the same time leaving room for the poor to devise choices of their own. Of course, this open-ended approach assumes exposure of the poor to all kinds of knowledge, both useful and harmful. For the worm to turn, however, the earth has to be loose, and no bird should sit there waiting to gobble up the worm.

Poverty alleviation is expensive as well as time consuming. The whole earth has to be loosened up and kept resilient so that each effort brings up something a little different by way of progress. In other words, a context of 'loose earth' should deliberately allow a diversity of worm tracks and endeavours. This is the reason why the often successful, apparently simple, low-cost, of-the-poor, by-the-poor, for-the-poor type of project is difficult to adapt for generalisation, either by NGOs or the state. Behind the apparent knock-down simplicity lies enormous expenditure—both material and non-material—but most of all, there is that loose earth encouraging diversity and innovation.

There are several reasons why these successful micro-level projects are not generalisable. One is the charisma and dedication associated with the 'first' experiment which usually cannot be replicated. Another is that the financial as well as ideological investment put into the original is often missing or hard to duplicate.

A third is that certain cultures absorb what others cannot. My view is that the inability to replicate stems from all of these and more. It is the innovative process itself that generates the first success which counts. The impetus, the consciousness raising, the leadership, the muscle and 'heavy weight' that developed the first project dissipates in succeeding ones that seek to duplicate. The well-known pattern of successful milk co-operatives based on smallholders in India—the so-called 'white revolution'—offers some positive guidance in this respect. It shifts responsibility from the state. But it undermines the notion of generalisability. It thus limits to very small pockets the ability of the poor to escape from the poverty trap. The key question is whether the lessons learnt from innovative NGO projects, the shift of focus from, say, merely targeting women to an emphasis on integrating methods and processes of alleviating poverty—the question is, can these processes ever be generalised?[13]

What system, in other words, can provide this loose earth, the space required to allow innovation to take hold? However prosaic it may appear, I suggest that for politics like India's, one more fully backed attempt at decentralised development generation and management is the answer. Mechanisms which encourage local decision making, local accountability, local political interplay between interests, are what is needed. Local NGOs fit this framework, but offer a marginal focus, in some ways a distraction from the real need for a broad political focus. What is required is an institutionalised support system backed by the state and society. In India, in 1985, one of the southern states, Karnataka, was attempting to develop a system that offered this environment.[14]

THE KARNATAKA APPROACH

The idea was to transfer the power of rural development design, financial resource allocation and personnel appointment and supervision to local representative bodies. There are three levels: (a) the gao sabha (village council) at the village level, comprising all eligible voters; (b) the mandal panchayat, an elected body representing a population of 15,000, or about 10 villages; and (c) the zila parishad, a district-level elected body embracing about 130 mandals. Karnataka has 27,000 villages, 2,600 mandals and 20 districts.

Election through adult franchise and secret ballot are held for seats in the mandal panchayat. Some 25 per cent of these seats are reserved for women and 18 per cent for socially disadvantaged classes, called the Scheduled Castes and Scheduled Tribes. In the zila parishad, seats reserved for women are 20 per cent, but those reserved for disadvantaged groups are the same as in the mandal panchayat. Political parties usually contest for approximately 56,000 seats in the mandal panchayat and about 1,000 seats in the zila parishad.

Traditionally, development schemes for, say, a mandal, were designed and implemented either according to a national pattern or by the relevant departments at the state capital. Teachers and health workers were state-appointed cadres. Any development activity for a particular village had to be sanctioned through a vertical hierarchy leading up to departmental heads at the state level.

Under the new structure, plans, decisions and appointments are made at the local level—what is called local/proximate accountability. Karnataka's Regional Planning Division has already noted encouraging results in the form of the improved attendance of primary school teachers and primary health functionaries at their posts. The elected bodies have also exerted a positive influence on the public distribution system, making it more equitable. They have given highest priority to primary education and pure drinking water supply in the new schemes proposed out of their discretionary planned allocations. These two are in accord with local sentiment, as is more appropriate development of natural resources. Results have already begun to appear after a period of one year during which the Karnataka approach has been under way.

The Karnataka experiment is nonetheless surrounded with hostility and scepticism. Even its own practitioners do not really appear to fully believe in its grassroots assumptions. In a sense, however, the Karnataka approach requires more sophisticated support than large and modern industrial projects. It requires self-restraint and non-interference from above, and deschooling from many of the older beliefs and practices of the development community, i.e., it requires trust and patience. These are states of mind contradictory to the development fever. But if Karnataka succeeds, it will likely become the most innovative institutionalised form of public administration in India.

REDISCOVERING OUR ROOTS

The problem is that modernisation is still associated with visible, large-scale industrialisation, export orientation, urbanisation, large organisations, visibility, formality, monetisation. Stereotyping the so-called less developed countries (LDCs) as being primary producers with informal labour, or as primitive economies with unexploited resources, has led to a second-class complex which strains to look West and North for its model. Low-profile activities are mocked as simulating the poor, as keeping the poor poor, and thereby carry the colonial legacies full circle. Looking to our own tradition is scorned as fundamentalist, obscurantist, feudal.

And, indeed, who would deny that these dangers lurk in our retraced histories? They are full of muck and misery. But impersonating the North is also not without its destructive much and misery. Manfred Max-Neef describes the process of analysis that was used to trace the constraints in resolving Columbia's economic crisis.[15] The analysis traced the roots of the malaise of fear. We need to learn fearlessness, and perhaps it is our poets and writers who can best teach it to us.

How can we keep our souls without dogma, our traditions without orthodoxy, and our cultures without chauvinism? Many in the so-called LDCs are making the attempt. The South Commission is also providing a platform for such practical reformulations of ourselves and our goals.[16]

COMMERCIAL NORMS AND NON-MATERIAL CHANGE

At the more operational level, commercial norms have increasingly been brought into anti-poverty programmes, particularly in the monitoring and evaluation systems. For example, a funder might finance income generation through credit inputs, as the International Fund for Agricultural Development does. The credit should enhance the income of the recipient individual or group. Thus, monitoring pays attention to: (*a*) increments to income; and (*b*) recovery of interest and reimbursement of credit. Viability is measured by the rate of return on capital. To make this economically feasible, investments are found where products can be marketed at competitive prices. The poor are then pushed into production and exchange which looks viable in the above terms, but which can suffer from pitfalls at both the micro and macro levels.[17]

Such production games become viable in the commercial sense. But there is the larger question of the backlash that such production and commercialisation create on natural resources and the environment. Issues such as market glut or national needs for basic goods can be overlooked.

Compounding this process of commercialisation is the demand for quick results—speedy implementation, speedy returns and speedy evaluation. Broad demographic, economic and social transformations are given gestation periods of 2 to a maximum of 5 years, whereas a cement or fertiliser plant, a road or a bridge are given 20 if not 100 years to be written off.

Non-material changes, which often are both more kindly and more pernicious, have little place in this economic monitoring and evaluation because they are mostly immeasurable. Thus, commercial viability and measurability, the ruling paradigms, quietly manipulate the poor into new but sometimes vulnerable ventures.

Good, hard rethinking is required to develop a system of monitoring and evaluation which will guide us towards long-term national and regional self-reliance, stressing improvements in the quality of life. The system needs to be more long term, more goal oriented, more inward looking and culture oriented, as well as more directly focused on poverty removal.

Dr Julius K. Nyerere, at the second meeting of the recently formed South Commission, provided an instructive example of the problem at the macro level.[18] Produce or perish, say the creditors, so Tanzania produces more of x, as does Brazil. As production increases, prices fall, the investment becomes unremunerative, the economy gets squeezed and indebtedness grows. Projections of the commercial viability of the loan are nullified by the ensuing glut. After all, the dealer of the cards is dealing the same device to several poor countries. Unless the recipients design a strategy to prevent their collective suicide through aggregate overproduction, this unequal game will continue.

In the context of current development approaches, which look towards NGOs and women for more effective development delivery and management, the views elaborated in this paper may sound discordant. But these views have emerged from observations about the limitations of NGOs and of women-oriented approaches. They reflect my own evolution from a champion of these two pegs of the development process to a more sober assessment of the necessary and sufficient conditions for the elimination of poverty.

To be sure, NGOs can act as pilots. The creative efforts of women can serve as a beacon light. But it is the state and society which must have the will to make room for the poor, to help them escape from their poverty trap using their own capabilities and creativity.

NOTES

1 ISST, *Integrating Women's Interest into a State Five Year Plan: Karnataka* (New Delhi: Ministry of Social Welfare, Government of India, 1984), 2 vols.

2 ISST, *Discussion Papers: Taluk-Level Conference in Gulbarga* (New Delhi: Institute of Social Studies Trust, 1982), 2 vols.

3 ISST, 'Inter-State Tasar Project: Report on a Field Survey', Chandrapur District, Maharashtra, 1982.

4 Devaki Jain, 'Country Paper—India', paper prepared for the Expert Group Consultation on Women in Planning, Asian and Pacific Center for Women and Development, Tehran, 1979. See also ISST, 'Women and the Planning Process: A Case Study from India', paper prepared for the conference 'Integrating Women into Development Planning', International Research and Training Institute for Advancement of Women, Santo Domingo, 1983; ISST, *Development of Women and Children in Rural Areas: Preparation of a Plan with Focus on Women, Block Chikmagalur (Karnataka)* (New Delhi: Ministry of Rural Development, Government of India, 1985), 2 vols; Devaki Jain, 'Attaining Plan Objectives: The Role of New Themes in Research', paper presented at the UN Educational, Scientific and Cultural Organization Symposium on 'Methods for the Integration of Women's Issues in Development Planning', Paris, 1987; Nalini Singh, 'Monitoring and Evaluation of Social Development Planning: Implications for the Women's Question', paper presented at the Consultative Meeting on 'Monitoring and Evaluation of Community-Focused Projects', Bangkok, 1979.

5 Devaki Jain, Nalini Singh and Malini Chand, *Women's Quest for Power: Five Case Studies* (New Delhi: Vikas, 1980).

6 Anupam Mishra and Satyendra Tripathi, *Chipko Movement: Uttarakhand Women's Bid to Save Forest Wealth* (New Delhi: Peace Foundation, 1978). See also Devaki Jain, 'The Natural Power of Women', *Sarla Behn Granth*, 1983; Diana Eck and Devaki Jain (eds), *Speaking of Faith: Cross-Cultural Perspectives on Women, Religion and Social Change* (New Delhi, Kali for Women, 1986).

7 Jennifer Sebatad, *Struggle and Development among Self-Employed Women: A Report on the SEWA Ahmedabad India* (Ahmedabad: SEWA, 1982).

8 U. Kalpagam, 'Organizing Women in Informal Sector: Discourse and Practice of Politics', *Mainstream*, vol. 25, no. 13 (1986), pp. 27–33. See also Robert Chambers, *Notes and Reflections on a Visit to the Working Women's Forum in South India* (New Delhi: Ford Foundation, 1985).

9 'An Autonomous National Credit Fund for Poor Women: A Conceptualization and Feasibility Study', Report of Meeting of NGO Consortium on Credit Fund for Poor Women, Surajkund, 1987, 2 vols.

10 M. A. Singamma Sreenivasan Foundation, Round Table on Development, 'Survival Strategies of the Poor and Traditional Wisdom: A Reflection', Bangalore, 1987, 3 vols.

11 Indian Association of Women's Studies, *Reports of Three National Conferences* (Bombay, 1981). See also National Conference on Women's Studies, Bombay, 1981, *Report* (Bombay: S.N.D.T. Women's University, Research Centre in Women's Studies, 1981); National Conference on Women's Studies, Trivandrum, 1984, *Report* (Trivandrum: Department of Sociology, University of Kerala, 1984); National Conference on Women's Studies, Chandigarh, 1986, *Report* (Chandigarh, Punjab University, 1986).

12 ISST, 'Technical Seminar on Women's Work and Employment: Papers', ISST, New Delhi, 1982. See also Economists Interested in Women's Issues Group, 'Reports and Papers of Four Seminars', Workshop on 'Women and Poverty', Centre for Studies in Social Science, Calcutta, 1983; Workshop on 'Women in Technology and Forms of Production', Madras Institute of Development Studies, Madras, 1984; Workshop on 'Occupational Diversification of Female Labour Force and Economic Development', Gandhi Labour Institute, Ahmedabad, 1987; Workshop on 'Women in Agriculture', Centre for Development Studies, Trivandrum, 1988. There are others, however, who believe that women in India and elsewhere do have to identify themselves and press their case for a better place in society, that the task of the women's movement is not yet over.

13 L. C. Jain, 'Role of Non-governmental Organizations in Development', paper prepared for the Workshop on 'Poverty in India: Research and Policy', Oxford University, 1987.

14 D. M. Najundappa, 'Decentralized Planning Problems of Administration and Coordination', paper presented at the Seminar on Decentralization, Bangalore, 1985. See also L. C. Jain, 'Central Planning and Karnataka's Decentralized

Planning', *Mainstream*, vol. 25, nos 32–33 (May 1987), pp. 15–19; Government of Karnataka, 'Panchayati Raj Law in Karnataka: A Bold Experiment in Democratic Decentralization', Department of Planning, Bangalore, 1984.

15 Manfred Max-Neef, The Other Economic Summit Panel, Society for International Development Conference, New Delhi, March 1988.

16 South Commission, 'Towards Development: Strategy and Action Programme for the South', Objectives and Terms of Reference of the South Commission.

17 Devaki Jain, 'Culture of the Poor: Is Equitable Development Possible?', paper prepared for the National Conference on Culture, Bangalore, 1986.

18 Mwalimu Julius Nyerere, Address to South Commissioners, Geneva, 3 October 1987; and Second Commission Meeting, Kuala Lumpur, 1 March 1988.

Chapter 2

Development Theory and Practice
Insights Emerging from Women's Experience

As I continued to explore the area of 'development and women', I was constantly confronted with the various errors—errors in design, errors due to not locating the issue, what can be called the 'problem', but even more seriously the errors in nomenclature. Words have meanings, and the use of a certain word—what I call 'vocabulary'—can distort the dimensions of policy and change. In order to illustrate this, I used a study that ISST had just completed on women in forest-based industry. I found that while women were engaged in what in economics is called the 'free collection of goods', namely, gathering berries and leaves, etc., it was actually a great source of employment, and in many ways a contribution to GDP. But because these goods were called 'minor forest produce', and had no particular status in so-called 'production' and 'employment' concerns, this activity did not get the attention that in fact it deserved. Further, women who collected and sold these goods were often exploited, and there was no particular legal protection for these collectors who were by and large forest dwellers.

Therefore, I argued that while lumbering was deforestation and therefore in one sense negative activity, lumber was termed a major forest produce. On the other hand, gathering gums and trees and leaves, berries and flowers as a part of production was considered a minor activity, though it provided not only value but more employment to women. In this way, I argued, the concepts, the vocabulary and the direction of development theory were full of contradictions.

As those engaged in research and action among women collate their information and experience, they find that the theories and strategies of development so far on the anvil are inconsistent with their findings. These findings relate to the characteristics of the economy and its operation as they observe it, the management of change, the possibilities as well as the constraints, apart from the priorities that women lay out as the substance of development, namely the satisfaction of the basic needs of food, health and education, of equity within the society. From their findings, these scholars and activists are able to construct specific plans and policies underpinned by theory, with institutions and methods that would not only bring the kind of economy and hopefully policy that would safeguard women's interests, but the interests of all, as well as of the planet as a whole.

What are these challenges that are posed and practices that are proposed? The challenges are posed to the description of the economic characteristics of the country and the evaluation and normative scales used in the conceptualisation of these descriptive categories. The practices proposed range from an emphasis on method and process rather than goals/targets, to revealing 'alternatives' in every field of development. At the level of action, most of the time and energy of women has been spent on resisting the kind of development fallout that is being generated. Taken together, the findings and ideas emerging from women's experience shows that the effort or the exercise of bringing women into the planning process, integrating women into development, earmarking funds and schemes for women, and making women visible appears trivial.

To illustrate: in a study undertaken to examine whether anti-poverty programmes and schemes, about 22 in number, were reaching women within poverty households—in other words, whether the class-targeted programme accommodated gender—it was found that the issue did not arise, as the class itself had not been reached. Thus, when the poverty households had not been reached, the question of whether the women had been reached became redundant.[1] Further, it appeared quite clear that the method by which the programme was being delivered, namely identification of the poor by the local development functionary, as well as the mounting of the scheme with a pattern of assistance that that had been designed far away from the place of action, had together led to a situation where inappropriateness was one of the major reasons for rejection.

The study had to move away from making recommendations to the effect that the roles of women and their problems should be more visible, or that women had to be educated and become more aware of their rights and the facilities available, or that more funds needed to be blocked for women functionaries and women's programmes. Instead it asked, if this whole programme and policy had failed poor men, why build a women's component into it? It seemed necessary to dismantle the whole programme and enable a reconstructive process, including access to resources and the opportunity to develop and implement self-defined programmes, whether for men or women.

Similar information along with similar responses and recommendations were coming from other investigations of women in poverty, not only from India but from all over the Third World.[2] It was clear that while women were a distinct subset of the poor,[3] with their own characteristics both in the economic as well as in the social field, and while their struggles for recognition and empowerment were legitimate and important, the larger or prior problem or need was to clear the undergrowth before expressing a specific gender concern.[4]

This undergrowth or overgrowth was the result of cumulative destructive pressures that had been mounted by development on the territory of the poor. It seemed that in the name of development, inequities of various kinds were being perpetrated. Soil, water, trees, productive opportunities, rights, institutions, cultural resources, and so much else that provides the support system for the underclass, were being encroached upon.[5] Here too, the solution that emerged was to use more democratic processes of formulating the development design, since process reveals content and makes the goal achievable.

Such affirmation of findings at the local level as well as at the national and international levels led to the feminist critique of the orthodox ideologies from the perspective of development. Feminists within certain ideological pockets were already critiquing Marxism, liberalism, Christianity, Islam and so forth—all the theologies of one or the other kind—from the point of view of the subordinate status given to women, and the lack of recognition of their roles or rights in existing literature, categories, analysis, predictive tools. The collation of and reflection on development experiences added one more arrow to the bow challenging these intellectual legacies.[6]

Another illustration emerges from research on the characteristics of the labour force and the inadequacy of measurement tools. Productive work, whether of men or women, especially that which is not monetised, does not get notified in the statistics of labour participation or domestic product. This is vividly illustrated by those who have been engaged in household surveys, with special reference to investigating women's roles and activities.[7] Probing these less visible workers, especially women who are engaged in labour, or workers from poverty sets, several important propositions present themselves.

The majority of the poor are engaged in some survival-level 'work', some income-earning process. These are in fact job slots, and those engaged in them could be called a severely underemployed labour force. Women predominate in this category. More interesting, however, is the fact that these jobs slots are 'good economics', namely, they are viable economic activities. Viable in that they provide some kind of reward which is higher than zero at the end of the day.[8] The policy that suggests itself then is to enhance the engagement *earnings* through backward linkages to raw materials, credit, training, amenities, and forward linkages to 'demand'—local and otherwise. Policy would need to make a serious gear shift then in employment generation. It would need to start from safeguarding and protecting existent markets like rural *haats* (markets), existing products like hand-processed items, existing habits, and 'commodity' banks, land, buildings and energy inputs would have to go into industry of another kind.[9]

Even identification of economic activity would need transformation. Production for self-consumption may need to be given a new status—it is usually not 'counted'; only production for sale and surplus is given economic legitimacy. Collection, e.g., of minor forest produce, of waste, is considered insignificant, but in fact offers a vast employment shed and a large undervalued domestic product.

There are various breadwinning activities unknown to international and national occupational coding. Further, the fluidity of occupation not only between seasons, but between dawn and dusk, makes categories like 'employer' and 'employee' inappropriate. Yet such categories are embedded in labour-related statutes and conventions, pre-empting the majority of workers from being included under the cover of labour laws. These 'categories' also permeate data collection, such as the census. It is almost as if those who co-ordinate and those who legislate are blind to the predominant reality.

Small business, the producers and vendors who predominate in the private sector and often are the backbone of trade in certain countries like Ghana or regions like the Caribbean—and in Indian states like Manipur—are marginalised as 'petty vendors'. But this is the manufacturing and trading sector of the South, not the big business (private and public) that gets centre stage in accounting and attention.

There is a gap between the ground reality and the conceptualisation of descriptive categories. This arises because the definitional and classificatory systems emerge from economic and social organisational arrangements and processes appropriate to the North—i.e., appropriate to industrialised, 'organised' economies. The existence of this gap has been systematically uncovered by women's studies and action.

INSTITUTIONAL INNOVATIONS

Women predominate in various types of groupings, many of which are unknown or unrecognised. These range from culturally derived formations such as those which gather around bhajans, festivals and rituals related to women, to economic formations such as traditional methods of saving, where money is not just put away but circulated. Some of these forms of social relations have provided the basis for larger, homogeneous affirmations of solidarity, especially in the field of resistance. These events of resistance have by and large been against policies of expansion of liquor shops, the cutting of trees, breaking of hutments and so on.[10]

Marketplaces, especially traditional ones such as the rural haats and shandies, and pavement vendors of handicrafts and vegetables or fish, are economic institutions too, though they have not been given legitimacy, perhaps as much because women predominate in them as because they are not part of the current Northern mode of production and trade.[11]

Women have formed themselves into unions of self-employed workers, namely workers who do not come under the category of pure employees, which seemed at one time to be a precondition of unionisation. From unions they have expanded into banking, showing that it is possible to create alternative institutions to those which are already established, and that these alternative institutions are designed to serve the needs of those who are outside the so-called 'mainstream'. The most well known of these innovative institutions in the field of women workers is SEWA, originating in Ahmedabad.[12]

In the field of thrift societies, Samakhya in Hyderabad has revealed the capabilities of women to make their savings into a fund without any support from the state. Reports from India and other parts of the world show that women not only are thrifty, but have an ethic of repaying loans because they take loans only for a specific purpose. Thus, innovative institutional arrangements created for a purpose, created as a response to needs, created with a will and in a sense not exogenous but endogenous to a particular group and its culture, are a part of the method, the instrument that women use for achieving some of their objectives.

These methods and these institutions are showing a way. Women choosing viable income-earning avenues even though they may provide only subsistence, or what is really underemployment, the fact that these choices are 'viable', that they do not require external energies to make them work, to make them yield results, that these institutions are already part of their life experience—all this shows a way of empowering and facilitating the poor, not only women.

These are only a few examples drawn from a large body of experience and literature. These examples show the need to look again at concepts and parameters; ultimately they reveal the possibilities of using historically derived institutions.[13] They also show that what we said in the beginning, namely that the largest and most dramatic use of women's energy has been to resist; and therefore there is a case for not integrating them into development, but reordering development so that it may be acceptable to women.

IN SUM

If we look, then, at women's perspective on development planning, three points emerge:

1. The planning process must begin with the grassroots and its knowledge of reality; it must be built on the choices of the group as to what they want and how they want to get it.
2. It must build on choices or an order of priorities which would satisfy basic needs such as income, food and health, a kind of minimum well-being as a first step.
3. Finally, if we look at what the body of literature reveals, it basically wants to stand most of the existing vocabulary of classification on its head. It questions scales, which would suggest that the major areas of production and trade as operated by the 'poor', the masses, is informal. It would say this is the central mode of production and trade from the employment point of view, from the output and turnover point of view. Thus, it would be called not a marginal activity but a main activity; it would not be called the marginal informal sector but the major manufacturing sector.

Such a change in perception would also apply to categorisations such as 'major forest produce' and 'minor forest produce'. It is now well established that the volume and value of minor forest products, not only in India but in the rest of the Third World, are greater than the volume and value of what is called major forest produce. Minor forest produce is not only an activity in which the majority of the masses engage, but it also produces products which are used by the masses. Further, its attack on trees is less vicious than that of major forest produce. Yet the words 'minor' and 'major' are used inappropriately.

And so it goes for so many of the inherited ways of looking at economic phenomena. Women's studies have challenged some of these descriptive categories and shown that by sticking to them, we are denying ourselves the opportunity to see the reality as it is and to build on people's capabilities as they are. A planning method which is acceptable to women is a method which starts by re-characterising social and economic characteristics in India to show the positive creativity of alternative local arrangements, and then begins to set out goals building on the predominant features.

NOTES

1 ISST, *Integrating Women's Interest into a State Five-Year Plan: Karnataka*.

2 Devaki Jain, 'Development as if Women Mattered: Can Women Build a New Paradigm?', lecture delivered at the pre-Nairobi consultation of the OECD Development Assistant Committee group, Paris, 1983; Gita Sen and Caren Grown, *Development, Crises, and Alternative Visions: Third World Women's Perspectives* (New York: Monthly Review Press, 1987).

3 Devaki Jain, 'Patterns of Female Work: Implications for Statistical Design, Economic Classification and Social Priorities', paper presented at the National Conference on Women's Studies, SNDT University, Bombay, 1981.

4 L. C. Jain, *Grass without Roots: Rural Development under Government Auspices* (New Delhi: SAGE, 1985).

5 Devaki Jain, 'The Culture of the Poor: Is Equitable Development Possible?', in Karuna M. Braganza and Saleem Peeradina (eds), *Cultural Forces Shaping India* (New Delhi: Macmillan, 1989).

6 Eck and Jain, *Speaking of Faith*.

7 Devaki Jain and Nirmala Banerjee (eds), *Tyranny of the Household: Investigative Essays on Women's Work*, Workshop on Women in Poverty (New Delhi: Shakti Books, 1985).

8 ISST, *Small-Scale Forest-Based Enterprises with Special Reference to the Roles of Women* (Bangalore: ISST, 1989), vols 1 and 2, prepared for FAO, Rome.

9 Shramshakti, 'Report of the National Commission on Self-Employed Women and Women in the Informal Sector', SEWA, Ahmedabad, 1988.

10 Devaki Jain, 'Need for a Larger Vision', *Manushi*, December 1983; Madhu Kishwar, 'Toiling without Rights: the Ho Women of Singhbhum', *Economic & Political Weekly*, vol. 22, no. 3 (January 1987), pp. 95–101.

11 Mahila Haat is a facilitation centre for women producers from poverty households, which enables women producers in Uttarakhand and markets their products in Delhi. See also Jolly Rohtagi and others, *Moonlight in Mithila: A Feasibility Report for the Empowerment of Women Producers in Bihar* (New Delhi: ISST, 1988), vols I and II.

12 SEWA, *SEWA in 1988* (Ahmedabad: SEWA, 1989).

13 M. A. Singamma Foundation, 'Integrating Women in Development Planning: The Role of Traditional Wisdom' (prepared for UNESCO), Bangalore, 1989.

Chapter 3

Gender and Poverty in India
Comment on a World Bank Country Study

The World Bank, perhaps for the first time, prepared a compre-hensive report on Gender and Poverty in India in 1991. This paper is a comment on that report. The World Bank report was a meticu-lous piece of work and gave visibility and voice to less prominent areas of concern and advocacy in the women's domain. However, I argued that while the report attempted to give a macro perspec-tive, it remained at the micro level. It pre-empted gender advo-cacy from influencing macro trends. I argued essentially that the notions of an inside/outside dichotomy, access and the market, highlighted by the report, were insufficient, even inappropriate tools for moving women out of their cruel condition.

The World Bank report *Gender and Poverty in India* is a meticulously done piece of work,[1] typical of the principal author Lynn Bennett. Such comprehensive surveys with an analytical peg and a policy direction are valuable in themselves as documents of reference, even if they do not begin to walk on policy and project feet. They give visibility and voice to less prominent areas of concern and advocacy. Other works in this genre would include the *World Development Reports* of the World Bank; the UNDP's *Human Development Reports*; the UN's *The World's Women: Trends and Statistics, 1970–1990*;[2] the United Nations Population Fund's (UNFPA) revealing *World Population Reports*; and the United Nations Children's Fund's (UNICEF) *Adjustment with a Human Face*.[3] All of these made a kind of 'big bang' upon their appearance. Such reports are taken notice of and widely referred to. The work under consideration too belongs to the same class of reports, that is, professional, macro, mainstream, 'big-bang'.

While we are here to deliberate on a report prepared by a team and presented by no less an institution than the World Bank, I may be allowed the liberty of personalising the report and addressing the principal author Lynn Bennett in my remarks.

The *Gender and Poverty in India* report contains an approach derived from intellectually worked-out premises, some quite strong. In fact, the report's advantage, liveliness and value lie in this expression of one mind which has reflected on and which cares about the issue it is writing about. And I suggest it is Lynn's viewpoint and analytical frame. Further, Lynn was a part of the Indian and earlier the Nepalese scene and has been witness to the evolution of research, analysis and advocacy in the subcontinent. In that sense, the report is as much if not more an outcome of Indian exercises in information gathering, of Indian (and possibly Nepalese) debates and viewpoints, as it is a World Bank investigation and report.

We can address ourselves to this report in terms of three categories: (*a*) the facts; (*b*) the analysis; and (*c*) the prescriptions.

THE FACTS

In terms of the facts, I think the report is a comprehensive reference book and sets a model of how to draw on data. Lynn's main thrust is to show that in the Indian context, women are important economic agents. To use an overused quotation from Mao Tse Tung, 'women hold up half the sky.' We would go further and say that in the poverty sets, women hold up *more* than half the sky. In the poverty sets, women's income often is the critical income for household survival; similarly, their fuel, water, cattle, soil, conserving and coping strategies are environmentally less dangerous. There is hardly any woman among the poor who is not trying to secure the 'survival kit' for her family by providing basic needs like food and care. Lynn wants greater recognition of this aspect of women's presence in the Indian polity. She states this strongly, partly to overpower the more widespread image of women being at the centre of the family as reproductive agents, needing support in their motherhood roles. The emphasis is on strengthening that part of policy which provides women access to economic resources, like credit, land, market signals, skill upgradation or organisation.

Lynn mobilises the data and presents them in the most telling formats to prove this point. Her route to the social inputs and causal analysis of social outcomes is through the incremental change in women's income. For example, she states that making women more productive—hence, more effective income earners—will reduce their dependency and enhance their status. It will also:

1. reduce fertility and slow population growth;
2. improve child survival;
3. increase the share of family income allocated to food and healthcare for children;
4. raise household income, especially in families below the poverty line; and
5. increase aggregate labour productivity and speed up growth in key economic sectors.

That these elements work this way is yet to be proved at the macro level, as Lynn admits.

Another example of fact-based analysis leads Lynn to critique the measurement techniques themselves:

> It is also possible that poor urban women are in fact economically active, but in an informal economy which is captured even less well by official statistics than the rural subsistence economy. Numerous micro-level studies carried out in poor urban areas show actual female participation rates of around 40%. Such findings suggest that problem of measurement and definition may make changes in urban female participation rates implied in macro-level data less than reliable.[4]

The second category of facts which the report mobilises and which is extremely useful is the listing of schemes in operation at different levels—overall, sectoral, poverty-specific, gender-specific, state-level, district-level, NGO-level, etc. These are well integrated in the report. There is also an assessment of these schemes. For example, on poverty alleviation: '[P]overty alleviation efforts in India are usually conceived as a three pronged effort:

- promoting self-employment among the poor;
- providing lean season wage employment; and
- addressing minimum needs such as nutrition, health, sanitation, housing and education.'[5]

The report continues: 'One such overall strategy is to concentrate on promotional efforts for self-employment among the entrepreneurial poor, while providing better targeted wage employment opportunities to the remaining able-bodied poor who do not have the skills for, or do not wish to take the risks related to, self-employment.'[6]

A third kind of facts relates to national reports specific to women, such as the Shramshakti report, the National Perspective Plan for Women, etc.,[7] again with reference to the debates and differences in viewpoints that these reports contain or have generated. The chapter on NGOs deserves special mention. Different typologies are presented, showing the landscape from different angles with consequent implications for development knowledge, action and public policy. Thus, the report updates all of us on whatever water has flowed under the bridge in the area of women and poverty.

ANALYSIS

The report rests its analysis on three concepts. First, the concept of the 'inside/outside' dichotomy, i.e., the idea that women, especially in Indian culture, are in some way screened from the public arena, even if they are hard-working wage labourers; for example, women from Rajasthan who dig, carry, etc., at construction sites but veil their faces. The inside/outside dichotomy therefore is not based on economic activity but on a cultural mode which inhibits women's participation in the public arena, including their assertion of power.

Second, the key word in Lynn's advocacy for women is to give them 'access'. The premise is that women have less access than men because of the inside/outside division of domains. Given access, women can improve their position both economically and socially. Lynn goes to the extent of saying that if access to economic strength is made available, then the incremental improvement in economic condition would automatically encourage women to reach out for and draw in what are called social inputs. The argument is that increase in women's purchasing power, articulation power and demand power would, through the pull of demand, draw investment in social infrastructure and basic needs.

Third, underlying this proposition is the macro-economic theme, that the 'market' is the best engine of growth. India needs this stimulus. The report writers must feel a sense of satisfaction that the current Indian policy towards development matches this belief. Following this proposition is the next, namely that growth provides and expands opportunities for all; i.e., there will be a demand pull. Finally, that this demand pull and this expansion of opportunity would draw women into further participation. And, if this demand is accompanied by good wages on the demand side and provision of access on the supply side, women will emerge and occupy their rightful place in the socio-economy.

The report thus explicitly states its faith in the market, in demand and supply, and the market's ability to settle transactions somewhat satisfactorily. In some cases, women come to work because of the push of poverty, in some cases they come to work because of the pull of certain fast-growing sectors.

PRESCRIPTIONS

A major recommendation is the organisation of women into groups. It is good that the report recognises that there is increasing acceptance of this instrument as one which is critical to women's advancement. Special elaboration is made of successful endeavours in the field of dairy co-operatives and credit co-operatives. Suggestions are made on how to improve the efficiency of schemes such as Development of Women and Children in Rural Areas, for instance by reducing the number of women required to start a project.

Another prescription is allowing women to exercise their full capacity in the economically productive sectors. There is insistence that not only women, but the rest of the society would be transformed for the better if this were implemented. It is suggested that currently, policy and programmes place stronger emphasis on women in their domestic domain. What is required if India is to take off is to shift that emphasis to women's economic roles and allow them to fully offer their potential to the economy and society.

A third prescription is with reference to NGOs. The report is wise in that while it recognises that NGO efforts in promoting women's advancement and in similar fields have a higher quality, they cannot substitute for large, central, national or macro policy instruments. The report recognises that NGOs are sparse even if their light shines brightly—even while it recommends generous funding support to the sector.

The research and development recommendations are outstanding. Note the section directed at research in agricultural and rural development, titled 'Agricultural Research and Technology Development':

Lacking land, female wage labourers will benefit from agriculture intensification and diversification that raise overall labor demand and reduce seasonal employment fluctuations. Among the measures to increase such demand are a shift to less water-intensive crops and wider distribution of available irrigation water in semi-arid regions; expansion of commercial crops like cotton, which require high female labor input and for which demand is buoyant, and diversification into high value non-cereal crops, vegetables, fruits, nuts and non-timber forest products.

Female cultivators who work on family land, will benefit more from laborsaving agricultural technologies that reduce their own investment time and the need for hired labor. In this regard their interests run counter to those of female agricultural wage workers. Even so, a shift in research priorities, from larger foodgrain yields to agricultural diversification would help both wage workers and cultivators, especially those on marginal holdings. Research on sustainability, risks and cost reduction and the links between various components of the family farm operation should lead to improved productivity. And since the role of women is greater in regions with harsh topography and climate, research on farming under rainfed conditions will also aid women farmers.[8]

Similarly, the recommendations in science and technology.

A recommendation which has already been part of the process of dialogue between the Government of India and the World Bank is with regard to a credit fund for women. There is place for all three approaches (agriculture intensification and diversification, less water-intensive crops, and diversification into high-value non-cereal crops) in a large, diverse country like India. It is important to note that the efficacy and vitality of this credit fund, which in some sense evolved in order to cover those 'errors and inadequacies' of the conventional credit routes, are advocated only because of a resistant 'methodology'. It has to be more like an NGO with sufficient expertise of a durable kind in its management, to be able to make its presence worthwhile. It is not to be one more governmental scheme. Mahila Samakhya, the national programme for women's empowerment, born out of the government but implemented in an innovative NGO style, is a good illustration of how to organise such women.

One aspect that struck me, for example, was the set of suggestions in the educational sector. There the report strongly advocates an all-out effort to bring little girls and adolescent girls into the fold of education as a minimum condition for all other recommendations, such as improved access, breaking of barriers, the inside/outside binary, organisation, and so on.

It is interesting to note that at the national seminar on school education held in Delhi in September 1991, the major recommendation was that the central figure, the goal or top priority in designing school education, should be the girl child. Thus, an appropriate allocation of funds should be made for infrastructural investment for drawing her into elementary and higher levels of education. The reason I make this comment is that many of the good ideas in these specific chapters are part of strategies which are now incorporated in the approach to the Eighth Plan, or at least present in the consciousness of policy makers.

COMMENTS

Though ostensibly the report is a 'macro' perspective document, in fact it remains at the micro level. This is a serious inadequacy, as it pre-empts gender advocacy from influencing macro trends and policies, just as it also limits the integration of gender into mainstream processes.

A related weakness is that the analytical frame of the report is not tethered in the current context of the Indian economy and policy. One cannot blame the report for not being contextual, since important changes have taken place after its preparation. But much of the operational clout of the report does need crucial recasting if it is to be rooted in today's context.

In my comments, I shall basically argue that the concepts of inside/outside, access, and the market are insufficient, even inappropriate tools by which women can be moved out of their cruel conditions. I will not be going into some of the other details, such as the fact that human resource development, basic needs, the problem of violence and so on are underplayed in the report.

The report does not acknowledge—naturally, because it was not in such active currency at the stage when it was being produced—the national consensus on decentralised management of development. Now that the Panchayati Raj Amendment Bill (72nd Amendment— now before Parliament) will come to pass, there will be not only in Karnataka and West Bengal, but at a more widespread official level, an institutional framework for development. The responsibility for not only implementation, but also deciding the design of development as well as mobilising some resources, accountability and so forth, will be devolved to local bodies.

These bodies are not as aseptic and anaemic as the Mahila Mandala, nor are they as few and peripheral as the NGOs. They are in fact an administrative system covering every nook and corner of the country. If the numbers in Karnataka offer any clue to the size of the female population that will be sitting on those bodies, it will be seen how necessary it is to take note of this institutional arrangement.

In Karnataka, in the last five years, 14,000 women (25 per cent of the total membership) have been sitting on these managing bodies, comprising a total strength of 56,000 persons. While they feel they floundered in the first two years, they now feel they are in the 'mainstream'. They know how budgets are built and dispensed. At a recent discussion in Bangalore in October 1991, many women felt that 33 per cent of the seats was not good enough, they should be given 50 per cent, as women were not sufficiently well regarded and a few women cannot overpower the men, and so forth.

True, women members of the panchayati raj may not always be considering issues related to poverty and gender. However, experiences such as the Institute of Education in Pune, Maharashtra, the Satyamurthy Foundation in Tamil Nadu, and in Karnataka the M. A. Singamma Sreenivasan Foundation, have shown that the demand groups embedded in panchayati raj are in fact speaking for poor women and minority women, and often have them on the boards.

As an illustration of how policy and programme would change, depending on how we 'cast' the institutional framework, I would give the following illustration. If we take note of the groups of women who will be participating in the panchayat raj, and see them as requiring to operate in the 'outside domain', it will be important for fund flows or financial flows, structures such as the credit fund for women, to be offered specifically to these women. They should have the opportunity to apply to the credit fund for their areas.

The fact that these women have access to a fund which men do not have would automatically raise their status, because 'money talks.' Several anecdotes from SEWA (Ahmedabad) and the Working Women's Forum (Madras) illustrate how credit membership cards have smoothened out unequal gender relations within the family. The same would prevail at an institutional level.

The process of political empowerment has begun, and approaches to gender in poverty and development need to take note of this important emerging Indian institutional framework. Built into this institutional framework is the capacity:

1. to take note of regional differences in everything, especially women's status, economic and social, of which the report under review takes admirable note;
2. to mobilise local resources, material and human;
3. to give access to accountability for policy and programmes. This is of crucial importance for women and other subordinate groups. 'Access' is a function of proximity for 'weaker' groups, as has been proven over and over again whether we talk of access to food or political power; and
4. most important of all, to provide the most effective basis for 'labour absorption' or sustainable 'full employment'.

There is much evidence to support the feasibility and importance of the fourth point above. Prof. M. L. Dantvala and others have argued that full employment, or a plan which can find productive engagement for every unemployed male and female, can only be achieved at the local level. This kind of view is further supported at the macro analytical level by economists like Prof. Krishna Bharadwaj, who have found that it is local clearing houses of demand and supply that, through innovative institutional mechanisms, have worked in the LDCs, and not macro resolutions of the unemployment or 'surplus' labour problem.

The importance of using these mechanisms to raise resources and to cope with the problem of livelihoods for the poor, especially women, gets magnified in the context of India's current economic position. There is no doubt that whatever long-term gains are to be gleaned, there is a severe resource crunch. As K. S. Krishnaswamy says in the *Economic & Political Weekly*:

> without a major change in the size structures and working style of the Central and State Governments, the programme of Liberalisation will soon be metamorphosed into something totally different in the process of implementation just as the Nehruvian concept of 'democratic planning' was in the past. This is a task which no political party in power has so far been prepared to undertake, for well known reasons. But unless this nettle is firmly grasped, neither the much desired reduction in the fiscal deficit, nor the change in the urban population's life-style necessary for a lasting 'adjustment' of the balance of payments will be

possible. And Manmohan Singh will have to wait much longer than he thinks for his package of reforms to reveal its 'human face'.[9]

By not taking this institutional framework as given, most of the recommendations of the report addressed to central government or centrist structures can in fact be misleading. For example, take the interventions that are recommended at the macro level, namely incentives, where the emphasis is on more macro schemes and macro fiscal policy (this is one of the key recommendations). To some extent, these suggestions conflict with the view that it is at the local level that restructuring as well as reordering of power needs to take place. While the report acknowledges the importance of diversity, and takes note of diversity in situations between states, regions, classes and sectors, it does not follow this up by saying that one of the best ways of reflecting this difference is by giving local bodies the strength and the power to design, decide and implement development.

Thus, the credit fund for women can in fact become a credit fund to be used by women for projects within the district level or *mandal* development plans.[10] There is also some concern among those who have been conducting 'credit only' programmes, such as Development of Women and Children in Rural Areas and the Integrated Rural Development Programme, that 'credit only' provides one line of support. Credit could be absorbed and made part of the whole project, i.e., the project should be a development project which sees the links between credit, production, marketing, and the whole capability required to implement the project.

Two examples could be given here. In trying to help women as *sikki* handicraft workers in the dry districts of Bihar,[11] it was found that there is a limit to how much this beautiful craft product can provide a sustained income to poor agricultural labouring women. What seems more important for these women is that the dry agricultural area needs to be made agriculturally productive—through either water or better extension research, as the report recommends for dryland farming. But it was found that unless their agricultural land gave them food and employment, marketing and improving the design of sikki products in aid of a needlepoint rehabilitation could only be a peripheral activity.

Similarly, in trying to understand the needs of women in the Kumaon district of the Himalayas, it was found that for a market support project to have significance, it was necessary to look at area development. Linkages with selling their own products (wool based) went all the way back to sheep rearing, which in turn went back to the use of land for different purposes. The strategy of giving 'credit only' funds needs to be reconsidered.

It is my view that we can have a National Fund for Women's Development, similar to the UN Voluntary Fund for Women. A national fund for women could be created to which applications might be made by various bodies. The national development fund could be broader than the credit fund: it might have a technical wing, e.g., which facilitates these projects in becoming viable.

But for all these forms of support to serve their ends properly, a strong technical planning support and training facility must be provided to local bodies (panchayats), as Prof. Dantvala has forcefully argued. This will enable women representatives to have their views, ideas and priorities written systematically into the local plans.

ADJUSTMENT

In the context of a country going through the structural adjustment process for the first time, it may not be improper to postulate a different conceptual framework to look at gender in poverty. For example, it could be suggested that one must anticipate now the specific impacts that structural adjustment might unleash. There are enough examples from Africa and Latin America on the special punishment of females adults and children enacted by such 'reform'. There are exercises which track the specific causes of distress under a structural adjustment programme, which might help India to do some remote sensing, even though those women and societies are of a different kind.

Where will the new reforms hurt? And within that, who will they hurt? If we can identify which technologies, which raw materials, which geographical areas, which kind of employment will be affected, we can then open that box to see who are the poor who will be hurt and, amongst them, how women would be affected.

I should imagine that the principal responsibility of those who are looking at a development plan for women in the next five years would be to design an anticipatory safety net for poor women which would help them to 'pre-empt themselves' when adjustment strikes. In reverse, the opportunity of adjustment could be used to move poor women forward. The bank, with all its worldly wisdom and information gathered from similar operations in other developing countries, should be able to provide analytical exercises which would help those who are designing macro policies in India to accommodate the IMF loan, to avoid the pain or enhance the pleasure of these macro-economic experiences. In other words, we cannot think of gender in poverty without rooting it in the current economic context.

Two seemingly contradictory responses may be called for here. First, a moving away from the 'sectoral' intensification approach, such as STEP.[12] We see already the distress signals of the domestic dairy industry in response to the new economic package. Would dairy be a safe bet for poor women? Warnings regarding other parts of the agricultural and allied sectors are also appearing as India globalises its economy. The second response involves delving into local governance, investing in the mobilisation of livelihoods for the poor in locally designed strategies, i.e., decentralised planning.

But economic safety nets by themselves may not be enough to avoid other 'debt traps', if IMF-assisted countries are any example. Large bailing-out operations may become necessary for women, for they are, as the report says, at the bottom of the pile.

WORK AND WORKERS: A JARRING NOTE

A jarring note in the report is its reference to the World Bank's 1989 Country Economy Report.[13] The latter report seems to argue that 'existing regulations have been responsible for impeding employment growth and manufacturing.' The argument is that protective laws will encourage a shift to more capital-intensive production. Further, that if the 'informal sector' simulates these worker protective measures, it will drive the economy even further into capital-intensive techniques. Among specific measures suggested is the 'dismantling of all but a few basic and enforceable regulations to protect workers. Applying these regulations to all workers can weaken the formal–informal duality.'[14]

Many of us would want the formal–informal duality to be weakened by giving workers in the so-called informal sector access to the security of formal sector workers. In fact, our thrust would be on having work in the informal sector recognised as full-fledged work. It would be further argued that if the predominant mode of production and trade is of a particular kind, as it exists in India and so many other developing countries, the word 'informal' is a misnomer. The 'formal sector' is a pimple or a sore on the body of the economy. Thus, our entire system of labour laws, labour ministries, trade unions, etc., needs to address itself to removing aspects of exploitation as well as the stagnation of workers in this predominant sector. Looked at this way, the argument that giving protective cover to the majority of workers would be detrimental to their employment, is disconcerting.

It is difficult to swallow this argument not only because of our perhaps philosophical approach to workers' rights and trade unionism as positive aspects of economic organisation; but also because of the very troubling experience that is reported from the fast-growing dynamic economies of the developing world. Those who have critiqued the growth path of Korea, Taiwan, Hong Kong and even Malaysia, if not some of the 'successful' Latin American countries, have deplored the complete lack of regard for the protection of workers. They have talked of sweat labour, hardship, low wages, forms of absorption of labour which create not only insecurity but social punishment. For example, studies in Korea suggest that rural girls brought at very early ages are removed from employment when they marry at a certain age, pushing them sometimes into prostitution. In Japan, hard lines are drawn in labour force absorption patterns across age and marital status, which has prevented women from climbing up to decision-making positions in the economic structure. This is only one aspect of the experience of these economies.

An illustration of what we can call the misleading aspects of nomenclature is provided by the status of forest produce. Timber, or lumber, is called a major forest produce. Leaves, berries, gums, roots and flowers are called minor forest produce. People who are engaged in free gathering of forest produce are not even considered to be workers. In fact, in India, the volume and value of output from forests is greater in minor forest produce than major forest produce. It is ridiculous to recognise this and still keep the same nomenclature.

Because of the nomenclature, both processes of production and trade in minor forest produce are totally neglected in terms of ensuring a certain amount of vigilance in terms of overexploitation of resources, regeneration of species, pricing, the interlinked chain of production and trade whereby tribal people sell large amounts of the now-fashionable raw materials for herbal medicines for a pittance, which are then picked up by contractors and sold to multinational pharmaceuticals like Lilly for preparing plant-based drugs. The condition of those who are 'workers' in this sector is totally invisible to minimum wage and other forms of protection. Thus, the plea here is not to get distracted by the normative aspects of language, which reverse the hierarchies of concern.

One sees such a normative comment in another section of the report, namely Chapter 7, 'Women outside Agriculture: Rural Non-farm Activities and the Urban Informal Sector'.[15] In comparing the shares of female employment in different sectors, the report states: 'Growth in women's share of employment in industries and services in India has lagged far behind not only that in the Southeast Asian countries, but... even behind the other South Asian countries.'[16] The term 'lag behind' is in relation to the fact that services have become an important sector for women in Indonesia and the Philippines.

Those who have been looking at women's participation in the services sector in Indonesia, the Philippines or even in Hong Kong, however, are appalled at the conditions under which women work in these sectors. We might ask whether women workers who are now in agriculture and not in the services, in the same proportion as, let us say, in Indonesia and the Philippines, are also lagging behind, or is it that the economic thrust of these two countries has made it necessary for women to seek work in services?

We know that the Philippines, like Kerala, provides a very large labour force of nurses and maids who are 'exported' to the richer developing countries (like Kuwait) as well as some of the developed countries. For example, in Kerala, we know that while women display the ideal social indicators—with high literacy and favourable sex ratios—they have to look outside Kerala for employment. The hardships that they face and their preference for staying in their own 'economies' is something to be considered when we are making such normative judgements. They do not prefer the 'outside' they are in. A deeper, open-minded examination of the consequences for poor women of structural shifts in the economy and various types of growth strategies is called for.

A CRITIQUE OF THE APPROACH TO GENDER AND DEVELOPMENT

Gender-based presentations which pinpoint the handicaps that are faced by women, or, to put it the other way, which pinpoint the discriminatory impact of programmes and policies of development, as well as pinpointing the jurisdictions occupied by men and women, whether in the domain of 'occupations' or in the domain of what Lynn calls the 'inside and outside', invite programmes and interventions on behalf of women. It is an approach which attempts to provide equal shares, level up the unequal, redress the balance.

A good example of what I call the 'equal shares' approach is provided in the Executive Summary of the report: 'if women are to claim a larger share of new jobs generated over the long-term, especially in the formal sector and in non-traditional occupations, the current disparities in male and female access to education... must be addressed immediately.'[17]

The approach of 'redressing imbalances', or of 'intervention on behalf of the unjustly treated', with the consequent policies and programmes, may be necessary but not sufficient in mitigating social distances due to disparities. Some of these distances get perpetuated due to certain growth and other fiscal and monetary strategies. Hence, they may give an appearance of 'curative' help, but may only be cosmetic or a form of firefighting. For transformation to occur, for the equalising to be sustainable, meaning not only 'ecologically sustainable' but for these groups to be able to sustain the intervention and move out of their unequal status, there may be need to look at the overall economic strategy and processes, the structure of the economy and polity, and its momentum.

There are many studies and analyses emerging from different sectors such as agriculture, industry, services as well as the environment, which suggest that one has to go beyond the shares or allocations of different groups and deal with the very nature of the policies and programmes of poverty alleviation as well as the methodology of implementation and the instruments used, and not only focus on gender balancing. What is produced, for whom, with what technology, the pricing policies, export/import policies and the mechanisms through which these are derived as well as 'put on the ground'—all contain built-in 'differentiating' if not discriminating impulses.

The report, in a sense, protects itself from this challenge or criticism by describing its recommendations as 'incrementalist' (as against 'structuralist'). The nature of the economy is given. The report's strategy is to nudge women from the inside to the outside—give them equal access with men to the 'public' arenas, especially the market. But even in the best of market economies, there are 'trade-offs'. The places women occupy are admittedly the least skilled, least powerful, lowest paid. Are organised demand groups of women and credit funds going to prevent these 'weak' groups from becoming 'trade-offs' in a burgeoning, 'modernising', globalising economy? It seems too optimistic.

One of the increasingly accepted views among women's groups, especially those who are analysing data on the experience of women in the economy, is that the response of women to economic macro policies, i.e., the gender-differentiated impact of these policies and the response to them, reveals the corrective measures required in the policy, in the methodology of design and implementation of development, and in the normative aspects of economic assessments. In other words, it is women and the environmentalists who are posing the most constructive but fundamental critiques of current development theory and practice. It is a pity if such a major professional exercise with Indian data and debates, as contained in the report, does not pull together its analysis to add to such 'structuralist' challenges, rather than remaining incrementalist.

Those who have been examining the various strategies of ensuring poor women's advancement or reduction of their burdens are increasingly dissatisfied with the 'equal shares' approach, or even an approach which proposes to redress gender imbalances. There is a growing sense that not only must women be involved in designing development and in the articulation of demands, but the space women occupy both in the economy and growth domain as well as in the family domain, and their livelihood strategies as well as choices in terms of alternative allocation, have to be understood and responded to in development practice.

In the literature on rethinking development, there is insufficient analysis of the relationship between trends in women's economic and social status, and trends in the mainstream economy. There is also not enough analysis of factors that generate economic growth and its relevance to those factors which generate a better place for women. Trends may have been tracked, but it is necessary to go beyond 'male and female' comparisons to a study of 'women and the economy'.

The World Bank report under consideration opens the door to undertaking such an analysis. But to link it to development theories, it would need far more complex exercises. It is for this reason that I suggest that an annotated catalogue or a directory of such documents be prepared, perhaps by the bank itself—a gathering of material so as to 'synthesise'. What is needed is a *World Development Report* based on the gender-differentiated analysis of development. We can then see that generalisations can be made across countries, cultures and economic histories on gender and development. We can perhaps see in a more informed way the relationships between types of economic growth strategies and women's well-being, gender equality and gender relations.

It has been one of my pet notions—and this approach may not have a place in the atmosphere of structural adjustment—that the experience of women in development, both in study and in action, reveals many useful theoretical strategies and methodological insights for redesigning development itself. In fact, I propose a 'women's plan for national development' or a 'women's perspective on global development', rather than an approach which talks of a plan for women within a national or global development plan, or, as it is usually called, 'a rational plan for women's development'.

NOTES

1   World Bank, *Gender and Poverty in India*, World Bank Country Study (Washington, D.C.: World Bank).

2   UN, *The World's Women: Trends and Statistics, 1970–1990* (New York: UN, 1991).

3   UNICEF, *Adjustment with a Human Face: Protecting the Vulnerable and Promoting Growth* (Oxford: Clarendon, 1987).

4   World Bank, *Gender and Poverty in India*, p. 92.

5   Ibid., p. 161.

6   Ibid., pp. 161–62.

7   Shramshakti, 'Report of the National Commission on Self-Employed Women and Women in the Informal Sector'; Government of India, *National Perspective Plan for Women 1988–2000 A.D.* (New Delhi: Department of Women and Child Development, Ministry of Human Resource Development, 1986).

8   World Bank, *Gender and Poverty in India*, p. xviii.

9   K. S. Krishnaswamy, 'On Liberalisation and Some Related Matters', *Economic & Political Weekly*, vol. 26, no. 42 (1991), pp. 2415–17, 2419–22.

10   A mandal is an intermediary elected council between the village and the district level.

11   Sikki is a dry long grass grown in the dry areas of north Bihar.

12   Support to Training and Employment Programme for Women, a funded scheme under the Ministry of Women and Child Development.

13   World Bank, *India: Poverty, Employment and Social Services*, A World Bank Country Study (Washington, D.C.: World Bank, 1989).

14   Ibid.

15   World Bank, *Gender and Poverty in India*, pp. 81–108.

16   Ibid., pp. 82–83.

17   Ibid., p. xxiii.

Chapter 4

Healing the Wounds of Development

In 1983, Michigan University organised a conference on education and women. By this time, I had begun to see how so many of the elements used as inputs into the progress of women and men, such as education, were problematic. At this conference, I argued that development as a means of bringing progress, of bringing change into the lives of men and women, had actually begun to hurt them because the tools used were inappropriate, and often destroyed whatever little belonged to the people at the bottom. I argued that the curriculum of education needed to be changed so that the design of development became healing rather than destructive.

In the global context, the term 'development' has been used to rank countries as developed, developing or underdeveloped based on various indicators and indices. Most are economic; they measure the output of goods and services, income, money supply and so on. Simultaneously, there is some concern with poverty and unequal distribution of wealth. The developed countries provide the yardstick by which all other countries are ranked. Implicit in this ranking is the idea that all countries should aspire to be like developed countries.

But what is it that the developed countries have achieved? Basically, they have achieved mass mechanisation and industrialisation, high levels of production of goods and services, super-affluence in material goods, an employer–employee relationship in all kinds of work, and high energy consumption. All are essentially forms of economic growth.

They represent one meaning of development, but only one. An alternative form of development would be the growth of people's capacities and strengths, their public involvement and their self-reliance, and their equal status. Why must development be equated with economic growth and, consequently, with mass industrialisation? This equation has not helped the majority of the people in so-called 'developing countries', and there is no good reason why the West should be our model, especially since India's historic pattern has been self-employment for the masses and its cultural concerns have been very different from those of a consumer society.

NEW STRATEGIES: NEW ORGANISATION OF WORK

We need to explore other options. Can we come out of poverty without damaging our ecosystems, our values, our identities? Can we avoid transforming all work into nine-to-five jobs? Can we structure our economies so that the majority of our workers remain self-employed, which is their historical and traditional form of employment? We must create our own options for progress and growth.

We must also trans-value 'backwardness' so that we can better understand what we want from progress and modernisation. We have to understand the functioning of traditional cultural institutions which have helped the majority of our people participate in decisions affecting them, and which are now being eroded. We have to understand the displacing effect of new technologies and their impact on the culture and identity of our people. We have to identify the forces that encourage the concentration of resources in the hands of the few and destroy the decentralised nature of our traditional systems. We have to develop and nurture a sense of pride in our own ways of living and our own value systems, instead of criticising them. We have to aspire to reasonable levels of consumption that can be sustained for the whole world, rather than pursue super-consumption at the expense of others. We have to change the direction of development, even in industrialised countries.

Efforts are under way to combat poverty and injustice at the grassroots level. They are, however, still scattered. Despite massive anti-poverty campaigns, we have not been able to improve the lives of our people. One reason for this is that we do not know our own people. There is a wealth of wisdom in their ways of work, their ways of communication, in the food they eat, the clothing they wear. Julius Nyerere, the former President of Tanzania, observed:

> Development needs to be rooted in the culture of a people, and the cultures of peoples. However slow or fast, real development will be 'organic' growth not the accretion of a foreign body. It will be compatible with ways of looking at the world which the society has evolved through historical experience. To the extent that this does not happen, the result will be discontent and possibly social unrest.
>
> ... Yet rejecting the concept that development is merely a matter of increasing the gross national income is not to reject development. Nor is it to say that the levels of production are irrelevant to development. Similarly, the inevitable uncertainties and social upsets which accompany change must not be used as an excuse for not trying to make changes. The present level of existence of hundreds of millions of human beings is an insult to the very concept of humanity.[1]

As women enter education and development, they must pause and reflect, then perhaps backtrack to advance again in new ways. The equality game that we played in the past decade is not leading us into green pastures; instead, it is leading us into the swamps in which our predecessors in progress, men, are trapped. Options that are foreclosed for them, and for advanced nations, are still open to us and to all women in developing countries who are planning and participating in their own advancement. But time is short and we urgently need to clarify and elaborate our goals.

In what follows I will present some areas of thought and action for feminists concerned with education, who see its link to women's endeavours for the healthy development of our planet and its people.[2] Specifically, I will identify areas for curriculum development, which, if introduced into formal or informal education, can facilitate these endeavours. They are:

1. providing a new theoretical and philosophical backdrop to the content of education;

2. providing information about the dangers of 'old' development and mobilising resistance to it;
3. building a curriculum suited to the local environment, culture and economic patterns and organising macro-educational systems that can accommodate this diversity; and
4. building women's self-worth by replacing myths with truth and building their confidence with thoughts on the nature of women's struggles for equality.

Many of these topics have already been addressed by feminists. Now it is time to consolidate them and to make a revolutionary effort to introduce them into the delivery mechanisms of education. Below, I present a case study illustrating the kind of consolidation I mean.

Lakshmi Ashram, nestled in the Himalayas at Kausani, is a residential school for girls of all ages, started by an Austrian woman, an environmentalist who was an associate of Gandhi. It has an enrolment of 80 to 100 high-school girls, a dozen teachers, and another dozen teacher trainees. The ashram has always been a focal point for 300 scattered hamlets and households in the surrounding mountains. The only way to get from hamlet to hamlet is on foot, over pathways that thread through the mountains.

Since the school follows the Gandhian mode of pedagogy, in which there are no divisions between childhood and adulthood, manual and intellectual work, or domestic and productive labour, all students live as they would in their homes and are aware of social and environmental issues. They wake at 5 a.m. and clean the school, cook, garden, or serve breakfast, according to the roster. They start their classes at 8 a.m. and read or work on crafts until lunch. In the afternoon they do homework, play, sing and dance. Their creativity and respect for labour, food and shortages are not dampened by the presence of electronic media, playing fields or adult servers. Students have graduated from the ashram to become street vendors, nurses and even air hostesses. Most return to live in their villages but remain agents of the ashram.

The tradition of Gandhian ashrams is not to proselytise or provide extension services. For example, *padayatra*, or travelling by foot, is associated with village-to-village preaching, like the activities of Vinoba

Bhave.[3] But, in fact, it is a way to make oneself accessible to others in the most humble way. The 'self' who is doing this for her own salvation must be a self-developed person who is fine-tuned to receive. As a receptacle, the *padayatri* (one who travels by foot) only reverberates. She strengthens the resolve of those she encounters and teaches the precept. She demonstrates the consistency between precept and practice.

Every outside development impulse the padayatri receives is injurious, and one of her tasks is to build up her resistance to these development impulses. Education policy, for example, which positively discriminates towards members of the so-called backward classes or the lower castes, requires that the school keep records of these children so that it can get special grants-in-aid. These children are entitled to a free education. Such identity keeping, however, carries the social stigmas of the village to the classroom, which should be the child's refuge from negative discrimination. In the case of Lakshmi Ashram, the school refused the grants and barred the inspector of schools from entering.

The school has evolved a curriculum suited to the environment, the ways of life and the aspirations of the hill people. The state has refused to certify the school, however, unless it changes its textbooks, courses and schedule. The school is striving to give its graduates the option of entering 'the rest of the world'. But it does not want to sacrifice appropriate education, education that does not alienate children from their environment, their creative intelligence or their past.

This curriculum issue, for which uniformity is demanded, is especially harmful for girls, something that has been demonstrated by the work of the Institute of Education in Pune and in many other field research and action reports.[4] Certain important conclusions emerged from the Pune research project:

> The reasons for non-enrolment and drop-out of rural children, particularly girls, are mainly two: (a) the indifference or irrelevance of the educational system to the needs and difficulties of the children, and (b) cultural, social and economic constraints which have not yet been clearly noted and dealt with by educational planners and administrators.[5]

Furthermore, the writers of the Pune report concluded, 'there was no lack of motivation among parents for sending children to school. Nor did children resist learning once the project tried to meet their convenience and basic urges for playing and learning.[6] The report's relevance is emphasised by the conclusions of Vina Mazumdar about the dropout rate of girls. 'According to 1981 figures', she writes,

> over 45 percent of girls in the 6–11 age group, over 75 percent in the 12–14 age group, and over 85 percent in the 15–17 age group were out of school, as compared to 20 percent, 57 percent, and 71 percent of boys in the respective age groups. The main problem of universalizing elementary education, is the problem of enrolment of girls. Girls constitute 80 percent of the total non-enrolled children in the age group of 6–14.[7]

Another researcher in education, Krishna Kumar,[8] has pointed out that 'together, the curriculum, the methods of teaching, and the teacher comprise an agency constantly threatening the child's, especially the poor child's, self concept.' In rural communities poor children develop many talents and abilities that are devalued by the formal education curriculum. Thus,

> the problem is not of a solely educational nature. It concerns a wider range of issues in children's lives, not just their learning behaviour....
>
> ... A child centred view of education, which is required for the progress of primary schooling, just cannot catch on in a milieu where children must work to feed the family and where they die of minor illnesses.

Instead, the curriculum must treat the realities of their lives, and the school delivery system must operate in a manner that recognises that the children work.

In a socio-economic survey of 100 villages prepared for an economic credit plan for women, the ISST found that the April examination coincided with coffee bean harvest time.[9] Children, both boys and girls, could not take exams during this period of economic demand. A request that school hours and examination periods be modified had been accepted by the government's education department. But the teachers, who wanted standard holidays, rejected it. In developing countries we cannot separate family, child and workplace. This transition did occur in the West, but it is not one we want to bring about.

Moreover, schools must integrate learning with productive work, rather than separate children from a valued craft tradition. Ashrams such as Lakshmi are licensed as production units for spinning and weaving. They receive benefits, such as looms and spinning wheels as well as the underpinning of all produce from the Khadi and Village Industries Commission (KVIC), a national, state-funded 'commodity' board.[10] Thus, the schoolchildren learn and earn. The khadi and other local industries have yielded, however, to pressures and have introduced mechanised carding, along with poor pricing and costing practices. The Lakshmi Ashram school wants to opt out of the KVIC umbrella because it is hampering its efforts to make khadi a way of life and not 'primitive' production.

The wider community around the ashram is facing other crises. The ecosystem is being destroyed through mining in mountain pastures. Alcoholism is growing because of an alliance between the state's exchequer and local politicians and merchants. Women of the villages are always resisting, in one way or another, the cutting of trees, the mining, the extension of liquor shops, and the civic bodies that do not provide drinking water. Battles for survival, legitimacy and peace surround and dominate their lives. They have little time for anything else; every mental and physical space around them is being wounded by one or another of these 'development' impulses.

It seems, then, that the content of education for the poor, especially for poor women, has to be information that can serve as an 'early warning system' to help them resist Western-style development, not education that will increase their participation in such development. They need a curriculum that enables them to value their own culture soundly and to look critically at the West, especially at Western science and technology.

Another major preoccupation must be how to resist science and technology. Advances in biotechnology will eliminate the livelihoods of millions of farmers and damage the health of millions of women. The poor need to be given reliable information about things that threaten their livelihood and also about how they can place people who understand these impending dangers in positions of political power. Early warning systems will build up resistance. In other words, our education must be for resistance, and our curriculum must inform people of cultural danger.

I can illustrate what such an education means by describing my own path towards my current assessment of the equation between education and development in South Asia. Because of my interest in adult education programmes for poor women, I had recommended that a curriculum be developed so that each programme (dairy, silk, fish, etc.) would design a module for adult education manuals. I felt that this would encourage women to attend the classes and would be useful to them in their economic tasks.[11]

In another forum, I proposed that the information gained through research could improve understanding of women's roles and give them infrastructural support.[12] One useful illustration is a project in which milk producers were to form a co-operative. After studying that site and the project, I proposed (because of my belief that participation in decision making would be a way to integrate women into development) that the project should first bring more women into co-operatives and also that the project should develop a social infrastructure for childcare, water and fuel support to reduce household drudgery. When both these suggestions were adopted I was thrilled and felt a sense of achievement. I wrote a paper for the mid-decade UN Conference on Women in Copenhagen in 1980, celebrating the possibilities of integrating women in development through research and advocacy. But, with hindsight, I now believe that the project should be resisted by women.[13]

A survey of 120 households at Kaira in Gujarat revealed that the introduction of this collective market support system for dairy households added 2 hours to the 12 hours a day that women already worked.[14] It took away the little bit of milk that had been kept for home consumption and ended the tradition of preserving milk by making butter, ghee and whey, the latter having been an important food. Household income had risen and become more reliable, but women had lost control of food resources. The money had been appropriated by the men of the household, the co-operative which was led by men, and the urban consumer. Introducing cash-generating projects does not help a poor family, which relies on 12 hours of women's labour a day for its food supply.

Another popular recommendation was to make the poor, especially women, aware of development services, of modes of organisation and of management. The radical edge to this is the awareness of rights. I prepared and designed schemes for government funding, including a proposal that 1 to 2 per cent of development funds should be spent on raising awareness about the programmes, especially programmes that credited self-employment, public works programmes for wage employment, and commodity promotion programmes in milk, silk, tea and textiles.

The end result of many of these programmes was to divert the poor from known options of sustainable development of highly vulnerable production, and a harsher, more deprived level of living, especially for women and children. In my own evolution I have gone from recommending sectorally specific 'employment-strengthening' curricula for adult women by taking literacy classes, to objecting to that very employment, be it in dairy farming or sericulture.

It has to be admitted that, while these worthy ideas were developed by researchers like myself through an 'ear to the ground' approach, we were leading our 'poor illiterate' sisters into the 'open world'. We were naïve and realised too late that this great goodness, 'development', integrating women into which had been our mandate, and this great public world which men occupy and into which we were to bring women through employment and health strategies, were dangerous, even devastating.

These experiences have shown me that we must teach ourselves and others the 'macro' consequences of 'micro' choices. It is such micro experiences of project impact—not only class and gender differentiation, but also the larger perspective of macro reverberations—that have made feminists engaged in development research step back and look at the macro policies of development.

A rural women's group may be encouraged by a national policy or a local development project to take up the farming of mulberry trees to provide fodder for silkworms. They may plant the trees on land formerly used for crops. The silkworms bring cash into the household, usually to its male members. In a low-resource household, this change in land use reduces food for the female members. Poor women are literally made to go around the mulberry bush.[15]

Looking back, the emphasis of the pioneers of the women's movement seems to have been on education. Development, however, challenges the whole foundation of education and its content. Today even specialists in the field of education have stopped looking for ways to bring more women into education. Instead of focusing on access, they are thinking again about the framework, goals and content of education.

Even men and women from within academic institutions are questioning the actual contribution of education to social development, because it can be and often has been a means of teaching the stereotypes of an unjust society. The Ministerial Conference of Non-Aligned and Other Developing Countries on the Role of Women in Development, held in New Delhi in April 1985, blamed educational systems for playing a subtle and powerful role (more powerful than the media or art) in promoting such stereotypes

> through myths like the supplementary nature of women's work.... In reality, there are extraordinarily few areas or circumstances where women's economic contribution could be dismissed as merely supplementary or optional or dispensable. But this myth has been very successfully practiced increasingly over the ages to keep women under subjugation politically, economically and socially.[16]

I suggest that building self-confidence and increasing self-worth are the pegs on which our knowledge is to hang. From the individual woman to the nation, we need to legitimate ourselves economically, politically, socially and culturally. Rethinking development requires a new body of thought, one that looks at new and existing political, economic and social theories, theories which include women's languages, values, descriptive statements, and the principles derived from them. Once this is done, the new indicators of progress will emerge.

There are many illustrations of the intelligence embedded in the cultural practices of the South, or of developing countries: the choice of crops and methods of water management in agriculture, the worship of trees which ensures their protection in forestry, the recycling of waste, herbal medicines, attention to diet, pollution, and the personal relationships between ages and genders. Carefully edited catalogues of these cases could become manuals for those designing local projects. Imagine a project formulator—his or her head full of the usual preconceptions that the local people are ignorant, unscientific and believe in voodoo and superstitions—opening a manual and finding references to local practices that are conserving and efficient. He or she may then design the project from that base. Imagine also the effect that this kind of documentation and approach would have on those who make up a 'backward group'. Their own self-worth would be enhanced.

For women, it seems to me that building self-worth requires a new look at the way we order human characteristics, or to use the old-fashioned words, our moral theory. I suggest that we are still mesmerised by male characteristics. Whether it is the women of Lakshmi Ashram or those women of Kumaon who prefer fuel trees to mineral mines or fruit trees, another view of agenda and of method exists. This is most evident among the poor, for whom the pressure for survival deepens gender differences and intensifies creativity.

One ideological or philosophical approach that seems to be consistent with the issues, concerns and characteristics of the women's experience in India is that of Gandhi. Gandhi concentrated on consciousness and the mind of the individual. Though his collection of do's and don'ts are often laughed at as being too austere, even perverse, they were immensely appealing to the people he addressed. They felt that they were being drawn into being better than themselves, into being mini-saints. Unity and homogeneity were built on personal ethics, not on class, gender, religion, race or political ideology.

Gandhi, not the -ism but rather the perspective and the method, offers a valuable lesson in how to use education to build both harmony and power in communities. It offers a way to link the individual to society. In his approach to equalising social and economic patterns, Gandhi released less aggressive moral, cultural and economic processes.

He attempted to bridge the gaps between social divides by stressing identification with others, experiencing the experience of the 'other'. He played the role of women as he saw them—as caring, moral and courageous beings. He wanted to be called 'Maa'. He identified with the poor by wearing clothes like theirs and living in their homes. He lived in Harijan colonies, in Muslim houses. He had great trust in human nature and in human imagination. He believed that, if one could see an injustice or a hurtful act from the side of the recipient, one would never be unjust or hurtful again.

He also sought to set up alternative styles of social relationships, not only in the ashrams, where inherited hierarchies and role allocations were replaced by new, equal relationships and bonding for social action, but also in alternative economic systems based on intimate, accessible production and consumption linkages. His perspective was to prevent any concentration of power in any one area—state, corporation, trade union, patriarch, temple or church—by building a basis for autonomy within each household.

This process of identifying with oppressed groups is one of the methods used today by female social activists in Gandhi-based institutions such as Lakshmi Ashram. In some respects, it removes the problem of outsider–insider, elite–mass, alienation. The women subscribe to the approach of letting each person's consciousness develop by offering a support system, often provided just by walking among the people as padayatri. They are patient. They do not push too hard to change class, caste and gender divisions, but instead live a life that rejects these divisions and shares with others the faith that, step by step, society will evolve, by adjusting and readjusting towards harmony.

Nai talim, Gandhi's philosophy of education; *sarvadharma*, his formula of transforming religious barriers into common worship; *sarvodaya*, his method of transforming class and caste barriers into communal harmony—all are used as slogans today. None of them will work, however, without the 'godly' men and women, or the mini-saints, that Gandhi trained. And these godly men and women cannot emerge without each one having developed a consciousness of self.

I suggest that, without rethinking and specifying the philosophy, the vision and the specific vocabularies, including the basic syllabus of education, it is not useful to draw women into education. The stance that poor women are forced to adopt, as it now stands, is one of resistance and struggle. To recycle that stance into more enriching 'building' roles requires going back, or down, and not going forward. It can be done. There is much material among us. We are also rich in resources. The question is to what use we will put them.

What we have been working at articulating is a vision of the new, educated woman. No matter whether she is a product of the formal or non-formal systems, she will embody important characteristics of a new, educated class. She will have the necessary knowledge to assist in saving the planet from environmental degradation. She will have learned to respect difference, but she will be rooted in her region and community, ready to accept sacrifice to preserve both. And, because she has been taught through texts that describe women's real contribution to economic and political life, she will no longer be a self-sacrificing servant of patriarchy.

NOTES

1   Julius K. Nyerere, message to M. A. Singamma Sreenivasan Foundation Round Table on 'Survival Strategies of the Poor and Traditional Wisdom: A Reflection', Rajmahal Vilas Extension, Bangalore, 17–18 May 1987. A full report on the round table is available from the International Institute for Environment and Development, London.

2   Tom Woodhouse, *People and Planet* (Hartland, Devon: Green Books, 1987).

3   Vinoba Bhave, disciple of Mahatma Gandhi who undertook a padayatra throughout India in the mid-1950s to redistribute land through appeals to the conscience of those who owned land. His campaigns were known as *bhoodan* (land gift) and *gramdan* (village gift).

4   Chitra Naik, 'Making Childhood Learning Happier', *Future* (UNICEF magazine), no. 20 (1987).

5   Woodhouse, *People and Planet*.

6   Ibid.

7   Vina Mazumdar, 'Education and Women's Equality', paper presented at the National Seminar on 'Education for Women's Equality', Vigyan Bhavan, New Delhi, 3–5 November 1985.

8   Krishna Kumar, 'Development of Women and Children in Rural Areas (DWCRA): Preparation of a Plan with Focus on Women, Block Chikmagalur (Karnataka)', proposal submitted by the ISST, New Delhi, September 1983.

9   Ibid.

10 The KVIC is a national structure which networks with all suppliers of khadi and with village industries, buying their products and selling them in retail shops.

11 On adult education see Devaki Jain, 'Five Year Plan Suggestions and Final Report: Task Force on Adult Education', ISST, p. 7; National Seminar on 'New Trends in Adult Education for Women, with Special Reference to Literacy', Indian Adult Education Association, New Delhi, 19–22 February 1980; Workshop on Educational Programmes for Adult Women, New Delhi, 1984; Rajkumari Chandrashekhar, *Aspects of Adult Education* (Madras: New Era Publication, 1982); ISST, 'Case Studies: Adult Education for Women', New Delhi, 1984. See also Devaki Jain, 'Women's Employment as Related to Rural Areas', paper presented at the Kulu Women and Development Conference, Copenhagen, 1980.

12 Jain et al., *Women's Quest for Power.*

13 Sen and Grown, *Development, Crises and Alternative Visions.*

14 Jain et al., *Women's Quest for Power.*

15 ISST, 'A Proposal on Household-Level Food Security', submitted to the FAO Nutrition Department, Rome, 1985.

16 *New Delhi Document on Women in Development*, Conference of Non-aligned and Other Developing Countries on the Role of Women in Development, New Delhi, 1985.

Chapter 5

Valuing Work: Time as a Measure
(with Malini Chand Seth)

A time-use study that was conducted by ISST in 1982—the earliest to be undertaken in developing countries—was basically intended to correct the figures for the work participation rate in the national statistics. The methodology used until then for counting workers had flaws. Thus, women's actual economic contributions were not counted. The ISST study was designed such that, through observation, investigators noted what women actually did for 16 hours a day for a week in a selection of households in Rajasthan and West Bengal. This study provided many insights, especially into the fact that when you measure work according to the time spent, you not only capture what are called 'economically valuable' issues, but also the time that women spend serving a household—fetching water, cooking, cleaning and looking after children. The present paper offers a detailed discussion of the ISST's time-use study, and narrates how we began to see how much work—sometime 18 hours out of 24—women and girl children do in a poverty household.

The UNDP's *Human Development Reports* (*HDRs*), initiated in 1990, have been taking up one cross–cutting theme each year. It is common knowledge that such reports—the *HDRs* of the UNDP, or the *World Development Reports* (*WDRs*) of the World Bank, or other global agencies' reports on the 'state of the world' in special sectors—are political documents: the quantitative measures through which they describe are prescriptive in their implications.

Gender discrimination is the theme of *HDR 1995*, which offers a very special illumination, an enlargement of the issue of inequality through a gender lens.[1] It makes the case that inequality between men and women cuts across all the usual divides—advanced, industrialised countries (G-7), developing countries (G-77), class, religion, race, geography. By revealing this discrimination as a worldwide, unmitigated phenomenon, the report provided the basis for women at the Fourth UN World Conference on Women at Beijing in 1995 to demand, for example, positive discrimination, a quota system in political processes and structures, as a universal instrument to redress the imbedded inequality in visible power. In other words, the politics of the report's insights was picked up and used by women in this matter.

The *HDR* of 1995 also makes some radical, insightful statements on growth and inequality. To quote:

> For too long, it was assumed that development was a process that lifts all boats, that its benefits trickled down to all income classes—and that it was gender-neutral in its impact. Experience teaches otherwise. Wide income disparities and gender gaps stare us in the face in all societies.
>
> *Moving towards gender equality is not a technocratic goal—it is a political process.* It requires a new way of thinking—in which the stereotyping of women and men gives way to a new philosophy that regards all people, irrespective of gender, as essential agents of change.
>
> The relentless struggle for gender equality will change most of today's premises for social, economic and political life.[2]

However, at the level of the actual measures used in constructing the Human Development Index (HDI), and thereby the Gender Development Index (GDI), the report does not measure up to its own radical statements quoted above. It is not able to get away from the politics of measurement, derived as it is from the bases of current theories of progress—money and the market.

There are many other inadequacies in the composition of indices, especially GDI and the Gender Empowerment Measure (GEM), from a Southern, feminist perspective, which have been addressed by Hirway and Mahadevia (GDI)[3] and Aasha Kapur Mehta (GEM).[4] This paper will specifically address the issue of valuation of work—a crucial element in the presentation of evaluative indices. It will take off from the ideas, facts and questions raised in chapter 4 of *HDR 1995*, and will end with some questions on measures, derived from a field investigation of the time use of individuals in a sample of 127 rural households.[5]

VALUING WOMEN'S WORK

Chapter 4 of *HDR 1995*, 'Valuing Women's Work', is sensitive, well informed, and raises issues that feminists, both academics and activists, have been grappling with for many decades—coming into international advocacy in Mexico in 1975 (the First UN Conference on Women), continuing through Nairobi in 1985 (the Third UN Conference on Women) and into the present time. To quote:

> Women's work is greatly undervalued in economic terms. This is due in part to the restricted definition of economic activity. But part of the problem is the notion of value itself.

> For the purposes of economic valuation, value is synonymous with market value.... But many goods and services with economic value are not marketed. In theory, this problem is resolvable if these items could be sold, for a market value could then be imputed to them on this basis—as is done for subsistence crops consumed by the producers themselves.... Yet much household and community work remains unvalued. The total product of society is thus underestimated—and the economic contributions of many people, especially women, are unrecognized and unrewarded.

> The general problem of unpaid or non-market work has long been noted.... But unpaid work goes far beyond housekeeping, and its omission leaves a major gap in national income accounting.

> An additional consideration is that the value of much household and community work transcends market value. This activity has *an intrinsic use value or human value* that is not captured by its value for exchange.[6]

Thus the observations in the chapter do in fact try to argue for a shift from market and money. The chapter then discusses the System of National Accounts (SNA) and its shortcomings, and also explores the possibilities of getting this 'unmeasured' contribution into the SNA, e.g.:

> The System of National Accounts was never designed to measure human well-being—only output, income and expenditures. But to accomplish this limited goal, the SNA should become more comprehensive, more encompassing in how it defines economic activity. The reason: much of the work of society remains 'invisible', and the people performing it do not get their proper economic reward or recognition.

> In many developing countries, production activities outside the household are difficult to separate from household work, and women's multiple tasks often combine the two. In other words, the distinction between SNA and non-SNA work is often blurred. Non-marketed output and the corresponding labour input are thus both underestimated.[7]

The chapter then presents information revealed from a review of time-use studies:

> A review of the 31 countries [shows that] women work longer hours than men in nearly every country.... Of the total burden of work, women carry on average 53% in developing countries and 51% in industrial countries.

> Of men's total work time in industrial countries, roughly two-thirds is spent in paid SNA activities and one-third in unpaid non-SNA activities. For women, these shares are reversed. In developing countries, more than three-fourths of men's work is in SNA activities. So, men receive the lion's share of income and recognition for their economic contribution—while most of women's work remains unpaid, unrecognized and undervalued.[8]

The report suggests that time studies offer a basis for valuating the 'invisible' contribution. Referring to an exercise conducted in 13 industrial countries to give a monetary value to 'non-SNA' production, it says: 'the value of non-SNA production in industrial countries is considerable, whatever the standard. *It is at least half of gross domestic product, and it accounts for more than half of private consumption.*' Of $16 trillion of global output which is 'invisible', $11 trillion is produced by women.[9]

The report then goes on to make a strong case for monetisation of non-market activities on the grounds that

> not giving an economic valuation to these activities risks seriously underestimating the contribution of women. There is no adequate reward or recognition for the burden of work that women carry.... The failure to value most of their work reduces women to virtual non-entities in most economic transactions—such as property ownership or offering collateral for bank loans. Because status in contemporary society is so often equated with income-earning power, women suffer a major undervaluation of their economic status. This is so despite their larger share of the total work burden and notwithstanding the reality that men's paid work in the market-place is often the result of 'joint production', much of which might not be possible if women did not stay at home looking after the children and the household.[10]

The report further observes:

> The monetization of the non-market work of women is more than a question of justice. It concerns the economic status of women in society. If women's unpaid work were properly valued, it is quite possible that women would emerge in most societies as the main breadwinners—or at least equal breadwinners—since they put in more hours of work than men.[11]

The report ends by suggesting that 'each working member of a family is entitled to a share of the income generated by market work proportional to her or his total labour contribution—including unpaid labour. For households to share income with their wives will become an act of entitlement rather than benevolence.'[12]

The field study of the time disposition/time allocation of individuals within a sample of rural households (the TAS study), while revealing this phenomenon of invisibility, concentrates more on measuring methods. It shows that by elaborating housework, breaking it into segments, it is possible to extract unmeasured economic activity, thereby making the enumeration of workers more accurate.

The TAS study suggests that while there is neglect of housework and its value in the current methodologies used by statistical systems, there is also a prior neglect in that even economic activity of the kind in which the majority of women engage in developing countries does not get reflected. It reveals that even if housework is not given recognition in SNA, elaboration of housework into its components, as well as across ages and classes, across occupations, across seasons in agriculture, etc., would help to identify the nature of participation or involvement of time and energy. Such identification, such profiles, are vital for index building and programmed support.

The TAS study also shows, amongst other things, the ways in which time disposition in hours can be incorporated into large-scale household surveys, and thus rectify the inaccuracy of the national data. Such an exercise is important as the basis of the calculation of income (which in turn affects HDI and GDI) derived from work participation rates (multiplied by wage rates). If the rates are higher due to better enumeration, the inequality between men and women, measured in GDI, will be reduced. (Maharashtra ranks first in India in GDI—and it has been observed that this could be due to the Maharashtra Employment Guarantee Scheme which provides waged work to women.) Such an outcome would in fact highlight that in LDCs, poor women are all working in conventional economic activities—a ground reality which needs to be highlighted as it shows physical hardship among poor women.[13] The TAS study also reveals that the female work participation rate (FWPR) is higher than the male work participation rate amongst the landless in India, highlighting the facts that focusing on the poor gives a different weight to the indices, and that class stratification is an important analytical tool in building measures, especially with a view to advocacy.

Going beyond the special features and utility of time-use studies, recommendations are made in the TAS study on how to improve the enumeration of women workers in national and international data production systems, e.g., by dropping the code 'domestic activity' from the Activity List of the International Standard; and by extending the time-use module in national household surveys to all members of a household so that activities are accurately notified.[14] The *HDR 1995* talks about income sharing within the family, so women can have entitlements and not be treated as 'beneficiaries'. Once again, going step by step, the issue need not be payment as much as identification of work participation in the LDCs in the first instance.

THE INDIAN TIME ALLOCATION STUDY

In the TAS study, 'housework' was elaborated, and the analysis provided ideas on improving the 'counting' or enumeration of women workers which could be used by national-level household surveys such as the National Sample Survey (NSS), as well as insights on measures in general.

The study involved household surveys in six villages, where time spent by men, women and children across a broad range of 42 activities was recorded largely through observation. The researchers visited each household six times during the 52-week period; they observed and recorded the activities of all members of each household above 5 years of age, in intervals of half hours.

In order to select the sample of 127 households for the detailed records, a full census was conducted of all the 860 households in the six villages. This was done through a questionnaire and one visit during which gainfully active persons were identified with the usual or standard method employed in India's employment surveys and labour enquiries—namely, giving an activity code to all persons in a household on the basis of their predominant preoccupation over the year and/or over the previous week.

This process of data collection, undertaken while living continuously in the village, offered an intimacy of experience both to the households and to the researchers. Conventional stratifications of society—whether of caste, class, age or gender—appeared and disappeared according to circumstances or issues. For example, the villages in Rajasthan looked like an undifferentiated mud heap, and it was difficult to know who was rich and who was poor from the size of the construction. But for the insider, it was the stocks of foodgrain that determined security and autonomy and their consequences—power. If you had enough foodgrain stored till the next crop, you did not get into debt, you did not have to struggle for wage work. Indebtedness and grain stocks emerged as the indicators of inequality more than land or homestead or consumption expenditure and jewellery.

Women's views on the priority needs of the village varied vastly from men's views, whatever the caste or class. Men identified a road, and women a health centre as the primary need. Men identified a school, and women identified training for employment as priority needs. The household or family seemed to be important units of social formation, useful for identification, but the internal dynamics seemed to provide equally important and useful information.

During the year 1977–78, the National Sample Survey Organisation (NSSO) surveyed 102,000 rural and 59,300 urban households across India for their periodic employment/unemployment data collection. This was the 32nd Round of the NSS. Responding to concerns about the accurate measurement of employment, especially of women, the questionnaire was extended to asking what are called 'probing questions'. These were a set of 24 questions addressed to those persons within a household who had identified themselves as being engaged mainly in domestic work only, or domestic work and collection of goods and services, i.e., activity codes 92 and 93.[15]

The TAS study also canvassed the 32nd Round questionnaire for the sample of 127 households to see the kind of profile of women's work this questionnaire provided, as different from the standard questionnaire canvassed earlier. The idea was to compare data emerging from the 32nd Round which used a standard questionnaire with the data provided by observed activity and recording among the same households.

THE DATA

Table 5.1 presents a broad spectrum of data on work participation rates from secondary and primary sources, as well as different areas and levels (state/village/sample households). The definitions and denominators are the same for all the numbers—however, strictly speaking, such data

Table 5.1 *Work participation rates*

Rows	Secondary Data: States					Primary Data: Selected villages			
	Census 1961	Census 1971	NSS 27R (1971–73)	NSS 32R (1977–78)		ISS Census 1976	NSS/ISS 32R (1977)		Time Disposition 1976–77
				(i)	(ii)				
Columns	1	2	3	4	5	6	7	8	9
Adults (15–59)									
Persons	81	55	–	71	83	81	72	96	87
Males	95	92	90	89	89	89	90	93	94
Females	64	15	66	52	75	71	49	98	80
West Bengal									
Persons	56	48	–	52	72	51	50	71	62
Males	90	84	81	87	87	91	91	91	93
Females	19	8	17	15	57	10	12	62	34

(Continued)

Table 5.1 (Continued)

Rows	Secondary Data: States					Primary Data: Selected villages			
	Census 1961	Census 1971	NSS 27R (1971–73)	NSS 32R (1977–78)		ISS Census 1976	NSS/ISS 32R (1977)		Time Disposition 1976–77
				(i)	(ii)				
Columns	1	2	3	4	5	6	7	8	9
Children (0–14)									
Rajasthan									
Children	15	6	–	–	–	28	14	34	56
Males	16	8	–	–	–	29	14	20	45
Females	14	3	–	–	–	27	14	48	69
West Bengal									
Children	4	3	–	–	–	4	11	17	45
Males	6	5	–	–	–	7	18	18	60
Females	2	1	–	–	–	1	2	23	30

Source: Jain and Chand, 'Report on a Time Allocation Study'; secondary sources as above.

are not comparable, as the size of the sample as well as the sampling frame, etc., are too small for statistically valid comparison. However, the tables are composed this way, with columns giving 'comparative' figures, for the insights they offer and the dramas they unfold. The last column of this table is computed by grouping the observed activities of all members of sample households involved at least in 1 hour, in each of the six rounds, of 'gainful activity', as defined by NSSO codes 0–71.[16]

What is striking is row 2 and row 5 (Table 5.1), that is, the percentage of male work participation. Whatever the method of investigation—the decennial census, NSSO 27th or 32nd Round, whatever the area or level of estimation—state or village or sample household, the figure for males remains 'constant'—around 89–90 per cent in Rajasthan, and in the range of 81 to 93 per cent in West Bengal. Whereas figures for females and children vary according to the methodology used, e.g., from 15 per cent to 98 per cent in the case of Rajasthan (columns 2 and 8), and from 8 per cent to 62 per cent for West Bengal children. The obvious inference is that the gainful activity of females and children—the tasks they engage in, their location—are not captured in the net cast by the existing investigation methodology with the same precision as for males.

It is not new to say that the difficulty in appropriately netting female labour is because of the nature/style of women's work. Many analyses of secondary employment data refer to the problems posed by including female labour figures, and some even exclude it in trend analysis to avoid 'irregularity'. The time allocation data helped to understand what brings in this 'irregularity'. Tables 5.2A and 5.2B summarise the data collected and averaged over six rounds from 127 households through observation, and distribute it across activities in terms of hours per day, by age and sex, covering about 9 hours a day. Time spent in 'personal activity' has been excluded from the tables, though it was collected, partly because of the focus of this paper and partly because it was based on recall data.

Predictable but interesting patterns emerge. Females, whether in Rajasthan, a high-FWPR state, or West Bengal, a low-FWPR state, report at least 3 if not 6 hours per day in domestic work. In Rajasthan, the women engage more in 'outside home' activities even though there

Table 5.2A Time allocation revealing segregation of activities by age and sex (Rajasthan)

Age	5–9		6–14		14–19		19–32		34–44		44–70	
No. of samples	M 97	F 87	M 154	F 138	M 63	F 58	M 180	F 215	M 91	F 98	M 160	F 91
1	2	3	4	5	6	7	8	9	10	11	12	13
Ploughing, digging,	–	–	0/05	–	0.57	–	0.75	–	0.87	–	0.79	–
Irrigation of fields	–	–	0.10	–	0.39	–	0.48	–	1.61	–	0.70	–
Harvesting	–	–	0.05	0.08	0.14	0.25	0.10	0.04	–	0.25	0.06	0.21
Groundnut picking	–	0.34	0.02	0.28	0.16	0.50	0.04	0.21	0.10	0.18	0.13	0.31
Vegetable picking	0.14	0.15	0.02	0.21	–	0.05	–	0.12	0.17	0.28	0.01	0.22
Cutting grass from fields	0.11	0.55	0.32	1.65	0.56	1.29	0.51	1.08	0.57	1.69	0.48	1.02
Weeding fields	–	–	0.12	0.42	–	0.54	0.06	0.66	0.69	0.71	0.63	0.83
* Total agriculture	0.51	1.63	1.38	3.06	2.00	2.98	2.75	2.44	6.31	3.62	4.04	3.05
Husking, winnowing, parboiling, grain husking	–	0.01	0.04	0.07	–	0.14	0.02	0.08	0.23	0.34	0.12	0.11
Cattle/goat grazing	1.12	0.87	0.61	0.81	0.54	0.20	0.35	0.12	0.56	0.05	0.30	0.18
Cattle milking and feeding	0.02	0.11	0.13	0.13	0.38	0.22	0.22	0.28	0.48	0.42	0.55	0.55
Making cowdung cakes	–	0.16	–	0.33	–	0.20	–	0.18	–	0.17	–	0.10
* Total allied	1.15	1.28	0.94	1.60	1.28	1.09	0.68	1.13	1.38	1.38	1.21	1.43

Service	–	–	–	0.06	1.29	–	1.35	–	0.36	0.03	–	–
Production of straw mats, ropes	–	–	–	0.02	–	0.02	–	0.02	–	–	0.03	0.09
Selling goods (stationery, grain, fish, etc.)	–	–	0.11	–	0.47	–	0.46	–	0.01	–	0.09	–
Manual labour	–	–	–	–	–	–	–	0.37	0.03	0.31	–	0.21
* Total non-agriculture	–	0.16	0.04	0.04	1.76	2.70	0.10	1.00	0.04	0.37	0.09	0.09
Cooking (grinding, cutting, etc.)	–	0.26	0.04	0.74	–	2.00	0.03	2.34	0.10	2.76	0.08	1.60
Sweeping, washing clothes and utensils	0.01	0.45	0.03	0.56	–	0.93	0.01	1.09	0.02	0.02	0.12	0.53
Fetching water	–	0.16	0.03	0.56	–	0.93	0.01	1.09	0.02	1.02	0.12	0.53
Fetching fuel	–	0.01	–	0.07	–	0.04	–	0.08	–	0.09	–	0.09
*Total household activities	0.01	0.89	0.10	1.75	–	3.66	0.05	4.05	0.14	4.33	0.25	2.47
Schooling	1.71	0.50	2.61	0.41	1.72	–	–	–	–	–	–	–
Playing—children	2.55	1.43	1.14	0.24	0.39	–	–	–	–	–	–	–
Total spent in childcare	0.16	1.71	0.40	1.23	0.20	0.31	0.07	1.13	0.17	0.69	0.15	0.91
*Total child activities	4.42	3.77	4.15	1.97	2.33	0.34	0.08	1.17	0.18	0.63	0.15	0.92

Source: Fieldwork conducted by ISST for TAS study.

Note: * Totals include activities that are not listed here.

Table 5.2B Time allocation revealing segregation of activities by age and sex (West Bengal)

Age	4–9		9–14		14–19		19–32		34–44		44–70	
No. of samples	M 146	F 124	M 152	F 151	M 81	F 88	M 191	F 257	M 150	F 124	M 127	F 140
1	2	3	4	5	6	7	8	9	10	11	12	13
Ploughing, digging	-	-	0.05	0.09	0.56	-	0.67	0.08	0.69	-	0.58	-
Sowing	',	-	0.03	-	0.32	-	0.43	0.04	1.29	0.08	0.32	-
Harvesting	-	-	0.63	0.03	0.84	0.05	0.98	0.16	0.81	0.07	0.10	-
Cutting grass from field	0.10	0.03	0.56	0.11	0.19	-	0.18	0.06	0.11	0.14	0.31	0.01
Weeding fields	-	-	0.03	-	0.39	-	0.36	002	0.46	-	0.26	-
* Total agriculture	0.14	0.05	1.87	0.38	0.47	0.24	4.12	0.59	4.54	0.49	3.77	0.07
Husking, winnowing, parboiling, grain husking	-	-	-	0.09	0.14	0.14	0.26	0.17	0.19	0.43	0.24	0.27
Cattle/goat grazing	1.37	0.13	1.97	0.44	1.12	0.07	0.20	-	0.06	0.09	0.02	-
Cattle milking and feeding	0.08	-	052	0.12	0.68	-	0.10	0.02	0.08	0.03	0.05	0.03
* Total allied	1.58	0.14	3.56	0.80	3.15	0.30	0.77	0.27	0.47	0.69	0.37	0.41
1	2	3	4	5	6	7	8	9	10	11	12	13
Production of straw mats, ropes	0.08	0.11	-	0.52	-	1.06	0.01	0.50	-	0.23	0.09	0.22

Activity												
Work as domestic servants	–	0.07	0.02	0.60	0.01	0.29	–	0.03	–	0.04	–	–
Selling goods (stationery, grain, fish, etc.)	–	–	–	0.02	0.73	0.08	1.04	0.17	1.47	0.01	0.37	0.05
Manual labour	–	–	0.06	–	0.19	–	0.46	0.14	0.70	–	0.32	–
*Total non-agriculture	0.21	0.18	0.31	1.72	0.99	1.44	1.62	1.20	2.58	0.76	2.16	1.59
Cooking (grinding, cutting, etc.)	–	0.26	0.04	0.74	–	2.00	0.03	2.34	0.10	2.76	0.08	1.60
Sweeping, washing clothes and utensils	–	0.06	0.04	0.57	0.03	1.05	0.03	1.45	–	0.27	–	0.52
Fetching water	–	0.05	0.06	0.27	0.07	0.59	0.01	0.39	–	0.29	–	018
*Total household activities	0.74	1.10	0.60	2.81	0.27	4.31	0.18	5.77	0.10	6.39	0.08	3.16
Schooling	1.25	1.30	1.12	0.83	–	0.06	0.09	–	–	–	–	–
Playing—children	2.80	3.28	0.73	0.72	0.06	–	0.01	–	–	–	–	–
Total spent in childcare	0.12	0.26	0.03	0.17	0.02	0.14	0.02	0.42	–	0.12	0.03	0.55
*Total child activities	4.19	4.92	1.90	1.81	0.08	0.25	0.11	0.48	–	0.19	0.04	0.62

Source: Jain and Chand, 'Report on a Time Allocation Study'.

Note: * Totals include activities that are not listed here.

is strict age-sex segmentation of tasks, whereas in West Bengal they engage in much more homebound work. In the Rajasthan villages, females engage in cutting grass from fields and weeding fields for up to 2 hours, going up to about 4 as the age level goes up. Cattle and goat grazing takes about an hour. Both these are outdoor 'male-type' activities, though regularly done by women and girls.[17] Per contra, in the West Bengal sample, home-based production of goods such as quilts and, of all things, begging, is relatively more 'intensive' (1 to 2 hours) than farm work for women.

Amongst the landed families in West Bengal, while most women declared that they were not gainfully active in that they were engaged in housework, during the harvesting season, the time spent in domestic work increased dramatically and regularly. Every household of a particular class showed the pattern of a hump in the harvest season (Figure 5.1).[18] Probing this, it was found that women in these households cooked and served meals to the extra farmhands who were engaged at this peak harvest time.

Though these women were actively engaged in what are identified as productive activities, the system does not have the techniques to capture this, because the activity is lost in the female domain of the kitchen. In Rajasthan, however, rural women, since they work on farms like men, appear in the labour force. (Manipuri women, who dominate in trade, appear in the labour force and are visible in statistics.) Prostitution, begging, working as housemaids, and processing paddy at home as is done by women in West Bengal, are on the other hand invisible in data. *Thus, the more male-like the activities of females, the more likely that they will be noticed and measured.*

Table 5.3 shows that in the Rajasthan villages, FWPR is clearly inversely related to landownership. In the West Bengal villages, such a clear relationship was observed only among males. In terms of hours of work, however, landed females in the Rajasthan sample show 2 hours more in economic activities than their landless sisters. They also work more hours at household activity (Figure 5.2).[19] In the Rajasthan sample, the women, across different age groups, weave in and out of economic and non-economic activity with the same range of 'intensity' (measured in hours of involvement per day) as West

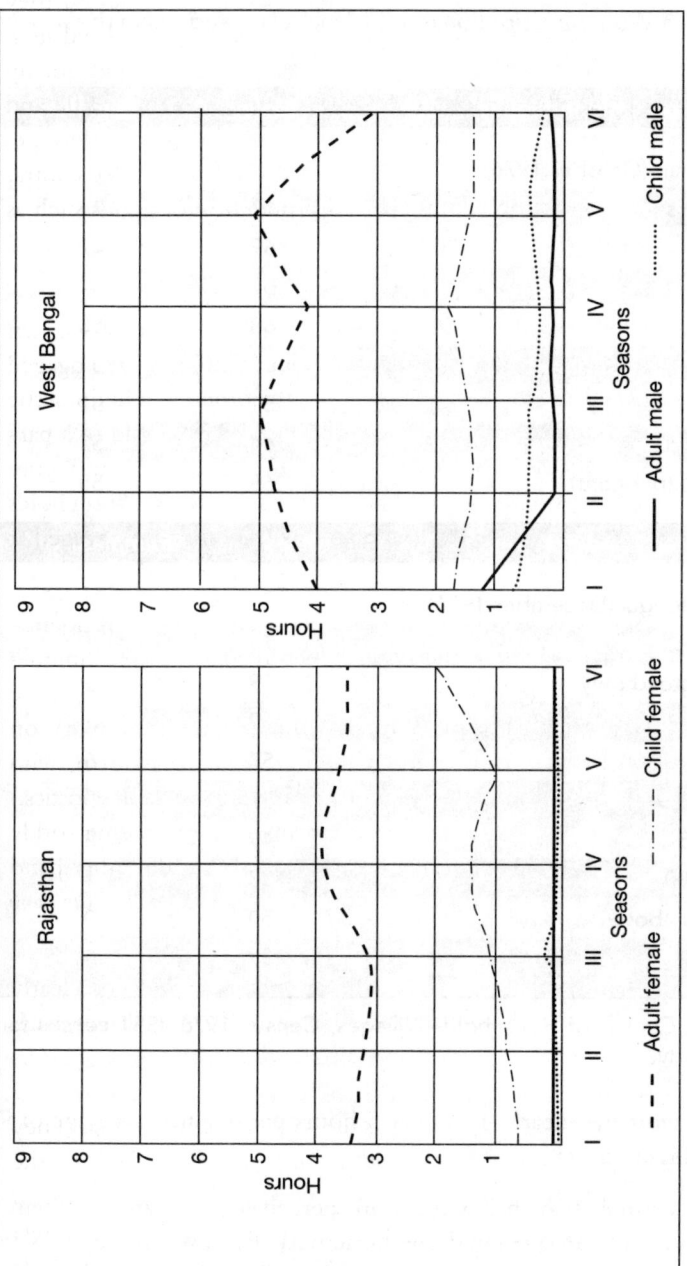

Figure 5.1 *Engagement in household activity by hours per day by age and sex across seasons*

Source: Jain and Chand, 'Report on a Time Allocation Study'.

Table 5.3 *Work participation rate by land, class and sex in the survey villages*

Operated Land in Bighas	Males	Females
Rajasthan (October 1976)		
Landless	67	74
0.1–2	69	47
2–5	67	67
5–10	68	58
10–15	67	54
15–20	51	52
20 and above	64	52
Overall (per cent)	65	55

Operated Land in Acres	Males	Females
West Bengal (December 1976)		
Landless	71	4
Homestead only	79	5
0.1–1	69	3
1–2	57	6
3.5–5.0	57	5
5.0–7.5	49	2
7.5–10.0	38	4
10 and above	50	0
Overall	59	4

Source: Census of Household—Villages, *Census 1976*; ISST census for TAS study.

Bengal women—nearly 4 to over 5 hours per day from the age of 9 to 14 (Figure 5.3).

It is natural then that women are perceived and perceive themselves as mainly engaged in domestic activity. Even when they also do income-earning work directly—that is, formally, visibly, as for example in Rajasthan, or indirectly, that is, unpaid family labour, free collection

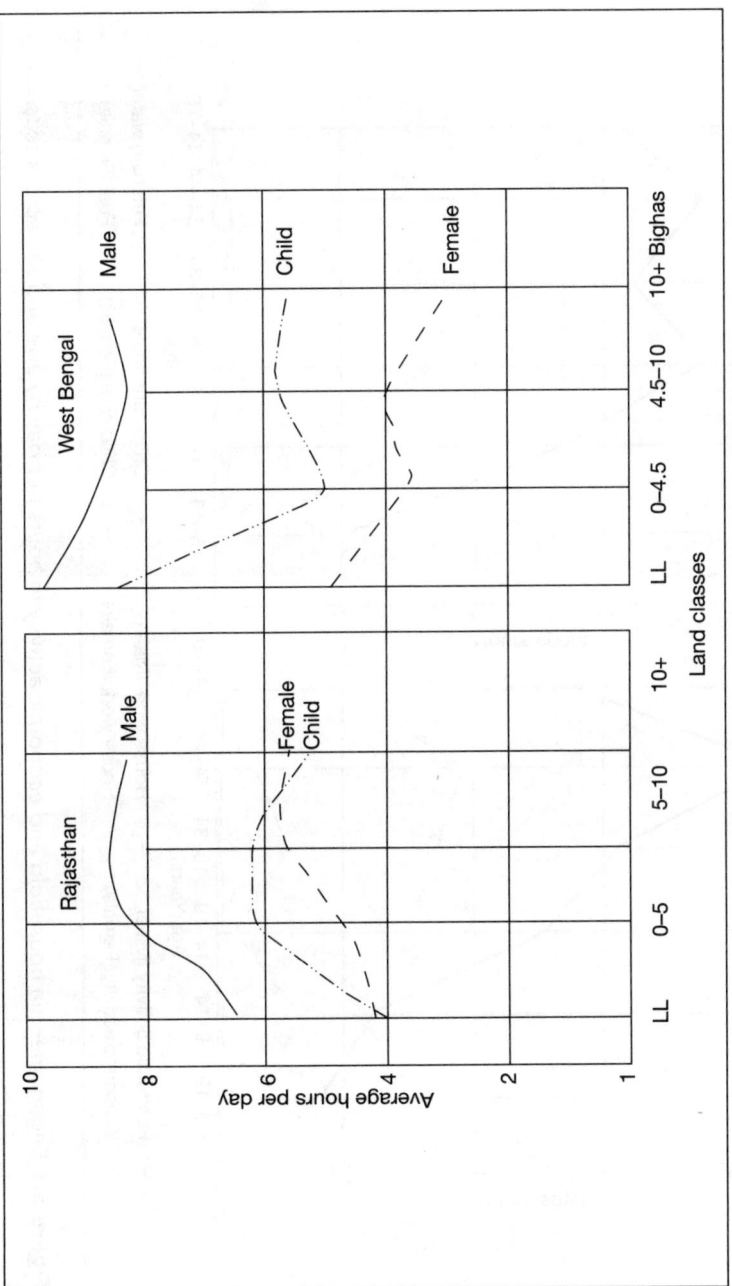

Figure 5.2 *Engagement in economic activity in hours per day by age, sex and land classes*

Source: Jain and Chand, 'Report on a Time Allocation Study'.

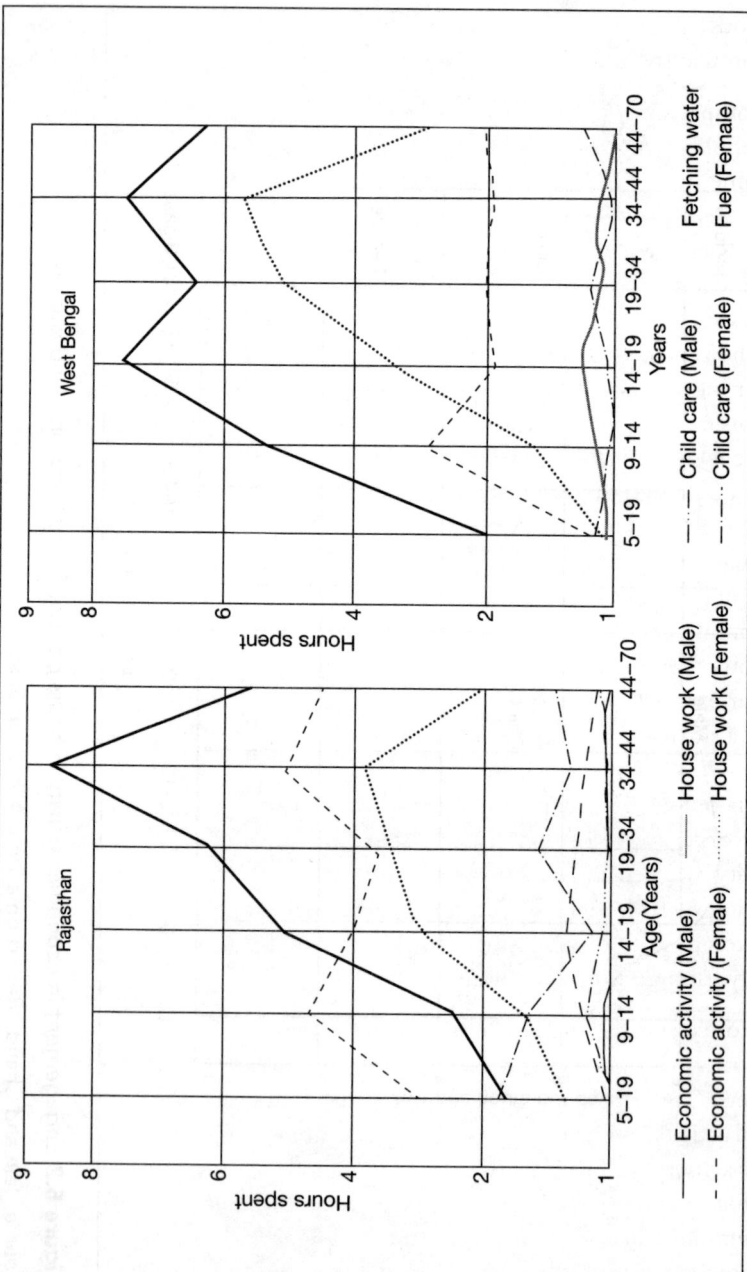

Figure 5.3 Engagement in household and economic activity in hours per day by age and sex across seasons

Source: Jain and Chand, 'Report on a Time Allocation Study'.

of goods and services, as in West Bengal, they cannot but be seen as predominantly houseworkers, which indeed they are.[20]

Comparison of data obtained from the questionnaire's census of households (schedule 1) and the time allocation data (schedule 2) for the same household revealed the following:

1. In Rajasthan, 4 out of the 37 women who reported as non-workers in schedule 1 were in fact spending up to 4 hours a day in activities such as groundnut picking and sowing the field. Nine others who reported as non-workers were grazing cattle and cutting grass for more than 1 hour. Thus, 13 out of 37, at least 30 per cent, fell outside the questionnaire net. Two of the 36 male children and 2 of the 34 female children who reported as non-workers were observed to be hoeing the field; 18 other female children were observed to be grazing cattle and cutting grass.
2. In West Bengal, 20 out of 104 females who reported themselves as non-workers were observed to be working in activities such as winnowing, threshing and parboiling, or as domestic servants in the homes of others, for as many as 8–10 hours per day. This emphasises our earlier point regarding the seriousness of measurement failure in a situation like that of West Bengal.

Fifteen out of 64 female children in West Bengal who reported as non-workers were also observed to be doing some gainful work. The majority worked as domestic servants; 10 females were reported as spending 8–10 hours begging, but were not included as workers in this exercise as the NSSO does not recognise begging as an economic activity, though it is recognised as an occupation.

Priority criteria, the concept of 'main activity', even the majority time criterion, puts these workers squarely in the category of domestic workers. The efficiency with which their 'other' activity—namely, gainful activity—is netted depends on the degree of visible marketability of this activity. In other words, the fact that they are uniquely responsible for a zone of work, viz., housework, gives them the distinction of being difficult to net. Is there a methodological innovation which can more satisfactorily handle this phenomenon?

The NSSO tried a new approach in its 32nd Round. Follow-up questions were addressed to all persons having a usual status of 01–93. In addition, further questions were addressed to persons engaged in domestic work (92) and those engaged in free collection of goods, etc., in addition to domestic work (93).

Tables 5.4 and 5.5[21] give data for selected states and all India. Table 5.5 tabulates the results of the 'probing questions'. Notice that where earlier counting shows low participation of women—such as the eastern region states, West Bengal, Orissa and Bihar—the percentage available for work at home rises. For example, in West Bengal, it rises from 9 to 27 per cent. Whereas in states where they are already reported as gainfully active, there is a lower percentage who report 'available for work' at home. In Rajasthan, the first category is 36 per cent (Table 5.4) and the second is 18 per cent (Table 5.5).

The special TAS study also canvassed the NSSO 32nd Round questionnaire with the respondents in the sample of households. Columns 7 and 8 of Table 5.1 give the results derived from the main questionnaire and from the probing questions from the 32nd Round questionnaire. It is found that in these calculations, the probing questions, be it in West

Table 5.4 *Percentage of rural females working according to current-day status in total females of age 5 years and above for all India and certain states*

All India	23
West Bengal	9
Orissa	17
Bihar	14
Rajasthan	36
Madhya Pradesh	33
Andhra Pradesh	34

Source: NSSO, 'Women's Activities in Rural India: A Study Based on NSSO 32nd Round Survey Results on Employment and Unemployment, Part 1', *Sarvekshana*, vol. 4, nos 3–4 (January–April 1981).

Table 5.5 *Percentage of rural females normally engaged in domestic duties, available for work if work is provided at their residences for all India and certain states*

	All Ages
All India	23
West Bengal	27
Orissa	26
Bihar	31
Rajasthan	18
Madhya Pradesh	9
Andhra Pradesh	25

Source: As for Table 5.4.

Bengal or Rajasthan, net larger percentages of women as 'available' for work from the 'dropouts' (i.e., 92, 93 code category).[22] Further to that, column 9, giving data calculated from the time disposition, also shows a lower percentage than in column 7 (32nd Round) simulation.

In other words, the additional females netted in the labour force by the probing questions (i.e., codes 92 and 93)—column 8—are greater than those netted by observation recording and grouping (column 9) in the TAS study. All that the respondent has to say is 'yes or 'no' for column 8, i.e., the probing questions; there is no time attached, as in column 9. Hence, a large number, perhaps larger than accurate, get netted. We would suggest that this kind of 'netting' would not only cast doubt on the figure, but would also suggest marginality of the workers who report as code 92–93, after reporting as domestic workers.

Whereas if a time value had been inducted right in the beginning, i.e., when netting the gainfully active, then instead of this two–step approach, i.e., first segregating the gainfully active from domestic work-ers (block 4, NSSO), and then probing to 'recover' them, always as a rather undefined 'lot', 'serious' workers could be generally segregated in one step. In other words, not having any kind of time attached to the answers to the probing questions, nor having any conceptual links with the activity codes which are grouped as representing gainful activity, the tabulation from the probing questions emphasises a certain kind of 'subsidiarity' or 'marginalness' which tends to lend women's activity a secondary role. If, however, time is also recorded with activity, then the relative 'value' of that activity gets 'weighed' in relation to other activities.

Another aspect of female participation in gainful activity that vitiates accurate enumeration, whatever the gainful activity status, is the intermittence across age classes. Figure 5.3 describes the 'age cycle' of males and females in terms of economic activities. It will be noticed that girls in Rajasthan begin participating at a very early stage with 1 or 2 hours in agriculture, which is more than the boys of the same age. As girls come to the reproductive age, they level off and the men cross over, becoming more than half-day and almost full-day workers in agriculture. But in non-agriculture activities, females are nowhere to be found.

In the Bengal sample, however, females never get captured at all. There is a low profile of women in agriculture and allied occupations. They get some significance in non-agricultural activities, but the duration of work remains less than 2 hours. Figure 5.1 brings out the explanation for this. Bengali females are deeply engaged in household chores (including sweeping, cleaning and cooking one's own food, and not including home production).[23]

HOUSEWORK AND ITS ELABORATION BRINGS WOMEN WORKERS 'IN'

The problem with housework is that it is sharply and universally associated with women and girls. If from time immemorial, it had been as strongly and categorically associated with men, then today it would not only have been a well-remunerated occupation, but architects and engineers would have relieved its odium. Perhaps it would have another name, and eminent housekeepers would have had international awards. In any case, there would have been no statistical debate about housework, its enumeration, valuation or boundaries—in other words, about the visibility of housework.[24]

One person who tried to 'masculinise' (as the equivalent of 'feminise') housework was Mahatma Gandhi. He saw this stereotyping of gender roles with women in the kitchen as an evil. He suggested to women that they should resist this male order—and refuse to marry, to have sex, refuse jewellery, and even refuse to cook. He wrote: 'To me, this domestic slavery of the kitchen too is a remnant of barbarism. It is high time that our womankind was freed from this incubus.'[25] In the ashrams or collectives that Gandhi built, in those days roles were constantly transposed to dismantle hierarchies. He persuaded men to cook, sew, clean dishes, knit—do what are called 'women's jobs'—in an attempt to transpose mental perceptions of the difference between men and women.

In the indexing and ranking undertaken by *HDR 1995*, Scandinavia comes first from the point of view of gender equity. According to Swedish sources,[26] only 10 per cent of fathers use parental leave, a facility which allows either the father or the mother to take one year off to nurse the child, showing that the law is not sufficient to revalue roles. While no data is presented for Scandinavia as such, Tables 4.3 and 4.4 in *HDR 1995* give the following figures for Norway only.[27] This data is cited here only illustratively. (Methods of calculation can be referred to in *HDR 1995*.) For example, time allocation by women in non-SNA activities is 62 per cent, compared to 36 per cent for men. This compares with women in rural Bangladesh,[28] among whom non-SNA work is 65 per cent compared to 30 per cent for men. Women's work burden compared with men (percentage difference) in Norway is 8 per cent. This compares, for example, with women in rural Bangladesh where the difference is 10 per cent,[29] showing that there is really not much variation in actual roles between these two regions.[30] The question might be asked as to whether the mental bending, the disciplining of the mind to perceive these chores as not lowly, the removal of mind–body hierarchies, has also taken place.

One of the most widespread presumptions in the description and analysis of labour force data—especially in relation to employment policy and programmes—is the denoting of women's economic roles as supplementary, subsidiary or secondary. The prescription has its base not only in mythology—patriarchal attitudes to the roles of women, that whatever they do can only be subordinate in status to men's roles—but also in the methodology which generates the facts. The link between the two, the myth and the methodology, is obvious. It also has its base in reality, in that women and girls are uniquely engaged in household chores or domestic activity, and many other similarly supportive activities, as well as in the production of goods and services which are usually the lowest-skilled, lowest-paid jobs, and predominantly household or household-proximate.[31]

Perception also plays a vital role in leading to this presumption. Women perceive themselves as mainly engaged in activities within the household, of which their most regular engagement is in what are called 'domestic activities'. These are cooking, cleaning, childcare: the three C's. Cooking implies water and fuel. Apart from reporting this fact, they also perceive these activities as having less value—which indeed is how society perceives them.

The time-use study not only provided some insights on how to disentangle this muddle, but also revealed some of the reality. It provided a close-up of women's activity patterns, and the factors that determine these patterns. It was suggestive of the importance both of culture and class in determining female work patterns. It indicated some methodological changes in survey design and implementation that could reduce the role of perceptions.[32]

FEEDING 'MICRO' FINDINGS INTO THE SYSTEM

Some of the first findings of the field study—such as the link between poverty and participation in economic activity; the heavy participation of children, especially female children, in tasks identical to female adults; the predominance of Rajasthani women in the weeding of fields for half a day in return for a wage; a predominance of women in Bengal in domestic service and processing of paddy for a non-cash reward among the poverty households—have been taken note of by statistical and policy agencies. The types of part-time activities in which women are engaged in rural areas, and how deeply these activities have been threatened by changes in technology, have also been made visible.[33]

For example, weeding was one of the main wage-earning occupations of women agriculture labourers in many parts of India (Tables 5.2A and 5.2B). The use of weedicides would threaten this source of income. Similarly, in searching for part-time employment for women, while schoolteaching was identified in rural areas, a wide range of options such as weeding, food processing, marketing vegetables and crop picking were not sufficiently mentioned in the statistics that were being released. Hence, policy tended to ignore this 'employment' of women, both in its attempt to strengthen and widen employment opportunities as well as in helping to prevent loss of employment.

The study underlined that the characteristics of the female labour force were markedly different from those of the male labour force, requiring far greater investigation and documentation and a far more sensitive response by the system. For example, female labour was concentrated in certain occupations which were by and large the least skilled, worst paid and most time consuming.[34] The study further revealed that within certain processes of production, there was a segmentation of tasks between men and women, and often the tasks performed by women were not identified. This lack of identification had many implications. These were the intra-occupational tasks which had the lowest wage levels and were the least unionised. Further, when these tasks were replaced by machines or other forms of technology change, the dropping out of women from such activity remained unnoticed. In other words, the baseline invisibility made displacement from employment an invisible, unquantified loss to women.[35]

The concepts of 'capital-intensive' and 'labour intensive', it was suggested, had to be further divided into male-labour-intensive and female-labour-intensive. The Sixth Five Year Plan, 1978–83, thus had a section on women's employment in the chapter on employment, which underlined the differences between male and female labour, and the acute pressure on women for income. An annexure listed occupations on the basis of the percentage of female workers.

Even using the conventional definition of gainful activity—there is a strong pressure by feminists to count domestic work, namely cooking, cleaning and childcare, the three C's, as gainful activity—even using the old, conventional, patriarchal definition, the percentage of women engaged in gainful activity, the female participation rate calculated by the TAS study, was almost twice that revealed in the macro data collection.

There were other important results also, such as the participation of children (ages 5 to 14), as well as the importance of class-based differentiation. It was found that amongst the absolutely landless, i.e., those who had no land, not even homestead land, the FWPR was greater than the male rate (Table 5.3). The average figure concealed the differences based on class, but there was more to this, that is, the data was not even being collected.[36]

The problem lay in the method of soliciting information as well as in the coding. In the activity codes which are used in international lists and which are attached to the question, 'What is your main activity?', code 93 refers to domestic activity. The majority of women, especially in the traditional sectors of the developing countries, would consider themselves mainly engaged in domestic activity, even if for several hours a day they were producing goods and services at home, or engaged in other income-substituting and income-earning activities. In the TAS study, it was found that the most regular activity, namely, activity which engaged several girls and women for all 365 days of the year for at least 4 hours if not more per day, was what are called 'household chores', i.e., the three C's. Naturally, for a woman who is a peasant or slum dweller and who collects water and fuel as well as weeds and milks, etc., the question 'What was your main regular activity in the last year?' would get the reply, 'Domestic activity'.

In the next section of the questionnaire, the investigators were told that those who identified themselves as belonging to code 93 should be left out. All the others were asked what they did in half-days during the previous week. Hence, the female worker becomes the 'missing woman'.[37]

A radical suggestion would be to drop the codes 92 and 93 from the questionnaires, thus pre-empting women from opting for that code and using block 4 (NSSO) alone for all the respondents. International advocacy is necessary to make any changes in a ground-level methodology because, unless domestic activity as a code is dropped internationally, no country-based statistical establishment will drop it as this would make it fall out of step with the standardisation of classificatory systems.

Simultaneously, the problem posed by women's self-perception is caused by the dominant economic values, namely, the idea that wage-earning labour is work, whereas non-wage-earning labour is not work. Such signals are generated from everywhere—from the political development paradigm of money and market, from the questionnaire and the investigator, apart from the mass media. It is linked to the scale of values in economic theory which, for example, sees the subsistence household—i.e., production for consumption—as something feudal or unmodern. Yet, today's thrust for conservation of resources, for reduction of wasteful consumption, is pointing to the importance of subsistence households, to those who are able to manage within the limits of resource availability. If subsistence households were given a positive value, it is likely that the contribution to women's inside-the-household work would get recognition in statistical definitions and classifications, and the stigma attached to housebound work would change or be blurred.

THE VALUE OF TIME-USE STUDIES

There is a growing body of literature which emphasises the importance of time as a measure. Its special relevance is underlined in situations where:

1. A large share of activities is non-marketed and/or non-monetised;
2. The reward for labour does not reflect what it is ideally supposed to reflect, namely, the value of that labour, wage rates/remuneration being extremely irregularly fixed.

Since these characteristics typify the resourceless household, the value of this kind of method is even more relevant to the study of poverty sets.

The data/relationships described so far from the TAS study and the insights or hints it offers would probably be weakened if they are overexploited by deriving strong conclusions or making strong assertions. However, these small sets of data only reaffirm what is now being observed and reported from other quantification exercises, from other researchers' insights and doubts.

Some of the statements most commonly made, some of the areas usually demarcated for reform in female labour force measurement and analysis, are under-enumeration, inadequate attention to unpaid family labour, home production and household work, and the relationships between these.[38] Some of the reasons given for this situation are poor conceptualisation of female work styles and mistaken perception of female economic roles by respondents and interviewers. Among the tools suggested for correcting this situation are: the recording of activities in various categories of detailed specification/identification, criteria for groupings/classification; ways of measuring them, for instance through time, apart from money and units of output, and so on.[39]

The field investigation described in this paper highlighted some of these points. It emphasised the following insights:

1. That identification of gainfully active persons through observation and recording of their activities, when matched with figures given through identification and through questioning, yielded a higher figure (Table 5.1) as anticipated. This emerged not only for females but also males, and especially for children, though the difference was lower for males than females and children; it was also lower in a state where female work styles were closer to male work styles than in a state where women were more homebound. In other words, the standard employment/unemployment questionnaire-based investigation revealed under-enumeration.
2. On the other hand, canvassing of the NSSO 32nd Round questionnaire among sample households, and adjusting the figure of economically active persons with the additional numbers released from the probing questions, by time allocation data, also yielded a higher figure, but much higher. This suggests that there may be over-enumeration if there is no 'control', by use of even a minimal time criterion of 1 hour over a reference week, or as in the case of the time disposition study, 1 hour on the day observed, six times in the year.
3. That whether the investigator is male or female, the questionnaires currently being used—with the activity codes, their classification

and the associated instructions to investigators—create some confusion especially in relation to female work.

4. That the main reason for this difficulty is the strong regular engagement of women in housework. Voluntary withdrawal notwithstanding (i.e., whether housework is extended or shrunk in response to labour demand), time is indented, usually for half a day or more, in the category of activities called 'domestic'. This clouds the clarity in reporting main activity by females even if they are doing other activities, say gainful activities, for 3 to 4 hours or more. In other words, the dominance of domestic work would lead to underreporting of other work.

5. That another reason for under-enumeration is the work styles of women, which are determined by history, biology, attitudes—a whole package. These work styles—characterised by intermittent participation over the life cycle as well as over a day or week; contribution to a productive activity but at the processing/pre-marketing, less visibly monetised stage; intermingling of production for self-consumption and production for sale—are not easy to disentangle, and the existing designs do not capture them.

6. That the resource base of households as well as their religion/culture, the size of the family, the number of infants—all affect female labour participation more than the male. The degree, the ranking of one over the other, would perhaps vary with region and landownership patterns, as well as the perception of opportunity. In other words, supply-side factors play a more important role in female labour supply than in male labour supply. The demand side—market pull, wage rates, wage differentials and type of work—also plays a vital role. The two are also interdependent, but to a lesser extent than among males.

7. That more than women, children and their work are underreported. Yet children, including those aged between 5 and 9, are strongly influenced by all the parameters described above, i.e., culture, asset base, seasons, distribution pattern and employment opportunities. In fact, children are even more vulnerable to these influences, as they are constantly being rearranged according to the pulls and pushes on adults.

RETROSPECT

The 'indicator' movement is an old story—the 'barefoot economics' of Manfred Max Neef, Hazel Henderson's 'beyond economics', the Physical Quality of Life Index of Morris David Morris,[40] all these are about 'new' indicators or measures of economic and social transformation. In the 1980s and 1990s, they did not seem radical enough as a means of reordering the content of development. But indicators are coming back, almost like a movement, and may become the tail that wags the dog. For example, a group in the US is illustrating that increases in crime, individualisation of family (absence of social support), etc., add to GDP in the USA. They have coined the slogan 'Growth in GDP is Social Decay'.[41] Their 'target' is the *Wall Street Journal* as the 'pace setter' for US growth. A worldwide network of indicator-wallahs is meeting in November to consolidate their power to demand new measures to measure progress. All of this is to reconstitute 'production', revalue its measures and influence consumption, as well as to show the political premises of measures.

That GDP growth does not necessarily trickle down is also an old story, which gets repeated in the *HDRs* of 1995 and 1996. But what is dramatically presented in *HDR 1996*,[42] is that the growth of GDP often exacerbates inequality: that it further stresses nations who are already besieged with poverty and inequality and political fragility. In *HDR 1996*, the inequality measures include not only the 'soft' indicators of health, education and gender, but the hard measures of per capita income, Gini coefficients and so on. Hence, the 'tail' is beginning to get more 'mainstream' and broad based in its advocacy through the *HDRs* themselves.

The ideas and prescriptions of the *HDRs* of 1995 and 1996 go back to the advocacy of the 1970s and 1980s, when liberalism was somewhat reined in by ideas of equality. The *HDRs* recommend full employment (if not phrasing it as the 'right to work') and the provision of a minimum level of basic civic amenities for a more 'humane' development. The interesting aspect of all this 'revival' is that the language of argument is not conventional 'ideology', but that of selectively using statistical indicators. But the real, radical steps are yet to be taken.

For instance, it is yet to be argued that poverty and the neglect of some categories of people, like women, are political issues (not economic issues). That the existence of poverty and discrimination reveals the inappropriateness of political systems, the lack of representation of these hard-pressed groups in the decision-making process. To 'choose' requires mechanisms for the choices to be effectively translated into actual 'receipts' or effective claims. Only the political frame and its sensitivity to these claims can provide such effectiveness. A 'political sensitivity' index giving values to representativeness and inequality incorporated into the HDI itself might take the bull by the horns.

Another radical step would be to enter the zone of current 'immeasurables'. If the indicators are to characterise the dominant or largest sections of the population of the 'poor' in developing countries—and the large sections of the population of adult women worldwide—then the indicators have to capture the non-monetised transactions too. Currently, however 'progressive' the *HDRs* may be, the values are based on money and the market.

While many attempts have been made to valuate non-monetised and invisible transactions, they are still measured against the 'standard' of money. Valuating women's work is linked to but not the same as measuring the labour force or developing unemployment/employment figures. All women's work yields an output, but all women's work does not provide an income.

For an assetless worker, it is her time more than her wage that measures her labour. Time itself can be used as a valuator. Time as a measure of value would reverse the values of men's and women's work—women would always come out on top as they spend more hours working than men, as the *HDR* has shown. *There is need to broaden the advocacy for using time itself as a measure—more statistical information on 'time spent' in the various categories—as has been attempted in the Indian time-use study.*

In India, the *HDRs* have evoked widespread interest. State governments wish to develop state *HDRs*; women activists want to emphasise GDIs and GEMs, as they provide a means of quantifying inequality. New indices for GDI and GEM have been developed by a group of Indian scholars in the Indian context of issues and available data. These will be constructed at the district level in eight districts to build accountability frames on behalf of women into the panchayati raj system. Such monitoring frameworks can be the tail that can wag not only the economic development dog, but the political process. However, efforts to bring in time modules into these indices—whether at the 'official' macro level, i.e., at the SNA level, the NSSO level, or the 'micro' level (the district-level efforts)—are yet to be made. The critical issue of inequality within the household between males and females, in everything including matters of life and death such as nutrition and health, is still difficult to measure. Sex ratio is being recommended for the South Asian region as a quantity that needs to be included. So too infant mortality rates, differentiated for males and females.[43] Anthropometric data provide one source of measured and measurable data for indicating this inequality, if not cruelty.[44] For the poor and especially for women, the integration of these new measures, especially hours of drudgery and hard labour, into national and international statistical presentations will not only transform the quantitative picture, not only call attention to what is needed in terms of interventions, but reorder the hierarchies embedded in the indices.

NOTES

1   UNDP, *Human Development Report 1995: Gender and Human Development* (New York: Oxford University Press, 1995). Cited in the text as *HDR 1995*.
2   Ibid., p. 1; emphases mine.
3   Indira Hirway and Darshini Mahadevia, 'Critique of Gender Development Index: Towards an Alternative', *Economic & Political Weekly*, vol. 31, no. 43 (1996), pp. WS87–WS96.
4   Aasha Kapur Mehta, 'Recasting Indices for Developing Countries: A Gender Empowerment Measure', *Economic & Political Weekly*, vol. 31, no. 43 (1996), pp. WS80–WS86.
5   Devaki Jain and Malini Chand, 'Report on a Time Allocation Study: Its Methodological Implications', paper presented at the Technical Seminar on 'Women's Work and Employment', ISST, New Delhi, 1982. Cited in the text as 'the TAS study'. The ISST undertook a study of rural households in 1976. The study was supported by the Indian Council of Social Science Research. In designing the study, ISST had the privilege of advice from several scholars, notably the late Prof. Ashok Rudra (who initiated and supervised a first

module in village Muluk in 1977), as well as the late Prof. Dandekar and several others. Dr Sudhir Bhattacharya worked in close collaboration with ISST in preparing the final results. The report in mimeo form is available at ISST, and acknowledges the several persons who helped in collecting and analysing the data.

The hypothesis on the basis of which this study was undertaken was that female work participation in India was under-enumerated because of the nature of female work and wage.

i)   The primary objective of the study was to test this hypothesis.
ii) A second objective was to try to identify the various determinants of female labour supply.
iii) A third was to regroup productive and non-productive activities and define gainful activity on the basis of the evidence.

However, as the study went along, many additional issues as well as strands of information were thrown up that both widened and reduced the scope of the investigation. Some of these changes will be reflected in the findings reported later in this paper.

The mode of investigation was observation and not recall. Each selected household was observed on two consecutive days, when the activities of every member of age 5 and above were recorded for a period of 15 hours, from 6 a.m. to 9 p.m. Clearly, observation was not continuous, since the investigators needed time out for their physiological needs. Such small gaps in observation were filled by questioning through recall. The frequency of observation of each household was once in two months, i.e., six times during the 52-week cycle. Kuita, Selampur and Thabgaon are a cluster of three villages in Birbhum, one of the poor districts of West Bengal. The main rural activity in the district is agriculture, and the main crop is paddy, followed by potato and jute. Etrampura, Mehtoli and Chentoli are a cluster of three villages in Bharatpur, a backward district of Rajasthan. The main rural activity in this district is agriculture. The main crops are jawar and bajra, which are adequate for household consumption. The chief cash crops are groundnut, maize and chillies.

6   UNDP, *HDR 1995*, p. 87; emphases mine.
7   Ibid., pp. 88, 90.
8   Ibid., p. 88.
9   Ibid., p. 97; emphasis in original. To aggregate the output of household goods and services and compare it with the aggregates of conventional national accounts, such as GDP, it is necessary to express its value in monetary units. The method chosen in the study of 13 industrial countries is to value household production at the cost of inputs—labour and capital. For unpaid labour, a market wage is imputed to the labour time needed to produce household goods and services.

The market wage selected is that of a substitute household worker—a worker who can perform, within the household, most of the economic activities carried out by unpaid household members. In industrial countries such workers tend to be women with low pay, therefore using their wage as a yardstick gives a conservative estimate of the value of household labour. After selecting this wage, the choice is among using net wages (after taxes), gross wages (before taxes) or extra gross wages, which include employers' social security contributions. The choice here is extra gross wages, because it is most comprehensive.

With extra gross wages as the yardstick, a conservative estimate of the value of non-SNA production is about half the value of GDP. A 1992 study of Australia estimates this production to be 86 per cent of GDP, and a study of Germany in the same year gives an estimate of 55 per cent. The lowest estimate of non-SNA output is 46 per cent in Finland. Most of the value of non-SNA output is attributable to labour. Labour valued at extra gross wages accounts for 72 per cent of GDP in Australia, 53 per cent in Germany and 45 per cent in Finland.

10 Ibid.
11 Ibid., pp. 97–98.
12 Ibid., p. 98.
13 Shram Shakti, *Report of the National Commission on Self-Employed Women and Women in the Informal Sector* (New Delhi, 1988).
14 In several small sample household surveys conducted by ISST, in order to understand the impact of specific development programmes, a block similar to the NSSO block 5—namely, recalling time disposition over the previous two days immediately preceding the day of investigation—was tried. All the activities were grouped into three broad categories, viz., gainful activities, household activities and personal. The further division of gainful activity sectors was related to the specific occupation or production process that was being developed by the programmes. Time was not restricted to any specific intervals, such as half a day, full day, etc., but left loose. It was found that often a programme or project, like dairying, added hours to this heavy workload on women. Most of the individuals in resourceless households work more than 8 hours a day even at conventional gainful activity for meagre income. Enforcing of minimum wage for these 'unspecified' occupations would in itself improve their economic status. The 8-hour day broken into two half-days tends to approximate the labour force for salaried or wage labour. Devaki Jain and Malini Chand, 'Importance of Age and Sex Specific Data Collection in Household Surveys', paper presented at the Regional Conference on Household Surveys, ESCAP, Bangkok, 1980.
15 Sudhir Bhattacharya, 'Women's Activities in Rural India: A Study Based on NSS 32nd Round (1977–78) Survey Results on Employment and Unemployment', NSSO, Department of Statistics, Government of India, June 1981. Information as to whether categories such as 'unemployed' or 'not in labour force' were engaged in more gainful activity of secondary importance,

in the sense that only a minor part of their available labour times was utilised for the purpose, was also collected. It indicates, for all India and for different states, the extent of subsidiary gainful activity performed by those rural females who have been classified by 'major time criteria' as either 'unemployed' (81 and 82) or 'not in labour force' (92, 93 and 95–98) according to usual status.

It is clearly seen that the change in the procedure of classification in the 32nd Round survey has affected quite substantially the labour force participation rates of rural females, whereas the effect was only marginal in the case of rural males. Further, the adjusted estimates are found to be fairly comparable with the corresponding 27th Round estimates.

16 V. M. Dandekar, 'Some Key Results in Employment and Unemployment', NSSO.

17 J. A. Mathaei, 'The Development of the Female Labour Force in the United States: An Historical Investigation', Department of Economics, Yale University, 1977.

18 Figures that have been drawn from the data do not in a technical sense lend themselves to the graphs that have been drawn. However, once again, liberties have been taken to reveal pictures in a telling way. The ISST TAS study was conducted in six rounds. It happened that the rounds approximately coincided with some agricultural seasons. Hence, Figure 6.2 can be indicative of this phenomenon. For example, in West Bengal one of the rounds coincided with the peak season for planting Aman rice, and another with the peak season for planting of Bodo rice—October–November. Hence, the tables may reveal seasonal changes in female work hours.

19 Gillian Hart, 'Patterns of Household Labour Allocation in a Javanese Village', paper prepared for the A/D/C RTN Workshop on Household Studies, Singapore, August 1976.

20 C. D. Deere, 'The Agricultural Division of Labour by Sex: Myths, Facts and Contradiction in the Northern Peruvian Sieria', Economics Department, University of Massachusetts, Amherst, 1977.

21 Bhattacharya, 'Women's Activities in Rural India'.

22 It was suggested to the NSSO that this identification be eliminated in block 4 (where a question is asked against codes 0–71), and be derived from block 5, which has a time disposition table, asking for recall of the previous week in half-days. This would imply that the time disposition chart is canvassed with all members of the household. It was suggested that many women would then recall what they did during other parts of their day, and thereby reveal their participation in 'economic activity'. At the stage of assigning codes, persons could be classified according to their time profile. It was also suggested that such a time profile would help to understand the time spent in activities such as fetching water and fuel, thus giving additional information for infrastructure planning (see suggested module), in lieu of code 92–93.

However, the technical committee of the 38th Round of the NSS rejected this proposal, arguing that the investigator would now have to collect charts for at least two more persons per household on an average, and that further, labour force data derived from block 5 would not be comparable with the data obtained from the 27th Round block 4. Attempts to argue that other sections of the schedule were cumbersome and known to be difficult to canvass, such as the details of expenditure and income, the probing questions on women dropouts (namely 93–93), the argument that one would sacrifice accuracy at the altar of comparability, were of no avail. The 38th Round persisted with the flaws of the 32nd Round.

23 However, a module could be added to the existing questionnaires, where time spent in a wide range of activities is slotted for all individuals (5 years and above) in a household, say for yesterday and today over four rounds, on the basis of recall of activities (covering both 0–71, but also household work, fetching water, fuel and so on). In this method, not only workers in terms of 1 hour's participation in gainful activity but also workers who are fully employed, underemployed as well as self-employed, could be quantified on the basis of time. To this time, if income, whether in cash or kind or output generated, is added, it may also be possible to tabulate workers by using the income criteria. The Philippines household survey attempted this in its economic activity block (see Jain and Chand, 'Report on a Time Allocation Study', minutes for modules).

It is true that data required for programme development would be of a different character from the data required for looking at aggregate trends to understand the impact of different types of sectoral or aggregate growth. It is also true that comparability will be affected every time there is a change in the questionnaire and the instructions to the investigators. However, it is also true that the impact of growth on the employment status of different sets of the population, not sectorally determined but determined in terms of different categories—especially class- and gender-differentiated—cannot be figured out with the existing data. See Jain and Chand, 'Importance of Age and Sex Specific Data Collection in Household Surveys'.

Time allocation recording need not only be through the anthropological method. Moreover, when recorded through recall as an additional module, the degree of error need be no more than is found in collecting other sets of data. On the other hand, it might provide the kind of information base necessary for understanding employment/unemployment both for trend analysis as well as programme development. A breakthrough can be achieved if some departures are made from the existing methodology even at the risk of not being able to track a trend.

24 Jain and Banerjee, *Tyranny of the Household*.

25 M. K. Gandhi, 'The Better Half', in *Everyone's Gandhi* (ed. Rita Roy) (New Delhi: Gandhi Peace Foundation, 1997).

26 Gunilla Sterner, Gender Specialist, Stockholm County Council, Lecture at the National Commission on Women (unpublished), New Delhi, 1996.

27 UNDP, *HDR 1995*, p. 94.

28 Ibid., p. 91, Table 4.2.

29 Ibid., p. 91.

30 Devaki Jain and Malini Chand, 'Domestic Work: Its Implication for Enumeration on Women's Work and Employment', paper presented at the Symposium on 'Women's Work and Society', Indian Statistical Institute, New Delhi, 1982 (reproduced in K. Saradamoni, ed., *Women, Work and Society*, Calcutta: Indian Statistical Institute, 1985).

31 Hart, 'Patterns of Household Labour Allocation in a Javanese Village'.

32 Devaki Jain and Malini Chand, 'Pattern of Female Work: Implication for Statistical Design, Economic Classification and Social Priorities', paper presented at the National Conference on Women's Studies, SNDT University, Bombay, 1981; M. Swaminathan, 'A Study of Energy Use Patterns of General Background Caste', Seminar on 'Women's Work and Employment', April 1982.

33 M. Mukherjee, Devaki Jain and C. P. Sujaya, 'Women, Work and Employment', paper presented at the International Workshop on Women's Studies, Trivandrum, 1989.

34 E. King-Quizon, 'Time Allocation and Home Production in Rural Laguna Households', paper presented at the Symposium on Household Economics, Manila, May 1977.

35 N. Birdsell and W. McGreevey, 'The Second Sex in the Third World: Is Female Poverty a Development Issue?', paper prepared for the International Center for Research on Women Policy Round Table, Washington, D.C., 21 June 1978.

36 P. Sundar, 'Characteristics of Female Employment: Implications of Research and Policy', *Economic & Political Weekly*, vol. 16, no. 19 (1981), pp. 863–71.

37 Jain and Chand, 'Pattern of Female Work'.

38 Deere, 'The Agricultural Division of Labour by Sex'; Bina Agarwal, 'Work Participation of Women in Rural India: Some Data and Conceptual Biases', *Economic & Political Weekly*, vol. 20, nos 51–52 (1985), pp. A155–A164; Sundar, 'Characteristics of Female Employment'; A. Beguin, 'Preface', in L. Goldschmidt-Clermont, *Unpaid Work in the Household: A Review of Economic Evaluation Methods*, Women, Work and Development no. 1 (Geneva: International Labour Office, 1982).

39 Deere, 'The Agricultural Division of Labour by Sex'; Monica Fong, 'Victims of Old Fashioned Statistics: Institutions and Agrarian Reform', *FAO Review on Agriculture and Development*, vol. 13, no. 3 (May–June 1980); Mathaei, 'The Development of the Female Labour Force in the United States'; Beguin, 'Preface', in Goldschmidt-Clermont, *Unpaid Work in the Household*; King-Quizon, 'Time Allocation and Home Production in Rural Laguna Households'; Birdsell and McGreevey, 'The Second Sex in the Third World'.

40 M. D. Morris and M. B. McAlpin, *Measuring the Condition of India's Poor: The Physical Quality of Life Index* (New Delhi: Promilla and Co., 1982).

41 C. Cobb, T. Halstead and J. Rowe, 'If the GDP Is Up, Why Is America Down?', *Atlantic Monthly* (October 1995), pp. 62–78.

42 UNDP, *Human Development Report 1996* (New York: Oxford University Press, 1996).

43 Indian team's collective recommendations, Karnataka Women's Information and Resource Centre (KWIRC), 1996. The KWIRC, a wing of the Singamma Sreenivasan Foundation, supported the process of critique and reconstruction by a group of seven women economists. This process received financial support from many agencies involved in *HDR 1995*—including the Department of Women and Child Development (Government of India), the British Council, the UN Development Fund for Women, UNDP and the State Government of Karnataka. The team continues to work on a district-level framework for GDI and GEM.

44 Anuradha Rajivan, 'Measurement of Gender Differences Using Anthropometry', *Economic & Political Weekly*, vol. 31, no. 43 (1996), pp. WS58–WS62.

Chapter 6

Nuancing Globalisation, or Mainstreaming the Downstream, or Reforming Reform

The Caribbean had a great leader called Nita Barrow, a citizen of Barbados, who served as the secretary general for the 1985 Nairobi Conference. The University of the West Indies had instituted a lecture in her memory, and I was invited to deliver one of these lectures. At this time, i.e., in 1999, the new liberal agenda had begun to show its face, arms and limbs much more, having been initiated in the early 1990s. The emphasis was on removing all regulatory mechanisms and on mainstreaming gender: in other words, bringing gender into the spaces of policy making, as well as liberalising and thereby undoing most regulatory mechanisms. The neoliberal paradigm really began as a message saying 'hands off, let capital move and let the state not be the initiator of development.' I argued against this hands-off policy, suggesting that once again, the 'reform', as the neoliberal economic paradigm was called, needed to be abandoned, and the poor and women amongst them needed to be enabled to design programme and policy.

I feel privileged to have been invited to give this lecture in memory of a person whom I knew well, and respected enormously. It was my good fortune to have not only worked with Nita Barrow towards and at the Nairobi Conference,[1] but also to have had good discussions with her right here in Barbados, when she was the governor general of the country.

Of her many outstanding attributes, one comes through in a story she told me during my last meeting with her in Barbados. We at Development Alternatives with Women for a New Era (DAWN) were preparing ourselves for the Fourth UN World Conference for Women at Beijing in 1995.[2] Peggy Antrobus had organised a DAWN meeting in Barbados. We were discussing the wrinkle or hiccup that we were encountering in relation to the Chinese government, which had indicated that it would be selective in granting entry permission to women from the NGO sector. It was seeking to prohibit those whom it thought would be 'difficult'. This had thrown the women's movement into something of a panic.

The ethic of the women's movement is inclusive of difference and respect for democracy. None of us could go until and unless all of us were included. There was a mobilisation of protest in New York and a sense of disappointment with Dr Gertrude Mongella, the Secretary General of the Fourth World Conference, for not appearing to tackle this issue head on.

As I was mentioning this to Nita, she said this was not anything new. It had happened to her also when she was organising the 1985 NGO Forum of Women in Nairobi. The Kenyan government put some conditionalities on the entry of NGOs. Nita said she did not confront it head on. Instead she got together some of the most important foreign ambassadors and agencies who were working in Kenya and got them interested in the World Conference on Women. They then called on the president of Kenya. They mentioned casually to him that Kenya's interest would be jeopardised if the impression was created among these various agencies and persons that Kenya, as the host country, was adopting exclusionary principles or procedures. He immediately caught the hint and the problem was resolved without any 'hoo-hah' or press conference or conflict-making confrontations.

It is interesting that the successor to Nita Barrow, Gertrude Mongella, instead of allying herself with an agitated movement and a confrontational approach, quietly negotiated a harmonious entry into China for all of us. As you know, we had a record presence there. This says something about women—not only the maturity and capacity of women leaders, but their way of handling confrontational situations. Women can walk around and negotiate a settlement; they tend to avoid head-on confrontations.[3]

Nita Barrow, like another great Caribbean woman, Lucille Mathurin Mair, was a part of what is called the 'mainstream'. Their constituency was the world and its well-being. Their historical memory of slavery, their experience of racism, of discrimination within that, and of colonisation made them strong voices for equality, for rights, and for broad-based change. These in fact are the basic issues 'downstream' too, that is, of the various people's movements, including the women's movement. What we see here is the link between mass mobilisation around the hardcore issue of economic empowerment of the poor and the reconstruction of political power.

What the international NGO movement, the women's movement and other transformative movements need is a fistful of salt, a symbolic unifying gesture to roll back the overwhelming force of the current paradigm of development.[4] This should not be done through essays and articles, but through international solidarity on a limited agenda of public action/opinion and ideology or philosophy. Thus, 'mainstream' and 'downstream', or what I prefer to call the mainsprings, the bubbling fountains of fresh spring water, have converged in these stalwarts, and I dedicate this lecture to them.

In this lecture:

- I review some of the major global development documents, paying attention to globalisation;
- I draw out what appears to me as some form of loose consensus;
- Finally, I pause at some of the relevant milestones in this discourse and point out the opportunities and directions for the women's movement and its allies.

The gender dimension is woven into the whole, in as much as I am a woman, a development economist and a feminist—therefore my language and my lens are inclusive of gender. Towards the end of this paper, I try to address the globe from the point of view of women. I try to elaborate on that area of my interest and what this review suggests with respect to it.

My basic argument is that a review of the global discourse reveals an opportunity for intervention and for negotiating on behalf of justice within that gung-ho, relentless march of markets and globalisation. I suggest that the leading players in global governance and the less visible ones are 'nuancing globalisation'. They are creating spaces for negotiating and recasting development. The missing parameters of this discourse are unity, the political ethic and the moral purpose. These must be included within the women's movement. If that could be forged, then there are enough examples of leverage which are encouraging.

I argue that we must revise the language used and the measures introduced in the discourse on globalisation. We need to rethink the spaces that the global system provides and the direction in which we develop our energies, and the purpose of movements dedicated to social justice. These are important elements in recasting the direction of development. For example, some of the changes in terminology that suggest themselves as more powerful in stimulating change include replacing the term 'showcasing' with 'snowballing'. By this I mean we should incorporate ideas emerging out of people's movements into the larger spaces to build public opinion, and therefore public policy. These are small flames that show promise of firing justice.

Like in South Africa, I would substitute the word 'transformation' for 'development'.[5] I suggest that we the people have to teach the UN and the national governments how to develop their analytical and monitoring frameworks, rather than work into or with the ones they have created. Attention has to be shifted from the state to the achievements of civil society in engendering transformation. These achievements need to be blown up into a storm to break down traditional structures of development.

A striking aspect of the review of the literature on globalisation[6] is that everyone in the system, be it the World Bank, academic economists or NGOs—everyone is nuancing globalisation. By nuancing I mean drawing out the subtleties or the details. Thus, in the last five years, the discourse has shifted from the 'mantra' stage (that is, sweeping statements about states and markets, liberalisation and reform), to a stage of qualification, to a concern with reforming the reform programme.

This transformation from rigidity to humility is of course due to actual lived experience, but also due to new interventions in the discourse such as those from the UNDP's HDRs. This transformation also includes the effectiveness of groundswell movements such as the NGO movement. Due to the inclusion of women in larger numbers than before in the various consultative and decision-making processes at the local and international level, I suggest the invisible hand is at work from the notoriously invisible people of the world—women.

REVIEWING THE GREAT GLOBE

The review of the global literature suggests, first, the importance of deconstructing, disaggregating or decomposing the term 'globalisation'. For example, Jagdish Bhagwati breaks the concept down into capital, investment and labour.[7] However, in a sense Bhagwati has left out the most important segment of globalisation. He has omitted the segment which has generated globalisation, namely information technology (IT). Interestingly, the UNDP *Human Development Report* for 1999 has a diagram which demonstrates that while much is being made of IT and internet users, the space in the whole circle of the world occupied by the internet-wallahs or internet folk is just a tiny segment. It is almost entirely located in the United States and Europe. There is no doubt, however, that a fourth player or fourth segment in the disaggregation of globalisation has to be communications. This development is picked up for examination in the 1999 *WDR* and the 1999 *HDR*.

Another classification to be introduced is the separation of process and outcome. The argument is that globalisation is a process, but it is often seen as a goal.[8]

A third classification distinguishes between 'global' and 'international'. International, with an emphasis on 'inter-', usually provides space for national identity and negotiations between nations.[9]

The issues that are being debated in the globalisation discourse are:

- The role of government: is there a conflict between the concept of globalisation and strong governments? What about our national boundaries?
- The role of 'national' as opposed to 'global': What is the role of the national effort? What is the space for national effort?
- Terminology and definition, that is, whether the term 'development' now needs to be replaced by the term 'transformation'.[10] Transformation is defined here as inclusive of political, social, cultural and economic change.[11] Was not the term 'progress' a better measure than its replacement, the GDP?[12] Measuring only material changes is insufficient. Whatever terminology or definition is used, it must be capable of measuring other variables.

This is what I call 'nuancing'. Each thinker, writer, actor is putting inverted commas, so to speak, around these themes of globalisation and sustainable development. Each is looking for the detail and rereading the small print,[13] rather than emphasising the big words. Within this nuancing of the globalisation and development landscape, one can also notice some movement towards a similarity of opinions, if not a consensus.

For example, the importance of participation by 'people' was highlighted in *WDR 1999*, by Stiglitz in 1998, Bhagwati in 1999, Norgaard in 1999, and in *HDR 1999*.[14] The intention of this inclusion may vary, from those who see it as more just, to those who see it as promoting more efficiency, or those who are interested in preventing breakdown and civic instability. But the accommodation of 'people' is seen as a necessary component even by the hard-headed, single-minded 'growth' generation. Another thread running through the literature is the reference to inequality. Most development experts flag equity and poverty eradication as the purpose of transformation, even though there exist severe differences on the 'how' of this transformation.

At one end, there are the bold statements by Bhagwati and Shroff that growth is the crucial variable to transform economies. They believe that whatever pains that it releases in its wake should not only be endured, but can in fact be managed. Thus Bhagwati, the *WDR* and the UNDP's *HDR* call attention not to the event or process of globalisation and liberalisation, but to a better management of the process especially in the layers in which he analyses, namely capital, labour and investment. However, the equity issue is focused around labour migration. Capital movements are supported on the theory of comparative advantage, but labour is restricted by the rich countries to their advantage. Inequity as expressed by the asymmetry of labour is also seen as an obstacle to the validation of free trade theory, especially the emphasis on comparative advantage, maximising of resources, output, profit and efficiency, and the justifying of a 'global' economy.

Regulation is another prescription around which there is convergence—regulation of financial institutions, regulation of labour movement, and the regulation of trade regimes within countries and between countries. Thus, from an earlier call to deregulate and liberalise, there is now a shift to regulate. This is often rephrased as 'governance' or 'management'.

Another 'common' element in the discourse is the call for attention to institutions. Whether it is for people's participation or for regulation, institutions are required. Naturally the greatest attention is paid to financial institutions, both local and global. This has led to the emergence of ideas for an international financial architecture. The proposals may range from a new international financial institution, all the way to the muting of the powers of certain global players such as the World Bank and the IMF for not being accountable. It may include also the upscaling of international institutions like the World Trade Organization (WTO).[15]

Finally, attention is focused on the nation. At every step, whether it is for an international financial architecture or for people-centred participatory transformation, the nation is identified as the critical theatre for action. National capacity, national procedure and natural political process are identified as aspects that have to be elucidated or moved centre stage for globalisation to be successful.

As the review progresses, the tensions are also discernible. For example, the 1999 *WDR* has two pillars, globalisation and localisation.

Localisation is valuable for participation and for ownership, as Stiglitz also claims. But the report also admits that globalisation disconnects with the 'local', often trampling over it. Localisation can create problems for what is called 'national consensus' on, say, the fiscal deficits. And yet national consensus on such items as fiscal deficit is almost a necessary condition for foreign direct investments (FDI) and multinational corporations (MNCs). Yet, there is an example from the state of Kerala in India, where women's groups have actually dealt with this disjunction and used localisation to deal with what are called the 'market forces' of globalisation.[16]

Another area of tension is between global agencies and international agencies. Many of us prefer international agencies since they not only accommodate national sovereignty and identity, but because international agencies, such as the UN family of agencies, seem to be more representative and seem to provide a theatre or a forum for negotiated settlements. On the other hand, global agencies like the World Bank and the IMF, apart from the MNCs, are driven by their main providers, namely the US and Japan, which are the main lending countries with surplus. Therefore, the politics or the political intentions of these countries will determine the stance of what look like world agencies, but are actually creatures of the rich. (Interestingly, Bhagwati dwells on this. He calls the relationship between the Bretton Woods Institutions and the nations asymmetrical, and thus reveals his preference for agencies like the WTO over the Bretton Woods Institutions.)

The countries of the South had at one time made a proposal for an Economic Security Council with elected members to be formed within the UN, similar to the current Security Council. They preferred this to another agency, as it would involve a greater sense of representative democracy. But like many proposals from the South, the idea withered. In a world where the UN is shrinking in its power, perhaps as a very result of the enlargement of global agencies 'untethered from the nation', its place is becoming increasingly marginal.

Sometimes the international fora have totally congested conduits due to the multiplicity of interests, especially narrow national interests, that they wish to focus upon. As a result, these conduits become dysfunctional.

A weakness in the analysis of the community of civil society organisations is the simplistic assumption that civil society is or should be the guardian of equity, even if market forces forage in the fields unscrupulously, and even if disparities increase due to the segmented entry of MNCs or the manoeuvres of the financial markets. It is as if the state and the private sector will release these forces of stress as a part of the journey of growth. In the meantime, the bandaging has to be done by the NGOs, like in the old theory separating growth from distributive justice. Non-governmental organisations must protest and resist this assigned role. Their role is to redirect the state and redesign transformation. It should not be to pick up the pieces in the aftermath of the destruction wrought by state and market forces.

There is nothing as validating as personal experience. When grass-roots organisations present an analysis, it directly addresses their own experience, but academia often finds such presentations unprofessional and anecdotal. However, I will take a risk and present a few milestones in the process of transformation. I have been a part of some of these initiatives, which point both to opportunity as well as impediments. These personal encounters have led me to the proposition that a unified moral purpose is crucial for all this self-appraisal and talk of renewal and movement beyond the state and towards civil society in which the mainstream analysis is currently indulging.

CLOSE ENCOUNTERS
The UNCTAD/UNDP Expert Group Meeting

In February 1999, the United Nations Conference on Trade and Development (UNCTAD) hosted an Expert Group Meeting.[17] Dr Eudine Barriteau and myself were amongst the feminist participants at the meeting. Fifteen low-income developing countries had been identified by UNTAD, and it wanted to develop a framework for their entry into the process of globalisation. A core group of experts was assembled to provide advice to these countries on the 'how' of globalisation.

The deliberations were driven by questions such as: How to globalise without being worse off? How to grasp globalisation opportunities?

How could capacity be built in these countries which had no experience of developed trade or manufacture? At the end of two days, the economists, drawn from the usual citadels of the Academy,[18] designed a process built on certain premises. These premises were:

- That the entry had to be gradual;
- That the national economy had to be strengthened almost as a precondition for entry;
- That the design of development had to be suited to the countries' political, economic and social situations, so there could be no universal formula;
- That the capability of the country had to be built into the very process of developing the country's assessment or country situational analysis;
- That no hard-and-fast attitude should be taken about protection— that infant industry protection had to be used.

This advice emerged out of the group's analysis of the different countries and regions which had already globalised, such as Brazil, Mexico, East Asia and Eastern Europe. They argued that the experiences of those countries which had globalised pointed to the need for a degree of caution about dogma and greater flexibility, apart from the need to pay more attention to national capacity to cope with globalisation. In some sense, it was a hushed and introspective meeting, and the Prebisch Lecture was very much a part of the aura of that meeting.[19]

Another Illustration of Hope: The Small Teaching the Big

Liberia, one of the most afflicted countries in the world, had not been included in the UNCTAD basket of 15 countries even though it qualified as a low-income and endangered nation. The reason given was that Liberia was extremely unstable, and also its leader was misbehaving and therefore there was an embargo on assistance.

Yet Liberia had been one of the countries that had moved me a great deal when I was a member of the Eminent Persons Group of the Graça Machel study sponsored in 1997 by the UN to assess the impact on children of armed conflict. So I decided to accept the invitation of UNDP in Liberia to initiate the process of building a national development policy and programme. I took the principles that had been decided in the UNCTAD/UNDP meeting in Geneva and tried to apply them to Liberia.

To my great joy it worked. Every Liberian agency, governmental, non-governmental, financial, political and cultural, welcomed my curiosity, informed me and loaded me with documents. They told me of their aspirations and the work that they had done before. I found that Liberia had the most capable people and institutions. They were quite capable of designing, defining and implementing their future without the outsider's help!

In fact, some of the most innovative demographic surveys were being conducted by Liberian citizens in collaboration with some technical personnel from the United Nations Family Planning Association. Whether it was at a women's meeting or the meeting with the chairman of the national bank, or the 'busy bees' in the street vending sector, the commitment of Liberians to pulling their country out of the aftermath of civil conflict was not only clear and alive, but ready to be released.

I served as a catalyst by mirroring to these persons what they themselves had said and what they knew. They did not need an outside consultant or new institutions. Under their own elected leadership, we drew up a group of institutions to prepare their 'country statement'. The only hitch was that there were sanctions against funding by the inter-governmental agencies, except for emergency relief. Living there for 15 days and seeing their capability, it was unbearable to think that these efforts would be crushed and perhaps Liberia would revert to child soldiers and war again. This was a distinct possibility, because the world was choosing to look only at the eggshell aspect of Liberia, its structural problems, and not the yoke, its people.

The point I am making is that it is possible to enable a country to strengthen itself and undertake globalisation on its own terms. It is also interesting to note that, even if not for Liberia, UNCTAD is thinking in this way. It reflects Stiglitz's position: 'The issue is one of the balance, and where that balance lies may depend on the country, the capacity of its government, the institutional development of its markets.'[20] In other words, development advice should be adapted to the circumstances of the country. Imagine what these 15 or 16 countries which have been 'basketed' by UNCTAD could accomplish with funds and expertise. Imagine if these countries were orchestrated to transform with these new ideas emerging from their experience, imagine their being enabled to build themselves into paradigms of just development. Imagine if this was pulled together as a showcase, not as individual countries but as a different 'G-15'. Isn't it possible that by learning from the mistakes of the big countries, the small countries could show the way?

Unfortunately, in spite of suggestions from the group that UNCTAD should set up a small steering group which ensured that the wisdom of that expert group was nurtured, and the theoretical insights in the lessons drawn, UNCTAD did not follow up.

Measures and Measurement: A Third Window of Hope

In its next *HDR*, South Africa has taken 'transformation' as its theme. Dr Stiglitz should be happy that they are highlighting 'transformation', though they have also added 'development' and 'democracy'. This language is widespread in South Africa where social segmentation and oppression have been seen in their most extreme, vulgar and cruel form, and thus the South African government thinks that without social transformation, there can be no talk of economic growth or globalisation. The segmentation of South African society would continue to vitiate any programme to build national unity, which should precede globalisation. This point is emphasised in *HDR 1999*. In preparing its human development report, however, South Africa wanted to find measures for the immeasurable.

I co-wrote a paper on how to measure in working towards transformation, especially non-material elements such as relations of power, access to political rights and access to participation and decision making.[21] We revealed that it was possible to find innovative indicators for what are called the 'immeasurables'. I was stimulated in my attempt by the work being done in the United States on measures of progress. For instance, Cobb et al. illustrate that increases in crime, individualisation of the family, accompanied by the absence of social support, add to the GDP in the US.[22] They have coined the slogan 'growth in GDP is social decay.' They criticise GDP for not only the inadequacies of the measure but for concealing the most unwanted elements. They have gone as far as to say that GDP is a measure of social decay.

These debates on measures have also been high on the agenda of those who are engaged in sustainable development. The International Institute of Sustainable Development held a conference in Bellagio in 1997 on developing a framework of indicators for worldwide use.[23] Richard Norgaard points out that the current rates of biodiversity loss, the appearance of climate change and the threat of its acceleration, and the accumulation of toxics in the environment provide ample evidence that we are living on our children's natural inheritance. Even if we included every possible interaction within the market system so that it worked perfectly efficiently, we would still have to grapple with what distribution of rights would get the system to go where we want it to go. My fear is that insights and mechanisms rooted in efficiency analyses will be accepted as sufficient given the dominant ideology, when in fact that ideology largely serves the purpose of protecting the current distribution of rights. A significant move towards an ethics of care for people and stewardship of nature is sorely needed.

Enriching Indices with Feminist Perspectives

As part of a group of women economists in India, we transformed the variables developed for the HDI at the UN. We paid special attention to the gender equity and inequity measures, changing them to suit the social and political conditions, goals and institutions of our country.[24] Measuring change is as important as change itself and what you measure. How you measure, sometimes almost invidiously if not openly, determines the values given to change. Thus, if growth is always measured as growth in GDP, then other measures will get second place. If a measure does not include poverty, the sex ratio or infant mortality, it will 'mute' these concerns. From a study I conducted on time use by women and men, including children in six villages in India, I challenged the work participation measure of the national data system.[25]

I argued that if time were used as a measure of value, it would upturn all the hierarchies embedded in valuation. For example, women would come out as the major workers in the economy, since they have the longest hours of labour. Their non-monetised work would get measured, and it occupies a higher rank than the conventional measure of money. Time as a measure of value would reverse the values of men's and women's work. Women would always come out on 'top' as they spend more hours working than men, as *HDR 1995* shows.[26]

Other ideas on measures are constantly emerging. For example, a corruption index has been developed by the Berlin-based anti-corruption watchdog group Transparency International in its fifth annual survey.[27] The corruption index ranks countries on the extent of corruption. For one of its variables, it measures the acceptance of bribes offered by corporations from the North.

Regionalism or Even Regionalisation: An Answer to Globalisation?

A fifth example I draw on arises from a series of discussions. They begin with a lecture I gave at the Asian Development Bank in Manila in 1998, and include meetings of the South African Development Community (SADC) meetings in Botswana and the NAM Summit in Durban.[28] I discuss the suggestion that regionalism (that is, geographically based continental boundaries of integrated economic development) can perhaps provide the kind of institutional arrangements necessary for coping with globalisation successfully.

It is now recognised that globalisation needs regulation, it needs governance and preparedness. Individual countries, like individual citizens, may not be able to manage the globetrotting of MNCs and international finance. But if individual countries link with others who are similar because of geography or history, then their internal capacities can be strengthened before taking on the global environment. This idea matches with the mainstream point of view that the most effective way of handling globalisation is to have it tethered in a national programme. The assumption is that the procedures within national institutions would facilitate transparency and the capacity to attempt to regulate financial markets. From there, national institutions can move to regional alliances to broaden the same procedures at that level.

At the Asian Development Bank, I not only proposed regionalism, by which I meant integrating economies rather than joint ventures, but I also offered it as the best bulwark against globetrotting by global players. In Botswana at the SADC secretariat, I suggested that we develop a model for the region, where against a goal full of employment, a maximisation model could be drawn up, taking natural, human and financial resources as 'givens'.[29] In South Asia too I have been canvassing for this idea. Initial explorations suggest that if we pool the resources (that is, the supply side) of individual nations and take the region as one economy, then we might be able to reach our very desirable goal of full employment without the hassles of external support.

If globalisation can treat the earth as one space untrammelled by national boundaries, why shouldn't the South try regionalisation with the same aim and have some roving regional economic giants, or regional MNCs, strengthening our own muscles with all the injunctions of free trade theory? At the NAM Summit in Durban in 1998, a policy document also proposed greater attention to regionalism.[30] In Manila and Durban this was welcomed. Though I may add that the further proposal that I am making for regionalisation has not been put in quite the same way.

THE CRACKS

Forging unity is where these positive examples break down or crack open. Like those gloomy robots in science fiction films, the witless march of less nuanced globalisation continues and in its wake mucks up the earth.

Building alliances is crucial to the success of nuancing globalisation if its positive effects are to be experienced by all. This requires snowballing such interventions into global opinion building. It should involve constructing and nurturing alliances across sectors such as women, workers and indigenous peoples. It should traverse domains such as civil society and the corporate sectors. To prevent cracks from emerging and to forge a workable unity, these alliances should link the regions of Latin America, Asia and Africa.

The proof that such mobilisation can take place and public action can transform policy, and can even enter the belly of a global agency, has been demonstrated by one of the most brilliant struggles I know of. The 'Save the Narmada' struggle originating in India is one of the most brilliant examples of 'think locally and act globally'. This struggle comes from the 15-year evolution of what is called in India the Narmada Bachao Andolan (NBA). The germination of the movement was around a very local issue, namely the inadequate or unsatisfactory arrangements being made for the resettlement of those who were being displaced by the construction of a mega dam called the Sardar Sarovar Dam. The struggle began with the impetus to protect homogeneous communities of tribal people comfortably living in the area, from being not only dislocated, but betrayed by offers of compensation. As the struggle proceeded, the issues changed from merely better resettlement of displaced persons to concerns about not only large dams, not only anxiety about environmental damage, the loss of precious forests and their species, but also about the process through which development was designed and engineered. It looked like there was no space at all for the people or animals that the project was going to affect, whether positively or negatively. Investments, designs and implementation were all made on calculations and ideas which were far removed from the soil and its people.

Thus, the people and the activists in the Narmada Valley began a dialogue and a march which was so clear, aware and strong that it was able to stop the World Bank from funding the project. It was able to induce the Japanese to withdraw the finance they were routing through the World Bank, and in the last few years it has been able to stop several corporations in Germany and Switzerland from providing the equipment. All of this was accomplished through the activism of local and international solidarity. The international solidarity around this struggle in the Narmada Valley has come from other groups which are working to protect people from mega projects. In Latin America, the movement is called People Against Dams.

The Philippines has a wide range of environmental movements. There are international committees to protect the rights of people

who live along the banks of rivers. There are committees to just protect rivers from the assault of development. Not only do the networks
mutually reinforce each other, but they also have been able to hold
back some of the most powerful world agencies. The lesson to note is
the vital connection between the global and local. Some of the major
principles of mobilisation had to be collectivity, solidarity and unity
to carry the message from the Narmada Valley to Washington. Yet
the idea to resist came from the local struggle in the Narmada Valley.

There are many more such illuminating examples of 'think locally
act globally', of people occupying spaces and recasting development; for
example, in India, the home-based workers movement and campaigns
against violence against women.[31]

GENDER AND FEMINISM IN GLOBALISATION

What about gender? Where is feminism in all this? For me, the current issue is not about gender differentiation, but about women's perspectives and women's advice, coming out of women's experiences.
The real issue is the consolidation of women's thought and therefore
women's opinion on the *what, where* and *how* of globalisation. To that
extent I could propose that since this lecture is by me, a development
economist, a feminist and a woman, it illustrates my point. But perhaps
that would not be fair to the opportunity that has been given to me by
the Centre for Gender and Development Studies and the University of
the West Indies to reflect more seriously on this aspect.

The UN brought out its *1999 World Survey on the Role of Women
in Development: Globalization, Gender and Work* in August 1999.[32] The
report finds that women's absorption into the waged labour force
has been higher than that of males, and that women have had greater
mobility. For example, women domestic workers from poor countries
are providing opportunities for women from the richer countries, like
the Middle East, to take on higher-quality, salaried professional jobs
by undertaking their reproductive work. There is a flip side. In the
informal sector, there is no worker protection either in wage laws
or job security, yet work in that sector is increasing and women are
bunching there. Women are increasingly working out of their homes

in the West. This may be an advantage in terms of not having a double burden and two shifts (working in the office or factory, and then coming home to work in the kitchen), but rather managing both in the same 'workplace'. The flip side of this 'advantage' is of course that there is further perpetuation of the stereotype and isolation from the formal organisation. Section by section, the report describes what is happening to women because of globalisation—seeing women basically as objects, as the pawns of globalisation.

In a sense, this 1999 UN World Survey on Women provides support to the analysis that the current preoccupation with impact, with monitoring according to the UN framework and its structures (including its counterparts in the nations), is, to put it mildly, the less creative role. It objectifies women. It does not give us agency. It does not ask, what have women done? What do women think on this subject?

Reflecting on the nearly 25 years during which I have been tracking developments and travelling with the women's movement, I am driven or directed by this experience to suggest that unwittingly we have slipped into a faultline. In the earlier era, 1975–90, it may have been necessary to develop exercises in gender differentiation to answer the question 'why women?' by developing databases which showed in what ways women and men were different, even as they participated in the labour force or made development choices. This was the 'gender in poverty', 'intra-household disparities' approach of the type of work we did, and appropriately so. In my opinion, the need today is to shift the question of women from the body to the mind.[33]

It seems to me that while the momentum for affirmative action in political structures, quota systems and representation is gaining ground, the inward-looking, searching question 'why women?' has not yet been answered, or even if answered, it has not yet been supported by a philosophy or ideology which makes clear and legitimate the demand that women should be in positions of leadership. I can visualise statements like 'going beyond the biological to the intellectual or ideational' and 'locating ourselves in relevance' as a way of describing what I am trying to develop.[34] I have been brooding over this idea for the last two years and testing it in papers. I am trying to work out an open-ended framework, philosophy or ethics of feminism under which women can unite.

Unity however has to have a moral purpose. In fact, the still graceful aspect of humans is that we are charmed by morality. In my view, the moral purpose should be poverty eradication. It is interesting that at the International NGO Conference at Seoul in October 1999, where downstream springs were gurgling, the most widely accepted thought was for NGOs to unite with a single-minded purpose for the removal of poverty.

Can we build up a cause in our countries that can unite all the downtrodden and disaffected people suffering from specific griev-ances, economic and political deprivations and inequalities, as well as social and cultural injustices, around a concept of freedom, equity and justice? Let us not have a grand theory to explain all the problems of the economy and society. Nor do we need one general and overriding answer or approach or plan to solve all these problems. Specific situ-ations need specific approaches. Each problem has to be solved in its own way. But there has to be one cause which may unite all groups, and one platform on which all those who are deprived, downtrodden and vulnerable can combine to give expression to their anguish and fury. I submit that that cause can be the championing of human rights, the cause of freedom, justice and equity which every individual has the right to claim by virtue of their identity as human beings. And elaborat-ing that cause, we have a new theory that propounds the principle that the right to development is a human right, where development means economic growth with freedom, equity and justice.[35]

However, taking poverty eradication as a unifying goal is not a sufficient condition for the removal of poverty. Once again, we may have to make another territorial leap, perhaps even a terrestrial leap, from the publicly moral to personal morality.

GANDHIAN PHILOSOPHY ON PERSONAL MORALITY AND EQUITY

A person who designed an effective methodology for serious engage-ment with the removal of poverty was Mahatma Gandhi. Gandhi provided the most doable and well-argued ideas. There is need for us to consider his ideas for the philosophical underpinnings of approaches to social and political transformation that they offer, be it at the local, national or global level. Gandhi offered a discriminating tool or norm that he called his 'talisman'. I have called this 'a bubbling-up theory of growth'. According to this line of reasoning, the criterion by which any political choice for economic change is made is whether it improves the condition of the poorest person. If we deal with removal of poverty first, then the improvement of other economic policies will follow. To quote Gandhi,

> Whenever you are in doubt, or when the self becomes too much with you, apply the following test: recall the face of the poorest and the weakest man or woman whom you may have seen and ask yourself if the step you contemplate is going to be of any use to him.[36]

My friend the late Mahbub ul Haq has also given the talisman pride of place in his South Asia *Human Development Report*.[37]

Like Marx and Hobbes before him, Gandhi saw the human being as a limited creature—capable of cruelty, narrow-mindedness, greed and violence, and requiring strong medicine to be socially manageable. Indeed, when we see starving people, especially women and children, marching in the thousands across national boundaries trying to escape from violence, when we hear that security personnel pick up girls to be sold into the flesh trade while child refugees are crossing borders, when we turn away from the expropriation of earth, water and mountains for 'growth'—then their perceptions seem correct.

While orthodox socialism addresses itself to inequalities based on the ownership of the means of production, Gandhi focused on inequalities in consumption. His argument, or his advocacy for austerity, for simplicity in lifestyle, was based on developing in Indians a consciousness of the problems of the poor. Gandhi believed that to consume too much food, or to own or display too much clothing when the neighbourhood was filled with those who could neither eat nor clothe themselves, was a form of violence.

There is a beautiful story of how a child living near the Sabarmati Ashram asked Gandhi why he only wore a dhoti and no shirt. The child offered to bring Gandhi a shirt. Gandhi is supposed to have said that he would wear a shirt when all the millions of shirtless Indians could also afford a shirt. Thus the practice of simplicity was in some sense an attempt to emulate or imitate the life of those who were needy, and thereby release resources to be able to provide for those who did not have enough.

Gandhi took this technique of identification with the deprived into many other domains. He saw it as a form of melting down hierarchies. There is an idea here for all of us to consider—it is perhaps the only strategy, namely the development of a personal morality and identification with the poor, based on which a united stand could in fact eradicate poverty.

DAWN AND THE DEVELOPMENT DISCOURSE

In the earlier years of DAWN, we relocated the analytical frame for understanding women in development by creating an alternative format which gave more leverage to poor women within their contextual locations. It is noteworthy that in the very beginning, DAWN focused entirely on poor women. The DAWN group felt that its basic ethic, its premise for existence, was its interest in rolling back the immiserisation—the distances between men and women, women and the earth, between women and their 'rights'—that was getting congealed by a certain type of North–South transfer. So DAWN aligned itself with the poor and did not inhibit itself in calling them 'poor women', even though we were teased about it.

When DAWN was preparing for the Social Summit again,[38] the DAWN family felt uncomfortable plugging itself into the stereotyped calculus provided by the Social Summit secretariat. We therefore stepped aside and put forward a policy document which challenged both the frame and the method by which the very aims of the Social Summit could be articulated. These were full employment, the right to work, the right to development, and the demand for justice.

Prior to the UN Fourth World Conference on Women, DAWN recast the framework from integrating women into development under the various categories of education, employment, etc., to looking at regional macro-economic contexts and locating the situation as well as the trajectory for change of poor women in that context. In that quest, DAWN recharacterised the regions and issues of the developing world as the Latin American debt crisis, the African continental food crisis, South Asian poverty and unemployment, and so forth. This re-landscaping of Southern continents and their issues provided what could be called 'levers' through which poor women could nudge themselves out of the crisis in which the broader landscape was located.

By looking at development and then women's role within it, rather than trying to bring women into the existing development processes, DAWN was challenging as well as transforming the theoretical and the practical base for understanding development. However, in Nairobi, DAWN had its own separate platform at the NGO Forum. It did not try to knit itself into 'advocacy' with the official process, the juggernaut of conventional categorisation of development. In fact, we stated that development was flawed, so we did not want a piece of that poisoned cake.

Three themes have been chosen by DAWN for the post-Beijing period, one of which, appropriately enough, is titled 'Political Restructuring and Social Transformation'. However, as I perceive the landscape today through a woman's lens, my impression is that in spite of the unity of political will that was almost tangible in Beijing, which crossed the divide between the NGO and the official confer-ence, there is a certain fragmentation in the women's movement. I argue that the fragmentation is partly because of the partnership with the UN and governments, which tend to ask for performance sheets based on conventional administrative procedures.

We need to start a process of consolidating women's experiences, to give a stronger, more visible voice to women's advice for nation build-ing, and for the political economy at the global level. We need to start a process of building unity in the women's movement around ideology.

There are many streams of thought and action by women which have led to transformation of policy and transformation of the outcomes of international conferences in Vienna, Cairo, Copenhagen, Beijing and so on. There are other arenas where women are influencing global approaches, as for example the World Commissions and the major world reports, be they from the World Bank, the UNDP, the International Labour Organization (ILO), UNICEF, the World Health Organization, the United Nations Population Fund (UNFPA) or the United Nations Educational, Scientific and Cultural Organization (UNESCO).

There is also much effort and some success in bringing women into political processes. This success has come about through larger numbers in assemblies as voters or through affirmative action policies. These activities are based on the premise that placing women in power structures would be a step towards bringing women's advice into the formation of policy, shaping the direction of social and economic development, as well as influencing the character of the state. However, there is yet no evidence of what can be called a striking presence of women's power at the international negotiations level. For example, one can compare this with the birth and emergence of a player in the global fields, such as the *HDRs* of the UNDP, where in 10 years an idea has emerged and captured the imagination of the world and is now a major influence. The women's movement, even though it has been in the international arena for a longer time, has not been able to provide or push for such a striking idea.

ABSENCE OF WOMEN'S INFLUENCE AT THE INTERNATIONAL LEVEL

There could be many explanations for this, and also many other kinds of views. For example, it might be argued that women have in fact influenced the *HDRs* and other such major ideas, but this is not explicit.

It is my view that one of the missing elements is the single-mindedness of an idea, a point of concern, an approach or even a basic agreement within the women's movement on what it is that women stand for or identify themselves with. This can flag attention to our experience in thought and action. For women to unite on a philosophy or a definition of feminism is not easy, and there is enough literature to argue for the importance of difference and diversity of opinion and choice.

It is my view that the time has also come for the question to be posed again: why women? However, it should not be posed in the earlier context in which it was not only posed but also answered: because of the significance for analysis, action and theory of gender differentiation. It must also be posed in relation to the current issues of women's leadership and in women's participation in directioning the political economy. We need to subvert the process and teach the system how to present a report on women, rather than have women's lives measured on conventional lines.

I have given an example from India of how a little flame can not only generate change in national policy but can bring different types of actors together. This was achieved only because of the moral position of the little flame that burns on the side of the injured. It is still a good thing in the world that even today it wakes up when the cause has a flavour of enabling the worst off, as in the case of the NBA. Similarly I have a dream that at the Beijing +5 meeting, we can begin a process culminating in a panel discussion. The aim behind this would be to argue for a basic premise, a basic ideology and method that justifies our calling attention to women's participation in governance.

The panel should give space to perspectives on the political economy of the globe. It should discuss global governance, and the movement from local to global by women. In other words, it would give space for women who have been generating ideas under the broad heading of 'transformation'. Many countries of the world have women entering politics and transforming the issues in politics. Other women have entered large structures, major organisations or bureaucracies and transformed them. This panel would be a means of putting forward, of stating simply, 'why women'.

Why women? What will we bring into the field that is different from men? Of course women will bring their choices in terms of priorities emerging from their particular experiences, largely drawn from women's biological experiences. What else will women bring? Are these issues being identified and reconstructed as women's particular opinions, views and ideology?

There is now literature on women in leadership and what they bring, on women as role models, on political and developmental choices and so on. Yet at the level of the globe there is still a gap, in that women have not released any effective message or projected a collective will on these global playing fields.

I recall a moment in Barbados at a DAWN consultation in 1995, when one of our colleagues, Gigi (Joseph) Francesca from the Philippines, dropped a pearl. We were going around the room identifying what were the major forces in the world which had to be dealt with in any treatise we would write on political economy and global governance. When it came to Gigi's turn, she said two words. She said, 'the globe' and 'Eurocentricism'.[39] There is a total truth in Gigi's postulating something called the 'globe', rather than the more amorphous and ambiguous term 'globalisation'. She personified it as a new player who would rule over the earth, untethered by the strings of nationhood, the world, the international and all other such terminologies. The great globe would have to be dealt with because it was something like, if you don't mind my saying so, that mindless 'exterminator' that we see in Hollywood films, who tramples over things with an ugly, glazed look in his eye.

Eurocentrism has also become a bugbear and an issue. The UNDP's 1999 *HDR* has a telling diagram on its very first page. It shows that more than 80 per cent of internet activity is located in Europe. Yet that is the least of the issues. Eurocentrism embraces the broader language of domination of culture, of political history, of obsession, of power, of phobias.

I would like to take this moment to grieve the passing of a brother, a comrade, a friend and a leader, Mwalimu Julius Nyerere, who died in London on 14 October 1999.[40] I was a member of the South Commission which he chaired, and all of us struggled to put forward a proposal[41] showing how our economic as well as political output would be maximised if we could efface some of our national egos and come together. The death of Julius Nyerere has invited very strange comments from the US-based newspapers—one even going so far as to say that he should have been prosecuted like Pinochet for the crimes that he perpetrated against his people.

During the tenure of the South Commission, I had hoped that the Third World women's movement and the attempts of the South

Commission could synergise each other—through the groundswell of intelligence and the willingness to bond. I had hoped that the intellectual analysis of DAWN could be picked up by the South Commission and the flames could be fanned. I had proposed that South–South co-operation should be built on existing bridges. One of the most valuable, lively, real bridges was the women's movement of the developing countries. But like many other leaders of the Southern countries, Mwalimu also was limited in his experience of these new changes, even though he had been the leader of his country for 27 years. The springs that were gurgling all over Africa were not fully known to him. Even though my sister and friend in the South Commission and one of the founders of DAWN, Marie-Angelique Savane, also a founder of the Association of African Women for Research and Development,[42] tried to draw his attention to this phenomenon. I can hear her saying, 'Mwalimu, you are speaking to the wrong people. You are speaking to the heads of states, you are speaking to the mainstream economists and you are getting depressed. Africa is bubbling and bursting with energy, but it is in the movements at the bottom.'

But neither Nyerere, nor at that time the secretary general of the South Commission who later became the finance minister of India, knew about these springs. I provide an updated illustration of what could be the leverage for an alliance between the women's movement and South–South economic agendas. The world is currently preparing to go to the WTO Conference and Summit in Seattle later in November 1999. India is one of those 'naughty' countries in the eyes of the United States because it is always putting forward resistance to some of their attempts at internationalisation or globalisation of trade regimes. The latest issue is in a reference that I have brought from an Indian newspaper. India and 11 other developing countries are insisting that there should be a discussion on implementation of the WTO on the grounds (which in my view is a feminist argument) that the problems that our countries are having in implementation point to changes required in the principles, that is, in the rules set up for WTO. The United States is unbending. It is saying that now we cannot redo the rules because these have been agreed upon. We can only do something at the 'implementation level'. Some countries like Japan or Europe are standing in between and saying, 'OK, let us take implementation in different bundles and handle it.' But the feminist point is that practice teaches theory, and it is only when you put an idea on the ground that you know what is wrong with it or what is right with it. This is the argument of the India-led group of 11 countries.

These countries argue that it is at the implementation stage that the rules become asymmetrical. For example, this is brought out clearly in the Anti-dumping Laws that the United States is using at every point to prevent imports from developing countries, and in the intellectual property rights implementation programme. Only 11 countries of the developing world have allied themselves with India. Imagine if the worldwide women's movement could provide support to these leverages of India and broaden that space, snowball it rather than showcase it? It could be a turning point in rolling back dominance, but we are not using such leverages.

Thus, a hope I had of bringing about convergence in two or three theatres fell through. I had hoped the South Commission and the Third World women's movement could concur on the issues of ideology, moral imperatives and a clear commitment to poverty eradication and participatory development. It would have been a perfect case of mainstream and downstream flowing together to roll back domination.

This is my story and these are the streams in which I swam with hope. You will not be surprised if I now feel intimidated or even negative, except that preparing this lecture gave me hope. As I scanned what is called 'the mainstream' and saw that our knowledge was at last being recycled back to us from the top, and that now there was a hope and opportunity for us, I felt the flame of energy and world mobilisation rekindled in me. I thank you for that rekindling.

NOTES

1 The Third World Conference on Women, held in Nairobi, Kenya, in 1985. Nita Barrow was the convener of the NGO Forum, called Forum '85. This meeting was held parallel to the UN World Conference to review the First Decade for Women (1975–85).

2 Devaki Jain was a founding member of DAWN, the idea for which came out of a meeting held in Bangalore, India, in 1984. She was also its first co-ordinator.

The initial base for DAWN was in Bangalore. Since then the network has been co-ordinated by Neuma Aguilar of Brazil and Peggy Antrobus, Barbados. It now has its headquarters in Fiji and is co-ordinated by Claire Slater.

3 Devaki Jain, 'Minds, Not Bodies: Expanding the Notion of Gender in Development', Bradford Morse Memorial Lecture, Opening Plenary at the Fourth World Conference on Women, Beijing, September 1995; reproduced as chapter 4 in Devaki Jain, *Journey of a Southern Feminist*, vol. 1 (New Delhi: Sage/Yoda, 2018).

4 During India's struggle for freedom from British colonial rule, Mahatma Gandhi undertook a long march accompanied by thousands of people and picked up a fistful of salt from the salt pans of the coast of Gujarat. This was a symbolic act of civil disobedience and affirmation of the economic rights of the people, which led to mass mobilisation.

5 Devaki Jain and Samia Ahmed, *Towards Just Development: Identifying Meaningful Indicators* (South Africa: UNDP, 1999).

6 World Bank, *Entering the 21st Century: World Development Report 1999/2000* (Oxford: Oxford University Press, 1999); UNDP, *Human Development Report 1999* (New York: Oxford University Press, 1999); International Labour Office, *Employability in the Global Economy: How Training Matters, World Employment Report 1998–99* (Geneva: International Labour Office, 1998); United Nations Population Fund (UNFPA), 'Population, Food Production and Nutrition in India', UNFPA, New Delhi, October 1999; Kirit S. Parikh (ed.), *India Development Report 1999–2000* (New Delhi: Oxford University Press, 1999); UN Women, *1999 World Survey on the Role of Women in Development: Globalization, Gender and Work* (New York: UN Women, 1999); Jagdish Bhagwati, 'Globalization Has a Human Face', Lecture at India Habitat Centre, New Delhi, 18 October 1999.

7 Bhagwati, 'Globalization Has a Human Face'.

8 Manu Shroff, 'Globalization: A Stock-Taking', *Economic & Political Weekly*, vol. 34, no. 40 (1999), pp. 2845–49.

9 Joseph E. Stiglitz, 'Towards a New Paradigm for Development: Strategies, Policies and Processes', Prebisch Lecture, United Nations Conference on Trade and Development, Geneva, 1998.

10 Ibid.

11 Devaki Jain, 'Home Thoughts from Abroad', University of Westville, Durban, 15 May 1999.

12 Stiglitz, 'Towards a New Paradigm for Development'.

13 Devaki Jain, 'The Role of People's Movements in Economic and Social Transformation', Opening Thematic Plenary at the 1999 Seoul International Conference of NGOs, 10–16 October 1999.

14 World Bank, *World Development Report 1999/2000*; Stiglitz, 'Towards a New Paradigm for Development'; Bhagwati, 'Globalization Has a Human Face'; Richard B. Norgaard, 'Beyond Growth and Globalization', *Economic & Political*

Weekly, vol. 34, no. 36 (1999), pp. 2570–74; UNDP, *Human Development Report 1999*.

15 Bhagwati, 'Globalization Has a Human Face'.

16 Jain, 'Home Thoughts from Abroad'.

17 UNCTAD Global Programme on 'Globalization, Liberalization and Sustainable Human Development', Expert Group Meeting, Geneva, February 1999.

18 Massachusetts Institute of Technology, Harvard, Oxford, Cambridge, the World Bank, IMF, Organisation for Economic Co-operation and Development.

19 Stiglitz, 'Towards a New Paradigm for Development'.

20 Ibid.

21 Jain and Ahmed, *Towards Just Development*.

22 Cobb et al., 'If the GDP Is Up, Why Is America Down?'

23 Norgaard, 'Beyond Growth and Globalization'.

24 'Enriching Indices with Feminist Perspective', Technical Workshop on Building a Framework for Measuring Gender Equity, ISST, Bangalore, 15–17 May 1996; Gender Audit at District Level, Karnataka Women's Information and Resource Centre, Bangalore, 13–14 February 1997.

25 Devaki Jain, 'Valuing Work: Time as a Measure', *Economic & Political Weekly*, vol. 31, no. 43 (1996), pp. WS46–WS57. Reproduced as chapter 5 in this volume.

26 UNDP, *Human Development Report 1995*.

27 *Asian Age*, 'India, Pakistan on Top of Bribe-Taker List', 28 October 1999.

28 Devaki Jain, 'Close Encounters of Another Kind: Women-Led Regional Economic and Social Cooperation', Seminar on the 'Relevance of Mainstreaming the Concerns of Women in Bank Activities', Asian Development Bank, Manila, 2 March 1998; Jain, 'Valuing Work'.

29 SADC Meeting, Botswana, 19 June 1999.

30 *Business Day*, 'Strengthening the South through NAM: The Opportunities', 13 August 1998 (published under the title: 'South Must Take Control of the Agenda').

31 Jain, 'The Role of People's Movements in Economic and Social Transformation'.

32 UN Women, *1999 World Survey on the Role of Women in Development*.

33 Jain, 'Minds, Not Bodies'.

34 Devaki Jain, 'Locating Ourselves in Relevance', colloquium series co-hosted by the African Gender Institute, University of Cape Town, and the Gender Equity Unit, University of Western Cape, Cape Town, 28 April 1998.

35 Arjun Sengupta, 'Delivering the Right to Development: ECSR and NGOs', *Economic & Political Weekly*, vol. 34, no. 41 (1999), pp. 2920–22.

36 Devaki Jain, *Minds, Bodies and Exemplars: Reflections at Beijing and Beyond* (New Delhi: British Council Division, 1996), p. 8.

37 *Human Development in South Asia* (Lahore: Mahbub ul Haq Human Development Centre).

38 World Summit for Social Development, Copenhagen, 6–12 March 1995.

39 Joseph (Gigi) Francesca, 'Shifting the Development Paradigm', Women 2000: Asia Pacific NGO Forum, Kasetsart University, Bangkok, 3 September 1999.

40 Devaki Jain, 'Tribute to Julius Nyerere', *Times of India*, 18 October 1999; *Hindu*, 'A Loss to the World: Tribute to Mwalimu Julius Nyerere', 31 October 1999.

41 Devaki Jain, 'Development South Style', paper prepared for a working party on development, South Commission, Geneva, 2–4 November 1988.

42 Marie Angelique Savane, AAWORD Meeting, DAWN, 1976.

Chapter 7

Food Battles, or Battling for Food

It has often baffled me that there is so much awareness of the hunger and basic lack of food amongst millions of people, and that nevertheless the price of food is forbidding for those at the bottom of the economic ladder. Yet the rhetoric prevails that agriculture is a second-class citizen in the economy. As one of our senior policy makers once put it, agriculture is a 'sunset industry'. This is in contrast to electronics, which is a 'sunrise industry'. Some of these dilemmas or paradoxes are vividly illustrated by the case of India, with its millions of tons of food and millions of hungry people. There is a whole discourse here on how such confusion can emerge, and so using India as an illustration, this paper goes over the complexities of putting on the ground a right to food programme as mandated both by the human rights framework as well as the equitable development framework.

To my mind, the issues being addressed by my sister panellists cover all aspects relevant to the theme of this session:

1. Gender, equity and rural employment.
2. Women organising for change in agriculture and National Rural Livelihood Mission (NRLM).
3. Impact of the food crisis on women at the grassroots.
4. Rural women as key to household food security.
5. Global perspectives on women and food security, the food crisis, nutrition, poverty, and the intersectionalities in gender/food issues.

The review and analysis presented by UN Special Rapporteur on the Right to Food Olivier De Schutter, in his report as well as in his presentation to the new committee set up by the Food and Agriculture Organization (FAO), also offer a complete profile representing the views of all of us—economists, feminists, agricultural specialists.

My paper covers the following themes:

- An outline of feminist macro-economic reasoning, particularly drawing on the work of the Casablanca Dreamers group;
- A perspective from the South with special reference to Asia;
- The argument that the recent Indian experience has lessons for our debate.

The paper includes sections on: the conflicts in the food security zone; a critique of global growth paths/ideas; what women need to address; ideas for another path to growth of the economy; an alternative to trickle-down theory, viz., the 'bubbling-up' theory of growth; building economic democracy; affirming the South; narratives from India; and food from the courts. In sum, what I would do is:

- List what I call the various sites of the battle for food, or food battles.
- Show how the major obstacle is the current growth model. The landscape we are addressing is dotted with landmines. Therefore, despite the best of intentions, we cannot walk safely on the existing road of global economic policy.
- Show the importance of recognising the difference between North and South feminist agendas.
- Provide arguments and ideas for reconstructing the economy towards an economic democracy.
- Present India as a case study of success and failure, with lessons for the way forward.

Gender concerns and feminist ideas, I would argue, are like a purple thread running through the stories that I weave. Further, many of us have recently been confabulating on what kind of healing touch we can bring to this conflict-ridden, violent and extremely insecure environment. We propose that our voice and our movement has to now go beyond gender equality, violence against women and gender budgeting, and begin to engage with global policy ideologies, challenging and reconstructing them with our gendered experience of political economy.

THE CONFLICTS IN THE FOOD SECURITY ZONE

The most telling language to understand what is happening, and to effectively advocate for the right to food, has been employed by the economist and Nobel laureate Prof. Amartya Sen. Many decades ago he coined the term 'food battles' to describe what was happening within households, especially in South Asia where food was distributed unequally within the household.[1] The term used at that time was 'sequential feeding'. Even as we thought this was a South Asian phenomenon, we were reminded by Ruth Dixon of the UK that at Sunday lunch in a British home, the first cut was for the male head of the household, and the last leftover was what mom ate! And indeed as has been pointed out by Special Rapporteur Olivier De Schutter, there are now many more battles that are impeding the effective implementation of the right to food, freedom from hunger, and food security.

Food battles do not only involve the intra-household battles for food between men and women that Amartya Sen talked about. They are also caused by the following conflicts:

- Battles over land use: (a) that pit farmers and fisherfolk (the traditional users of land) against entities like real estate developers, miners, resort builders, export-led industries called special export zones, tourist resorts, etc.; i.e., land battles between agricultural use and industry use and export sectors; (b) that involve the question of what to grow: biofuels or food, basic cereals, or exotic food for the rich.
- Battles between environmental projects like growing trees and growing food crops.
- Battles on how to grow food: industrial, technical, mechanised, plantation-type farming or peasant farming.
- Battles on trading rules: financial speculation with agricultural products leading to artificial price rise.

- Battles between farmers of the North and the South on subsidies—
  i.e., protection versus free trade.

In listing the various sites of the battle for food, I am basically providing evidence to support my later argument that there are very many global forces and, what is more, forces driven by economic theory, that have to be tackled in order to articulate ways in which we can provide food security. It points to the immensity of what needs to be changed.

The food crisis, hunger, food deprivation, and the battles listed above have emerged as a result of a particular model of GDP growth. This economic model has led to five important shifts:

- The global shift of the sectoral distribution or sourcing of GDP from agriculture to services (see Figure 7.1 and Table 7.1).
- With implications for the relative positions of capital and labour[2] (see Table 7.2).
- Shifts in the centres of power, from the local and national to the global.

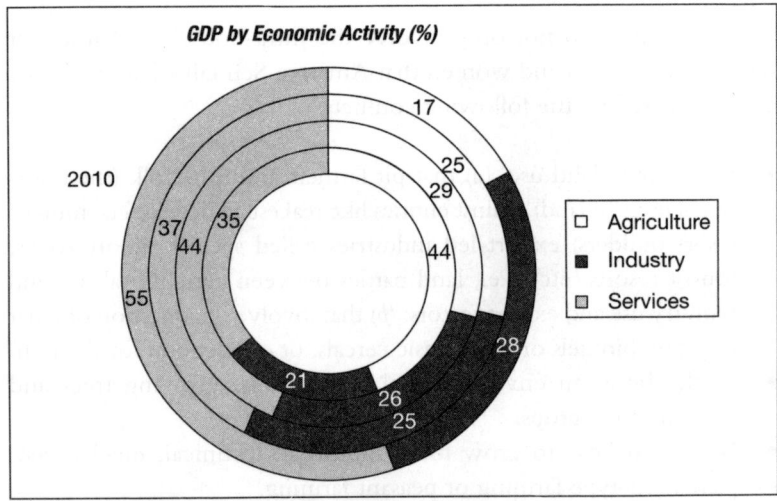

Figure 7.1 *Shift in GDP composition, India, 1973–2010*[3]
Source: NAS.

Table 7.1 Global shifts in composition of GDP from agriculture to services, 1970–2001

	Percentage of Economic Activity by Sector											
	Economic Activity—Agriculture				Economic Activity—Industry				Economic Activity—Services			
	1970	1980	1990	2001	1970	1980	1990	2001	1970	1980	1990	2001
World	27	7	5	4	32	38	33	29	41	55	62	67
Developed countries	7	4	3	2	35	37	33	26	58	59	65	72
Developing countries	27	17	15	11	32	42	36	37	41	41	49	52

Source: UNCTAD Handbook of Statistics Online, http://www.unctad.org/Templates/Page.asp?intItemID=1890

Table 7.2 Labour force in agriculture

	Total Labour Force (Millions)			Labour Force in Agriculture (Millions)			Percentage of Labour Force in Agriculture		
	1980	1990	2001	1980	1990	2001	1980	1990	2001
World	2,051	2,498	2,993	1,067	1,221	1,327	52	49	44
Developed countries	559	610	658	75	62	47	13	10	7
Industrialised countries	364	408	448	29	23	16	8	6	4
Transition economies	196	202	210	46	40	31	23	20	15
Developing countries	1492	1887	2335	993	1,159	1,280	67	61	55

Source: Summary of Food and Agricultural Statistics 2003.

- In control over knowledge, from women and communities to corporations and international institutions;
- In cultural values, from sustainability to consumerism; and
- In identity too, as the categories of rural and urban are blurred.

CRITIQUE OF GLOBAL GROWTH PATHS/IDEAS

The first area I will address is the theories of growth or the growth model in operation. In what follows, I will elaborate on the theory that the global shift from agriculture to services, from wage-, labour- and employment-led policies to capital- and export-led policies, has been one of the important reasons for hunger, as seen for example in India. I refer to landmines, as the obstacles on the road are often not visible. For instance, the FAO makes the strong argument that the rise in prices of oil due to the turbulence in the Arab region might encourage those who grow crops for fuels, namely biofuels. This is a landmine.

It is argued that this moving away from agriculture has been responsible for the worldwide crisis in food security. The UN in its *World Economic Situation and Prospects* report[4] estimates that the total number of food-insecure people is probably closer to about three billion, or about half the population of the world. The early years of the 21st century saw hungry people rioting in 37 countries.

There is a shift towards greater market orientation at the macro level, which is also reflected at the micro level with people increasingly moving out of subsistence production and towards production for the market. This trend is also being reinforced by micro-level interventions, such as credit delivery programmes that encourage poor households to engage in market-oriented production.

WHAT WOMEN NEED TO ADDRESS

To my mind, unless the above model is displaced, everything else will be nibbling at the edges. The Casablanca Dreamers group, a loose formation of feminist scholars and activists,[5] also argues that it will not be enough simply to distribute more land to individual women farmers. There would be a need to direct the entire economy towards supporting small farms and the kind of farming that women engage in. If the current trend continues, then within the space of a couple of decades, land would be concentrated in the hands of large commercial farmers. Better land rights for women need to be embedded in a system of equitable public support.

In other words, they point to the link between women's roles and values in a political economy and the changes that are required in macro-economic policy. They argue that in order to bring about freedom from hunger for all, the necessary mechanisms to be set in place are: a complete reorientation of the production schema, i.e., the role, location and share of food-based, not fuel-based, agriculture in the GDP, and thereby a revision of the selection/prioritisation of the triggers of economic success, and the political philosophy underpinning such a policy. But the question is: can we put these systems in place?

IDEAS FOR ANOTHER PATH TO GROWTH OF THE ECONOMY

Is it possible to generate the same growth rate of GDP from other sources and in other ways? Can the demand generated by, say, millions of incomes at the lower end of the economy be an engine of growth, and to some extent relieve the managers of the economy from generating surplus for social spending? In other words, can distributive justice be built into the growth path? It would not seem impossible, but it certainly would need abandoning the current over-the-top belief in corporate and FDI-led growth.

I would therefore argue that despite the best of intentions— pro-poor programmes, the right to food, and women's schemes (a complete feast currently on the table in India)—there is no way to relieve the various aspects of hunger and deprivation except by changing the model of growth and the measures of progress and well-being.

While much of the work and evaluations, including those being undertaken in India, by the FAO, and globally, on how to make food accessible, how to free people from hunger, etc., are seen as the management of food supply and its distribution, the case being made is for the deconstruction of production and distribution systems. In other words, a case for small farms, land rights for farmers, especially women, with extraordinarily strong support to enable them to become communities and co-operatives that can maximise their output and income.

This is possible, and the Casablanca group in their paper 'Vision for a Better World: From Economic Crisis to Equality' have proposed the 'bubbling-up' theory of growth.[6] The bubbling-up theory of growth argues that the process of removal of poverty can itself be an engine of growth. That incomes and capabilities among those who are currently poor have the potential to generate demand, which in turn will engineer production, but of goods that are immediately needed by the poor and that are currently peripheral in production. The oiling of this engine will bubble up and fire the economy in a much more broad-based manner. Unlike export-led growth, this approach will not skew production and trade into the elite trap, which is accentuating disparities and creating discontent.

BUILDING ECONOMIC DEMOCRACY

The Casablanca Dreamers group states further: 'In our view, there has been much advocacy and effort to introduce political democracy worldwide by the UN and other agencies, but not enough to introduce Economic Democracy.' Economic democracy, just like political democracy, would entail participation in economic decision making by 'people', with equality of power to decide. Like the political vote, there would be the economic vote, and transparency in drawing up public policy, budgets and deals. If we had such a system, there would not arise the phenomena that have driven many countries to economic and political trouble, with secret deals and corruption.

Not surprisingly, Mahatma Gandhi had laid out the framework for economic democracy in the ideas he provided for what he called the 'second freedom', the first being liberation from British rule over India. Gandhi called the idea of a full-employment or wage-led growth model 'economic democracy', where every individual would exercise his or her economic vote, with every purchase, on what to produce and how.

AFFIRMING THE SOUTH

I also propose that no matter how well we bond as women, working for and with women, almost transposing our consciousnesses with each other across all boundaries of geography, culture, race and economy, there is a need for us to affirm our differences, especially in analysis and agenda setting. I would add that unless we do this, we as women's lobbies would fail to deliver justice to the women of the South. There are issues particularly related to women, and there are other issues related to what is happening in the South regions. Both need to be foregrounded visibly and tangibly.

In many of the papers being written especially by African development-oriented feminists, the question being asked is: when did violence against women appear on the agenda? They ask this rhetorically, essentially questioning how the women's development agenda got replaced or moved off the screen.

Now many of us are asking similar questions regarding the high profile given to 'care', the measuring of household work and unpaid work. The depth of poverty—the kind of poverty that unfortunately people especially in India experience, where death is an event that can take place at any time of any day—has made this particularly clear and vivid. In such a circumstance, what would be the choice of a woman at the edge of death—giving recognition to the fact that she does household work? Or giving recognition to the fact that she may be a victim of violence? Or giving recognition to accessible food and a decent livelihood? It is for this reason that I would like to argue that if we are looking at the poorest of the poor in India, the livelihood and food agenda needs to be given a direct push. Therefore, while violence against women and the care economy are important agendas, priorities in these regions would still lead to highlighting economic security issues.

The *Economic Survey* for 2011–12 reveals not only the ongoing transfer of economic power to South countries, but also their increasing negotiating power in economic debates and institutions.[7] Again, it is critical that the women's movement in these countries creates knowledge to inform, intervene and to transform the rules, but this is not happening. This knowledge is also not flagged during the global meetings on women and development.

The South countries are mobilising themselves into regional economic clubs. These economic clubs tend to have similar objectives and similar economic models as the earlier clubs such as the European Union. But they are in the process of forming themselves and their agendas currently, therefore it is critical that the agenda for women must include engaging intellectually with these formations and with their networks. For example, suggestions to these clubs could include a South–South convention on wage fixation, with special reference to garment workers and domestic workers. These workers are highly exploited by multinationals for the cheapest labour. These issues have been written about at length. The South can take a view on small farms and women's land rights, going against the current that emphasises commercialisation and the plantation mode of agriculture.

Another aspect of South–South engagement which in fact speaks directly to food security involves some of the proposals coming out of groups such as IBSA (India, Brazil, South Africa). One of IBSA's meetings in New Delhi proposed what in fact had been advocated by the South Commission as early as the 1990s, that the South needed to replace the North-based food cartels. (Wheat, rice and cash crops like cocoa are all orchestrated by global markets and cartels and by signals from Northern countries.) It was suggested that there should be South–South grain banks. Through electronic media, South countries could signal each other regarding stocks of food and share a common market for foodgrains.

Another new economic group is BRIC (Brazil, Russia, India, China)—a mix of East and South—and now they are uniting in their work at the UN Security Council, most recently against the resolution on armed intervention in Libya. In my experience, these aspects are not covered in the women and development meetings, especially those convened by the UN and its agencies or by global research institutions.

FOOD FROM THE COURTS: INDIAN INITIATIVES AS PEACE BUILDING IN THE BATTLEGROUND

India is a good example of both success and failures. The Indian paradox of high rates of GDP growth despite crisis, mountains of food lying in silos and millions of hungry people, is interesting to study, because the Indian state has engaged with the presence of poverty and hunger for decades. Further, despite deep flaws in its performance, it does function under the rule of law and continues to have space for the affirmation of rights, free press, etc.—the characteristics of an embedded democratic nation.

But India also, both in the past under a more socialistic, centrally planned economy, as well as now with a very liberal, market-oriented economic policy, attempts to do the right thing. India has for many decades had a network of more than 0.4 million fair price shops claiming to annually distribute commodities worth more than ₹150 billion to about 160 million families. The Public Distribution System (PDS) in India is perhaps the largest distribution network of its type in the world.[8] These shops distribute a total of 35 kilograms of wheat and rice to about 65 million families below the poverty line at ₹4.2 per kilogram (10 cents in US currency) for wheat and ₹5.6 for rice (the present market rate is about double the PDS price). Another 25 million of the poorest families get 35 kilograms of foodgrains at a highly subsidised rate of ₹2 per kilogram for wheat and ₹3 per kilogram for rice. In addition, there are welfare schemes such as hot cooked midday meals for schoolgoing children, and supplementary nutrition for preschool children.

Our five-year plans for the first two decades were directed towards broadening employment. We had a radical land reforms agenda. Yet we did get into the situation often characterised as mountains of food and millions of hungry people, with assessments showing shocking deprivations.

However, the latest budget proposals by the Indian Finance Minister on 28 February 2011 are full of grant-in-aid funds for farms and rural labour, a big boost to revive the rural economy and ensure self-sufficiency in food. The incentives are directed to farmers to grow foodgrains and vegetables and non-farm foods. Further, they are giving special financial and technical support to women farmers, even women who may not have land titles.

A food security bill is being drafted and hopefully the Right to Food Act will get passed by the Parliament this month. The motivation for the proposed National Food Security Act to provide a guarantee of adequate nutrition is derived from the right to food as an aspect of the right to life under Article 21 (interpreted by the Supreme Court as a right to life with dignity). In fact, the Indian efforts to bring in a food security bill started with the writ mandamus on the right to life, as people were dying of hunger.

Democratic governments the world over guarantee all people who live within their boundaries the most essential and basic of all rights, and this is the right to life. The fundamental right to life is understood to imply that, for instance, if a person is detained by the state, and dies while in its custody, either because of torture or extra-judicial killings, state authorities are criminally liable for the death. The actual realisation of this right, especially by powerless and disenfranchised people, remains of course flawed and often bitterly contested in many countries. But the theory of such state accountability is rarely contested within the framework of liberal democracy. But assured food to live should also be part of the fundamental right to life, because life itself is impossible without food. The courts in India understand this, and it is the courts that have led the government to move forward its campaign for the right to food.

The act is amazingly sensitive to all the issues that have been raised by my fellow panellists. It targets almost all services, even at the household level, to women. All fair price shops will be in the hands of women and women's groups. Cash transfers will go to the oldest woman in a family. Special and cost-free cooked meals will go to mothers and young girls, apart from the large midday meal scheme that is already operating in schools.

But more significantly, the Government of India has put on the ground, with an annual budget of ₹100 crore (US$25 million), a grant-in-aid scheme called the Mahila Kisan Sashaktikaran Pariyojana

(Women Farmers Empowerment Scheme), a sub-component of the National Rural Livelihood Mission. This means funds to enable women farmers to improve their capabilities so as to produce more and better, and to market it. This will also enable household and village-level food security. Funds have been put aside for women to form co-operatives among themselves, for consolidating their production, and for training in improved farming techniques including non-farm production! The programme has already come into action and is being enabled by the participation of civil society organisations, women's self-help groups, etc.

HOW DID THIS HAPPEN?

I would like to suggest that it is a result of the interplay between civil society, interest-based groups, and the government and the judiciary. Some of you know that we in India have not only a lively women's movement, but we also have a special group called the Working Group of Feminist Economists, which includes several women whom many of you would know, such as Jayati Ghosh, Bina Agarwal and myself and so on. This working group was set up by our Planning Commission during the 11th Plan. The report of the group is available on the website of the Planning Commission.[9]

We were invited to scrutinise the sectoral chapters—and not only the women and development chapters—such as infrastructure, agriculture, industry, employment, etc., which specifically address macro-economic domains. In examining the agriculture sector, we advised that not only should women be given landownership rights, but they should also be recognised as farmers, as there has been an exodus of men from rural areas seeking employment in cities, and very often women are sole cultivators. We also argued what is universally true, that women are not only good farmers but generally engage in food farming for household food security. All this is now enshrined in our grant schema! This is to demonstrate how group advocacy with knowledge can influence budgetary outlays.

Similarly, the right to food security bill and the later act have been influenced by work being done by groups for more than 10 years. The judiciary has been helpful in flagging food security as a constitutional right related to the right to life. And now the lobbies have managed to get the bill into Parliament to frame the act. Thus, in conclusion, I think we need to take our interest in rights language and practice, basically a legal domain, into the legal spaces, into the macro-economic spaces within countries, and into the regions.

In Beijing, the international women's movement identified gaining political power and engaging in political structures as a priority goal, as the minimal or necessary condition for reaching the goals of gender equality. We demanded quotas in political spaces, and have moved forward a great deal since gaining this entry. Now, 17 years after Beijing, responding to the changes in world and regional order, our efforts on behalf of gender need to be directed to gaining or enabling democratically constructed economies and economic policies and institutions. We would need begin from the labour or worker point of view, and then move upwards, emphasising economic democracy as a necessary condition for political democracy to work.

APPENDIX: FEMINIST NOTES

In a paper written for the Beijing +15 meetings at the UN in March 2010,[10] the informal group called the Casablanca Dreamers proposed that the global meltdown and the crises of contemporary development that were highlighted in 2009–10 did not only pertain to finance and employment, but also involved deprivation of food, water, energy, fuel and care. They further stated that growing environmental devastation was a phenomenon that had been evolving for decades, much before the Lehman Brothers affair.

Further, responding to the devastating food crisis that also appeared in full fury during the same years, the Casablanca group pointed out that food economies are by and large led by women farmers. They added that 'in many developing countries, women make up over half of the agricultural work force. In some countries they are the majority of farmers.'[11] But there is a gender caste operating here, whose case for recognition as farmers is still a submerged issue— even when a woman farmer commits suicide, it is not seen as a 'farmer's suicide'. Women who produce 'our' food are adulated, but work such as domestic work is taken for granted and even seen as a cultural value in patriarchal societies.

The distribution of land rights and of public investment and regulation of markets (including international markets) needs to take note of these aspects of women as farmers, for them to be able to enjoy the recognition as well as to make their contribution to food security. Further, it needs to be recognised that the rural woman now is not only a rural citizen; she is also the urban poor migrant and road construction worker, the migrant to other lands in search of work, and so on. However, sectoral interest has moved from agriculture, food, water and livelihood, to making a mark on the world through focusing on the percentage of tradable, foreign exchange reserves and military power.

NOTES

1 Amartya Sen, 'Food Battles: Conflicts in the Access to Food', *Food and Nutrition*, vol. 10, no. 1 (1984), pp. 81–89.

2 S. Seguino, 'The Global Economic Crisis, Its Gender Implications and Policy Responses', paper prepared for the interactive expert panel on 'The Gender Perspectives of the Financial Crisis', 53rd Session of the Commission on the Status of Women, UN, New York, 2–13 March 2009, p. 10.

3 I am grateful to Dr Pooja Sharma for this diagram and data.

4 *World Economic Situation and Prospects 2008* is a joint product of the Department of Economic and Social Affairs, UNCTAD and the five UN regional commissions. See UN, *World Economic Situation and Prospects 2008* (New York: UN, 2008), https://www.un.org/en/development/desa/policy/wesp/wesp_archive/2008wesp.pdf (accessed 8 April 2018).

5 Devaki Jain and Diane Elson, in Collaboration with the Casablanca Dreamers, 'Vision for a Better World: From Economic Crisis to Equality', UNDP, 2010, http://www.inclusivecities.org/wp-content/uploads/2012/07/Jain_Elson_UNDP_Crisis_to_equality.pdf (accessed 8 April 2018).

6 Ibid.

7 Government of India, *Economic Survey 2011–2012*, Chapter 2: 'Microfoundations of Macroeconomic Development', https://www.indiabudget.gov.in/budget2011-2012/es2010-11/echap-02.pdf (accessed 8 April 2018).

8 The targeted PDS scheme caters to 65 million families below the poverty line, and 115 million other families above the poverty line, to act as a safety net for the vulnerable sections of Indian society.

9   Planning Commission, *Engendering Public Policy: A Report on the Work of the Working Group of Feminist Economists during the Preparation of Eleventh Five Year Plan 2007–2012* (New Delhi: Government of India, May 2010), http://planningcommission.nic.in/reports/genrep/rep_engpub.pdf (accessed 8 April 2018).

10 Jain and Elson with the Casablanca Dreamers, 'Vision for a Better World'.

11 Ibid., p. 20.

Chapter 8

Are We Knowledge-Proof?
Development as Waste

At least since the 1960s, I had been 'walking' with development. The term 'development' was coined basically for what were called 'underdeveloped' countries, or the former colonies. It was different from economic progress or economic growth. Development was supposed to include more than economic advantage. My journey in understanding, redesigning and arguing with regard to our development policy and programme had depressed me, and had shown me that in the name of development, nothing had changed for my constituency, namely women in poverty households. It seemed like mere rhetoric, with no transformation. Hence my argument that while research and analysis were revealing that the design and the thrust areas of what was called 'development' were not making any difference, we still continued to run on the same track.

It does not feel nice to be doing a lecture in memory of Lovraj Kumar. We were not only contemporaries and very good friends, but Dharma and he took me in as a waif and a stray in Bombay in 1956, sharing every thing they had—home, car, facilities, friends, picnics, parties, and the most precious of all, their daughter Radha, and Dharma's parents Amma and Appa who lived in Matunga. On returning from my work some days, I would play with Radha in their flat on Peddar Road. Even as I grew up—a phrase that may make you laugh as you see a 70-year-old woman in front of you talking of 'growing up'—Lovraj maintained that same tender caring and enabling concern for me as he did, I know, for many of us, if not for every one of us. I could ask anything of him and Dharma and they would say, 'Of course, come on over, have a meal and we will talk.' And so my parasitic relationship with them continued forever. I can almost see him laugh with his beautiful eyes crinkled, at the thought that I, the convent girl from Bangalore, was giving a memorial lecture in this pompous city of Delhi!

The title of this lecture, or at least a part of it, is stolen from another colourful character of our times, the late Raj Krishna. All of you know him as the author of the term 'Hindu rate of growth'. But here is another of his gems. When he was a member of the Planning Commission in 1977–78, he was once present at a cabinet meeting. Those of you who have known Raj Krishna can visualise the following story, as he could, like Dharma, tell a story out of an experience which would make it absolutely hilarious and yet substantial. 'Bhai,' he said, *'wahan kisi ki bathi nahi jalti hai.'*[1] They are 'knowledge-proof'. And then the loud roar of laughter. How many more 'Raj Krishnaisms' he would have generated if he had been alive to see this 'leading light' of the 'knowledge industry', namely India, being knowledge-proof?

We have lost Pitambar Pant, Dharm Narain, Sukhamoy Chakravarty, Ravinder Kumar, not to forget Bhanu Pant, Sheila Dhar, Sarasamma Raj and Kamla Rajkrishna, even more luminous and politically astute than their men, and so many others who, in that era of the 1970s and 1980s, were engrossed in India, before our social circles burst and, in my opinion, got lost in the amorphous amalgam of the 'new' Indian global society—the non-resident Indians (NRIs), the corporate icons, the media 'brats', film and fashion, the Sensex, and our very own builders of 'modern' India that occupy the government spaces. How could all those wonderful, noble people, really 'devoted to India', the 'resident Indians', as I would like to call them, leave us in such haste? I wish they were here and we were doing a celebration of our half-century friendships and our claiming of India as its citizens, rather than offering memorials. Our gangs seem to be dropping off the planet quite rapidly now, most recently Prof. Khusro. Perhaps it's just as well. We don't belong.

We now have an emerging, vibrant and almost homogeneous world community in India which is interconnected and globalised and feeds on that interconnectivity. This global society is caught in its own web of lifestyles related to consumption and opportunity, to the point of turning away from the more multiple-layered, interdependent and moral connectivities that communities had in our times. This neo-global community is called, in India, 'the middle class'. It feeds on itself, it is a vote-money bank, it determines policy, it attracts media, it is the face of India—the face that is used politically to project moder-nity, momentum, dynamism, an India 'emerging as a world power', a 'developed nation', and other similar sentiments and images.

The emergence of this amoral, self-propelled class of men and women, unattached to roots, circulating in the 'other economy', the global goods, services and opportunities economy, has distorted the earlier moral concerns and impulses, however much faulted, and the intimacy with deprivation, injustice and inequality that we had harboured. The corporate is the contemporary icon, not public work or public service or constructive work, as Gandhiji used to call it.

INNOVATIVE INDIA

Some of the most interesting innovations in India, via our IT-savvy community, are that an Indian living in Cambridge, Massachusetts, can ask for a specific ritual puja to be performed in one of the most popular temples in India on his behalf, and see it on his screen being performed in his name. Since he is able to pay almost 100 times what his equivalent in India can pay, he gets the first priority. This in turn has commercialised our temples and our priests, who see so much money in this hunger of what we call the 'NRI' for his roots in religious practice.

I suggest that this search has also regenerated dogma and rigidity in a religion that was at one time not only open, but a non-religion, a way of life, a consciousness of the divine, a minimalist religion. Today its shape, its contours, mimic other structured religions, as without structure, there can be no boundary for practice. It is practice that this NRI would like to feed to his alienated children to keep up his memories of his own childhood. And of course there are the Bollywood films—*Kabhi Khushi Kabhie Gham*[2] and others—to feed him to us, and his imagined India to him.[3]

This lecture has other connectivities for me, as wasteland development was one of my father's (Late Sri M.A. Sreenivasan) obsessions—and I am sure Kamla Choudhry and V. B. Easwaran and other friends here will recall his pestering them, as he pestered chief ministers, revenue officials and the food secretaries of the Government of Karnataka, to get on with it. He must have designed at least five schemes and written at least 25 articles on how food security and employment could both be achieved through wasteland development. He abhorred waste of any kind.

His other pet waste utilisation project, which he called 'Pankajalakshmi',[4] was to use the methane gas that comes out of sewage treatment plants for energy, to be cylinderised like the CNG cylinders now in vogue, or used as energy to treat the wastewater so it could be used for industry, and leave the other water for drinking. As long as there are humans, there will be this energy, he would say, and like the lotus rises, beautiful, from the swampy tank beds, so does energy out of night soil.[5]

For evoking all these memories of joy and sorrow, I thank the Society for Promotion of Wasteland Development (SPWD), especially Amrita Patel for honouring me with this invitation to deliver the Lovraj Kumar Memorial Lecture of 2003.

'BEFORE-MIDNIGHT' CHILDREN

In what follows, I would like to argue that my generation, the 'before-midnight' children, has known that the course we followed—whether in the technologies we used, the economic policies that we released, the political processes that we ignored—would not only pollute our rivers and our soil, not only create chaotic towns, soak us fully in corrupt practices—life taking, like counterfeit drugs, or financially endangering, like stamp paper scams—but also generate the kind of disparities, pollution of nature and people, that hold within them time bombs waiting to further blast away what is left of peacefulness in the Indian landscape. I would illustrate this with three examples of that 'knowledge-proofness' within the discourse on development. Two illustrations emerge from national policies on population and employment; and one from my current research into the intellectual history of the UN, with special reference to its efforts to provide equality and justice to women worldwide.

I will then suggest that we have not only generated waste in creating development, but we have wasted development. And here I use the term 'wasting'[6] in its harshest meaning of 'devastating' (*Webster*) and, in criminal parlance, 'finishing off'. We have made development into an unwanted impulse. When we hear our leaders exhorting us to make India a 'developed country' in so many years (by 2015, for instance), shivers run down my spine. What does that mean? Look at the 'developed' countries. They generate enough waste to poison the atmosphere and change the temperature of the earth. Their momentum for sustaining their political power and their economic path requires them to invade other countries, to cannibalise business, to break all moral and international conventions. Their development drive is terrifying. It has become so scary that even its luminaries and its gods are rethinking. Revisionism is the order of the day. Here is Nobel laureate Joseph Stiglitz, Economic Advisor to the World Bank for three years (1997–2000), saying:

> Disillusion with the international system of globalization under the aegis of the IMF grows as the poor in Indonesia, Morocco, or Papua New Guinea have fuel and food subsidies cut, as those in Thailand see AIDS increase as a result of IMF-forced cutbacks in health expenditures, and as families in many developing countries, having to pay for their children's education under so-called cost recovery programs, make the painful choice not to send their daughters to school.... The net effect of the policies set by the Washington Consensus has all too often been to benefit the few at the expense of the many, the well-off at the expense of the poor. In many cases commercial interests and values have superseded concern for the environment, democracy, human rights, and social justice.[7]

NEW EMPRESS

Then there is the 'New Empress', the World Bank,[8] which revealed just last month (August 2003) that privatisation of civic amenities and 'public goods', namely water, power, etc., has been a failure on both counts: of profit and recovery of investment (key to the banks and the private sector); and efficiency of delivery. The report found 'that private ownership did not solve problems in government-run enterprises'.[9] Further,

> consumers can threaten not to re-elect a government that fails to provide adequate services. They have a harder time holding private companies to account. A Latinbarometer poll that covered 17 countries in 2001 found that 63 per cent of respondents felt they had not benefited from privatization.... the most difficult enterprises to privatize successfully are traditional monopolies that sell essential services to consumers, such as water and electricity.... The World Bank report concludes that selling a water or electricity system to the private sector does not solve the essential problem—which is how to pay for such systems in the first place.[10]

Yet we are 'walking the talk' with 'globalism' and privatisation of basic services and public utilities—a process euphemistically called 'Reform'. Alarm bells ring when there is a suggestion either by the trade unions or the court that decisions need democratic processes of decision making. 'Reform slows down' is a frequent headline, supposed to create panic. 'Unemployment' and 'disparities' and 'deprivation increase', however, are not headlines. I once suggested that instead of the Sensex there should be daily index of the number of people disengaged from jobs, the number who got jobs and the number that need them. Maybe now we can add, the number of farmer suicides, the number of deaths due to starvation! Or the number of girls sold and the number of new AIDS victims. But that would not interest the money holders.

In the vocabulary of the people's movements in India today, movements to which I currently belong, the slogan used to be 'save us from development'—*vikas hai vinash*, development has become an enemy. Development tramples over centuries-old rich alluvial soil that supports farming in the Narmada Valley, displacing people; it encroaches on coastal land, ruining it forever with shrimp farming and tourism; it cracks the carefully balanced formations of the Himalayan range; it invents new crimes such as truck prostitution, globalises the flesh trade, apart from other economic and political crimes. Then the people's movements replaced the word 'development', *vikas*, with the term 'transformation' or *badlao*, which seemed attractive. Now the *naras* (slogans) are *badlao se bachao*—save us even from transformation.[11]

What does that say to 'development'? Leave us alone—just let us be where we are. In pop language, 'Cool it, man.' We are better off without your hands reaching out to us. We will cope. Development is not, as Amartya Sen would say, 'freedom'; to use his own coinage, it would be to these groups 'unfreedom'. Its touch is seen as the kiss of injury, if not of death. The repercussions of this 'leave us alone' attitude, apart from reinvoking traditional wisdoms and non-conventional scientific alternatives, which is welcome, sometimes turns into affirmations of narrower cultural and religious identities, a retaliation against change, a conservativeness leading to unhealthy 'new' conflicts.[12] That is why I say we are wasting development. More on this later, as I now come to my illustrations of 'knowledge-proofness'.

OUR DESIRE TO REDUCE INDIA'S POPULATION

The most vivid, current and raging example of our knowledge-proofness is what is being believed, suggested and implemented by some states as a population reduction programme based on various 'incentives and disincentives', as these useless, i.e., ineffective and unnecessary, yet cruel and discriminatory constitutional violations are euphemistically called. Every fact emerging from official statistics and field reports is revealing.

There is a substantial demographic transition under way in the country—a secular trend of falling total fertility rates (TFRs). The TFR has declined by almost half a child in the six and half years between the National Family Health Survey-1 (NFHS-1) and NFHS-2. Replacement-level or close-to-replacement-level fertility has been reached in Kerala, Tamil Nadu, Karnataka, Goa, Andhra Pradesh, Himachal Pradesh, Delhi and Punjab. It is true that the TFR is high in Uttar Pradesh, Bihar, Madhya Pradesh and Rajasthan. But even in these states, it has declined between the two NFHS surveys in 1992–93 and 1998–99 respectively, from 4.82 to 3.99 in Uttar Pradesh, 4 to

3.49 in Bihar, and from 3.90 to 3.31 in Madhya Pradesh. Rajasthan is the only large state where the TFR has increased from 3.63 to 3.78 (see Tables 8.1 and 8.2).[13]

Interestingly, NFHS–2 also reveals that the fertility rate that is currently sought, 2.13, is lower by 0.72 child (that is, by 25 per cent) than the current TFR of 2.85. This is to say, if unwanted births could be reduced, the TFR would drop to the replacement level of fertility. Indeed, this is acknowledged in the National Population Policy, which has therefore made its priority meeting the unmet need for health and family planning services. To propose punitive measures, in this context, is thus clearly absurd.[14]

The evidence gathered from all these places and worldwide reveals that there is a fall in the TFR:

Table 8.1 *Fertility by state, NFHS-2: TFR for the three-year period preceding the survey*

Sl No.	States	NFHS-2 TFR
1.	Goa	1.69
2.	Karnataka	1.89
3.	Kerala	1.51

Source: IIPS, *National Family Health Survey (NFHS-2), 1998–99.*

Table 8.2 *Disparities in well-being*

	SC	ST	OBCs	Illiterate Women	Better-Off Women	Others
TFR	3.15	3.06	3.47	3.47	1.99	–
IMR	83	84	76	–	–	62
Under-5 mortality	119	126	103	–	–	82

Source: IIPS, *National Family Health Survey (NFHS-2), 1998–99.*
Note: TFR: total fertility rate; IMR: infant mortality rate.

- When there is a wage or labour absorption programme where women are accessing employment;
- Where there is better survival of children (which in turn depends on provision of not only health services but also clean drinking water, sanitation, mothers' health—something that pioneers like Dr Shanti Ghosh[15] have been dinning into our ears from the 1950s); and when there is overall education, not just women's education, as is often peddled.

In the developed, industrialised countries, those countries that experienced the largest increases in female labour force participation rates in the 1980s also tended to have the largest declines in TFRs.

Data on women's employment in the developing world reveal leaps forward in their absorption into the labour force over the period 1970 to 1990. Some regions like South Asia show a leap from 25 per cent to 44 per cent, and Latin America from 22 per cent to 30 per cent, while in the same regions, the male employment percentage declined from 88 to 78, and 85 to 84 respectively. Most of this addition is in the service sector, but also in the informal economy. Some of this leap could account for the remarkable secular downswing in the rate of population growth in South Asia.[16]

Amartya Sen, in a presentation at a seminar in Delhi this year on 'Development as Freedom: An India Perspective',[17] referred to studies done both in India and abroad which tried to see what were the major causes or impulses or policies or triggers that brought down fertility. In his book *Development as Freedom*, Sen refers to

an important statistical contribution by Mamta Murthi, Anne Catherine Guio, and Jean Drèze [which] deals with data from 296 districts in India in the census of India of 1981.... These variables [including fertility rates] are related to a number of other district-level variables with explanatory potential, such as female literacy rates, female labor force participation, incidence of poverty (and levels of income), extent of urbanization, availability of medical facilities including family planning services, and the proportion of socially underprivileged groups (scheduled castes and scheduled tribes) in the population.[18]

The analysis reveals that it was basically two items—employment and education—that influenced the fertility rate. Sen referred in his presentation to the remarkable trend in Bangladesh where the population growth rate had tumbled down from over 6 within 10 years to 2+. He referred to many parts of India where there have been dramatic falls in the growth rate of population, in the absence of targets, norms or 'disincentives'. He argued that such incentives do not work; they are not as effective as other inputs such as employment and education. Instead, they lead to corrupt practices, apart from cruelty (like the practice of disposing of females, from the foetus to girl children), or prevent those deprived of either health and contraceptive services or self-determination from engaging in political institutions (see below)—an undemocratic policy and a violation of rights, unworthy of India.

The Government of India in 1992 set up an expert group of scientists, demographers and economists to prepare a draft of a National Population Policy. The group also consulted a large number of grassroots and specialist organisations. The Swaminathan Report on population policy emphatically rejected the targeted and two-child norm approach, and pointed to the need for a social amenities base and women's empowerment, and the use of local self-government agencies to reduce the growth of population or for population stabilisation.[19]

Restrictive Practices

Imposing 'restrictive practices', as I call the idea of banning persons with more than two children from contesting elections, leads to corruption and falsification by functionaries, and provides another reason to attack the female of the species inside the womb or outside. China is full of examples of girl children being sold off or dropped into a well or abandoned when the inspectors came to see if the norm had been maintained. Kerala and Dakshina Kannada have achieved the same levels of reproduction without those pressures, as Amartya Sen has been exhorting for the last decade or more.[20]

If one reads the private members' bills pending in Parliament on what they would like to do to the people of India, it is unbelievable—they read like Gestapo orders. And all this 'wasting' (again, using the criminal parlance of 'finishing off') of people is wasteful as such policies do not deliver. The solution lies elsewhere and is not only simple, but will yield the additional benefits of a more capable population!

'Mindset' is the word used these days, and indeed if a mind is set, hardened, and unwilling to respond to knowledge, even if it is screamed from the trenches and towers, there is certainly cause for worry. No use just tapping away at the keys of computers and sharing all sorts of knowledge and creating all kinds of IT systems opportunities for learning, and then being dumb, deaf and thick-headed when it concerns such large numbers of the most underprivileged, deprived and powerless sections of society.

Commenting on such data, Prof. Mohan Rao says: 'Obviously then, demographic transition not only has geographical features, but is a deeply social phenomenon, imprinted by existing social inequalities. Clearly, to impose two-child norms under such circumstances is to widen inequalities among our people.'[21] Rao continues:

> In the States where these laws have been imposed, as in Haryana, Madhya Pradesh and Rajasthan, scores of cases have been documented where women have been deserted, or forced to undergo sex selective abortions. Children have also been abandoned or given up for adoption. In general, such a norm provides an impetus for an increase in sex-selective abortions, worsening an already terrible child sex ratio in the country....

> It also needs to be recalled that, given the age structure of the population, there is an inbuilt momentum which coercive measures can do nothing about.

Three colloquia on National Population Policy 2000 have been organised with all stakeholders in collaboration with the Government of India's Ministry of Health and Family Welfare.[22] Letters based on their findings were sent to all the members of Parliament—750 or so. The finale was a colloquium bringing this whole process of dialogue and harvest of knowledge into the halls of the National Commission of Human Rights, which then issued a declaration and also a show cause notice to the states to stop these repressive policies.

Self-Determination

The policy, I suggest, should find ways of giving women the right to self determination, by granting more power to the panchayats or enabling women's access to wage and education. As Bina Agarwal and Pradeep Panda have most recently pointed out, owning property could work as a deterrent to spousal violence.[23] If I relate to you the stories about men, their desire to express their virility through the bloated wombs of their wives, or their fear that if the woman uses contraceptives, she might cuckold them, and so on, it would be both comical and grotesque.[24] And in such situations, to bring in all kinds of legal punishments to a family, which ultimately gets to the woman's body and her rights, is really abominable to say the least. And yet that is what is obsessing the bold and the beautiful who are in power. Ignorance? No. Knowledge-proofness.

PURSUIT OF EMPLOYMENT: DEFYING THE LESSONS THROWN UP BY PERIODIC REVIEWS

After a review of progress in combating unemployment in the first two decades of planned development (at the end of the 1960s), Raj Krishna concluded: 'The grave national problem of unemployment has defied solution in spite of two decades of planned development.... reason is the tragic phenomenon of positive unemployment growth associated with a positive output growth.'[25] After four decades of planned development, i.e., by 1987–88, the tragic phenomenon of disjunction between output growth and employment growth pointed out by Raj Krishna two decades earlier had not only continued, but had been further compounded. During the period 1983 to 1987–88, GDP shot up from 3.5 to 5.3 per cent, but the employment growth rate fell from 2.82 during 1973–79 to 1.55 in 1983–88. In agriculture, the employment growth rate declined from 1.8 to an insignificant 0.07 in the 15-year period ending 1988.[26]

The reforms introduced in 1991 were precisely aimed to slim the state and correct the distortions attributed to over-centralisation. Dismantling of controls, liberalisation, privatisation, disinvestments, marketisation, transparency, exit policies were all packaged to move the economy and to reduce poverty and promote employment by making the pattern of industrialisation labour intensive. After 10 years of reforms (1991–2001), a review was provided by the Planning Commission in its 2002 paper on targeting ten millions jobs a year in the Tenth Plan.[27]

The report reveals that the employment-generating capacity of the economy and especially the organised sector vis-à-vis GDP growth is declining fast over time (1983 to 2000), in spite of the fact that during the same period GDP growth accelerated from 5.2 to 6.7 per cent per annum.[28] The explanation: There has been an even more significant decline in the labour intensity—employment elasticity to value added has declined from 0.52 to 0.16.[29] The report makes the devastating observation that in the late 1990s, the organised sector reached 'almost a near jobless growth', and in agriculture, 'employment growth touched near zero.'[30]

The Planning Commission's 'Approach Paper to the Tenth Five Year Plan (2002–07)', while referring appreciatively to the average growth rate of 6.5 per cent in the Eighth and Ninth Plan periods, making India one of the 10 fastest-growing developing countries, says:

> These positive developments are, however, clouded by other features, which give cause for concern.... More than half of the children 1–5 years old in rural areas are under-nourished, with girl children suffering even more severe malnutrition. The infant mortality rate has stagnated at 72 per 1000 for the last several years.[31]

Employment, job creation: if it is to happen it has to be a goal, integrated into the choice of technology and use of economic spaces. The most promising segment where jobs admittedly are, as M. S. Swaminathan keeps reminding us, and as my father persistently pointed out, are in the semi-arid and rainfed areas.[32] The SPWD has played a significant role in highlighting this. Two-thirds of our cultivable area is semi-arid or rainfed, but the holdings are marginal and run into over 100 million in number. A precondition for raising their productivity, and hence their employment intensity, is an exacting, appropriate institutional framework. This has been repeated time and again by periodic studies. But the Tenth Plan is not touched by all that knowledge.

We have lessons like the experience of the Maharashtra Employment Guarantee Scheme, which with all its warts and holes not only provided a base for rural labour, but interestingly provided a lifeline to poor rural women. A study we did at ISST for ILO,[33] in which the great late Shri Pagay partnered, found that the percentage of women who availed of the employment offer was greater than that of men. The *Human Development Report* for Maharashtra showed a more even GDI, i.e., disparities between men and women were lower due to this wage earning on the part of women.

In Karnataka, we resonated this by initiating the Karnataka Employment Affirmation Scheme. Dr Nanjundappa, deputy chairman of the Karnataka State Planning Board, and I even set up a committee on 21 October 1995 to try to undertake district-level planning for full employment. Kamaladevi Chattopadhyay added to this by showing how we could use even the skills of crafts people, for instance, theatre prop and costume makers, for job creation in designing our labour absorption programme for each district.

Right to Work

This concern was also addressed in a conference on the right to work in Delhi, sponsored jointly by the Planning Commission, the Institute of Advanced Management and Research, ISST and SEWA, in 1990.

From Nobel Laureates to ordinary citizens concerned for the poor in India, today there are loud, informed calls to give the right to work and right to food pride of place in the policy area,[34] and to banish 'illfare',[35] the name given to a book which appraises India's efforts to provide welfare and to honour the Indian Constitution.

But no, we have to continue with glamorous centrally designed schemes, each named after a prime minister or other luminary. Catchy names like Stree Shakthi, Mahila Abhivrudhi Yojana, etc., are used for these shot-in-the-dark schemes, which are often the same wine in other bottles, schemes which marginalise the poor.

And now the latest vogue is the 'self-help group' (SHG)—women as the 'survival package' for poor families, the sherpas, applauded for being good borrowers, thrifty, able to roll over bank credit as collectives (there are no SHGs for men—they can continue to be the legal holders of titles to assets, to borrow not repay). Banks love the SHGs and boast of how much they have lent, and how women have rolled over the money. But evaluations show what hardships these women are facing given that the socio-economic milieu has stayed the same.

So today we have every kind of leakage: from massive unemployment and hunger, to the sale of women, kidneys, you name it. Flea-biting-flea conflicts, for a piece of an unavailable cake. I could go on like this, singing a litany of knowingly ignored, useful, protective knowledge—for example, how we have ignored the best-in-the-world evaluations of poverty reduction programmes from the Planning Commission itself. We have ignored finance commissions, e.g., the Tenth and Eleventh Finance Commissions, which gave strong mandates for the devolution of finance to local self-governing bodies so that they may be what they were meant to be. We have also ignored grounded advice such as how to handle the pollution of the Yamuna.

Rising to the Situation

Once, 20 years ago, when the environmentalist Anupam Misra from the Gandhi Peace Foundation made a presentation on the filth and silt that were being poured into the Yamuna and how therefore it rises dangerously in the monsoons, I asked in panic, 'so what will happen Anupam, we don't seem to be rising to the situation?' He said, 'Jamunaji will teach Delhi a lesson, she will flood and destroy Delhi some day—we deserve it.' That made my flesh creep—visions of the science fiction movies where jelly-like creatures and substances spread endlessly, burying everything in their wake—but I did nothing.

One more example of very serious knowledge-proofness I must share with you. This is about our overenthusiasm for the IT highway to the moon, to modern India, ignoring every kind of warning regarding the dangers of oversubscription to this milky way. Listen to this horrendous report about the run on the IT highway from an IT genius, Joseph Firmage, who was one of the geniuses from Silicon Valley (and who was also praised for having donated one million dollars to enable this big-bang meeting called the State of the World Forum at the Millennium Summit in New York in 2000). He made a technocrat's presentation on the IT highway, especially what can be forecast by the innovative research and development edge of physicists, who are continuously bringing in new inventions to make the IT road even more brilliant every day.[36]

Firmage moved from technology to economics and from technomics to environment, and came up with two options, which, using the language of computer software, he called 3.0 and 4.0. He then presented what he called 'footprints', where he showed how the economics of the onward road—physics triggering technology and technology choices to maximise profits, and then back to physics to trigger technology and so on—was such that it would definitely have to lead to both a dropping of people and a dropping of the earth and its natural resources from the plans of the world, and from the earth itself! I quote: 'Our ideologically programmed, technologically equipped economy—ideotechnomics, as I call it—is growing a nervous system and increasingly intelligent, muscular, mobile, and information-rich extensions programmed to wipe us all out.' Like Anupam Misra's 'Jamunaji'?

Shib Shankar Dasgupta, writing in the *Deccan Herald*, says:

> Bill Gates is very hungry these days. So is Carly Fiorina along with the whole army of decision-makers of the modern digital corporations. There is no food scarcity in Silicon Valley but they are still hungry. Out of the total human population of 6 billion only 580 million are hooked to the Internet. What an opportunity loss! Bridging this digital divide could improve their sales figures by almost ten-fold. That's the hunger among the digital corporations. Their drive for more business is destined to transform the world of hunger into a world of opportunities....
>
> ... An NUA Internet survey reports that nearly 90 per cent of all Internet users are in the industrialised countries. In contrast, Internet users in Africa and the Middle East, together account for only 1 per cent of the global Internet users.[37]

Jumping to the conclusion that bringing people to the internet will bridge the digital divide is shallow. Dasgupta quotes Amartya Sen, who has argued in one of his works that 'the tendency to think of growing more food as the only way of solving a food problem is strong and tempting, and often it does have some rationale. But the picture is more complex than that, related to alternative economic opportunities and the possibilities of international trade.'[38] Reality is more complex. Proactive institutional support, both at the national as well as international levels, is vital to transform the present predicament. The debate on what a hungry man will do with an internet connection remains, says Dasgupta.

My last illustration is close to my heart; though it does not quite fit into the same type of knowledge-proofness we have been discussing, it is certainly relevant to wastefulness. I am now writing a book as part of the UN Intellectual History Project, which hopes to bring out 14 volumes each on a different theme. My theme is gender. I am to trace the history of ideas which has engaged the UN for 50 years and have been worldwide in their coverage (www.unhistory.org). It is a work in progress.

DEVASTATED, DEPRESSED, DISGUSTED...

I was devastated, depressed, disgusted, angry, immobilised by some of the learning. While women gave brilliant, meaningful suggestions coming out of their lived experiences, the system ignored their advice. For example, women, based on their lived experience as well intellect, as well as something that we could call the ethics emerging out of their experience, have not only been taking stands physically—say against war, or tree felling as in the Chipko movement, or against the removal of pavement vendors as in the Manek Chowk struggle of SEWA Ahmedabad, against the rebuilding of the Keithel market in Imphal, or even arrack addiction by men and boys, against the laying of oil pipes as in Nigeria, or the resistance to the drug lords in Colombia—i.e., not only have they been literally practising satyagraha, but they have also been explaining why it is important not to wage war, and instead to find ways of overcoming, negotiating, resolving, dissolving conflict, why it is important not to fell the trees, exposing the fallacies in the argument that excise revenue compensates for loss of lives, health, disposable income, and damage due to domestic violence triggered by arrack, and so on.[39] In other words, they have been giving 'intellectual' advice, generating alternative theories of development,[40] explaining new methods of landing development with justice—both to humans and to nature—for decades, all over the world.

I also found that the engagement of women in any schema—intellectual, legal or institutional—broadens that concept and moreover makes it inclusive. It enables the aspirations of those other than women. Extraordinary illuminations have been brought in by women, whether one traces the history of ideas of equality, equity/poverty, work, or fiscal policy. Women have not only had the most significant ideas, but have worked hard to have them listened to, for purposes that were broader than their own emancipation.

But the finding of the research is also that women's ideas, their experience, were not absorbed by the UN or by the governments. There seems an unwillingness to recognise women's intellection, a desire to stick to the notion of women as bodies, not minds.[41] Just as for population policy we are wombs, not people. In another book that I have just co-edited with Dr Pam Rajput, *Narratives from the Women's Studies Family—Recreating Knowledge*,[42] where 19 scholars in women's studies have narrated both the value of such studies as well as their difficulties, there is universal complaint that their knowledge, their epistemology, is not accommodated or absorbed by the 'main' disciplines. This knowledge remains in the ghettos. This is not quite the same as 'knowledge-proofness' or the bulb not burning; it is a conscious refusal, a mindset, an unwillingness to perceive, to see the value of women.

The Neglected Factor

It is not uncommon for the obvious to be unnoticed, but a persistent neglect of the obvious in the analysis and response to ground-level realities in India and South Asia is the neglect of the *factor of woman*. The factor of woman, as a single nucleus, or the power-filled genome, or this 'last person' that Gandhi talks about, contains the secret for turning around a downswing into an upswing. Charging this factor, starting from this factor, analysing the disparity, discrimination, exclusion as well as creativity and brilliance of this factor, can reverse the tide of deepening poverty as well as the political and economic culture.

The neglect of this factor expresses itself in many areas of academic and policy work—sometimes enabled and sometimes disabled by international initiatives and ideas. In an amazing feat of blindness, the system refuses to 'see' and thereby loses and wastes this multiplier.

Gopal Guru, in an article 'How Egalitarian Are the Social Sciences in India?', makes a parallel point on how knowledge is created or built in exclusion—the case in point is with reference to the Dalits—and then this 'distant' knowledge is used in preparing laws, programmes, analysis, etc.[43] Are you not reminded of Alice and the Red Queen?

> 'I don't understand you,' said Alice to the Red Queen. 'It's dreadfully confusing!'
>
> 'That's the effect of living backwards,' the Queen said kindly: 'it always makes one a little giddy at first.'
>
> 'Living backwards!' Alice repeated in great astonishment. 'I never heard of such a thing!'[44]

What this review, I hope, is suggesting is that it is time to reconsider the term and the value of development itself. I am not suggesting a rethinking of development, bringing in another avatar of it, but suggesting that it be dropped. Since we have wasted it, killed it off, let us bury it. Not try to reinvoke it in various new forms. We need to find other ways of envisioning our future, not development.

Vinash se Bachao

I have been sharing with you what can be called several narratives which reveal our unwillingness or incapacity to apply knowledge, particularly highlighting that by ignoring this knowledge, we are actually damaging, hurting or devastating both people and the earth, and have opened up doors if not tunnels to unpredictable violence stimulated by rage and so on. Yet one of the most valuable narratives of what can be called early warning systems, conscience raising, not only consciousness raising, has been provided by the organisation which has brought us together here, namely SPWD, through its work and the lecture series. I must thank Mr Pramod Tyagi for providing me with 13 of the earlier lectures in this series, which drew my attention to the kind of *vichar prachar* (dissemination of thought), as Vinoba Bhave used to say, that SPWD has been doing, trying to save us from self-destruction. So instead of *badlao se bachao* (save us from change), SPWD says *vinash se bachao* (save us from destruction).

Bharat Dogra in the 1998 Lovraj Kumar Memorial lecture said that the mission statement of the SPWD was to 'prevent, arrest and reverse degradation of life support systems, particularly land and water, and to expand livelihood opportunities in a sustainable and equitable manner through people's participation.' According to Dogra, implicit in this statement is an understanding that land, water and other natural resources have to be protected, and the livelihood of people based on these also has to be protected; we should not create a conflict between these two objectives. Bharat emphasises that the word that is being used is 'protection'.[45]

Ponna Wignaraja's[46] lecture in 2001 talked of the value, for both protection of the environment as well as protecting the poor from poverty, of social movements, something I have referred to. Then the lecture by N. C. Saxena[47] in 1999 emphasised the value of the participation of people in designing their own future as crucial for the effective landing of the design. The fact that in spite of all these lectures and efforts, I still need to call attention to the same concerns, I think confirms what I said in the beginning, that our generation knowingly brought this upon ourselves.

However, going back to the SPWD mission statement, it prompts me to suggest that maybe we have to think of other terminology to be able to walk into the future, maybe we should replace the word 'development' by 'protection'.[48]

But Why Should We 'Use'?

The word 'development' is synonymous with use. And indeed, when I learned or taught economics, the understanding of development was to use resources, to put them to productive use, which usually was also associated with sale or valuation in terms of market and money. A country was underdeveloped when her minerals and her other resources were not used to produce products, preferably for exchange. Just as it seemed normal to put idle resources to use, similarly human resource development was intended to educate people and develop their skills. And then there was human development, first to ensure that human beings had health and education, which was then expanded to include rights, and then later the capability to access those rights, and so on.[49] But all the time the basic premise is to use, not to allow to lie idle. It is the pressure to 'develop', that is, 'to use' human beings, natural resources, land, sky and all the wealth that grows between the sky and the earth and the water, the pressure which suggests that without use, this is wasted, that has led to so much waste, a wasting of the treasures. But why should we use? That is the question that seems to confront us as we see the devastation to which this purpose, i.e., to develop what looks like an idle asset, be it human or natural, has led us. Leave us alone, cry the people of the Narmada Valley, and so do the last of the forests, the lakes, the mountains, and often the people.

Thus, if we say 'protect', for instance, protect the environment, protect the poor from being further pauperised, protect the citizen from being deprived of democratic rights through the corporatisation of public goods and so on, we might find a way to shift our attention from tinkering with 'development' to becoming really the guardians of our planet.

Long, long ago, in July 1992, I was so gripped with the notion of waste that I presented a paper on 'Women, Waste and Planet Safety',[50] which was much appreciated by the late Julius Nyerere and republished in many places. In this paper, I had asked that nations of the world need not be classified according to GDP growth rates or even HDI, but according to three categories of waste, i.e., societies can be divided into three categories associated with waste:

- *Waste-generating societies:* These are usually associated with affluence, with high-tech production and, until recently, with ignorance of processes of recycling material into consumable goods.
- *Waste-recycling societies:* Here waste utilisation becomes an art, a craft, a source of income and wealth creation. By and large these societies have low access to trade, to exchange. They have dispersed, isolated populations.

- *Waste-avoidance societies:* These are not dissimilar from waste-recycling societies, but they are usually on another economic and cultural plane. For example, in acute poverty, there is a perception of wasting as sinful. Scarce resources have to be stretched. Thus, choices of both production and consumption are made that do not allow waste.

There is an associated, but not necessarily associated, culture of barring wastefulness as sinful, and taboos which bar people from use of certain materials and so on.[51] I had then of course become somewhat sentimental and gave the highest 'marks' to those societies which were not waste generating and to those that were waste recycling, and argued that the non-waste-generating societies were those which were poor, which managed to use every scrap or which made other people's waste become useful. So they were worthy.

Over the years I have realised that there is a trap in this classification also. Because we became such experts in waste recycling, we poor countries and, amongst the poor countries, the poor people, waste is being dumped in our countries, so that the worst off could poison themselves in recycling it. I hear that in China, there is huge dumping of used computers from the United States and little children dismantle the insides to get that little piece of radioactive material which can be reused, obviously in the process inviting danger to their own lives. Similarly, we know that children and the poor in India go into the waste dumps often, exposing themselves to infected needles apart from other horrors.

I have decided not to make waste recycling into a virtue because it also has its hazards. But certainly, societies which do not generate waste because they simplify their lifestyle could have a double-edged advantage—less environmental damage but greater levelling between people. In other words, greater reduction of inequality. All of you know as I do, that Gandhi's formula for the economic regeneration of post-colonial India, and for building a less unequal society, was based on muting difference through transposing identities; put simply, putting oneself into the other's shoes.[52] Greater simplicity in consumption is one of the techniques, I believe, to reduce the gap between the poor and the rich, in some sense, by levelling down lifestyles to the poorest.

One hesitates today in quoting formulas like those that Gandhi gave, because while people are invoking him a great deal these days, from left to right, from state to civil society—because there is something healing about invoking Gandhi—the possibilities of realising his views are, in my view, extremely dim, with this gung-ho 'global society' being extolled as the future of 'developed' India.

Somewhere, we, those who are gathered here, need to puncture this balloon, this postulating of the IT-savvy country, 7–8 per cent GDP country, as a progressive country, belonging to the new millennium: of the middle class as a value. We gathered here could at least reinvoke some of the values that were so much at the front of the minds of what I call the 'before-midnight children', Lovraj's generation—the ones that are marked for disappearance, the ones that don't belong. We could reinvoke inequality, class differentiation, the dangers of such gross blindness to the increasing disparities, by public denouncement of 'development', by the public ringing of alarm bells—at the thought of a 'developed' India in 2015.

We do not need to go to Seattle or Cancun because sometimes when you see the crowd there and their methods of agitation, you feel somewhat inhibited, but we could shame our own people. We here could be the vanguard for not rethinking development, but abandoning development and seeking a platform to protect not only the environment, not only the deprived and the assaulted, but India from further 'wasting'—a platform to make the SPWD mission into a vision for the new India, maybe renaming it Society for Protecting Natural Resources and People.

NOTES

1   Literally, 'The light doesn't shine there.'
2   Sagarika Ghose, 'E-mail Nationalism' (a review of the popular Hindi film *Kabhi Khushi Kabhi Gham*), *Indian Express*, 28 December 2001.
3   Devaki Jain, 'Perspectives on Peace', Women and Public Policy Programme, John F. Kennedy School of Government, Harvard University, 5 May 2003.
4   M. A. Sreenivasan, 'Pankajalakshmi: Energy from Sewage', *Indian Express*, 23 July 1982.

5   M. A. Sreenivasan, 'Ah! Bangalore: Turning Chellaghatta into Pourambudhi', *Deccan Herald*, 24 June 1984.

6   Devaki Jain, 'Women, Waste and Planet Safety: Proposal for a North–South Alliance', *Wide Bulletin*, no. 3, 1992.

7   Joseph Stiglitz, *Globalization and Its Discontents* (London: Penguin, 2002), p. 11.

8   Madelaine Drohan, 'Now They Tell Us: Privatization Is No Panacea', *Globe & Mail* (Canada), 6 August 2003.

9   Ibid.

10 Ibid.

11 Jain, 'The Role of People's Movements in Economic and Social Transformation'.

12 Devaki Jain, 'The Many New Faces of Economic Development and Some Questions on How to Land Justice', North–South Round Table on 'Imperatives of Tolerance and Justice in a Globalized World', Cairo, 27–28 November 2002.

13 Indian Institute of Population Sciences (IIPS), *National Family Health Survey (NFHS-2), 1998–99* (Mumbai: IIPS).

14 Communication from Dr Mohan Rao, 22 September 2003.

15 Shanti Ghosh, 'Revaluing Women's Roles', paper presented at the conference 'Population Trends and Family Planning in South Asia', New Delhi, 14–20 March 1989.

16 Devaki Jain, 'Enabling Poverty and Inequality Reduction in South Asia', UNFPA Retreat, New York, 30 September–2 October 2002.

17 Amartya Sen, presentation at seminar on 'Development as Freedom: An India Perspective', New Delhi, 31 July 2003 and 1 August 2003.

18 Amartya Sen, *Development as Freedom* (New York: Anchor Books, 1999).

19 M. S. Swaminathan (ed.), *Draft National Population Policy* (New Delhi: Government of India, 1994).

20 Amartya Sen, 'Population and Reasoned Agency: Food, Fertility and Economic Development', paper presented at the seminar 'Population, Environment, Development', Royal Swedish Academy of Sciences and Beijer Institute, Stockholm, October 1993.

21 Mohan Rao, 'Two-Child Norm and Panchayats: Many Steps Back', *Economic & Political Weekly*, vol. 38, no. 33 (2003), pp. 3452–54.

22 *Report of the Colloquium on National Population Policy*, Singamma Sreenivasan Foundation, Bangalore, 19–20 October 2000; *Report of the Second Colloquium on National Population Policy*, convened by Karnataka Women's Information and Resource Centre and Centre of Social Medicine and Community Health, New Delhi, 20–21 April 2001; National Colloquium on Population Policy, Development and Human Rights, New Delhi, January 2003.

23 Bina Agarwal and Pradeep Panda, 'Home and the World: Revisiting Violence', *New Indian Express*, 7 August 2003.

24 Based on six case studies conducted by ISST in Banwasi Sewa Ashram, Uttar Pradesh, and other sites, for the International Conference on Population and Development, 1994.

25 L. C. Jain, 'The Government's Employment Policy Disappoints', 25 September 2008, http://www.rediff.com/news/2008/sep/25guest1.htm (accessed 8 April 2018).

26 Devaki Jain, 'How Women's Leadership Can Transform the Nation: Durgabai Showed the Way', Lecture in Honour of Smt. Durgabai Deshmukh, 15 July 2004.

27 Planning Commission, *Report of the Special Group on Targeting Ten Million Employment Opportunities per Year over the Tenth Plan Period* (New Delhi: Government of India, May 2002).

28 Ibid., p. 15.

29 Ibid., p. 37.

30 Ibid., p. 52.

31 Planning Commission, 'Approach Paper to the Tenth Five Year Plan (2002–2007), Government of India, New Delhi, 1 September 2001.

32 See also L. C. Jain, 'This Job Package Is Empty', *Hindustan Times*, 11 June 2002.

33 ISST, 'Impact on Women Workers: Maharashtra Employment Guarantee Scheme', mimeograph, New Delhi, December 1979.

34 Jean Drèze, Aruna Roy, Amartya Sen, 2003.

35 Barbara Harriss-White and S. Subramaniam (eds), *Illfare in India: Essays on India's Social Sector in Honour of S. Guhan* (New Delhi: SAGE, 1999).

36 Devaki Jain, 'Inequality and Information Technology: Reducing Global Players' Role', *Deccan Herald*, 29 September 2000; Devaki Jain, 'Inequality and Information Technology: Caution for Karnataka, Andhra', *Deccan Herald*, 30 September 2000.

37 Shib Shankar Dasgupta, 'Digitising the World of Hunger', *Deccan Herald*, 17 September 2003.

38 Sen, *Development as Freedom*, p. 176.

39 Jain, 'Development as if Women Mattered'.

40 Sen and Grown, *Development, Crises, and Alternative Visions*.

41 Jain, *Minds, Bodies and Exemplars*.

42 Devaki Jain and Pam Rajput (eds), *Narratives from the Women's Studies Family: Recreating Knowledge* (New Delhi: SAGE, 2003).

43 Gopal Guru, 'How Egalitarian Are the Social Sciences in India?', *Economic & Political Weekly*, vol. 37, no. 51 (2002), pp. 5003–9.

44 Lewis Carroll, *Through the Looking-Glass* (London: Penguin Popular Classics, 1994 [1865]), p. 79.

45 Bharat Dogra, 'Protecting Forests and Livelihood: Creating Harmony, Reducing Conflict', Lovraj Kumar Memorial Lecture, SPWD, New Delhi, 1998.

46 Ponna Wignaraja, 'Fundamentals of Poverty Eradication in South Asia: The Poor Are Not the Problem, But Are Part of the Solution', Lovraj Kumar Memorial Lecture, SPWD, New Delhi, 21 September 2001.

47 N. C. Saxena, 'Participatory Issues in Joint Forest Management in India', Lovraj Kumar Memorial Lecture, SPWD, New Delhi, 18 September 1999.

48 A word that is being used a great deal these days is 'security', which has now been extended to human security with a whole global commission, of which Amartya Sen and Sadako Ogata were the co-chairs. But I do not like the word 'security', just like I do not really like the word 'development'.

49 Sakiko Fukuda-Parr and A. K. Shiva Kumar (eds), *Readings in Human Development* (New Delhi: Oxford University Press, 2003).

50 Devaki Jain, 'Women, Waste and Planet Safety: Proposal for North–South Alliance', Institute of Development Studies, Sussex, 9–12 July 1992.

51 Ibid.

52 Jain, 'Minds, Bodies and Exemplars'.

Chapter 9

A View from the South*
A Story of Intersections

Some of the most well-known scholars on development and women were putting together a book, Developing Power: How Women Transformed International Development. *Edited by Arvonne S. Fraser and Irene Tinker, the volume was to have contributors from all over the world. The editors associated me not only with the founding of DAWN in 1983 but also with the fact that I had been a member of the South Commission. Hence they asked for a contribution. But they wanted a personal story of how my perspective had evolved, how I had come to my choice of passion—something biographical. Hence this paper became really a description of my journey and what I had learnt over those decades, both from the research I was doing as well as the various meetings and conferences that I attended.*

In her last book, *My Professional Life and Publications, 1929–1998,*[1] Ester Boserup traces her intellectual history by describing her various encounters, whether at a teaching post or a job at the UN or a field assignment, and lists her articles and books that expound the theories and propositions she arrived at because of that stimulus. Her book is only 62 pages long, but it reveals how much we are influenced by the journey of our lives, especially by visual, physical encounters, direct observations. I was fortunate to be considered a friend by Ester; both of us had worked on the *Asian Drama* by Gunnar Myrdal between 1958 and 1960,[2] and shared some of the learning as well as the discomfort of that experience. Ester later contributed a chapter to my first book, *Indian Women*, published in 1975, which attempted to capture the status of Indian women.

This value of the visual is reflected in my own journey with development. Living in India, side by side with not only poverty but also the sight of women bending, carrying, walking, breaking, cutting, *doing* all the time, threw up themes about women's lives that became the areas of my research. The historical period in which I graduated from college also defined my perspective. Indian independence was less than 10 years old in 1956, when I took up my first job, and there were many post-liberation initiatives and experiments to efface the pains of colonisation.

One of my formative experiences was walking from village to village following Vinoba Bhave, a disciple of Mahatma Gandhi, as he asked landowners to gift land to the landless as a moral act. This approach to levelling the inequality in the ownership of land, the most desired and valuable asset, had attracted idealists and the young from all over India and the rest of the world.[3] This walk, and the hope in the human spirit that it evoked in me, were instrumental in my selection for a seminar at Harvard University in 1958 and my admission to St Anne's College, Oxford. Both institutions were impressed by the nature of my experience of participating in this transformative movement.

Subsequent travels to various countries of the global South made me aware of the potential for unity among its countries and continents. This awareness underlined another aspect of my politics, and accounts for many of the initiatives and positions I have taken, including my presence on the South Commission. This commission of 28 eminent economists from the global South was set up by Julius Nyerere, former president of Tanzania, in 1987 to assess the possibilities of building an 'economic South'.[4]

When I met Dr Julius Nyerere, I told him that he was two years behind us, the women of the South. Back in 1984 we had created a South–South network, DAWN, whose focus was on finding our own framework for understanding the location of poor women in our development trajectories and offering approaches for their emancipation. When Dr Nyerere gave me the names of the people he had chosen to be on the commission, I exclaimed, 'What are you doing with a bunch of tired old men?' (I was 53 years old at that time.) That very evening, I was invited to join the commission. Two other women also became members: Marie Angelique Savane, who had founded the Association of African Women in Research and Development, and Solita Colles Monsood, an accomplished macro-economist.

Most of the members of the South Commission, however, were influential men who tended to see the world of the South through the columns of the *London Times* or the *New York Times*. I repeatedly protested against their stereotypical images of our societies. I pointed out that the continents of the South were not as separated as the media and scholars of the North perceived. Rather, many lines, threads and habits bound us together. Strong intellectual and political energies were bubbling in our countries, and a process of self-definition was occurring.

This pulse of change was palpable to those living the South.[5] I contend, therefore, that the lived context is a crucial tethering for that amalgam of thought and action that characterises those engaged in transformation, including feminists. Myriad corners and colours shaped and lit my journey. Three perhaps are most significant: first, women in poverty (and therefore, the question of women and work); second, Gandhi's brilliance in thinking of and working towards a just and compassionate society and economy; and third, my location as one who belongs to a developing and thereby ex-colonial and relatively poorer country in the South.[6]

A WOMAN'S BEGINNINGS

None of these co-ordinates can be directly traced to my upbringing, either at home or in the educational institutions I attended. I was born in 1933 in the city of Mysore. My mother provided a home rich in culture while raising seven children. She had been married at 11 years of age to a brilliant civil servant, who later became the premier of a state in India.[7] She ensured that her three daughters learned to speak English, the language of power at that time, a skill she did not have but tried to acquire as an adult. As the wife of the mayor of the city of Mysore, she went to a convent for private tutorials. My own schools and colleges were rather aseptic places. The nuns steered clear of politics for their own protection.

Higher education for her daughters was not on the agenda, though it was carefully planned (including training abroad) for my four brothers. I was being prepared for marriage after I finished high school, since female puberty in my family meant marriage. No one in my family or in school discussed this discrimination; we lived it. It was not even perceived as unfair. The allocation of roles and futures was all part of the given. Its objective reality had not yet become the vivid and articulated issue it is now. I escaped this destiny using cunning and subterfuge, but my motivation was more an innate stubbornness than any feminist consciousness. Furthermore, even in my case, postgraduate education was not possible, since all the postgraduate courses were in co-ed colleges, which were out of the question for me.

BECOMING CONSCIOUS OF GENDER ISSUES

Nonetheless, it was not these facts that pushed me into the domain of women. After college, I had become a self-confident young woman who, as a university lecturer in economics from 1963 to 1969, found the company of male colleagues far more interesting than that of women colleagues. By 1974, however, I had resigned from a later post to care for my two infant sons. Until this time, I had been a queen bee. Then a friend asked me to work on replacing an old book, called *Women of India*.[8] She wanted the new book in time for the International Women's Year, 1975. Since it was to be home-based work I accepted, although I knew almost nothing of the subject. I drew on my various academic friends and asked them to go beyond the strict boundaries of their disciplines and consider the status of Indian women. We welded together the book *Indian Women*, which was released by the then president of India.[9]

The introduction to that 1975 volume marks the start of my journey towards understanding the dynamics of gender. Even at that time, struck as I was by the injustice of gender discrimination, I sensed that women need not become men (a desire I had had as a girl) to set things right. Women needed to fight for their place in this scenario, as women.

It seemed to me that it was a recognition of the distinctive features of womanhood and the identification of its advantages, its special value, and then the use of that identity by women that would strengthen our place in the construction of gender. I was troubled by the words 'status' and 'liberation', and tried to clarify them. I was also overwhelmed by the data. Women were bearing the greater share of the burden of poverty, whether measured in terms of scarce resources, food, clothing, shelter, medical care and education, or social hierarchy. I found women beautiful. I wrote that I would like men to join us, not the other way around.

ISST: BUILDING A BASE FOR RESEARCH AND ACTION

In the 1970s, an energetic intellectual and political environment prevailed in India, with the interweaving dynamics of coalitions and platforms across diverse, distinct social and political movements. Most of them were dedicated to deepening democracy and eliminating poverty.[10] It was possible to get support for unorthodox ideas from orthodox people. For example, I received an unusual fellowship from the Indian Council of Social Science Research (ICSSR) to conduct a field study on women's use of time, though I did not have an advanced degree nor was I attached to any recognised institution.[11]

With this fellowship, I went on to investigate a phenomenon that was taking place in Ahmedabad, the capital of the state of Gujarat. A large mass of women working as cart pullers, vegetable vendors, rag quilt makers and so on, had been organised into a trade association. A visit to SEWA, the now famous women's trade union, and the uncovering of the difference between poor men and poor women in their economic domains, generated the idea that women had to organise separately around their economic activity if they were to claim recognition in all spheres: under the law, in social status and in economic services. Organising around work as the first pillar of any process of empowerment of poor women became the creed, not only for me, but in the policy-making arenas too.

Thus began my research about what I called the 'worksheds' of many women, leading to the book *Women's Quest for Power*.[12] I examined five endeavours built around women's stereotypical work to assess how far the genesis and ideology of the effort and the nature of leadership influenced the agency of women workers. All work did not necessarily empower women, nor did all organisations empower them. It took something more, and that seemed to be feminist leadership.

Since I was looking for an organisational base from which I could continue my engagement with these issues, I resurrected an organisation called the Institute of Social Studies Trust, pioneered in 1963 by an economist whose main interest had been poverty, inequality and employment. Over time, ISST became the bedrock from which my studies, the sensitisation of sister organisations, and the birth of other networks were generated.

In 1974, the concept of time use was not known in India, though the methodology was being used in the North. I came to it intuitively, out of disbelief in what I saw, namely women working everywhere in the fields and on roads, but whose work was not being counted in the national economic statistics. Something was wrong with the method of measurement of work. My study of time allocation by men, women and children in six villages in India provided data in support of a different form of measurement; it also revealed the difference between the nature of men's and women's economic activity, especially amongst the poor.[13]

Differentiating between men and women among the poor, now known as gender differentiation, became the theme of all the research and advocacy of ISST. This uncovering of women among the poor as a class by themselves was of crucial importance to my journey, as it challenged political ideology from a perspective that was not that of economic programmes.

Role differentiation revealed the kinds of burdens, such as time spent fetching water or fuel, that women bore which had not even been identified, much less counted as work. In a different study I pointed out not only that women were the majority of the workforce in what the ILO called 'emergency employment',[14] but the seasons when women were not engaged in agriculture were different from those of men, thus challenging the perceptions of seasonal unemployment. At ISST we then moved on to examine the differing choices made by men and women. We drew on the narratives of the Chipko movement, in which the men were willing to sell the existing trees to lumber mills and replant the hill slopes with commercial fruit trees, while the women did a 'hug-in' and saved the trees for their fuel and fodder value. Thus, the class issue, and the plea for class before gender, was somewhat moderated by the uncovering of these hard disparities and differences between poor men and poor women. We also conducted the most elaborate study of female-headed households to determine the various causes of female-headedness.[15]

My first foray into public lecturing from a podium that represented the intellectual establishment was in 1982 at the Nehru Memorial Museum and Library in Delhi, to deliver a memorial lecture.[16] This gave me a chance to wave our findings from the rooftops, so to speak, and to challenge social scientists. What was this sociological family they talked about, with rules and regulations that created a bonded unit? In contrast, we found many non-families among the poor, families in which women battled for survival. What was this counting of workers, and the hierarchy of work, that the statisticians were putting forth that left out women's work?

The intellectual environment at the time was such that these ideas and findings were taken seriously by the mainstream. Women did get identified as a subset of the poor for both statistical and program-matic purposes. Their occupational characteristics, with a man and a woman within a poor family often having different sources of income, was taken note of by the Planning Commission. Also, India's Sixth Five Year Plan (1976–81) for the first time had a separate section on women's employment, with tables showing the sectors where women were bunched in particular occupations. These data also revealed that women were the least-paid workers.[17]

Responding both to the notion of integrating women into development—a message from the UN's 1975 World Conference on

Women at Mexico City—as well as the concern for women in poverty, ISST undertook a study of the planning process of the government of the Indian state of Karnataka. This endeavour was called 'integrating', or 'mainstreaming' as it would be called today, women into a state five-year plan.[18] The study brought into focus the question of development transfers to the poor and what their real impact was, and also brought into sharp relief the conditions and the contexts within which poor women could be enabled to escape their poverty.[19] The study also made the more fundamental observation that the development design and development transfers themselves were flawed. The ways of ending women's poverty could not be considered in isolation from the mechanisms used to deliver the services intended for them. They were a political matter that had to be located in a broader critique of the system, the method, and the local macro-economic, political and social context.

Between 1977 and 1987, ISST went into overdrive; its output of research, its outreach to grassroots organisations of women, and its organisational strength both financially and in numbers of team workers grew tenfold. We were publishing annotated bibliographies of women and work studies in India, reviewing the statistics on women in agriculture in India, and training statisticians in other countries. We were invited to participate with many international agencies to design studies on women and poverty. We were also enabling the birth of an NGO network with our expertise. This period saw the birth of the Indian Association of Women's Studies; Kali for Women Studies, the feminist publishing house; and Mahila Haat, an association of women producers.

BUILDING THE BASE FOR THINKING ABOUT DEVELOPMENT

During the 1970s and 1980s, the women's movement in India and abroad was lively and active. The Mexico conference of 1975 was a defining moment for many of us. It linked us to many friends and networks and gave us visibility within the international community, including the UN. The Indian government brought representatives of women's organisations onto its national preparatory committees for the World Women's Conferences in Copenhagen (1980) and Nairobi (1985), and at the NAM conference on women in Cairo prior to Nairobi.

In 1983, I presented a paper on the impact on poor women of development transfers at a meeting of the Women in Development group of the Organisation for Economic Co-operation and Development (OECD) Development Assistance Committee in Paris. To prepare for this lecture, 'Development as if Women Mattered: Can Women Build A New Paradigm?', I requested Karin Himmelstrand, then the Women in Development programme officer of the Swedish International Development Cooperation Agency, to send me evaluation reports of all the donor grant projects throughout the continents of the South. Reviewing this literature, I concluded that all was not well with development programmes, be it an area development project in Ethiopia or an income-generating project for women in Sri Lanka. Development transfers had pushed poor women into deeper corners, just as they had in India.[20]

At a 1983 seminar at Harvard University convened by Diana Eck, called 'Women, Religion and Social Change', I explored the possibility of a Gandhian feminist perspective on development.[21] In the book *Speaking of Faith*, co-edited by Diana and myself, we concluded that there was universality in the attitude of religions toward women, as they all sanctioned an inferior position for women, but there was also universality in the potential for a common spiritual consciousness.[22] Women can take the best of each religion's essence, establish this consciousness, and be the builders of bridges across religions because of the similarity of their experience of patriarchy, bigotry and discrimination.

The year 1983 was a landmark because it became the year of many streams which eventually led, among other things, to the pool from which DAWN sprang the following year. One significant event was a meeting with Katherine McKee, the programme officer for women's affairs at the Ford Foundation. She was looking for ideas to fund at the forthcoming UN Conference on Women to be held in Nairobi in 1985. I shared with her my concern as expressed in my Paris lecture at the OECD Development Assistance Committee meeting and in my critique of the 'catching-up-with-men' approach that was embedded in the UN framework for reporting to the Nairobi conference. I suggested panels and platforms from which women from the developing countries could present their own act, a presentation of views from the South, recalling those moments of distance and discomfort that we from the Third World had felt in the North. Kate's response was encouraging, and we decided to begin the process by having a consultation. I insisted it should be in the South. Women from all the continents of the world were invited to Bangalore in August 1984.

In three unforgettable days, the group transformed the framework given by the UN for Nairobi and, as we realised later, the experience transformed each individual. On the first day we took the UN framework and put up the usual paper charts for jotting down ideas. The day ended in deep frustration. On the second day, Fatima Mernissi of Morocco, tired and angry, said, 'Off with all those wall papers. This is not the way to think, against someone else's framework.' In a flash we started to identify the various crises in our regions starting with Africa, where the flashpoint was hunger, a food crisis. Soon Latin America's debt, South Asia's poverty, and the Pacific Islands' militarism were identified as the major preoccupations. Poor women in these regions were not only totally engaged in the economies of these countries, but were both suffering from and responding creatively to these onslaughts. The framework began to emerge. Next we thought about how it could be captured in panels and in a document for the Nairobi conference.

A process plan for accomplishing these things was prepared. The title for the idea for this project we called DAWN—Development Alternatives with Women for a New Era. The DAWN follow-up cell was located at ISST and remained there until September 1985, when the cell rotated to Latin America. For the next 10 months, ISST not only began to manage the process, but also raised funds to support consultations regarding the document as well as for the Nairobi panels. Meanwhile, I travelled wherever I was invited to mobilise support, drafting proposals en route. Besides Ford, support was provided by the Population Council and the Norwegian and Finnish governments.

The first round of drafts emerged in Bergen in the spring of 1985, drawn up by small working groups. The drafts contextualised the analysis of poor women's responses to development in their regions, but moved on to generalisations; combined, they recognised the women's movement as the crucial vehicle for change and offered an alternative vision for development. The final draft was then worked on by Gita Sen and Caren Grown and published as *Development, Crises, and Alternative Visions: Third World Women's Perspectives.* This book, which reflects a new development paradigm, has been widely quoted by development agencies and is often used in university courses.

This process and its outcome have taught many lessons and uncovered many ideas. First, it showed that thinking should not be structured. In the traditional societies of the South, thinking together happens through open-ended, unstructured conversation. This permits the emergence of the most creative aspects of a group's thinking, whereas structuring would groove their thinking along pre-established channels. Second, it demonstrated that when an idea resonates in other minds and hearts, then the flow of support—moral and financial—happens readily. It takes off, perhaps demonstrating a feminist view that an idea is born in many places at the same time and cannot be individually claimed. The third lesson emerged when feminists in the North showed delight at the initiative of women of the South to claim their political identity, and actively supported the effort.

ROADBLOCKS TO TRANSFORMATION

In assessing the advancement of women, many things must be taken into consideration. At the start of the 21st century, their achievements are being stressed as part of significant benchmarks and the end of a millennium. Women are writing their histories, claiming to have generated an idea or prompted a programme. Women are being honoured for bringing about change. Such celebration, however, has also raised difficult questions. Who really removed the shroud, coined a phrase, or fostered a movement? Because the written word and its dissemination are dominated by the English-speaking North, the South often is denied the credit it is due for the many discoveries made there, especially in the field of development.

Most significant and more troubling are questions about the extent of accomplishments. Statistical evidence documents the unyielding nature of poverty amongst women, along with the unyielding nature of men's control over every domain, whether in society, government, the intellectual world or the UN. The transformation that women are seeking seems to be on hold; our endeavours to highlight the power and value of women's presence in any space have still not yielded significant relief from the overall assault on women, in the form of physical violence at home or in the theatres of conflict.[23] It may not simply be a matter of men being reluctant to change; some have said that we have failed because of our own virtues. We like to be free, different; we stress individuality and emphasise cultural and other forms of group diversity among ourselves. Has this meant that we cannot be that tidal wave which crashes with a united force, smashing received ideas and practices?

At international conferences and within global agencies, other processes are taking place. Since these theatres of activity are located in the North—New York, Washington or Geneva—those who are close to these cities remain close to power. In these theatres, there seems to be a growing trend to replace the concept of 'development' with that of 'rights'. With sleight of pen and mind, Amartya Sen has called development 'freedom', and the UNDP's *Human Development Report* has enshrined this change in its 2000 reports, which describes development as freedom from basic horrors like hunger and illiteracy.[24] Because most of those working for social justice are now engaging with laws, the courts and the judiciary rather than the state, the rights framework looks more attractive and is easier to glide into than the development approach. But after all the litigation, the issues nonetheless come back to economics and development, as resources are also required for that freedom. The rights framework easily becomes a transnational actor, a characteristic that, while it has many positive values for women, also has some troubling edges in the realm of affirming national sovereignty in an increasingly globalised and polarised world. Significant changes are taking place in international financing arrangements and ideologies regarding what constitutes economic success, apart from global governance, with significant shifts in the role of the UN itself in the global arena. Many of these trends are not to the advantage of the South.

As feminists we need to reflect on these phenomena. Feminists are known for challenging the inherited theories of knowledge and practice. Whether through theology, psychology, social anthropology or history, we are continually exposing the error in the information base, in the understanding and reconstructing of these sciences. Now we need to define a way forward that enables us to make that quantum leap into the mindset of the 'Other' as well as to participate with eyes wide open in the international politics of economics.

Feminists working in development across the North–South divide have formed wise alliances against economic, social and cultural injustices, but the North-dominated political-economic plans still dominate. Closer alliances and struggles within national bounds, which press for the deepening of democracy and the strengthening of national sovereignty, are called for. Globally, we feminists must foster regionalism and work for the creation of institutional frameworks for decentralising economic and political power.

NOTES

1   Ester Boserup, *My Professional Life and Publications 1929–1998* (Copenhagen: Museum Tusculanum Press, 1999).

2   Gunnar Myrdal, *Asian Drama: An Inquiry into the Poverty of Nations* (London: Allen Lane, 1968).

3   It is interesting that Ujamaa in Tanzania and the kibbutzim in Israel were similar post-liberation ideas around the concept of attempting to replace inequality through collectivity—not through force, as in the erstwhile Soviet Union, but as a form of 'voluntary mobilisation'.

4   Nyerere had relinquished the presidency of Tanzania in 1985, and had been invited by the chair of NAM to convene such a commission.

5   South Commission, *The Challenge to the South: The Report of the South Commission* (New York: Oxford University Press, 1990).

6   My preoccupation with poverty and the importance of building solidarity amongst the like-minded propelled me to call a meeting of all those who had received the Right Livelihood Award, known as the Alternative Nobel Prize. Given to those who had worked at the grassroots on the basic issues of life and livelihood, my friends and I called this round table meeting 'Survival Strategies of the Poor and Traditional Wisdom: A Reflection'. It was held in Bangalore in May 1987.

7   M. A. Sreenivasan, *Of the Raj, Maharajas and Me* (New Delhi: Ravi Dayal Publishers, 1991).

8   This volume, by Tara Ali Baig, was published by the Government of India in the 1950s.

9   Devaki Jain (ed.), *Indian Women* (New Delhi: Publications Division, Government of India, 1975).

10 Political upheavals like the Jayaprakash Narayan movement occurred, starting with the Bihar famine of 1966 and climaxing in 1975 with the declaration of Emergency and suspension of the Constitution. The Emergency was declared while many of us were at the First World Conference on Women at Mexico City in June 1975. I left Mexico before the conference ended for fear that India would be closed to returnees. Side by side were technical responses, from that of the National Planning Commission in the shape of the Fifth Five Year Plan (1971–76)—a landmark in India's economic evolution, signalling consumption restraint, austerity and transfer from the rich to the poor—to various review committees like the Commission on Education, and the Committee on the Status of Women, which was preparing the now famous report, *Towards Equality*. Government of India, *Towards Equality: Report of the Committee on Status of Women in India* (New Delhi: Department of Social Welfare, Ministry of Education and Social Welfare, 1974).

11 This was a fellowship for people like myself who had dropped out of the university and become housewives. It offered a support of ₹500 per month in 1974.

12 Jain et al., *Women's Quest for Power*.

13 Jain, 'Valuing Work'.

14 ISST, 'Impact on Women Workers: Maharashtra Employment Guarantee Scheme'.

15 Devaki Jain and Mukul Mukerjee, 'Women and Their Households: The Relevance of Men and Macro Policies—An Indian Perspective', ISST, New Delhi, 1989.

16 Devaki Jain, 'Indian Women Today and Tomorrow', Padmaja Naidu Memorial Lecture, Teen Murti House, New Delhi, November 1982. The lecture was in honour of Padmaja Naidu, a woman poet and a participant in the Indian nationalist struggle.

17 Jain, *Indian Women*.

18 ISST, *Integrating Women into a State Five Year Plan: Karnataka*, vols 1–2.

19 Anisur Rehman, 'Some Dimensions of People's Participation in the Bhoomi Sena Movement Followed by a Discussion on the Issue', Popular Participation Programme, United Nations Research Institute for Social Development, Geneva, 1981.

20 Devaki Jain, *Income Generating Activities for Women: Some Case Studies* (New Delhi: UNICEF, 1980).

21 Later published as 'Gandhian Contributions towards a Feminist Ethic', in Eck and Jain, *Speaking of Faith*, pp. 255–70.

22 Eck and Jain, *Speaking of Faith*.

23 Jain, 'Valuing Women: Signals from the Ground'.

24 Sen, 'Population and Reasoned Agency'.

Chapter 10

Women, Public Policy and the New World Order*

It was thrilling for me to receive an invitation from Jagori, a progressive and collective organisation that is an exemplar of what we call 'feminist resource centres', to give a public lecture in Delhi. I was living in Bangalore at that time, and this seemed to me a great honour. Also, I could use the opportunity once again to remind the women's movement, especially the game changers like Jagori, that global economic programmes were like the sky that could come crashing down on the masses. The women's movement should be aware not only of these macro forces but also of ideas and actions which can replace them with a more benign 'sky'.

THE CROSSROADS

It seems to me that this is a crucial juncture in the history of this nation and of women's engagement with this history. For there is still space and opportunity for those of us in the women's movement, those who worry about equality and social justice, to turn the traffic around and deflect the march of current policy in political economy. The time has come, I believe, for women's movements to renew the power and politics of their foremothers, to sharpen their tools, demonstrate the power of their collective action, and bring themselves from the margins to the centre where a great void is visible. And should we choose not

---

* This paper could not have been written as well as completed on time without the untiring help of M. V. Jagadeesh and Perce Bloomer.

to stand up and be counted, we would be unworthy of the remarkable, brilliant and brave journeys we have ourselves undertaken. We would be unworthy of the identity we claim for ourselves, one defined against discrimination, against the demeaning gaze and the prejudices which cut across class, caste, creed, race and location.

In April 2006, a wide range of people—political leaders, concerned citizens, lawyers and artists—could be seen demonstrating their support of Medha Patkar's stand and the work of the Narmada Bachao Andolan (NBA) at the ground level. It is evident that we still have a live constituency of those who 'care', even as the democratic space for the negotiation of justice and honour is rapidly shrinking.[1]

There has been a dramatic shift of the very sky—not merely the landscape, but the sky underneath which we live. What I am saying is not new. Thinkers national and international have commented on the changes in global politics and global economics since 9/11, as September 11, 2001, is often referred to.[2] Commentators have underscored the shifts in coalitions, the rise of narrow identities, what Amartya Sen calls the 'miniaturising' of people.[3]

Arundhati Roy has offered her own perspective on the narrowing of the concept of civilisation into exclusively religious identity:

> Increasingly, Indian Nationalism has come to mean Hindu Nationalism, which defines itself not through a respect or regard for itself, but through a hatred of the Other. And the Other, for the moment, is not just Pakistan, it's Muslim. It's disturbing to see how neatly nationalism dovetails into fascism.... Fascism's firm footprint has appeared in India. Let's mark the date: Spring, 2002. While we can thank the American President and the Coalition Against Terror for creating a congenial international atmosphere for its ghastly debut, we cannot credit them for the years it has been brewing in our public and private lives.... In no time at all, the godsquadders from hell have colonised the public imagination. And we allowed them in.[4]

There has been a sharp increase in inequalities everywhere, in every theatre—within nations, between nations and between regions. That is one dimension of the sky. It has been mapped by the reports of such prominent actors as the World Bank. The *World Development Report*

2005 states in bold terms, 'inequality is not only unfair—it also wastes resources and stifles economic progress.'[5] It warns nations who imagine that, given time, the effects of 'trickle down' will be apparent, that the source of the trickle will dry up. Let us illustrate this.

As a global society emerges, inequalities of income and distances between people are increasing. We see this by looking at poverty rates between 1985 and 1998. While they did decline slightly in South Asia, the absolute numbers of those below the poverty line increased. Poverty rates in Africa rose, and there was an especially sharp rise within the so-called 'transition' economies of Eastern Europe and the former Soviet Union. In Latin America, poverty rates doubled before they declined. In other words, the overall decline was far less than had been projected by the majority of development economists. And wherever a decline was apparent, it was much slower in the 1990s than in earlier decades.[6]

As indicated above, outside the rich countries, the numbers of those living in poverty in the LDCs rose steadily during the last two decades of the 20th century. This increase is part of the phenomenon of growing global economic inequality, both between and within countries. The incomes of LDCs and transition economies have stagnated while those of rich industrialised countries have risen, producing increased inequality.[7] Again, within most countries, the less well off became poorer while the rich got richer. This is confirmed even by traditional measures of household income or consumption, which, as will become evident, miss crucial aspects of impoverishment. Summing up the trends visible in many countries over an extended period of time, Ravi Kanbur and Lyn Squire state, 'inequality has been surprisingly persistent, and where inequality has changed rapidly, it has increased.'[8]

Investigations of ground realities confirm the increase in immiseration and disparities. Statistics on inequality have been provided by Abhijit Sen and Himanshu,[9] while vivid descriptions of the debt ridden turning to suicide are found in the articles of P. Sainath[10] and increasingly also on television.

Another great change in the sky is the unrolling of thrust areas of an economic programme based on what I would call 'acute liberalisation', where trade-led growth is made the mantra for all problems.

In such a sky, how and where are interventions made on behalf of women and justice? What do data and reports reveal on the location and condition of women, especially the deprived majority? To pose my question differently, in what ways and to what degree has the women's movement been able to bear upon this sky? This new sky and the phenomena it is generating, the viruses it is breeding, make it imperative that we work out the position of the women's movement in relation to it.

I have reflected on my own history to decide what constitutes my USP (to use the latest jargon), in which domains my participation has been valued, to see how my individual experience suggests insights into these questions. Given the number of sites in India where information is currently processed—listservs, blogs and big-scale information dissemination programmes addressing every topic possible, including women, policy and the new world order—it is necessary for me to situate myself for my words to carry significance.

I have identified some contexts for learning that I might claim as unique. One relates to my age. The second has been my involvement in the politics of affirmation of nations of the South (that is, areas formerly under colonial empires). This brought me into the NAM arena, not just at conferences on women's issues, but also as a government delegate at the NAM Conference on Culture in Columbia in 1991. The third related item is my considerable participation in international spaces, including high-profile confederations like the South Commission. Fourth, my involvement in the population policy, which was launched in 1992 on what proved to be a bumpy journey, and which continued to weave in and out of my life until 2003.

The fact of my having been born in 1933 and having attained adulthood in 1953 is responsible for more than what is often said about those like Vina Mazumdar, Neera Desai and myself—that we were pioneers of women's studies, who made prominent the 'equal but different' debate in the landscape of knowledge. It has also influenced how the idea of India entered my imagination. Belonging to the generation before 'midnight's children' made certain political ideas part of our lives, regardless of whether we arrived at these via the journey of the formal left, Gandhi's passage to India, or the early years of internationalism in the women's movement. The India of our dreams is actually the India that we lived in. On returning in 1956 from my first educational experience in Oxford, India was represented, for me, by Nehru and Gandhi. Gandhi, as in the idealist vision of Vinoba Bhave, and Nehru, as establishing a role for India on the international stage.

It was at this time that I undertook a comparative study of government programmes for rural India—the area-based planning of the Khadi and Village Industries Commission, the government's Community Development and National Extension Service programme and, for my second sponsor, the Indian Cooperative Union headed by Kamaladevi Chattopadhyay, the Gramdaan reconstruction programme.

This study entailed extensive travel all over Bihar, Orissa, Andhra and Maharashtra. It was thrilling to be walking in India's fields of reconstruction—the atmosphere was charged with dedication and hope. When we met visitors from other South Asian countries or attended meetings of delegates from Palestine and South Africa, we realised that, despite colonisation, India had developed extraordinary capacities for self-reliance during the freedom struggle and after. In Thailand and Bangladesh, they were using Nestlé's condensed milk, imported soap and imported cars with air conditioning for people like us. While there was India, producing its own milk, soap, cars, bicycles. We were the envy of liberated countries who had not yet achieved what Gandhi called the 'second freedom' of liberation from economic colonisation.

There was in this period an embarrassment, what we may call a *sankocham*, at the idea of living ostentatiously while surrounded by the poverty starkly manifest in malnutrition and high mortality rates. Indian bureaucrats were reluctant to display their wealth through consumption, and money was not valued as a means to a lifestyle fitted out with luxurious consumer goods. There were, of course, those who hoarded wealth or were concerned only to accumulate it, but this too was accompanied by an overlay of embarrassment.

What I call the 'Gandhi touch' made for the belief that consumer preferences could be directed to benefit the have-nots. The conscious favouring of khadi shops and the revival of handicrafts were aspects of this policy, which extended to mandating state governments to buy exclusively from producers identified as especially deprived. Municipal schools were supposed to buy their school uniforms from the refugee women's co-operative which had an outlet in the old building of the Cottage Industries Emporium. Many government departments made their purchases from certain groups of producers in the same way that Congressmen were expected to show their patronage of khadi spinners by wearing khadi suits and caps. Distinctions were introduced in the textile industry to ensure a market for the labour-intensive handloom sector, which had the exclusive right to produce bordered sarees. In this way, public policy sought to secure a more substantial share in the national income to those of its contributors who belonged to the 'classes living in poverty'. The vision behind the plans was the protection and promotion of employment and livelihood.

Turning our attention from policy makers to producers, there emerged at that time remarkable trade unions and associations of work-ers, like the Mazdoor Mahajan of Ahmedabad (whose first president was Anasuya Sarabhai) and the Dastakar Anjuman of Kashmir. Some of these associations had been set up by Gandhi. This was a fascinat-ing India, and if you look back today, it does seem difficult to not be attracted to it. But it could also be said that we failed India, as what I see now of the nation is not comforting. More on this later, but it is enough to suggest that we failed to engage fully in the reconstruction of India by using what we had learned from our historical experience. We enjoyed what our history had given us and stood by watching. My generation has come to rethink the course we followed, whether with regard to the technologies we adopted, the economic policies we allowed, or the political processes we ignored. These choices have led to the pollution of both nature and people, for it has destroyed our rivers and our soil, created chaotic towns and steeped us in corrupt practices, whether life taking like counterfeit drugs or financially threat-ening like stamp paper. This has generated disparities that hold within themselves time bombs waiting to blast away what is left of peace and security in the Indian landscape. We should have unselfconsciously gone into politics, and tried to initiate mass participatory dialogues, as indeed the NBA is now doing.

Apart from the era in which I grew up, another part of my history I cherish is my participation in the South Commission set up in 1987. I cannot begin to tell you what an experience it was to be a member of a commission meant solely for economists from developing countries, led by a man like Julius Nyerere, who drew inspiration from the socialist vision and was also a leader of a remarkable freedom movement in Tanganyika (now Tanzania). We represented a cross-section of experience, for besides economists there were people who had retired as heads of state or heads of banks or as members of the UN or the foreign service. We three women (Marie Angelique Savané, Solita Collas-Monsod and myself) represented the academic activism that characterised the feminist movement.

It was a serious attempt at what I call 'striking back at the empire', prompted by the need to respond to the Brandt Commission, which had initiated the process of making rich countries into an economic club. Interestingly, it was Mugabe who, as chair of NAM, mooted the idea of having a South–South Economic Commission. This idea of 'retaliation' was developed into a constructive proposal by Julius Nyerere. He proposed that we develop our sinews by sharing knowledge, co-operating on economic matters and setting up new institutions like a debtors' forum, a bank for nations of the South as well as information systems within the South. This would enable us to harness our power and to overcome our differences.

We had consultations in Cuba, China, India, Kuwait, Mozambique, Malaysia and Tanzania. In Mozambique, we learned of the extraordinary way the Portuguese pulled out. Before leaving, they destroyed all infrastructure that would have been of use to the 'free Mozambiquans', such as power lines and basement pipes in high-rise buildings. When I left Mozambique I swore that I would never again admire Portugal for the maritime genius that is celebrated in their museums and their history books. They were the worst of the colonisers.

In East Africa, Nyerere appealed to leaders to abandon their turf wars and fight the enemy together. This carried resonances of the trade union language—just as the workers of the world had been exhorted to unite and overthrow their chains, leaders and people of the South were being asked to unite against all odds. We were shown the way by Cuba, which we visited towards the close of our term. As we were listening and learning from various voices in Cuba, in the company of Fidel Castro, with whom I had such memorable conversations and for whom I came to feel such affection, Nyerere looked at us and said, 'We have the South Report here.' In other words, we had what we wanted to say—Cuba had done it. And in China, Nyerere shared his hopes openly. He urged me to tell the premier that if China and India combined, the South would have no difficulty in proving its power against the North.

It is worth analysing the failure of our work to achieve its aims. First of all, it may have been too late. Many countries in Africa were already entangled in structural adjustment programmes, or what is called economic reform, and their leaders had been 'bought over'. As Latin America was reeling under debt, here too it was impossible to unknot the process. Second, many of the commission's members being retired 'leaders', they had little or no experience of what we now call people's movements. Their understanding of governance was limited to their own area of jurisdiction, and did not comprehend the extraordinary energy, clarity and ability to identify the 'how' of institutions that characterised the groundswell of people's movements.

Interestingly, this recognition of the need to abandon Western intel- lectualism and forge a separate identity to rethink development from the vantage point of the poor and marginalised in former colonies had been identified much earlier in the 1980s by those of us in the women's movement. It was this that led to the founding of DAWN.[11]

The UN's framework of gender equality measured progress by comparing statistics in education, wages and political participation, without going behind the scenes to investigate what was responsible for the disparities between men and women and between the rich and the poor. What DAWN brought into the discourse on women and development in 1984–85 was this will to uncover the roots of inequal- ity. At the founding meeting, representatives identified their regional crises in a matter of minutes, within which it was possible to situate the problems of poor women. Thus DAWN shifted the discussion from what we call the 'ladder game' to harnessing macro-economic policy for the advancement of women.

The South Commission in many ways followed up on DAWN in trying to recast the development paradigm. The interesting issue is that what DAWN could do, the South Commission could not. And this has lessons for us.

Firstly, the fact that, without the backing of a huge commission or the UN, a group of women had created an intellectual ferment and developed a new analytical frame which was widely celebrated and used, shows that women are capable of collective strategising, overcoming inhibitions and establishing what are called the necessary conditions for making 'a strike'. This confirms the willingness and eagerness of women to come together if there is a possibility of creative efforts at transformation and their energetic use of new ideas. It also affirms their collective concern about poverty and inequality—a kind of ethical imperative. It also reveals the fact that women's creative intellect is often in advance of men's intellect, given that DAWN preceded the South Commission.

The South Commission could not come up with what it sought, namely a path-breaking development theory which was intellectually acceptable and could be sold to leaders and people. It was hamstrung by its lack of unity and by the inherited understanding of its members that the old order had to be actually discarded. It was also trapped in men's ways of working, which demanded big structures with posts and funds, a 'big deal' to squeeze the toothpaste out of the tube. Following the South Commission's Report,[12] the South Centre that had been set up as a hub for energising the South collapsed and was replaced by bureaucratic management of South–South communication.

In my view, unless we dismantle the symbols of the new economic order that carry such overwhelming power, and forge new structures through processes that are democratic and inclusive—and only learned by plunging into the women's movement—there is no way of holding back the collapse of the sky we see around us. Although I came out of the South Commission disappointed, I also came out of it knowing that the way forward would be shown by women-only spaces and collective strategies led by women. Brought up against the old dilemma that public policy is given, and is not for us to shape or negotiate, I affirmed the need to create new public policy.

This said, I will now gather these points under the three heads addressed by the title—women, public policy and the new world order. Under 'women', I propose to take up both the political story of women's history that is bound up with issues of identity, as well as the intellectual story of women's engagement with knowledge. I will illustrate engagements with public policy through stories of women's work. I will also deal with the dilemmas, what I call the *problematiques*, of women's participation in public policy and especially of what is now called 'gendering public policy'. Finally, I will share with you my ideas, as indeed my anxieties, regarding the new world order.

The experiences I will be drawing on to address my topic include my years of work at the ISST and the research for my recent book, an 'intellectual history' of development thought in the UN, illuminated by the parallel history of the struggle of women to be addressed on more equal terms in the international theatre of justice.[13] Work on this book helped me discover much about intellectual domination. Those like myself, who have been associated with the women's movement for over 30 years, keep struggling to reconcile two of the most visible realities of today's world. On the one hand, there is the strong political presence assumed by the women's movement, locally and globally. There is now widespread recognition that a gendered analysis bringing out difference and inequality is necessary to development design. Yet we cannot escape the fact that development thought has been unable to prevent the situation on the ground from worsening sharply in recent years for many women, particularly those living in poverty or in sites of conflict.

I suggest we need to ponder on what our response to this disjunction is to be. My lecture comprises five sections: (*a*) the women's movement; (*b*) knowledge; (*c*) women and work; (*d*) the new world order; and (*e*) some reflections on engaging in public policy.

THE WOMEN'S MOVEMENT

Representing what even several 'outsiders' have acknowledged to be the last surviving global social movement,[14] and the most sustained in its reflection on such a wide spectrum of issues, the women's movement's most remarkable achievement consists of having established the reality of women as a social configuration over and above their plural identities. We have old and new examples of how women have transcended differences of class, caste, religion, ideology or location. They have mobilised around issues like the anti-arrack struggle in Andhra Pradesh, or within other struggles, like the Dalit Women's Federation. Once I even suggested that identity is like liquid, for it flows into differently shaped containers depending on its use, although I have subsequently abandoned that 'model'.

In my presidential address to the National Conference on Women's Studies in 1993 (Mysore), I presented a chart of collective action by Indian women to highlight the issues they are raising at the ground level, the strategies they adopt, and what that tells us about the 'what and how' of development. A long and diverse list, it referred, among others, to vegetable vendors in Manek Chowk in Ahmedabad, market women in Imphal, the anti-arrack movement in Andhra Pradesh, women in a settlement in Assam, and the Chipko movement. The review described how women experiencing poverty and other forms of deprivation are putting their bodies on the line.[15] Their struggle could be for livelihood, for the preservation of their shacks, for water or for protection from physical violence. The review suggested that such collective action found opportunity and indeed success only when women organised as women. Put the other way, they have to organise themselves as women, across other social divisions and political formations, in order to survive, to find a 'way out'.[16] This finding was decisively confirmed during my research for *Women, Development and the UN*.

Writing history from the perspective of the 'South' is a rewarding but challenging task. The available knowledge base is overwhelmingly Eurocentric, both in its choice of sources and in its presentation of history, so that it is easy for such perceptions to dominate discourse elsewhere. Yet if World War II constituted a defining event for the northern hemisphere and provided the context for founding the United Nations, such events were not the most significant externalities for nations of the South.

The histories of the colonised countries were defined by slavery and indentured labour, by economic exploitation and the denial of cultural and intellectual recognition. Historical landmarks for black citizens of

South Africa are the dates punctuating the period of apartheid, like the years 1964 and 1990 which mark the 27 years Nelson Mandela was incarcerated on Robben Island.

Eurocentrism is also true of the history of ideas. Accounts of the course of intellectual currents and claims for the influence of intellectual contributions refer to a world whose contours are viewed from the West. Yet to Indians experiencing the everyday economic constraints that were a condition of colonial rule, Mahatma Gandhi appeared more relevant than John Maynard Keynes.

I learned a great deal on how women claim power for themselves. I found that whenever women did achieve success and broke through male bastions of knowledge and power, it was by building on their collective identity as women. I called this 'a place of one's own', or the 'women's tent', both powerhouse and ghetto. As Virginia Woolf argued, a 'room of one's own' is where we women are free to think and can husband our resources to confront the world outside.[17] From such a powerhouse, if even one woman is enabled to represent the political will of women, she can make that difference.

My book provides examples of such strategising, beginning with the Universal Declaration of Human Rights, through the NAM conferences, all the way to the Committee on the Elimination of All Forms of Discrimination Against Women and to Beijing. It often provides a perspective from the inside out, describing how women bureaucrats collaborated with women in civil society, or occasions when North and South came together to achieve their larger goal of equal rights together with equal treatment. The politics behind these celebrated interventions reads almost like a thriller. Minerva Bernadino from San Domingo, Helvi Sippila from Finland, Vida Tomsic from the former Yugoslavia and our own Hansa Mehta at international fora, and Kamaladevi Chattopadhyay, Renuka Chakravarty, Sarojini Naidu and Durgabai Deshmukh among others from India, were all concerned with the liberation of both the nation and of women—all their tireless political activism was directed towards getting what really should not have needed so much time and energy to establish, that we exist, have minds, that we are different but must be treated as equal citizens.[18] A disgraceful revelation, that we needed to do so much just to prove that.

Collective strategising through a place of one's own has now become a feature of all world gatherings, such as the World Social Summit, or the 'peace tent', which I would like to suggest is an extension of the women's tent, the symbol of women's politics. The caucus, the bonding across conventional divides of region, ideology, race and position, was and continues to be a powerful tool.

But dilemmas persist. While a place of one's own has been necessary to work out plans and develop the confidence to face the bigger world, it made 'outsiders' see our 'tent' as a separate enclave. This perception perpetuates the 'women for women by women to women' formula, which prevents women from revisioning development and withholds from development discourse learnings from the lived experience of women.

Thus, a place of one's own can be a powerhouse or a ghetto—or both. We need to be on our guard against simplistic solutions such as increased funds for women, for it can go into the basket that is a means of hiving off women and simultaneously impoverishing movements for equality and justice.

The tenability of the political identity 'woman' is constantly contested by many women themselves, who insist that identity is determined by caste, class, race and sexuality at the same time—and to at least the same degree—as it is by gender. The very sophistication of the feminist movement has come to challenge this identity as 'essentialist'.

Yet the reading of history has convinced me that there is a strong case for affirming such an identity. Lord Meghnad Desai speaks of the various ethnic, religious, regional and linguistic identities within the Indian nation and says that 'Indian democracy was shaped by these ignored identities as they asserted themselves in the daily course of electoral politics.'[19] He asserts that the growing assertion of multiple nations within the Indian state is the reason the country lags in development. He traces the changes in definitions of nationhood from subjecthood to citizenhood. In a debate on these ideas of his, I suggested that women's identity has not been recognised as a boundary for citizenship.[20]

This predicament of a group still in a state of subjecthood is similar—though not the same—as that of another set of people whose nation 'is also a question'. Here I refer to the Dalits. Partha Chatterjee and Lata Mani have shown how women's bodies were central to both colonial and nationalist discourse on India. I suggest we have not yet set out a theoretical basis for understanding how women constitute their own nation within India.

Another less-discussed aspect of the elusiveness of the possibility of theorising women—or the elusiveness even of women theorising—is what I call the *neti neti* syndrome. In the Upanishads, the quest for 'truth' proceeds by rejecting every provisional definition with the phrase 'not this, not this'. In other words, it is definition by negation. It often occurs to me that feminists deny every attempt at a definition or a conclusive statement of their politics. It is extremely difficult to navigate gendered spaces and to unpack gendered concepts. The recognition that women are located within nested hierarchies throws into question conventional political alignments. In an entire book contesting one-dimensional identities, Amartya Sen has not addressed this complex issue of women's identity, which one cannot help feeling would have enriched his discussion.[21]

What is current today is the celebration of pluralism—the affirmation of identities based on colour, caste, class and gender, of shifting identities and of unpredictable intersections between identities. It seems to reflect the pressure for representation, for democracy, but also could be a consequence of the deepening of divisions based on colour, class, religion, caste, gender and location. When coupled with increased deprivation, this leads to a search for quick escape routes, so that solidarity occurs around the more obvious givens of ethnicity or religion, rather than through creative coalitions across these categories. Such thinking has made inroads into both the women's movement and government bodies, making consensus building more difficult. The fragmentation of women's identity as a collective has led to some reluctance within the UN to emphasise gender. This trend also makes room for expressions of cultural relativism—an unwelcome development.

To consolidate forces in the battle against racism, the 'other' had to anchor identity on a single pole. Attempts to highlight differences between male and female, rich and poor, urban and rural, educated and uneducated or Christian and non–Christian would have impeded the mobilisation of political will. It was this will which made possible the acts of courage and sacrifice that eventually undid the power of the white regime in South Africa. The more the oppressor strained to assert power, the more the weakness and absurdity of his or her position was apparent to the oppressed. It was the power of this knowledge that the adversary was creating myths, or trying to seek protection in a glass cage, which inspired the anti-apartheid movement and eroded the self-confidence of the white minority.

It may be stretching the point, but the women's movement needs to learn from this single-minded politics the strategic value of mobilising around a single identity when the walk to liberation is going to be a long one. Just as white supremacy was sustained by the belief that customary ethical constraints could be set aside in interactions with black people who were used and abused—as was brought home to me the year I lived in South Africa—the mindset that women are valueless and deserve ill treatment is deeply embedded worldwide. It is true we have made many dents in this rock. The history of the world is full of heroines and rebels who have challenged these perceptions and values. Fatima Mernissi and Elizabeth Amoah have described cases from Morocco and Ghana where strong women who became leaders were branded as witches, so that they could be burned as Joan of Arc had been, or removed from the scene in other ways.[22]

I believe that to achieve women's emancipation, the many identities we bear must be transcended by bonding, by emphasising the identity of woman. The challenge is to use this identity, without granting it enduring relevance, to make the larger claim for liberation from discrimination and exclusion. This strategy has to be considered if we are to make a more significant dent, if not in fact undermine the powers against which we are pitted.

KNOWLEDGE

The problems of knowledge are central to feminist theorizing, which has sought to destabilize androcentric, mainstream thinking in the humanities and in the social and natural sciences.

—Helen Longino (1993)

While researching my book, one of the areas I found most fascinating to read up on was women's engagement with knowledge—their production of new knowledge, often by exposing fallacies in existing knowledge, but also by developing new methodologies for deriving and processing knowledge. These discoveries were empowering in themselves, but they also did much to convince the 'other' of the salience of that (not simple) slogan 'equal but different'.

Analysing the foundations of modern scientific knowledge, the feminist philosopher Sandra Harding claims that traditional social science has typically asked questions about nature and social life that certain (usually privileged) men wish to see answered.[23] Harding traces the relationship between the development of modern Western science and the history of European expansion. Challenging the claim of modern science to value neutrality, she argues that European voyages of discovery went hand in hand with the development of modern science and technology. Europeans who were colonising the world needed to know about winds, tides, maps and navigation, the construction of ships and firearms, as well as botany and the means of survival in harsh environments. Such questions acquired intellectual interest because of the need to solve colonialism's everyday exigencies.[24]

To quote Ann Tickner,

> Feminists in all the disciplines have been acutely aware of the relationship between knowledge and power and the ways that traditional knowledge has been constructed in the interests of the powerful. Feminist scholarship has emerged from a deep skepticism about knowledge which, while it claims to be universal and objective, is not. In reality, such knowledge is usually partial, created by men and based on men's lives. Sensitive to gendered differences in these regards, feminists see their scholarly responsibility as creating new knowledge that is less androcentric, more genuinely universal, and that produces research that is useful to women.[25]

It was in this realm of ideas that women fighting different battles found themselves on common ground. They came together to protest against untenable distinctions—between public and private or between theory and practice—and false hierarchies between development and human rights or between human rights and women's rights. They found they could create alliances with 'the umbrella of thought' providing a shared space.

One of the few advantages of exclusion from history is the determination to end exclusion; thus, women's history has tended to be more inclusive by race, ethnicity, class, sexuality, religion, ability and region than other histories.[26] However, 'bringing women in' was no simple act of insertion. It meant that the fields of study had to change in multiple ways, which included the unpacking of certain central assumptions of the discipline. Divisions between disciplines were also shown to disable investigation. Such questioning created a 'politics of disturbance'.[27] It meant undertaking to 'plough up inherited turfs without planting the same old seeds in the field'.[28] Feminists insist that it is the experiential and the collective that give birth to an idea. And further, that no one theoretical construct can do justice to all situations. The revelation and unpeeling of the several layers around the notion of equality, for example, challenge the notion of one dominant construct.[29]

The contribution of women's studies has been critical. Women have redefined the meaning of work. They have questioned the models of development being promoted and even revisioned what the new world order should be. Knowledge has been created and disseminated through multiple sources. It came from those working in communities as well as those debating the givens of the academy. There has been research that has documented grassroots success stories and research that has provided wider contexts and more sophisticated theories.

I argue that it is their very difference from men in the realm of thought that has prevented women's views from being accommodated within policy, and also inhibited women from participating in the framing of policy. For a long time, this difference in their perceptions of knowledge/truth and women's rejection of the idea of the 'final word' made for a conscious distancing from the world of the mind.[30] This changed as women's research on subjects related to development started to draw attention to how patriarchy operated in all its sites. A gendered perspective questioned the very premises of theories. In all fields of inquiry, it transformed the definition of categories, the tools of measurement and the interpretation of data, which came to have major implications for policy and practice. For when the difference that defines gender was uncovered, the seemingly self-evident categories of 'work', 'the household' and 'the poor', measures such as money, the domestic product and caloric requirements for types of work, and the valuation of contributions to economic, social, political spaces and intellectual spaces were all revealed as inadequate and in need of substitution, and were in fact replaced by women's studies.

The perspective provided by gendered experience revealed the presence of other economies such as the unpaid economy. Then there are other political spaces—there is politics behind the closed doors of the household, in terms of both discrimination in the provision of basic amenities, and the power to take decisions. There are other social relations and behaviours, other values and other measures of value, as we see when women's collective actions, whether economic, social or political, whether covert or overt, reveal choices different from the choices of their 'own' men.[31] In the realm of medicine, it is now recognised that women's diseases are often trivialised or misdiagnosed.[32] As women succeeded in unsettling the definitions provided by the establishment, there were consequences at the level of policy, like the adoption of social indicators, the prioritisation of human development, and the reclassification of domestic space as open to judicial intervention.

Gender as an analytical tool has a revelatory quality. When a 'gender lens' is applied to matters of inequality and discrimination—central to issues of governance and in the social sciences—there become visible not only the many instances and dimensions of inequality, but also the many difficulties of doing away with them. For inequalities of gender work within more encompassing domains of inequality, whether mapped by class, race, caste, age or occupation. Among minorities, indigenous peoples and refugees, the experience of women needs to be specifically addressed. Gender inequalities are also brought to light by studying agency in different locations—the family, institutions and the power to access services like food, health, education. Discrimination works on multiple levels.

We may say that almost all the debates and events of the last 50 years are captured in the single notion or aspiration of equality. The women's movement traces numerous configurations of this kaleidoscopic concept. Women's studies has exposed the many facets of inequality, its pervasive presence as well as its particular circumstances. In doing so, it sometimes seemed that 'equality' may be understood better without our being closer to achieving it, as it retreats like a will-o'-the-wisp before attempts at theoretical definition or actual establishment. Legal and extra-legal struggles and theories drawing on both philosophy and politics, both economics and sociology, served to enrich the understanding of equality but did not always achieve it. But the exposition was worth the journey, for it illuminated other inequalities and sought to redress these.

Perhaps the defining feature of these explorations is that women are at the centre of the theories discussed and also the active practitioners of these theories. Women are both subjects of study and agents. Theory then is not an 'abstract intellectual idea divorced from the lives of women, but seeks to explain how those lives are lived'.[33] Yet on the other hand, one disturbing feature was that most of this new knowledge was produced by women. It did not attract the participation of both sexes. In contrast, research or politics that addresses class or race has been taken up by those outside the race or class in question as well as by its members.

I would like to conclude this section by saying that it is crucial that all examples of the entrenchment of patriarchal thought in the theory and terminology of every discipline be made accessible to women engaged in struggles and action. It would give them the confidence that their own objections to the system are legitimate. As Gerda Lerner has said, 'Every thinking woman had to argue with the "great man" in her head, instead of being strengthened and encouraged by her foremothers.'[34]

WOMEN AND WORK

I first undertook research to investigate women's work, and in my view it is still this area that shows us how the cookie crumbles as far as poverty, inequality and the condition of women are concerned. An understanding of inequality and discrimination requires us to probe and unravel what has been called the 'gender knot'.[35]

The core issue is taking women into account as a subset of all social categories, whose roles are decided by both biology and the inter-pretation of the biological role by cultural tradition and by religion and appraised according to a hierarchy of values. The re-evaluation of women's work is an area of knowledge consolidated over the last 50 years in which all players have participated. The UN and national bodies have considered and sometimes adopted the ideas generated. These range from the immediately intelligible—the value of non-monetised work, the dignity of care work and the reproduction of humans—to new measures of work such as the time invested in it; new modes of research, through collective identification of a measure; and even to renaming domains of experience, as in formal and informal economies. The modes and hierarchies of valuation in different domains of knowledge—economics, statistics and other social and physical sciences—are to my mind the keys to understanding why women, girls and female infants still experience incarceration of different kinds.

The ISST, supported by the ICSSR, conducted between 1975 and 1977 a study of time allocation by men and women in the households of six villages which exposed many dimensions of valuation.[36] The study was partnered by NSSO. Everyone was absorbed in the imple-mentation and outcome of the study, from field investigators up to the chairman and the chief executive officer. This was a pioneering study in many ways. The hypothesis was that female work participation rates are underestimated in India owing to methodological inadequacy, what we may call a failure of measurement. The first field trial, conducted by Professor Ashok Rudra in Muluk, a village in Shantiniketan, established that women and girls earned bread in ways not accounted for, since it was accomplished under various species of 'subterfuge'.

The study described how among the poor, the work participation of women was greater than that of men. It showed that children, especially girl children between the ages of 8 and 12, were engaged in significant economic activities. It also showed that the activity code 'domestic activity', canvassed in the opening block of the NSSO schedule, was a stumbling block for women for it created the perception that the activity that took up most of their time was only 'housework', even if it meant 4 hours a day weeding, or 6 hours a day attending to animals and milking, or 12 hours a day chopping mulberry to feed silk worms. The study did not just call attention to the invisibilising of women's work, but sought to devise research methods which did justice to this work.

The discovery that among the poorest (usually landless) households women's work participation rates were higher than those of men led us to conclude that 'all poor women are women workers.' No poor woman can afford not to work, as she and her family would perish. Women were responsible for the household's survival and would do anything, including selling their bodies, to bring home that daily bread.

The ISST teams led by our first and very worthy research assistant Malini Chand (now Sheth) lived in the villages for a year and recorded what poor people—women and men and children—were actually doing. The information was shocking. Women and girls were working 18 hours a day. While boys played or went to school, girls cooked, cleaned and carried. Among the poor, girls were often the breadwinners for the entire household. 'Development interventions' had often led to an increase in the workload of women with no accompanying increase in their incomes or well-being. The realisation that men preferred to be idle rather than work for poor wages explained intriguing statements about the low rate of the labour participation of females in West Bengal. Poor women and girls in West Bengal were working, but 'under cover' of 'feminine' work—as domestic help, as beggars rather than in the fields, often for non-monetary rewards.

This 'time-use' study, which challenged assessments of women's economic contribution and concentrated on the poorest, attracted the interest of many well-known economists and social scientists apart from Prof. Ashok Rudra. Professors Pranab Bardhan, Pradhan Prasad and Ashok Mitra offered suggestions for stratifying the sample by class. Prof. V. M. Dandekar directed the NSSO to partner with us in the selection of villages and households and in canvassing the questionnaire of the 32nd Round, with which our fieldworkers visited the same households as the NSSO. He also saw to it that we had access to the raw schedules of the NSSO. This allowed us to present our (not strictly comparable) data in columns alongside NSSO data for the 27th Round as well as on the tables for the 32nd Round. This strengthened our case for under-enumeration and its causes.

This single study by the ISST had considerable impact, as it came to be known by a constituency of people expert in the collection and use of data, especially data concerning employment outside and inside the official system. We participated in all the conferences of the NSSO, the Central Statistics Office and census. Our contribution in terms of action as well as in the redesigning of systems of data collection consolidated our position as the focal point for women and work concerns. The Padmaja Naidu Memorial Lecture in 1982 was a chance to challenge social scientists by, so to speak, waving these facts from the rooftops. What was the sociological family they spoke of? What were all these tracings of kinship organisations with their rules and regulations? These were fragmented non-families in which women were struggling for survival. Who were these workers being counted and placed in hierarchies of work by statisticians? Among assetless households, rates of work participation were higher for women than for men.

These differences came to be understood as 'gender differentiation', which was to underpin all the research and advocacy of ISST. This uncovering of women as a 'class' by themselves within the poverty sets was of crucial importance in our journey, as it challenged political ideology besides economic programmes.[37]

The next point of entry was into spaces where women predominated as workers, and where their engagement in work had been recognised and organised to increase their economic and social power. This research was initiated following a case study of SEWA funded by the ICSSR. At that time, SEWA was the women's wing of the Textile Labour Association, a strong trade union in Ahmedabad, and organising workers in the informal sector had given them vital negotiating power. This led the ICSSR in 1979 to sponsor a survey of similar successful endeavours to organise masses of women, which was published in 1980.[38]

The design of the book pioneered a style of case study research—investigating experience on the ground, introducing primary data from field surveys of households, and following these up with the narratives of women. It proposed that poor women were able identify spaces where they could eke out a bare livelihood, but that their incomes would multiply considerably if they were provided linkages back and forth, such as organisation, market intelligence and access to raw materials or wholesale goods through collective purchase. It was thus a critique of current income-generating projects for women like Development of Women and Children in Rural Areas that were supported by the government and even agencies like the Central Social Welfare Board and UNICEF. The suggestion was essentially that development design could learn from the survival strategies of poor women.

Thus began the search for clusters of women already in a particular occupation, so that that particular space could be expanded. This led to a Government of India programme called STEP (Support Team for Employment Promotion). It also led to the birth of the Mahila Haat at ISST, a market for women producers. The initiative was based on the idea of starting with the traditional *haat*s, viable marketplaces where the turnover of trade was greater than in modern markets. Here women could usually sell their products, the suggestion for what was to be produced having come from the marketplace.

The fact that ISST's first study was partnered by mainstream agencies including the Planning Commission enabled it in 1980 to hold a round table with 50 to 60 senior economists at the Institute of Economic Growth, Delhi University. It was called a 'statistical dialogue between micro and macro', and, being a first, some of the economists were initially sceptical. Micro studies were presented by different agencies to official bodies concerned with data collection, which led to the inclusion of a gender focus in the Central Statistics Office, NSSO, the National Board of Statistics as well as by the Registrar General.

This partnership with official bodies continued, and ISST was part of the Indian delegation at the first international conference on household surveys convened by ESCAP in Bangkok. We carried the day, arguing that women should feature not just as a subject in the category 'social welfare' but in their economic and social roles. This was the seed of the recognition that the household cannot be the primary unit of analysis, given that within households individuals hold different occupations and may experience development differently.

These 'micro–macro interactions' on data encouraged us to form a network of economists called EIWIG, a clumsy acronym but one that sought to be inclusive of both women and men involved in gendered research and economists interested in women's issues. The core of our work involved field studies concerned with poor women's work in different industries and sectors: forest based, marine products, hand-looms, khadi and village industries, mulberry and tassar sericulture and public works programmes. The households at which we looked were stratified according to class (in terms of landownership or its lack). The most elaborate study attempted to understand female-headed households, choosing field sites that pointed to different 'causes' for this phenomenon.[39] This study was commissioned by the ILO, just as many others were commissioned by the government or by UN agencies.

The findings gave a clear message regarding hierarchies of value. For a worker without assets, it is her time rather than her wage that is a measure of her labour. The adoption of time as a measure of value would entail a reversal of the values ascribed to men and women's work. Women would always come out on 'top' given that they spend more hours working than men, as shown even by the *HDR* of 1995 in its time allocation survey.[40]

While many attempts have been made to put a value on the non-monetised and invisible transactions, these are still measured against the 'standard' of money. Valuating women's work is related to but not the same as estimating the labour force or producing figures for unemployment. For all women's work yields an output, but all women's work does not provide an income.

Today, the Central Statistics Office and many other agencies try to gather more statistics on 'time spent' in their various categories. This tool has also helped in conducting a gender audit at the district and subdistrict level. It remains difficult to measure the inequality between males and females within the household in all matters including those of nutrition and health, which affect life and death. The sex ratio is being recommended as a factor to be included for the South Asian region. Similarly, we need to integrate into national and international statistics the different rates of infant mortality for males and females, and quantitative measures of female drudgery and hard labour. These will transform the quantitative picture and call attention to what is needed in terms of interventions. They will also reorder the hierarchies defining the indices.

These studies led to increased awareness of the many other hierarchies embedded in the terminology of various theories.[41] Classificatory systems and definitions contain implied hierarchies which place women lower down the scale than men. Take household work and work of economic value done within the home. If we call the home a workplace, every homemaker or home-based producer becomes a worker and may therefore avail of labour laws and thus social security.[42] Comparisons can be drawn with the way in which the recent International Convention on Torture recognised the home as a possible site of torture and enslavement, which had to be covered by the laws for custodial violence that apply to police stations.

THE NATURE OF INEQUALITY

Here is the profile of a little girl that I presented at the Padmaja Naidu Memorial lecture in 1982:

> Naini is an eleven-year-old Mina girl of Etrampura, a small village of 57 households in Bharatpur, Rajasthan. Hers is a joint family of nine people, including her parents, uncles, an aunt and a younger brother. The family lives by the produce of the eight bighas of land it owns. Depending on the season, they hire outside labour or hire out their own labour. The father and the uncles plough and dig land which Naini, her mother and aunt weed and pack together.
>
> Naini's uncle, nineteen-year-old Kardiram, attends high school in Bhusawar, five kilometres away, and her younger brother Chuttanlal is in the third standard of the school in the neighbouring village, Chentoli. Naini, who assists her parents in household chores, asks when questioned, 'Who will do all this if I go to school?'
>
> Rising at six in the morning, Naini's first task is to spend an hour making cowdung cakes. This is followed by going to the well to fetch water. Returning to the house she sweeps the courtyard. At 7.30, she sieves the wheat flour, lights the fire and assists her mother in preparing rotis. The family sits down to eat daliya and bajra rotis in brass thalis. It is Naini's daily task to clean the utensils after breakfast. After packing

some lunch for the family, she sets out with her mother to their field which lies on the border of Mehtoli and Etrampura, about 3 kms away. In September, a quarter of the field is covered with capsicum while the rest is ploughed and made ready for the next crop. She and her mother are assigned the task of weeding the field. She does this from nine in the morning to noon, then goes home with her mother to cook lunch while her father and her uncle remain back in the field.

She cuts the potatoes while her mother prepares the rotis. After eating lunch, she washes the utensils and again goes to the well to fill another pitcher of water. From quarter to three in the afternoon Naini is once more to be seen on her field, cutting grass for her cattle. By four in the evening, she has collected a big bundle which she ties up and carries home to deposit in the cattle-shed. Her uncle will cut it later and feed it to the cattle. Adjoining their mud-hut next to the cattle-shed is a little store-room, from where Naini takes out the cowdung cakes which are prepared by her every morning, and the firewood which she and her aunt had collected last week. With the help of these cowdung cakes Naini fires the oven and cooks daliya. She then sweeps the house for the second time.

The food is usually prepared by her aunt. As she is very sick these days, the task is shared by Naini and her mother. Once dinner is ready and Naini's daily tasks are completed, she finally finds half an hour to sit down and relax, chatting and teasing her brother Chuttan who has set aside his books. At 7.30, she serves a dinner of daliya, boiled milk and bajra rotis to all the family before sitting down herself. After cleaning the fireplace at 8.30, Naini rolls out her own and Chuttanlal's mattress and gets ready to sleep, to prepare herself for another such day of work.[43]

Such patterns of labour are found even today, for example in the study conducted by Seiro Ito, a Japanese economist, on time use among children in some villages of Andhra Pradesh.[44]

Time as a measure of value has taken hold in all domains of the social sciences. The ISST continued its investigation into the domain of work, undertaking studies of women in various sectors of production— dairying, *pappad* making, *bidi* making, sericulture, the gathering of minor forest produce, the manufacture of envelopes, Zardozi embroidery, *chikan*, carpets, prawn peeling—as well as of vendors and the workers in SEWA and what were called emergency sites (in this case, the Maharashtra Employment Guarantee sites).[45] We found many concealed hierarchies persisting in even the formal domain of economic measurement, which especially affected acknowledgement of the work of women.

I have indicated other areas where language or vocabulary implies hierarchies which neglect important values, and affect marginalised groups in particular.[46] I have argued there is a lack of fit between ground realities and descriptive categories. This is because the definitions and classificatory systems emerge from economic and social organisation and processes appropriate to the North, to 'organised' industrial economies. The entire research in women's studies has served to expose this disjuncture. Small businesses, the producers and vendors who dominate the private sector and form the backbone of trade in countries like Ghana, in regions like the Caribbean, or states like Manipur in India, have been marginalised as 'petty vendors'. But this is the manufacturing and trading sector of the South, not the big businesses, private and public, that occupy centre stage in accounts and in policy decisions. It should be renamed the 'business sector'. In fact in Liberia, which liberated itself from a dictator just a few months ago and elected a woman president, it was the women vendors, called the 'market women', who brought about this change. What is more, they hold the economy together—they are the business hub and the bankers and money rollers of Liberia.[47]

It is now well established that in India and the rest of the Third World, the volume and value of what are called 'minor' forest products are greater than those of 'major' forest produce. Minor forest produce sustains an economy in which the masses are the main contributors as well as the main users. Its impact on tree cover is also less violent than that of industries concerned with major forest produce. Workers in this sector are not recognised as workers, their wages are not negotiated, most of them are forest dwellers and are women. Today, because of the increased interest in plant-based medicine, their products are in demand, but all this has meant is that they are being exploited terribly. Yet the use of the words 'minor' and 'major' continues, and such vocabulary serves to occlude the degree to which those gathering or processing 'minor forest produce' are being exploited.[48]

The very definition of economic activities must be transformed. 'Production for self-consumption' may need to be given a new status. It is usually not accounted for, as only the production of surplus for sale is seen to have economic relevance. Collection of waste (for example, some items of minor forest produce) is considered insignificant but in fact offers a vast employment pool and is a substantial component of domestic production.

Another instance of the entrenchment of linguistic hierarchies is the term 'informal' sector for modes of production or trade that lack a shop floor or waged work. This sector contains more workers, indeed 92 per cent of women workers belong here. At a conference on the informal sector convened by the UNESCO and the Asia Pacific Center for Women and Development in Kuala Lumpur in Bangalore, the participants named this sector the 'first sector'. Not only does it contain the largest proportion of workers, in the history of production and trade it also appeared earlier than factory work and waged work! It is another misnomer to describe such workers as 'unorganised'. This term is misleading, for even if the workers may not be unionised, the putting out of work by contractors and enterprises is highly organised, as we see in the *bidi* industry in Karnataka.

The household had been the primary unit of classification during the collection of data concerning the poor (including estimating numbers), and was also the target of programmes for the poor, like the provision of employment and services such as credit and food. When research started to investigate this 'black box', it was found that within the household differences prevailed in every area for women and children, whether with regard to bread-earning activities, access to services like health or education, or the availability of time or leisure. Concepts like household-level food security were changed to individual food security within the household, as the practice of sequential feeding in several cultures meant that a smaller share of food was given to children, especially female children, and to women among the adults. This was discussed at the World Food Conference organised by the Food and Agriculture Organization, where ISST presented a paper arguing that it had been a mistake to see the household as the primary unit of analysis, and one should recast the proposition thus: 'The food security of a household is dependent on the food security of its individual members.'[49]

Further, it is necessary to recognise that households among the poor may not consist of closely bonded individuals collectively optimising their activities. They are often fragmented and scattered. Many are headed by women who have to fend for their own and the family's survival.[50]

This attention to intra-household inequality in every aspect—power, earnings, service utilisation, workload and the availability of time and leisure, and finally mortality rates—led to many transformations in the perception of 'development as freedom', to borrow from Amartya Sen.[51] For example, the importance of individual rights affected the perception of the family as unjust in its dealings with its members. The condition of women revealed the importance of universalisation, a vision that characterises the human rights approach. Also affirmed was the necessity of social inputs and social security, public goods that would go some way to redress embedded inequalities. Recognition that conventional assessments of economic achievement obscure achievements in social protection, and that the two often do not go together, directed attention towards social development, going on to human development and its deviation from standard economic growth paths.[52]

To sum up the implications of the above, the fact that women often work within the household, sometimes as self-employed traders, has drawn attention to the importance of what is known as the 'informal sector' of the economy.[53] And the recognition of gender difference within poor households—essentially the individuation of household members—has effected changes in the collection of statistics, the nature of employment offers, the understanding of employment trends, efforts to unionise labour, and the nature of credit offers, including demands for collateral.

Another area where the understanding of the economy has expanded is with regard to the 'gift economy'. The concept arises from the fact that the logic of the market, of the exchange of equivalents, takes the place of and conceals the logic of gift giving. The system of gift giving is omnipresent, and is as creative as it is unrecognised. The direct satisfaction of another's need appears to be so simple as to be uninformative. Yet it is transitive, whereas exchange is intransitive. That is, it gives value to the other and creates bonds between giver and receiver, making the receiver as important as the giver (an idea with resonances of Gandhian thought). According to the theory of gift giving, exchange places people in adversarial positions and emphasises self-interest and separation, whereas gift giving emphasises connection and community. Proponents of this idea say that women's free labour in the home, which if it were counted would add at least 40 per cent to the gross national product of most countries, is actually gift labour. Women have been assigned the social role of mothering, which entails unilateral gift giving. It is this experience or practice that they suggest could be developed into an alternative to the market.[54]

Voluntary tasks, including free job training and home-building organisations, are harder to classify than other activities associated with charity. In 1984, women in New Zealand argued that while monetary contributions to charity (made largely by men) are tax deductible, this was not true of the contribution of time (made largely by women). This mobilisation led to the introduction of a question concerning 'time dedicated to volunteer work' in the 1986 Census on Population.[55]

Each of these ideas seeks to create a space less destructive of human relationships and the environment, and less vulnerable in the face of shocks to the system, than could be envisaged within earlier theories of production and trade. In all the ways outlined above, distortions of value and hierarchies implicit in terminology were brought out by exploring the work spaces and narratives of women, and through the investigative methods and the style of researchers on women's issues. Their reassessment of the usefulness of the available measuring tools led women to become vital participants in inscribing justice and equality in development design and implementation.

WOMEN, PUBLIC POLICY AND THE NEW WORLD ORDER

We're an empire now and when we act we create our own reality.

— A senior adviser to President George W. Bush[56]

Definitions belonged to the definers—not the defined.

— Toni Morrison, *Beloved*[57]

The role of the intellectual is to say truth to power, to address the central authority in every society without hypocrisy, and to choose the method, the style, the critique best suited for these purposes. This is so because the intellectual produces a kind of performance that continues for years, whose main goal is to give utterance not to mere fashion and passing fads but to real ideas and values.

— Edward Said[58]

THE NEW GLOBAL ORDER: DEBATES ON DEFINITION

For many, the new global order is more than globalisation. It is the economic strength of what is now known as the coalition against terror. An apt description of this new powerdom was offered by the editor of the *New Indian Express* in January 2002:

> The important thing is not that we have changed. But that everything, the world around us, has changed so completely that no one, not China, not Russia, not even Cuba, is protesting. There is, however, more to this new world than mere unipolarity. That would have been simpler to deal with. You can always stand up to hegemony. But what do you do with a world where the big boys cartelise in a manner unprecedented in history? They think and act together, with a remarkable common sense of purpose and, ostensibly, towards greater common good.... The US, China, United Europe and Russia, are the four powers that circumscribe this world.[59]

I call it the new 'powerdom',[60] to emphasise that the controlling regime is more like a monarchical than a democratic regime. I propose that describing the new face of power this way is most relevant to considering women's location in the general landscape and how women can link with the elements in the sky, even if it is to bring them down and replace them with more elements that sustain peace.

I have also asserted that what started as the modernisation project in the form of bailing out developing nations through offers of capital was later formalised into the new liberal paradigm.[61] Here, capital-driven economic growth was offered as the panacea for all times and all 'problems'. The modernisation project thereby reinvented itself as Empire. I use the term 'Empire' to refer to the overwhelming power of one culture and one set of values, a symptom of which is the use of the term 'civilisation' with fundamentalist overtones.[62]

'Empire' is now an intelligible word. It has emerged from various gatherings of those concerned with the overwhelming domination of some global forces, political and economic, as a new avatar of older imperial conquest. As a term it has been used more recently at the Social Forums in Brazil, Hyderabad, Mumbai.[63] However, it has been used in two opposite senses. I have used 'Empire' to refer to the resistance movement. For example, in my piece on the value of the Social Forum, I invoke science fiction with the phrase 'Empire Strikes Back', i.e., the 'good' striking the evil. But, as Ann Tickner has observed, 'The term "empire" is now being used with approbation by neo-conservatives in the Bush administration and by its critics with alarm.'[64]

Empire has spawned a new wave of scholarship which marks the early stage of imperial self-recognition. This did not become apparent for the first time with the Bush administration, but as far back as 1945, when the US emerged from the Second World War with enormous power and self-confidence.[65] Following the events of September 11, 2001, the United States has been engaged in a global war against evil which demands a full-spectrum global response to any imminent threat. This strategy, articulated in the National Security Strategy of 2002, has been backed by military budget outlays of $465.9 billion in 2005, with an additional total of $346 billion in special supplementary funding appropriations for the war on terrorism between 2001 and 2006.[66] Besides its military component, this strategy calls for the promotion of a neoliberal global economy and the globalisation of Western-style democracy.[67] As Ronald Steel sums it up:

> A nation possessing this kind of power—the world's dominant economy, the currency with which the world reckons and pays its bills, the most powerful armed force with bases around the globe and a budget that nearly exceeds that of all other nations combined, and with a

messianic desire to spread its ideology and to mold the lives and minds of the rest of the world in its image—is, by any honest reckoning, an imperial state.[68]

Ben Fine affirms that macro-economics is being pressed into the service of imperialism:

> ... a third intellectual trend, is the emergence of a new virulent strain of economics imperialism based on market, especially informational failure. Whilst mainstream economics has become absolutely intoler-ant of dissent within its own discipline, it has increasingly sought to colonise other disciplines, understanding both market and non-market phenomena as the rational, historically evolved response to market failures.... this approach has been applied to development, alongside more or less everything else, and underpins the shifting rhetoric and scholarship of the World Bank in its move from Washington to post-Washington consensus.[69]

We can now see how the sky has been collapsing on people, as I opened my lecture by declaring. This collapse of the sky has most severely affected the less privileged, and among these the women, as we shall now examine.

IMPACT OF THE NEW GLOBAL ORDER ON WOMEN

Shahra Razavi suggests that 'the consolidation of a market-led devel-opment model denies vast groups of women the opportunity to claim entitlements and achieve more secure livelihoods.' Macro-economic decision making remains 'particularly resistant to feminist incursions'.[70] One finding that emerged from research conducted by the United Nations Research Institute for Social Development (UNRISD) is the tendency for women to be confined to the less lucrative segments of the non-farm sector, in the form of survivalist strategies, which do not offer good long-term prospects.

Economist Diane Elson points to the shrinking of public dialogue on macro-economic policy: 'Macro-economic policy is constructed in neoclassical economics as something beyond social dialogue and public debate.' She adds, 'Technocratic calculation has become independent of democratic deliberation.'[71]

Data on women's employment in the developing world reveal that in the period 1970 to 1990, their absorption into the labour force increased dramatically. Regions like South Asia show a leap from 25 per cent to 44 per cent, while in Latin America female absorption in the labour force rose from 22 per cent to 30 per cent. In the same regions, the male percentage declined from 88 to 78 per cent, and 85 to 84 per cent respectively. Most of this addition is in the service sector, but also in the informal economy. The nature of the expansion in employment opportunities globally is such that women are preferred as workers in many of the fast-growing sectors of production and export.[72]

The flip side to this 'absorption' is that the work is usually offered under the most exploitative, unprotected and underpaid schemes. A UNICEF study of five Asian countries found that job slots often emerge for home-based women workers only because of the retrenchment of men from what is called the low end of the production pyramid.[73]

Informal occupations provide the livelihood (paid or otherwise) of more than 80 per cent of women in low-income countries and 40 per cent of those in middle-income countries. These countries combined account for 85 per cent of the world's population.[74] Yet these jobs are sought by women because of the primary importance of sustaining their families.

The overriding importance of this is declared again and again, in interviews with and hearings of a wide range of women, whether they are in Sonagachi, in Mumbai's dance bars, in interior villages, or participants in the Maharashtra Employment Guarantee Scheme, willing to take up hard labour. Reporting the words of women in relief camps following the riots of 2002 in Gujarat, Ela Bhatt said all they wanted was *kaam* (work)—any work, wherever it might be.

Women are in the worst spots in even the fast-growing export sectors. They are also confined to the worst spots in the agricultural sector. A study conducted by the World Bank in Uttar Pradesh, which, with 160 million people, is India's most populous state, reveals that female workers form the greater proportion of those involved in low-paid casual work, primarily in the agricultural sector. This means that there has been a feminisation of the agricultural workforce, as the relative proportions of both female cultivators and female agricultural labourers have grown. Three-fourths of women's employment days are spent doing agricultural work, as compared to only 40 per cent for men. Women are also three times more likely than men to work as agricultural labourers—work that is backbreaking, insecure and of low status. In contrast to men, women rarely hold regular jobs or jobs in the non-farm sector as these activities are left to men. When they do obtain such employment, women are again underpaid and confined to unskilled activities.[75]

The following statistical profile shows how deep run the relations between women, agricultural work, informal work, landlessness and poverty. According to the census of 2001, there are 10.75 million agricultural workers in India, of whom 99.4 per cent work in the informal sector. Conversely, 64 per cent of the informal sector work-force depends on agriculture. More than 90 per cent of the rural poor engage in agriculture. Women form 38 per cent of all agricultural workers. Although women constitute over one-third of the agricultural workforce, they own less than one-tenth of agriculture land. Dalit and tribal women account for half of female agricultural labour and almost half of them are landless.[76]

The shift from farm to non-farm employment in the agricultural sector among men has not occurred among women. This has been a disadvantage, as they have lost out on higher wages in the non-farm sector. It also indicates that they enjoy less mobility than men.

A close look at 'backward' districts and regions would confirm what is even otherwise well established: the links between low literacy for women and high rates of unemployment; poor water and sanitation facilities and high maternal and infant mortality; and most importantly, a high proportion of households living in extreme poverty and high fertility. If we took a map of India and, having drawn a circle in the centre around the four BIMARU states (Bihar, Madhya Pradesh, Rajasthan, Uttar Pradesh), coloured the map in increasingly dark shades of grey to correspond to the proportion of the population to whom the 'negative' indicators above apply, the circle in the centre would be black. All 'bad' roads lead to this black hole. I once called this configuration of states 'the black heart of Mother India', as it was right in the centre of the map of India. And data reveal that women are at the bottom of this black hole.[77]

THE MARK OF INDIA'S NEW MACRO-ECONOMIC POLICIES ON THIS LANDSCAPE

The sine qua non of India's economic development has historically been the small farm and the small business. These have been not only the most important sources of employment in India, but they have shown their sustainability, and it is so moving to see how people take a little credit and open a shop, or vend on a pavement, as if there were always space for one more vendor—and yet they survive and they take home something. Ela Bhatt has been declared the businesswoman of the millennium by the Confederation of Indian Industry, and that is because she drew attention to the value of such traders—own account petty traders and vendors.

But now the state wishes to open retail trade to FDI.[78] It is my view that if we open it to FDI, the Walmart syndrome will exterminate us. It is a monster and is eating up other small monsters like Kmart in America. This has been admitted by the monster itself, and I quote from the journal of the retail trade consortium:

> India is the hottest retail spot.... India's retail industry, both food and non-food, is the second largest employer, after agriculture, and the second largest untapped market.... Retail market worth 330 billion dollars... As grand ambitions materialize [i.e. the entry of global players], the retail space will become increasingly concentrated, as smaller players are forced out or bought up by larger companies and the new companies change the face of the market... capture non food spending...[79]

This was unselfconsciously affirmed by Bush during his recent visit to India in March 2006. Trying to appease the discontent of US citizens about job slots in the US being given over to Indians, he said this would be overwhelmingly compensated by the market for US products in

India: 'We just have to find out what Indians want, and then produce it, and then we have a million consumers buying it! It is a great and expanding market for the US.' He went on to say:

> We see those opportunities here in India. Americans who come to this country will see Indian consumers buying McCurry Meals from McDonald's, home appliances from Whirlpool. They will see Indian businesses buying American products like the 68 planes that Air India recently ordered from Boeing. They will also see American businesses like General Electric and Microsoft and Intel who are in India to learn about the needs of local customers and do vital research that makes their products more competitive in world markets. The United States will not give into the protectionists and lose these opportunities. For the sake of workers in both our countries, America will trade with confidence.[80]

Here is some rough data on the current values of retail trade in India. There is more data available, disaggregated according to gender as well as size and ownership, but I am presenting this data only to give an indication of the treasure we have built up.

Percentage of retail trade in enterprise

    Total: 39.8 %

    Rural enterprise: 36.1 %

    Urban enterprise: 44.2 %

Number of workers (in millions)

    Retail trade: 18.54

    Rural: 7.88

    Urban: 10.65

Further, out of 30.35 million enterprises, 80.4 per cent are self-financing, 5.15 per cent do not use fuel of any kind, and 5.14 per cent do not need premises. The percentage of those financed by institutional finance, the Integrated Rural Development Programme and other poverty alleviation programmes was less than 1 per cent! It is incredible what is done despite shortages of power and other infrastructure!

The entry of FDI would exterminate this treasure, and not just our traders but our scattered consumers may well figure in the statistics of suicides. We would have thrown away our sine qua non, small farms and small businesses. Opposing FDI is a cause that those gathered here can rally around.

At the beginning of the 21st century, over two million women were estimated to be working in East and Southeast Asia. They accounted for one-third of the migrant population of the region. Most female migrants are in reproductive occupations—domestic work and sex work, in private households and informal commercial sectors. Despite the great need to protect their welfare and human rights, the governments of their destination countries view migrants merely as a workforce which meets labour shortages, and disclaim responsibilities for undertaking protective measures and gender-sensitive policies.[81]

Feminised migration in East and Southeast Asia has its roots in the region's rapid but uneven economic development, which is marked by the inequalities and conflicts produced by differences of gender, class and nationality.[82] Existing gender inequalities and economic injustice have been exacerbated and ethnic discrimination has increased with the migration of women from low-income economies like the Philippines, Indonesia, Vietnam, Pakistan and Bangladesh to high-income economies like Singapore, Malaysia, Hong Kong Special Administrative Region, Taiwan Province of China, the Republic of Korea and Japan. The latest report of INSTRAW on women migrants confirms that women are the majority of the migrant workers. They accounted for 69 per cent of overseas migrant workers in the Philippines and 70 per cent in Indonesia in 2000.[83]

Hair-raising facts are presented in the latest report on employment of the ILO and the report from UNIFEM.[84] Junya Lek Yimprasert, a woman trade union leader from Thailand, gives a chilling description of how transnational corporations like Nike stride across the globe looking for cheaper and cheaper labour at increasingly more vulnerable terms of employment, dropping one country and moving to another, thereby pushing those women to migrate with the company for a poorer deal in terms of wage rate and security rather than lose their livelihood.[85] So we have the free movement of capital looking for profit, being followed by endangered, unprotected female labour.

We may imagine this phenomenon not as an 'Asian Drama' (after Gunnar Myrdal) but the international drama of corporate capital.[86] As capital tramples down the people of country after country in its hunger for cheaper and cheaper labour, its behaviour is essentially similar to that of the predator of ancient legends, or of Hollywood's 'Exterminator'. The phenomenon began with 'putting out' work in Latin America, where what happened in the sweatshops is well known, and in Hong Kong. It moved to East Asia, then China, followed by Thailand, afterwards to Bangladesh and Sri Lanka, and is now moving into Pakistan and India. In each case the multinational is looking for cheaper and less organised labour. And each country offers more and more incentives to the MNC to invest—land tax relief and other exemptions from nationally binding laws, including those for the protection of labour. All over the world these predators, in collusion with our leaders, are driving down labour protection and eroding national sovereignty.

REGIONALISM: AN EXTENSION OF THE TRADE-LED GROWTH MODEL

Another area that needs our attention is the trend towards economic regionalism. We must make it more widely understood that this trend develops from the trade-led growth model that is currently the paradigm within which all our economies are functioning. The world is increasingly moving towards regional agreements, and as neighbours realise that the Indian economy is taking off, there is greater interest in working out a South Asian arrangement. I suggest that we examine some of the trade agreements, especially IBSA (India–Brazil–South Africa), SAFTA (South Asian Free Trade Area), Mercosur and perhaps SADC (Southern African Development Community) to see how we can build in a strategy for absorbing 'people', particularly women, into the outcomes planned.

Why focus on women? First, they are already in some senses gaining from the opportunities offered by the processes of free trade and globalisation. I say 'in some senses', having just discussed at length the adverse implications of this, but we must recognise that these are still seen as worthwhile opportunities by the women who avail of them.

Second, women also actively participate in opportunities for collective employment like SHGs. They have also networked across countries to change policies. Apart from building coalitions like Home Net and Women in Informal Employment Globalising and Organising (WIEGO), such mobilisation has also helped to frame policy (Home Workers Convention, ILO) and the establishment of resources like Women's World Banking.[87] If the women's movement manages to use what has been achieved so far as the thin end of the wedge, it might indeed be able to use reports, analysis and advocacy to overturn the existing paradigm.

I think such subversion would be important even for the other struggles of countries of the South. If it is carried out by the women's movement, women's leadership in ideas would be visible, which is what I think would really succeed in countering male prejudice against women.

DILEMMAS OF INVOLVEMENT IN PUBLIC POLICY

There are inbuilt difficulties in gendering public policy. We first face the question of how the term 'woman' can be the basis for coherent identity, given the heterogeneity it represents. How is it possible to forge an identity that can claim a political voice and can effect change? Women belong to all classes, castes, religions, political ideologies and cultural configurations. Thus, 'woman' ceases to be a meaningful identity, except when defined by physiological difference from men, which is mostly associated with the womb, with reproduction and its concomitants. It is thus simpler to forge an identity on reproductive rights, or even violence against women, as these are related to the body. When it comes to mainstream political choices, there are irreducible differences. Since the voice that women need to develop to influence public policy has to be political and have a presence in power structures, these strong differences in their primary political identity impedes solidarity. For women, to forge an identity in terms of ideology appears unviable.

From the time women began to group themselves together as an international and national women's movement around the 1970s, they were forced to confront the implications of 'development'. Development can be defined as any kind of design for the improvement of the well-being of human beings, whether in the North or the South. For the women's movement, the basic approach or argument has been that people on the ground do not just know what they want best, but also know best how to achieve it. They built the 'development house' around two pillars: collective viewpoints and locally designed 'development' programmes. That was the core of women's policy proposals, and became known as the 'bottom-up approach' in engineering national economic progress.

A mass base and ground-level struggles can bring us once again to what we are looking for—influence in the public space. If we want to make a difference, in my view the politics for us is not being visible in the top zone of macro-economics, but to represent the poor in the top zone.

Another issue concerns participation, also seen as mainstreaming. Does effective participation mean sitting at the table of power or separately? The question that haunts those who wish to jump into what is called the 'mainstream', and 'integrate into existing policies', is captured in Hamlet's timeless words, 'To be or not to be?' Translated into the concerns of this paper, the question is, 'Do we join the mainstream or remain apart, contesting its legitimacy and its values?'[88] Trying to integrate oneself within an existing framework has problems. If the nature of public policy arising from the given theories and frameworks of data and analysis are unacceptable to women or to Dalits, then, as Gopal Guru argues, integrating into that setup is surrender. Apart from being flawed in principle, it may lead to undesirable results.[89]

But this abstention from participation has its own negative effects in terms of exclusion. In the language of the feminists, the dilemma is often formulated as 'Do we want a piece of the poisoned cake?'[90] Or put another way, do women want to join the 'polluted stream'?[91]

There are innumerable dilemmas in attempts to 'gender' macro-economic policy. Even as I lay out my arguments, I would like to present my conclusion—that the concept of 'gendering', valuable as it may be in many domains, cannot, when it comes to the domain of development and public policy, work as a way to achieve women's quest for equality.[92]

I would say that gendering as an idea has obstructed our movement because it brings us into an existing macro-economic frame. For example, there is now a desire to 'engender' the 11th Five Year Plan. Many of us have taken up this cause with enthusiasm. We have even shown ourselves to have learned from the experience of trying to gender the previous Five Year Plan, in resisting ghettoisation in the form of a chapter by women for women. There should instead be a way of including women in the design as both subject and object of sectoral planning. We are trying to have a gender perspective inform different sections of the Five Year Plan. We have even conceived the idea of seeing India's major outlays during the 11th Plan directed towards the poor and social development, such as the outlay on the National Rural Employment Guarantee Act, the Development Fund for Backward Areas, and the National Rural Health Mission. We are looking at it as a canvas and thinking out how we can put women's footprints on the canvas. We would like to ensure that the ideas of women brush onto the canvas a life which permeates it throughout.

Today as women ask to be included, there is no clear ideological vision with which they are associated. They are instead often associated with complaints of being excluded or with appeals for money for their economic, political and social security. We are not yet known as a worldwide movement for justice, although our efforts since 9/11 against war did in fact signal a worldwide revolutionary movement.

Looking back, I would say that gendering public policy is a trap. Our involvement in development plans prevents our rethinking the whole idea of development. In the past, our brilliance consisted in drawing on women's experience to challenge prevailing wisdom. Entering into the exercise of gendering this or that item pre-empts that possibility. It is like sleeping with the enemy.

But we would then be left with the problem of exclusion. If you do not participate, the likelihood is that you will be left behind. That is why I value the opportunity for reflection offered to us today within the atmosphere generated by the NBA's protest in Delhi. We can recharge ourselves for the task of building another India, whether we speak of the legal system, the criteria guiding our development choices, or the prevailing perception of people and the environment.

TOWARDS A CONCLUSION: CRY THE BELOVED INDIA, OR 'DESH BACHAO'

'If you are not with us, you are against us.' This is the logic President Bush introduced into the world, a simple either/or that leaves no space for other positions or for debate. This simplistic categorisation has crept into our own political analysis. Harish Khare has used the phrase 'nationalist ethos' to describe an ethos nurtured during the anti-colonial struggle but still widely prevalent in India.[93] He declares that 'the middle classes in India remain wedded to the Nehruvian ideal of total autonomy in the pursuit of science and technology.' I would add that this constituency includes those concerned also with economic policy and foreign policy, among whom I belong.

There are a whole range of people and agencies, who belong to neither the left nor the right and may have no clear politics at all, who are in favour of safeguarding natural resources and livelihoods and the principles of sovereignty and social justice. Those who hold such view-points do not necessarily belong to people's movements but may be academics, civil servants or members of business houses. It is extremely important for those who influence public policy in India—including the media—to see this kind of opinion as a genuine, fact-based, nation-alistic opinion that is held by a very broad range of actors.

There is need to make room for this other space, for opinions that move India away from 'Bush-ism'. Given that this is an energetic and vocal society, one that protests when squeezed, it is not only unjust but dangerous to abandon the established tracks of our economic development. In another 10 years, we will not have with us even the few of us who experienced the excitement of the India of the 1950s and 1960s. With that loss of memory there will disappear an important dissenting voice against what appears to be the unthinking exposure of India and its struggling citizens to the overwhelming power of corporate capital.

In terms of the metaphor of the sky I have been using throughout, this would correspond to the naked forces of the cosmos. And if there continues the present trend of issues becoming so polarised as to shrink the space where difference can be sorted out openly, we will lose the space that defines our ethos as 'argumentative Indians', to use Amartya Sen's idiom. All these factors may lead to civic breakdowns that hamstring our democratic culture. In other words, the democracy that has sustained India would be threatened.

In his inaugural speech at the meeting of Asian parliamentarians to discuss population and development, Lok Sabha Speaker Somnath Chatterjee observed that the forces driving the new world order 'must recognise that there is no easy solution. Each country has to develop its own approach based on its native realities, historical factors and social mores.'[94]

Decades ago, in the 1970s, Thandike Mkandiwe (an eminent African economist who now heads UNRISD) described Africa's predicament in the throes of what was then called structural adjustment. He said that capital markets, including lending agencies like IMF and World Bank, would put pressure on the state to engage in market-driven economic policy as well as to improve what we call 'governance'. This led to the state assuming disproportionate power, pushing African countries from a semblance of democracy towards fascism.

We can see this happening in India today. While on the one hand there is the rhetoric of liberalisation, of building competitive markets both internal and external, the state has become the major arbitrator of matters affecting the private sector. Without the state today, no corporate, national or multinational can take a step. State policy determines positions regarding the capital market, currency, land allocation, preferences to be given to some sectors over others or to large over small sectors. Therefore it is understandable that everyone including the children of wealthy business families would like to join politics, as it is through the state that they can access the benefits of the liberal economy.

These policies were first adopted in Africa, then in Latin America. They led to widespread corruption in politics, to disparities, and finally to a breakdown of civic order. Street battles were succeeded by dictatorial regimes, which gave way before revolution, which was followed by revival by way of the return of a semi-socialist state. This cycle has been enacted in Brazil, Chile and Venezuela.

These examples have lessons for India which boasts of being a knowledge-driven country, a thoughtful country. Yet with her eyes wide open, India is entering the same historical process that led to convulsions in neighbouring continents. The senior economists who currently hold power in the government are aware of the international theatre and aware of the experience of other countries. Does it not seem treacherous to use the hope of prosperity to force into such tracks India, which is that much more vulnerable because of its huge population, its extraordinary diversity, its many scars through history and the great proportion of the poor?

Many have said that this is the most culturally democratic country, accommodating, tolerant of pluralism, capable of producing everything under the sun, and with a market which can absorb its own entire supply of goods and services. The Indian economy can accommodate the production and consumption cycle within itself if it wished, and so give everyone at least enough food and livelihood before thinking of other lands. However, even if a more modern system of production, trade and consumption had been possible, it would seem bizarre to invite man-made disaster, the likelihood of which is so tangible and proximate. It is the same tangible inequality that has led to civic and economic breakdown in many Latin American countries.

Unrest and violence is fermenting in Karnataka, pinnacle of the IT industry. Scams on land use are proliferating. Land was obtained from the three-month-old H. D. Kumaraswamy government by Gandhi City for Advanced R&D Ltd, under the pretence of being concerned with IT. One of the company's directors is M. S. Balaji, a student's union leader from the Bharatiya Janata Party. Land was received by another little-known company, Sapphire Infrastructure Developers, promoted by the well-known contractor Reddy Veeranna, who has several contracts to his credit including those for the Krishna Bhagya Jala Nigam. The two companies together are now in possession of 2,200 acres of land.[95]

The recent violence and riots in Bangalore after the death of the matinee idol Dr Raj Kumar have been attributed to the increasingly visible disparities in the city. Those who have prospered from the IT industry include young people with large disposable incomes, working in banks and multi-storey business houses through whose glass windows a whole range of consumer goods and fashions are visible to those outside—who might be called the 'indigenous' population, less privileged, educated only up to matriculation, and unemployed. Both Prof. Ananthamurthy and one of the senior executives of Infosys saw the riots as a product of sharp inequalities and their effects on the psyche. The riots expressed the frustration and also the anger of the poor.

The increase in Naxalism in parts of the country is evidence of the unwillingness of the young people in these areas to accept the oppression and exclusion they are experiencing. As confirmed by the council of ministers looking at Naxalism, it is a phenomenon concentrated in tribal areas. In its characteristically uneven-handed way, the government wants to protect itself from the increasing violence of the Naxalites and wants, on the other hand, to push land now occupied by tribal people into the hands of corporates.

In my opinion, it is not too late to withdraw from such a 'program'—I say 'program' deliberately, as this kind of devastation of densely populated areas of India through a vision of development in terms of mega projects, mega roads, capital inducement and FDI inducement will destroy these populations and their sense of self and hope. This will turn them from tolerant, beautiful citizens into the terrorists we have seen in so many regions.

Recently we have heard that if the height of the Sardar Sarovar Dam is raised by another 10 metres, it will lead to the submergence of land occupied by 35,000 families, who will have to move out of the Narmada Valley. But this is only one example. There are many other areas in India where there has been massive displacement from existing livelihood spaces. According to the mid-term appraisal of the Planning Commission in 2000, 25 million people, mainly tribals, have been displaced. Half of them have not been rehabilitated—they have in fact been pauperised. Just a few days ago, the police opened fire on fisherfolk on the Vizag coast, to protect the transfer of a government yard on the coastline to a private company. Bullets summoned in aid of development.

I saw this in Brazil, at the public hearing organised by the World Commission on Dams.[96] A whole clan of forest dwellers was shot dead when they objected to the construction of a dam—and Brazil had plans to build another 50 in their valleys and forests.

The recent public dialogue initiated by the protest of the NBA has raised the consciousness of a wide range of people in India. They demand that the process of development respect the aim of the Indian Constitution to provide justice to its citizens, that it be transparent and democratic and work to remove poverty. It has made people question the process through which such decisions are taken, as well as the extraordinary neglect of the knowledge pouring out not just from the NBA and the extensive data India has on the value of small water-harvesting projects, but from the government's own reviews. This includes, for example, the knowledge of the adverse impact of the Bhakra Dam and the salination of some of the fields it was meant to irrigate.

India is rich in its experience of water management, whether through check dams, ponds or lakes. It has developed incredible water harvesting and water management techniques that are locally created, locally owned and locally used. There is also a persuasive argument that people make optimum use of what is locally developed and owned, whereas they waste what comes through no effort of their own.

As we have marched for parliamentary quotas or for the famous Mathura case, as we have managed to get passed bills on domestic violence and on rape, we need now to engage with the politics of development. We also need to battle with increased vigour the trends towards inequality. We have to restore a sky that protects our people and does not collapse on them.

I would like to end with a request for a discussion of some ideas that strike me as possible bases on which the women's movement can rebuild its political presence and make the best use of its ability to build concepts from ground-level realities and to work together despite differences. While there may be other priorities in each of your minds, I am putting down some of those that concern me in the domains of action and theory.

Action

Of primary importance is worker protection and preventing the dismantling of trade unionism. In an era of corporatisation, the only countervailing power available belongs to those who work for the corporate sector or even the state. The larger and stronger their organisation, the greater their capacity to resist. Many of us may feel that trade unions have often been irresponsible as regards what are called the needs of the public when public services break down, or feel that issues related to remuneration are secondary when there are so many without even the basis for remuneration. But such criticisms should not distract us. We have to strengthen the institution as an institution and prevent any erosion of its power. This is going to be extremely difficult, given that the trend is for 'flexi-labour', something even some workers have learned to find convenient (certainly workers in the higher levels of employment prefer it). However difficult, I believe that women must stand solidly behind worker organisations.

We have before us much scope to build worker organisations from below. The NREGA scheme is going to generate millions of wage labourers, who will be located in areas analogous to the shop floor, namely the gram panchayat. A substantial proportion will be women workers. It is necessary that they organise into co-operatives and associations, initially to make sure that the package arrives as promised, that their wages are paid and the laws related to compensation and facilities such as water and crèches are adhered to. One can then build up a massive federation of NREGA workers across the nation, within which women's unions may lead, which would be the revolutionary force that bears upon current economic and political ideologies.

The second task is unhesitating resistance to the entry of FDI in retail trade and in projects of 'linking the farmer to the supermarket'. We need to understand the implications of, and argue against, free currency convertibility. Here is an area for those gathered here to carry out a satyagraha, a 'fistful of salt' for the women's movement today.

Third, I believe that however anti-national it appears, we need to address the issue of militarisation. Various protocols India has been signing—with South Africa, Russia and Israel—concern largely defence items. These deals are necessarily bound up in secrecy. The militarisation of international relations has led to a loss of transparency that betrays democratic principles. We are definitely giving way on this front. And it is one of the major causes of the increase in the power of the state, of corruption and the deflection of finances from investment in basic amenities.

Thought

Feminists have marshalled examples from every discipline, including theology, of the hierarchies embedded in theory and language, and it is crucial that this critique leads to a rearrangement of hierarchies. It should also be made available as a body of knowledge to women engaged in ground-level struggles or public action. It would give them both the confidence that their own critique of the injustice of the system is legitimate, besides equipping them with the new language and theories for their struggle. The reconstruction of theory can be a unifying agenda for women, an umbrella of thought.

Further, what is needed now and can be attained if women put their minds together, is establishing the brilliant struggles of women as a body of knowledge, chiselled into theory, which challenges the dominant ideas of national advancement. We cannot minimise the importance of gaining acceptance for theory grounded in experience. This exercise should lead to a book which would be as profound and as illuminating and have as powerful an impact as, for example, Marx's *Das Kapital* or Adam Smith's *Wealth of Nations*, two classics of economic thought whose enduring influence has in many ways led to the circumscription of thought.

NOTES

1 'There was a massive support from people from all walks of life, including Sharad Yadav, Surendra Mohan, Arundhati Roy, Vandana Shiva, Rajinder Singh, Prabhash Joshi, B. D. Sharma, Abani Roy, Mohini Giri, Primila Loomba, Swami Agnivesh, B. N. Yughandar, Mungekar, Vimal Thorat and Raj Babbar.' Gargi Parsai, 'Medha Won't Relent Despite Soz' Plea', *Hindu*, 5 April 2006, http://www.thehindu.com/todays-paper/Medha-wont-relent-despite-Sozs-plea/article15734220.ece (accessed 16 October 2017). 'DU, JNU, Jamia students, even school students with lemon and water, academics, artists, women's groups, filmmakers are streaming in, even while relay fasts, road blocks and street protests are being held across India.' Amit Sengupta, 'Anatomy of a Satyagraha', *Tehelka*, 17 April 2006. This paper could not have been written as well as completed on time without the untiring help of M. V. Jagadeesh and Perce Bloomer.

2 See for example, Louis Emmerij, 'Development Thinking, Globalization and Cultural Diversity', paper prepared for the North–South Round Table 'Imperative of Tolerance and Justice in a Globalised World', Cairo, 27–28 November 2002; John Toye, *Dilemmas of Development* (Oxford: Blackwell, 1993); Lant Pritchett and Michael Woolcock, 'Solutions When the Solution Is the Problem: Arraying the Disarray in Development', *World Development*, vol. 32, no. 2 (2004), pp. 191–212; Ben Fine, 'Globalisation and Development: The Imperative of Political Economy', paper presented at the conference 'Towards a New Political Economy of Development: Globalisation and Governance', Sheffield, July 2002; and Susan Moller Okin, 'Things That Don't Count', mimeo, 2001.

3 Amartya Sen, *Identity and Violence: The Illusion of Destiny* (New Delhi: Penguin, 2006).

4 Arundhati Roy, 'Democracy: Who's She When She's at Home?', *Outlook*, 6 May 2002.

5 World Bank, *World Development Report 2005: A Better Investment Climate for Everyone* (Washington, D.C.: World Bank, 2005). See also Heather Stewart, 'Why Equality Is the Best Policy', *Hindu*, 26 September 2005.

6 The poverty line was set at $1 in 1985. By 1993 it had risen to $1.08, due to inflation, but it is still referred to as the '$1/day line'. The data in this paragraph draws from Shaohua Chen and Martin Ravallion, 'How Did the World's Poorest Fare in the 1990s?', Development Research Group, World Bank, 2000, p. 6; and Shahid Yusuf and Joseph Stiglitz, 'Development Issues: Settled and Open', in Gerald Meier and Joseph Stiglitz (eds), *Frontiers of Development Economics: The Future in Perspective* (New York: Oxford University Press, 2001), pp. 227–68; see pp. 228 and 232.

7 William Easterly, 'The Lost Decades: Developing Countries' Stagnation in spite of Policy Reform, 1950–1999', World Bank, Washington, D.C., 2000, p. 7.

8 Ravi Kanbur and Lyn Squire, 'The Evolution of Thinking about Poverty: Exploring the Interactions', in Meier and Stiglitz, *Frontiers of Development Economics*, pp. 183–226; see p. 193.

9 Abhijit Sen and Himanshu, 'Poverty and Inequality in India: Getting Closer to the Truth', *Economic & Political Weekly*, vol. 39, no. 38 (2004), pp. 4247–63.

10 P. Sainath, numerous articles in *Hindu* between 2003 and 2006.

11 Devaki Jain, 'A View from the South: A Story of Intersections', in Arvonne S. Fraser and Irene Tinker (eds), *Developing Power: How Women Transformed International Development* (New York: Feminist Press, 2004), pp. 128–37.

12 South Commission, *The Challenge to the South*.

13 Jain, *Women, Development and the UN*.

14 I refer to the remarks of Peter Niggli at the international conference 'Gender Apartheid as a Hindrance to Development', convened by Alliance Sud (the Swiss Alliance of Development Organisations) and the Swiss Agency for Development and Cooperation, Berne, 15 November 2005; and to Desmond Tutu's J. R. D. Tata Memorial Lecture at Bangalore, 12 December 2005.

15 Devaki Jain, 'Minds, Not Bodies: Expanding the Notion of Gender in Development', Bradford Morse Memorial Lecture, Opening Plenary at the Fourth World Conference on Women, Beijing, September 1995; reproduced as chapter 4 in Devaki Jain, *Journey of a Southern Feminist*, vol. 1 (New Delhi: Sage/Yoda, 2018). The chart of women's collective action is reproduced as an appendix in chapter 3, 'The Leadership Gap', in Jain, *Journey of a Southern Feminist*, vol. 1.

16 Devaki Jain, 'Removing Discrimination and Poverty: The Importance of Exemplars', Convocation Address, University of Tirunelveli, October 1995.

17 Virginia Woolf, *A Room of One's Own* (New York: Fountain Press, and London: Hogarth Press, 1929).

18 See Kamaladevi Chattopadhayay, *Indian Women's Battle for Freedom* (New Delhi: Abhinav Publications, 1983); Radha Kumar, *The History of Doing: An Illustrated Account of Movements for Women's Rights and Feminism in India, 1800–1990* (London: Verso Books, 1993); and Aparna Basu and Bharati Ray, *Women's Struggle: A History of the All India Women's Conference, 1927–2002* (New Delhi: Manohar Books, 2003).

19 Meghnad Desai, *Development and Nationhood: Essays in the Political Economy of South Asia* (New Delhi: Oxford University Press, 2004).

20 Devaki Jain, 'What Does It Take to Become a Citizen? Some Neglected Collective Identities in Building "Nation"', presented at the seminar 'Democracy, Communalism, Secularism and the Dilemmas of Indian Nationhood', New Delhi, January 2005.

21 Sen, *Identity and Violence*.

22 Mernissi, 'Femininity as Subversion'; Amoah, 'Women, Witches and Social Change in Ghana'.

23 Sandra Harding (ed.), *Feminism and Methodology* (Bloomington: Indiana University Press, 1987), p. 6.

24 Sandra Harding, *Is Science Multicultural? Postcolonialism, Feminisms and Epistemologies* (Bloomington: Indiana University Press, 1998), pp. 39–54.

25 Ann Tickner, 'On the Frontlines or Sidelines of Knowledge and Power? Feminist Practices of Responsible Scholarship', Presidential Address at the Annual Meeting of the International Studies Association, San Diego, 23 March 2006.

26 Wilma Mankiller, Gwendolyn Mink, Marysa Navarro, Barbara Smith and Gloria Steinem (eds), *The Reader's Companion to U.S. Women's History* (Boston and New York: Houghton Mifflin, 1998), p. xxi.

27 William Connolly, 'Democracy and Territory', in Marjorie Ringrose and Adam J. Lerner (eds), *Reimagining the Nation* (Buckingham: Open University Press, 1993), pp. 49–75; see p. 61.

28 Christine Sylvester, 'Homeless in International Relations? Women's Place in Canonical Texts and in Feminist Reimaginings', in Anne Phillips (ed.), *Feminism and Politics* (Oxford: Oxford University Press, 1998), pp. 44–66.

29 Jane L. Parpart, M. Patricia Connelly and V. Eudine Barriteau, *Theoretical Perspectives on Gender and Development* (Ottawa: International Development Research Centre Canada, 2000); and Devaki Jain, 'Development Theory and Practice: Insights Emerging from Women's Experience', *Economic & Political Weekly*, vol. 25, no. 27 (1990), pp. 1445–54.

30 Yasuko Muramatsu, 'Gender and Economics in Japan: Japanese Women's Position in Economics and Activities of Japan Association for Feminist Economics to Advance Gender Perspective', paper presented at the Sixth Science Council of Asia Workshop, 'A Comparative Study of the Research Conditions of Women Scientists and the Present State of Women's/Gender Studies in Asian Countries: Towards Human Centered Sustainable Development', New Delhi, 17 April 2006.

31 Hazel Henderson, *Creating Alternative Futures: The End of Economics* (Connecticut: Kumarian Press Books for a World That Works, 1996). See also Devaki Jain, 'The Leadership Gap: Challenge to Feminists', Presidential Address, Indian Association of Women's Studies Conference, Mysore, 1993; and Jain, 'Development as if Women Mattered'.

32 Devaki Jain, 'Power through the Looking Glass of Feminism', in Kathy Davis, Monique Leijenaar and Jantine Oldersma (eds), *The Gender of Power* (Leiden: Vena, 1987) (republished in *Vocabulary of Women's Politics* (New Delhi: Friedrich Ebert Stiftung, 2001).

33 Stevi Jackson and Jackie Jones, 'Thinking for Ourselves: An Introduction to Feminist Theorising', in Stevi Jackson and Jackie Jones (eds), *Contemporary Feminist Theory* (Edinburgh: Edinburgh University Press, 1998), p. 1.

34 Gerda Lerner, *The Creation of Feminist Consciousness: From the Middle Ages to Eighteen-Seventy* (Oxford: Oxford University Press, 1993), p. 12.

35 Allan G. Johnson, *The Gender Knot* (Philadelphia: Temple University Press, 1997).

36 Jain and Chand, 'Report on Time Allocation Study'.

37 Devaki Jain, 'Are Women a Separate Issue?', *Populi*, vol. 5, no. 1 (November 1978), pp. 7–15; see p. 9.

38 Jain et al., *Women's Quest for Power*.

39 Devaki Jain and Mukul Mukherjee, 'Women and Their Households: The Relevance of Men and Macro Policies—An Indian Perspective', paper prepared for the first ISST study on 'Indian Female Households', ILO, 1984.

40 UNDP, *Human Development Report 1995*.

41 Devaki Jain, 'Interrogating Disciplines/Disciplining Gender: Towards a History of Women's Studies in India', 20th Anniversary Seminar, Centre for Women's Development Studies, New Delhi, 19–22 February 2001; Jain, 'Development Theory and Practice'.

42 Devaki Jain, 'Advances in Feminist Theory: An Indian Perspective', paper presented at the International Sociological Association Conference, New Delhi, August 1986.

43 Jain, 'Indian Women Today and Tomorrow'.

44 Seiro Ito, 'A Survey of Recent Economics Literature on Child Labor', in Seiro Ito (ed.), *Agricultural Production, Household Behaviour and Child Labour in Andhra Pradesh* (Chiba: Institute of Developing Economies, Japan External Trade Organization, 2005).

45 ISST, *ISST 25: Reflections* (New Delhi: Institute of Social Studies Trust, 2005).

46 Jain, 'Development Theory and Practice'.

47 Devaki Jain, 'Challenges and Opportunities: Liberia Looks Forward', draft of a diagnostic analysis to initiate a situational analysis, June 1999.

48 Jain, *Women's Quest for Power*.

49 See UNICEF, 'Income Generating Activities for Women: Some Case Studies', 1980.

50 Devaki Jain, 'Through the Looking Glass of Poverty', paper presented at New Hall, Cambridge, 19 October 2001.

51 Sen, *Development as Freedom*.

52 Devaki Jain, 'Women's Work and Rights: An Overview', paper prepared for the National Conference on 'Engendering Macroeconomics and Macroeconomic Policies', Centre for Women's Studies, Department of Economics, Mumbai University, 29–30 September 2005.

53 Marilyn Carr and Marty Chen, *Globalization and the Informal Economy: How Global Trade and Investment Impact on the Working Poor* (Geneva: ILO, 2002).

54 See the publications of the Center for the Study of the Gift Economy, Austin, Texas.

55 Marilyn Waring, *If Women Counted: A New Feminist Economics* (San Francisco: Harper & Row) (first published in New Zealand as *Counting for Nothing: What Men Value and What Women are Worth* [Wellington: Allen & Unwin, 1988]).

56 Quoted in Ron Susskind, 'Without a Doubt', *New York Times Magazine*, 17 October 2004.

57 Quoted in Zillah Eisenstein, 'What's in a Name? Seeing Feminism, Universalism, and Modernity', *Wagadu*, vol. 1, no. 1 (Spring 2004), p. 188.

58 Edward Said, *Representations of the Intellectual: The 1993 Reith Lectures* (New York: Vintage, 1996).

59 Shekhar Gupta, 'Welcome to Moscowashington: After September 11, the Big Boys Are Joining Hands, How Do We Play Ours?', *New Indian Express*, 19 January 2002.

60 Devaki Jain, 'For Whom the Bell Tolls: Democracy and Development in South Asia', *Cambridge Review of International Affairs*, vol. 15, no. 2 (2002), pp. 299–310.

61 See Jain, *Women, Development and the UN*.

62 Devaki Jain, 'The Value of the Particular to the General', paper presented at the conference 'South Asia and the United Nations', United Nations University, Tokyo, 26 May 2002; Devaki Jain, 'Globalism and Localism: Negotiating Feminist Space', paper presented at the seminar 'Rethinking Gender, Democracy and Development: Is Decentralisation a Tool for Local Effective Political Voice?', Ferrara University and Modena University, Italy, 20–22 May 2002 (reproduced as chapter 7 in Devaki Jain, *Journey of a Southern Feminist*, vol. 1 [New Delhi: Sage/Yoda, 2018]).

63 Devaki Jain, 'The Empire Strikes Back: A Report on the Asian Social Forum, Hyderabad, 2–3 Jan 2003', *Economic & Political Weekly*, vol. 38, no. 1 (2003), pp. 99–101, later published in Jai Sen et al. (eds), *Challenging Empires* (New Delhi: Vivek Foundation, 2004), pp. 289–92; Arundhati Roy, 'Confronting Empire', Porto Alegre, Brazil, 27 January 2003, published in Sen et al., *Challenging Empires*.

64 Tickner, 'On the Frontlines or Sidelines of Knowledge and Power?'

65 Ronald Steel claims that there is widespread acceptance of the idea that the US is an empire, defined not in terms of formal acquisition of territory, as was the case with earlier European empires, but in terms of economic and political control. He traces this imperial legacy back to the early days of American history and claims that it became global after 1945. See Ronald Steel, 'Totem and Taboo', *Nation*, vol. 279, no. 8 (2004).

66 These figures were given out by the International Institute for Strategic Studies and by the Stockholm Institute for Peace Research in 2005. The report of the International Institute for Strategic Studies put supplementary defence-related spending at $346 billion since the attacks of September 11, 2001. The Stockholm Institute for Peace Research broke down supplementary spending on the war on terrorism by year: in the fiscal year 2001, it was $20 billion; in 2002, $44 billion; in 2003, $88 billion; in 2004, $87 billion; in 2005, $107 billion.

67 In a recent article, neo-conservative Francis Fukuyama writes that the second Bush administration has been distancing itself from the policies articulated in the Strategy and is in the process of rewriting it. He terms the neo-conservative foreign policy described in the Strategy as 'benevolent hegemony', but admits that neo-conservatism has become associated with coercive regime change, unilateralism and American hegemony, and, therefore, is unacceptable to

and unpopular in much of the rest of the world. He claims that he himself can no longer support neo-conservatism. See Francis Fukuyama, 'After Neoconservatism', *New York Times*, 19 February 2006. Since Fukuyama's article appeared, the new National Security Strategy has been released. Its military component remains largely unchanged.

68 Steel, 'Totem and Taboo'.

69 Fine, 'Globalisation and Development'.

70 See 'Introduction' in Shahra Razavi (ed.), *Shifting Burdens: Gender and Agrarian Change under Neoliberalism* (Bloomfield, CT: Kumarian Press, 2002).

71 Diane Elson (ed.), *Male Bias in Macro-economics*;(Manchester: Manchester University Press, 1991).

72 Devaki Jain, 'Are We Knowledge Proof? Development as Waste', Lovraj Kumar Memorial Lecture, New Delhi, 26 September 2003, reproduced as chapter 8 in the present volume.

73 UNIFEM, *Progress of the World's Women 2005: Women, Work and Poverty* (New York: UNIFEM, 2005).

74 Marty Chen, 'Women and the Informal Sector: Realities, Statistics and Policies', paper presented at the Economic Policy Forum, International Center for Research on Women, Washington, D.C., 15 March 1996, quoted in 'Rural Producers: Trends, Issues and Challenges for Socio-Economic Development', in Food and Agriculture Organization, *Filling the Data Gap: Gender-Sensitive Statistics for Agricultural Development* (Rome: Food and Agriculture Organization, 1999), http://www.fao.org/docrep/X2785e/X2785e00.htm (accessed 22 February 2018). See also Rekha Mehra and Sarah Gammage, 'Trends, Countertrends and Gaps in Women's Employment', *World Development*, vol. 27, no. 3 (1999), pp. 533–50.

75 Valerie Kozel and Barbara Parker, 'A Profile and Diagnostic of the Poverty in Uttar Pradesh', paper presented at the Poverty Monitoring and Evaluation Workshop, Planning Commission of India and the World Bank, New Delhi, 11 January 2002.

76 See Reema Nanavaty, 'Women Agriculture Workers', *Seminar*, no. 531 (November 2003), http://www.india-seminar.com/2003/531/531%20reema%20nanavaty.htm (accessed 22 February 2018).

77 Devaki Jain, 'Enabling Poverty and Inequality Reduction in South Asia', UNFPA Retreat, New York, 30 September–2 October 2002.

78 Elissa Braunstein, 'Foreign Direct Investment, Development and Gender Equity: A Review of Research and Policy', Occasional Paper 12, UNRISD, January 2006.

79 A. T. Kearney, '2005 Global Retail Development Index: An Annual Study of Retail Investment', *Financial Express*, 9 July 2005.

80 George W. Bush, in a speech at Purana Qila, New Delhi, 1 March 2006.

81 Keiko Yamanaka and Nicola Piper, 'Feminized Migration in East and Southeast Asia: Polices, Actions and Empowerment', UNRISD Occasional Paper 11, December 2005.

82 Ibid.

83 UN, 'Gender, Migration and Remittances', report of the UN International Research and Training Institute for the Advancement of Women (INSTRAW), 2004. See also UNIFEM, 'Migration Has Women's Face: Women Are Now Half the Migrant Workers in Asia', Migration Posters Series.

84 UNIFEM, *Progress of the World's Women 2005*.

85 Junya Lek Yimprasert, 'Trade-Led Growth with Regionalism and Bilateralism: The Implications for Women's Decent Work', Opening Plenary, International Forum for Women's Rights in Development, convened by the Association for Women's Rights in Development, Bangkok, 27–30 October 2005.

86 Gunnar Myrdal, *Asian Drama: An Inquiry into the Poverty of Nations* (New York: Pantheon Publications, 1968), 3 vols.

87 Devaki Jain, 'Women's Rights between the UN Human Rights Regime and Free Trade Agreements', International Conference on 'Globalising Women's Rights: Confronting Unequal Development between the UN Rights Framework and WTO Trade Agreements', Bonn, 19–22 May 2004.

88 For an overview of the promises and threats of gender mainstreaming today, see Susanna George, 'Mainstreaming Gender as a Women's Movement Strategy: A Critique from a Reluctant Gender Advocate'; Sunila Abeysekara and Marilee Karl, 'Gender Mainstreaming: An Obsolete Concept? A Conversation between Two Longtime Feminist Activists'; and Agnes Atia Apusigah, 'Gender Mainstreaming: The Ghana Poverty Reduction Strategy, or Is It?', in *Women in Action 2004-2: Examining Feminist and Social Movements* (Manila: ISIS International, 2004).

89 Guru, 'How Egalitarian Are the Social Sciences in India?'

90 Devaki Jain, 'The Role of People's Movement in Economics and Social Transformation', paper presented at the Opening Plenary on 'Economic and Social Development', International Conference on 'The Role of NGOs in the 21st Century: Inspire, Empower, Act', Seoul, 10–16 October 1999.

91 Bella Abzug, 'Women Will Change the Nature of Power', Bradford Morse Memorial Lecture, Opening Plenary, United Nations Fourth World Conference on Women, Beijing, 5 September 1995.

92 Devaki Jain, 'To Be or Not to Be? The Location of Women in Public Policy', in Gopal K. Kadekodi, S. M. Ravi Kanbur and Vijayendra Rao (eds), *Development in Karnataka: Challenges of Governance, Equity and Empowerment* (New Delhi: Academic Foundation, 2008), pp. 107–24. Reproduced as chapter 10 in Devaki Jain, *Journey of a Southern Feminist*, vol. 1 (New Delhi: SAGE/Yoda, 2018).

93 See Harish Khare, 'Selling the United States of America in India', *Hindu*, 21 July 2005.

94 See *Hindu*, 'Somnath: Factor Population in Development Strategies', 24 April 2006, p. 13.

95 *New Indian Express*, 'Contractors Pocket Land in the Name of IT', 24 April 2006, p. 3.

96 World Commission on Dams, *Dams and Development: A New Framework for Development* (London: Earthscan Publications, 2000).

Chapter 11

Growth, Poverty and Inequality
The Linkages and Relevance of Macro-economic Policies

For two decades, I had been arguing that the UN's goal of gender equality was a non-starter, that the macro-economic system, the growth theories, the methods by which poverty was being eradicated were flawed, and that to ask for gender equality from a flawed system was both misleading and perhaps unethical. In my paper, I referred to the Indian ground-level experience with local self-government and other such grounded measures which foreground the question of what kind of macro change is required.

In my presentation I will basically argue:

- That poverty, whether it is of men or of women, cannot be reduced or eradicated, unless the very theories of growth are undermined or redone.

- Thus, ideas which are now the new mantra, such as 'inclusive growth' as elaborated currently (by the World Bank, UNDP, national leaders and economists), will not heal the pain of poverty. Inclusion needs to be reconceptualised as the 'agency' of the excluded, the think side of action.

- Further, that poverty and inequality are inextricably linked, and without attention to inequality, which is now a ferocious presence in our countries, poverty cannot be attacked.

- And that gender inequality is linked to overall inequality, so we need to address the overall presence of and increase in inequality when we intend to remove gender inequality and poverty.[1]

- That in reorienting growth into an engine of poverty removal, we need to create new indicators of poverty and of development vision.
- That macro-economic policies, to be just, need to be woven into institutional arrangements.

Thus, there needs to be serious rethinking on how we go about poverty eradication and women's empowerment.[2]

I will use the current Indian experience to support my argument, presenting the macro picture of the dilemmas India is facing as a 'success story' in economic growth, then following it up with what you would call a women's 'best practice' on the ground, called 'Women Advise Fiscal Policy', which points to the link between political and economic governance. This practice could lead to an alternative paradigm, linking macro-economics to institutional arrangements for democratic decision making.

THE PROBLEMATIQUE OF THE INDIAN EXPERIENCE

Everyone has heard of the miraculous appearance of India, within the last five years, as a leading economic power, now racing next to China, something that was not so tangible even about six years ago, though India set out on the road to liberalisation, euphemistically called 'economic reform', with the budget of 1993. The real GDP in 2004 was 10.3 times what it was in 1978, and in the post-liberalisation period the average annual growth rate of the GDP has been around 6.2 per cent. Its implications, as in many other countries, have included a shift in the share of GDP from agriculture to services; a shift in labour absorption and increase in the rate of joblessness; a third impact has been on inequality; and a fourth impact, which is emerging in frightening proportions, is violent conflicts.

Shift in the Share of GDP from Agriculture to Services

Figure 11.1 describes the shift away from agriculture and towards services in terms of contribution to GDP. This is a global trend, and many explanations are floating around on why this is taking place. My own

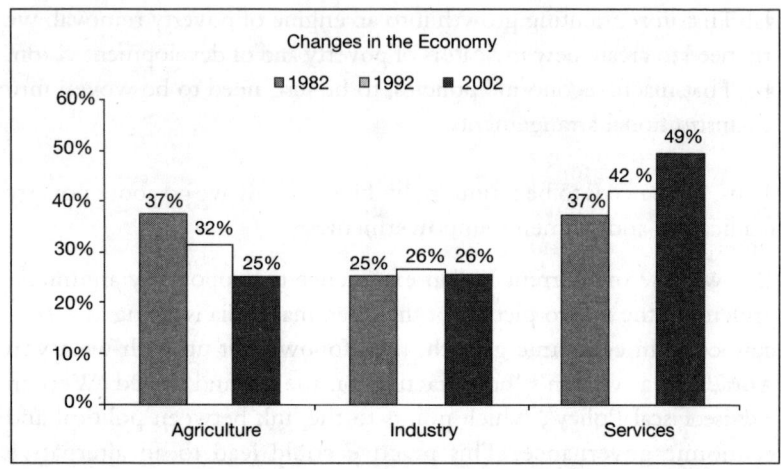

Figure 11.1: *Changes in the economy*
Source: World Bank and India Infoline.

hunch is that as inequality increases, the better-off sections are seeking more urban services, including domestic workers, the entertainment industry and health services.

Rate of Joblessness

After 10 years of these reforms (1991–2001), the Indian Planning Commission admits that the employment-generating capacity of the economy and especially the organised sector vis-à-vis GDP growth is declining fast over time (1983 to 2000), in spite of the fact that during the same period GDP growth accelerated from 5.2 to 6.7 per cent per annum. There has been an even more significant decline in labour intensity: employment elasticity to value added has declined from 0.52 to 0.16.[3] At the end of November 1999, there were more than 4.1 crore registered job seekers compared to nearly 3.92 crore at the end of 1997–98.[4]

According to NSSO data during 1995–96,[5] 1.8 per cent of rural men, 0.9 per cent rural women, 4 per cent urban men and 3.6 per cent urban women in the labour force returned their status as 'usually unemployed'. With nearly 8 million new entrants every year, the labour force at present may well be around 400 million. According to the latest NSSO data for 1998,[6] the usual-status unemployment rate has gone up to 2.49 per cent of the labour force, which is the highest ever reported so far except for the year 1987.

As for 'employment' in the unorganised sector, it is mainly own-account, decentralised, rural or small town based. The growth rate of enterprises (numbering 237.82 lakh)[7] during 1990–98 declined from 2.264 to 2.23 per cent, and the growth rate of employment (at 650.45 lakh) in these enterprises during 1990–98 came down from the 1980s rate of 2.68 per cent to a mere 1.30 per cent.[8] The contagion of low employment growth in the organised sector has spread to the unor-ganised sector as well.

Compared to the nearly 30 per cent share of wages in industrial value added in 1988–89, according to the *Annual Survey of Industries* data, in the year 1997–98 the share of wages came down to as low as 20.24 per cent. In China and India, the two largest developing coun-tries, the sharp fall in the employment intensity of growth has been a problem. This is due largely to a sharp, sudden shift away from labour-intensive economic activities towards capital-intensive ones.[9]

Most Asian countries experienced inadequate employment growth, and the problem has become worse in recent years. 'This has been a major factor in weakening the impact of economic growth on the earnings of the poor and in making growth less poverty alleviating than it might have been.'[10]

For women, agricultural work, informal work, landlessness and poverty mesh into a connected web, the sheer magnitude of which is apparent in the following statistical profile (based on the 2001 census):

- There are 107.5 lakh agriculture workers in India.
- Of all agriculture workers, 99.4 per cent work in the informal sector.
- 64 per cent of the total informal sector workforce depends on agriculture.
- 38 per cent of all agriculture workers are women.
- More than 90 per cent of the rural poor engage in agriculture.

- Although women constitute two-thirds of the agriculture work-force, they own less than one-tenth of agriculture land.

Growing Inequality

The globalisation process is premised on creating winners and losers, and thus leads to greater inequality. The recent study by the World Institute for Development Economics Research of the United Nations University (UNU-WIDER) on the world distribution of household wealth takes wealth (rather than mere income) as the parameter, and finds resounding evidence that the distribution of wealth is highly concentrated—'in fact, much more concentrated than the world distribution of income'.[11] It also states in unequivocal terms that 'corporate globalisation has been marked by greatly increased disparities, both within countries and between countries.'[12]

The gender dimension further complicates this—women most often do not share in the wealth of men, even within the same household or family.[13] Therefore, the gender distribution of wealth matters. The deep, widespread, asymmetrical gender relationships lead women to experience greater inequality than men, and similarly not only are more women poor, but their experience of poverty is also markedly different.

Within India, the sharp and appalling rise in inequality is evident in the fact that while until 1993–94, the all-India Gini coefficient of per capita consumption expenditure was fairly stable, it has shown a marked increase since then (Figure 11.2). The magnitude and rate of change of inequalities is quite substantial as very sharp contrasts are evident between the rural sectors of the slow-growing states and the urban sectors of the fast-growing states.[14]

Multiple inequalities lock in income levels of the poor and disadvantaged and of populations in backward areas, and the trickle-down effects of growth are limited to the margins of the high-growing enclaves and urban conglomerations.[15]

The rise in inequality appears to be the result of three factors: (a) a shift in earnings from labour to capital income; (b) the rapid growth of the services sector—particularly the FIRE sector (finance, insurance

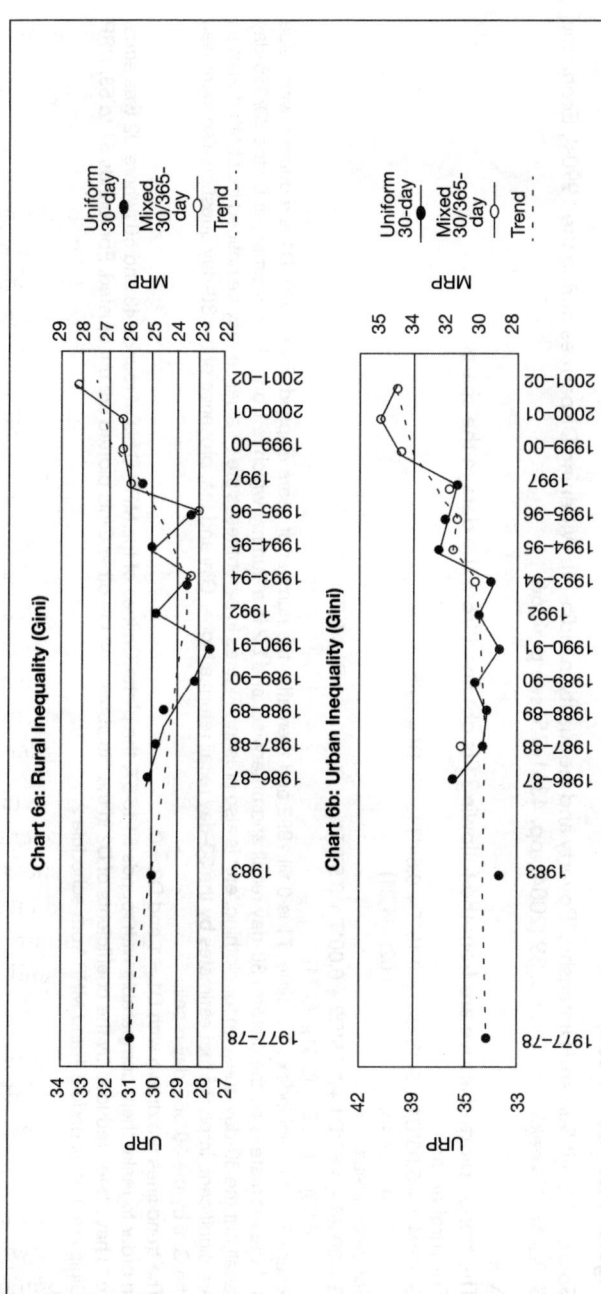

Figure 11.2 *Rural and urban inequality*

Figure 11.2 (Continued)

Source: Abhijit Sen and Himanshu, 'Poverty and Inequality in India—II: Widening Disparities during the 1990s', *Economic & Political Weekly*, vol. 39, no. 39 (2004), pp. 4361–75; see p. 4366.

Notes

The trends plotted above are from the following fits obtained from the data in the charts:

For rural areas:

$G = 394.7 + 5.05*D1 + 2.33*D2 - 0.19*T + 0.64*T1$: $R^2 = 0.85$

    (7.14)   (2.45)   (3.02) (4.21)

For urban areas:

$G = 29.26 + 4.67*D1 + 1.58*D2 + 0.00*T + 0.57*T1$: $R^2 = 0.79$

    (6.50)   (1.67)   (0.01) (3.71)

where G is the Gini index . T is time. T1 is 0 till 1992 and thereafter the number of years elapsed since 1992. D1 is a dummy with value 1 if the estimate is by the uniform 30-day recall and otherwise, and D2 is a dummy which is 1 only if the estimate is by the 30/365-day recall but the 30-day question for clothing, etc; is also present. Figures in parentheses are t-values. It may be noticed that both dummies are significant. implying that estimates by the 30-day recall return a higher Gini and that presence of the 30-day question also increases the Gini by the 30/365-day recall.

The trend lines are drawn with D1 = 1 and D2 = 0.

In order to make them comparable with rounds 51 to 57, the plotted values of the MRP Ginis of rounds 43 and 50 (where D2 was equal to 1) have been reduced by the coefficients of D2 in the fits above . All the other Ginis plotted are unadjusted. For rounds 51 to 53. URP Ginis are from schedule 1 and MRP from schedule 2.

and real estate)—with a consequent explosion in demand for skilled workers; and (c) a drop in the rate of labour absorption during the reform period. There has also been an increase in regional inequality, especially in the incidence of rural poverty. This rise in inequality has implied that, despite better growth, poverty reduction has been sluggish.[16]

Violent Conflict Attributable to Rapid Rise in Inequality

A case study of Ahmedabad, once known as the 'Manchester of India', illustrates how the rise in economic insecurities can create a fertile ground for social and political instability. Eighty per cent of workers in the city of Ahmedabad were employed by the textile industry in the 1960s and the 1970s.[17] The closing down of the mills pushed the workers into partial employment, insecure employment and unemployment. These long years of loss of livelihood and a way of life created frustrations, tensions and anger that became one of the main triggers for communal riots in the city in 1985 and later again in 2001.

Similarly, numerous cases of substantial disruption and rising vulnerabilities in people's lives are evident:

- deep recession in the powerloom sector in Tamil Nadu,
- crisis in the edible oil industry after the slashing of import tariffs,
- collapse in coffee prices and farmer suicides in Kerala,
- bankruptcy among the cotton farmers and farmers in Andhra Pradesh leading to an increase in farmers suicides,
- the displacement of traditional fishing by commercial shrimp farmers in Kerala and Orissa.

Arundhati Roy, commenting on the eruptions of violent resistance scattered all over India in the last six months, says:

> Some will agree to be herded around, humiliated, starved, kicked around. Some are going to stand up and fight. My prediction is that we are going to see a paroxysm of violence. Most of it will be committed by the state. Some of it will be just an outbreak of common criminalism fuelled by desperation. Some will be part of a political insurrection.[18]

The 2005 Philippines *Human Development Report*, with the theme *Peace, Human Security and Human Development in the Philippines*, reveals that the bottom 10 provinces in almost every aspect of human development (including human survival, income, access to knowledge) are always the most conflict-ridden. This report was 'the first quantifiable documentation to show that cultural isolation, discrimination, and a lack of basic services, such as electricity, water, roads and education, can be *predictors* of armed encounters.'[19]

THE ENGINES OF GROWTH

There is now an argument that the engines which generated India's growth are not really FDI and business production.

> The rising share of economic surplus in output has been accompanied by greater consumption by the surplus earners themselves and also by greater investment that has been stimulated by such consumption. The ability to introduce technological-cum-structural change through imitation of what prevails in the metropolis is what has kept up the level of aggregate demand in the Indian economy leading to an increase in the rate of economic growth.[20]

This analysis points to several dangers to the Indian economy, reminding us of the time in the 1960s and 1970s when Brazil was described as 'two economies', one a circular production–consumption cycle of the rich for the rich, and one down under, leading later to explosive political situations.

The headlines in an Indian newspaper after the G-8 summit read, 'The Davids Took On the Goliaths'.[21] Here the Davids are the G-5 (China, India, Brazil, Mexico and South Africa) who were invited to Germany as 'outreach' partners. The G-5 countries are increasingly coming together despite their strong differences. This needs to be taken note of by the UNDP in its gender work, as this is where macro policies will be decided collectively, not at the UN or at G-8 meetings.

Brazil's income inequality, along with South Africa's, is among the highest in the world, far greater than China's and India's. But the magnitude of poverty in the latter two is greater—with more people in 'extreme poverty' in India than Brazil's population. Further, rising regional differences are a serious concern for China.

Among the leaders of the G-5, Lula da Silva, president of Brazil, said he would seek to reduce Brazil's huge gap between the rich and the poor and ensure economic growth in his second term following his landslide re-election. He said his second term would be marked 'by economic development, better income distribution and quality educa-tion'.[22] According to South African president Thabo Mbeki,

> None of the great social problems we have to solve is capable of reso-lution outside the context of creation of jobs and the alleviation and eradication of poverty and therefore the struggle to eradicate poverty has been and will continue to be a central part of the national effort to build the new South Africa.[23]

Manmohan Singh, India's prime minister, in a speech to the Confederation of Indian Industry said:

> I clearly stated that the guiding principle of our Government has been to ensure that, while sustaining higher rates of economic growth, the improved performance of the economy must contribute to employ-ment generation, poverty reduction and human development. The aim of each of our flagship programmes is to ensure that growth is more equitable and that it empowers the most deprived of our citizens.... I do recognize that we have a long way to go in addressing the needs and concerns of all sections of our society, especially the poorest among us.[24]

'INCLUSION' NEEDS TO BE RECONCEPTUALISED AS 'AGENCY', THE THINK SIDE OF ACTION

So where do we go from here? In the quest for 'taming' the harshness of rapid economic growth, the term 'inclusive' has become the mantra that is being used as well as challenged from many diverse quarters. Within India, the idea of 'inclusion' is enshrined in national docu-ments, such as the 11th Plan Approach Paper titled *Towards Faster and More Inclusive Growth*.[25] Resonating again and again in other official fora including speeches by the Indian prime minister Dr Manmohan

Singh,[26] who perhaps initiated this language, and in the global arena among institutions like the Asian Development Bank,[27] the 2006 *World Development Report*,[28] or the latest UNDP and ILO joint effort,[29] it is now the popular currency.

By and large the term 'inclusive' is being seen as a way of carrying the 'excluded', usually denoting the poor or the unemployed, along with the energy of rapid economic growth. This idea of inclusiveness as 'making the opportunities available to all including the poor',[30] or as 'one wherein the distribution of income moves in favour of the poor as a part and parcel of the growth process itself',[31] permeates most texts.

However, there is need to reconceptualise inclusion as not only recognising the usual marginalised communities or sections of society as beneficiaries, but as including them as thinkers who think and 'know' differently, and whose presence in designing is the real inclusion. There is need to give the excluded agency, to use Prof. Amartya Sen's language.[32] Inclusion should involve the inclusion of the knowledge and analysis and experience of minority groups, women and other excluded groups in development design. Nowhere is this proposition more clearly validated than in the 'exclusion' of women, despite the desire to include women.

The collective voice of various women, their experiences, their insights have been translated by the agencies of the women's move-ment, and have become a body of knowledge which has increased and improved 'understanding'. It is this knowledge that we have within us and amongst us, that has to find a place in the planning process in ways in which it can be adapted and made into a real mission to transform the stressful conditions which these sections of society are facing today.

In response to such reasoning, in India we have set up a feminist economists' group as an advisory body to the Planning Commission. Twenty of India's best-known feminist economists are members and are mandated to examine the draft chapters of the plan, and introduce their ideas into it, as well as to make a presentation on their perspectives on the current macro policies. This might be a first in the world, but basically it serves to prove that there is a case for using the intellectual powerhouse that women's scholarship and activism generates. This represents a sea change in understanding inclusion—a best practice for consideration by the UNDP.[33]

ECONOMIC POLICIES TO BE JUST NEED INSTITUTIONAL ARRANGEMENTS: A FIELD EXPERIENCE

What follows is a micro illustration of how we can upturn the pyramid, create transformation from below. In this field experience, the positioning of subject and object suggested by gender-responsive budgeting is shifted. Here,

- Women design area development.
- Women advise on fiscal policy.
- Women participate in macro-economic decision making.
- Women reveal, put forth the knowledge derived not only from academic studies, where in any case feminist research is known for drawing its inspiration from ground-level research, but also from the lived experience of women.

Giving agency to women reveals that institutional design can perhaps be a useful tool for transformation of macro-economics by women.

In 43 gram panchayats[34] scattered across four districts in Karnataka, the Singamma Sreenivasan Foundation undertook an exercise to enable the elected women (who are 35 per cent to 40 per cent of a total number of around 900 elected members in these four districts) to design the area plan drawn from the budget allotted to their respective gram panchayats.

An expert group of the Planning Commission,[35] while reconceptualising inclusion at the grassroots level, said that special attention had to be given to women and disadvantaged groups so as to enable them to take a lead in planning. The current means of inclusion of women in development planning and implementation as well as in the allocation of funds in India is to offer a special women's component plan to ensure that a part of sectoral funding is available and used for women. This is known as 'gender-responsive budgeting'. However, what is needed is for equality to be built into the envisioning process as a whole, by ensuring that women have an important role in the design of the entire plan rather than only in the women's component. For example, in surveys involved in the planning process, it needs to be ensured that women's views are especially sought, including through focus group discussions. Women community leaders will need to be identified and included on committees that may be formed under various sectors, to ensure that women are included in planning for sectors other than social development, such as infrastructure, use of common lands, natural resources and employment. As a member of the expert group, I argued that in ensuring meaningful participation of traditionally muted and excluded groups like dalits and women in the envisioning exercise, there is need for special capacity building for them. Networks of elected women members ought to be encouraged so that they can exert collective pressure as well as throw up leadership for a meaningful development of village and district plans with women's views embedded in them.

Here we see women being given an opportunity to actually design development, not simply to gender a given development. The main premise here is that women's minds and experiences have to direct development, and this idea is slightly different from gender-responsive budgeting. For collective strategising, and for organised and politically savvy interventions, it was suggested that we need 'a place of our own', that is, a separate area to draw attention to women's political views, political in the broadest sense of the word. The women's movement for decades has argued for an emphasis on grassroots experience and the community's need to define and implement development. This 'bottom-up' approach is possible and has a chance to happen in India.

In 1993, India amended its Constitution with the 73rd and 74th Amendments that provided 33.3 per cent reservation to women in elected local councils. Under this amendment, the locally elected councils are accountable for designing and implementing the use of billions of dollars, and this provided an opportunity for women to design economic policy at the local level. Studies reveal differences in their choice of development, especially in priorities such as water, sanitation, health, education, issues of the girl child, location of roads, bus stops, airports, liquor shops, etc.

However, macro policies can inhibit this process. That is, if the power of the state and the macro-economic model are given over to international capital and corporates, then all this devolution of power would be, and is being, wiped out. For example, several acres of the coast of Gujarat have been bought by non-Indian private companies, making area planning by the women of the area impossible. Therefore, shifts in macro policies have overrun the efforts to build the capacity of women to plan for their area.

These experiments suggest that if a political economy puts decentral-ised governance in place (and many economies such as the Philippines, Ghana, Bangladesh, India and South Africa have done this), and the budgets are then summated from the village level to the districts, to the state level, and to the nation, a national budget can accumulate from local budgets. Then instead of asking for a share of a budget, which is what actually happens in the conventional gender-responsive budgeting process, women can direct development and its financing This would fulfil a long-standing feminist dream of what is called the 'bottom-up' approach to development, and perhaps usher in that alternative para-digm we are seeking.

TACKLING GROWTH: STARTING WITH THE POOR

In 1928, Gandhi, seeing the condition of the poor of India, drew up what he called the 'economic constitution of India':

> According to me the economic constitution of India and for the matter of that of the world, should be such that no one under it should suffer from want of food and clothing. In other words everybody should be able to get sufficient work to enable him to make the two ends meet. And this ideal can be universally realised only if the means of produc-tion of the elementary necessaries of life remain in the control of the masses. These should be freely available to all as God's air and water are or ought to be; they should not be made a vehicle of traffic for the exploitation of others. Their monopolisation by any country, nation or group of persons would be unjust. The neglect of this simple principle is the cause of the destitution that we witness today not only in this unhappy land but in other parts of the world too.[36]

The argument here is basically that there needs to be serious rethinking on how we pursue poverty eradication and women's empowerment. The idea that has gripped our minds in the last five years can be summed up as 'money matters', that funding could make a difference to the crisis that women in poverty are facing, namely hunger, deprivation in terms of basic needs like water and food, apart from domestic and other forms of violence, discrimination, etc. There is a big push for the idea that the Millennium Development Goals can be achieved by bringing in large chunks of money. In fact, in the paper prepared by Caren Grown, Chandrika Bahadur, Jessie Handbury and Diane Elson,[37] the authors analyse the scenario to present the specific amounts necessary to achieve this, and conclude:

> We find that the cost of interventions that aim directly to promote gender equality is $7–$13 per capita, on average, from 2006–2015 for the five countries. The first result of the analysis is not surprising: achieving MDGs costs money—a fact often overlooked by governments in rich and poor countries alike.

They further translate this in per capita terms and arrive at the following finding:

> We also find that between 35–52 per cent of the total costs of the MDGs, which translates into $37–$57 per capita per year, can be attributed to the achievement of gender equality objectives in the five countries. These costs represent 9 per cent of 2003 GDP in Bangladesh, 15 per cent of 2003 GDP in Cambodia, 18 per cent of 2003 in Tanzania, and 19 per cent of 2003 GDP in Ghana and Uganda.[38]

What we need to do is to set our own table—to re-create the paradigm of development itself, the identification of the engines of growth. Instead of seeing the poor as a target group who need special ladders within a framework of economic development, enabling the poor to become economic and political agents could itself become the engine of growth. Thus, departing from the 'trickle-down' or social net approach, it would be useful to look at what can be called the 'bubbling-up' theory of growth. This alternative theory would argue that putting incomes and political power in the hands of the poor could generate the demand and the voice that would direct development. The purchasing power and the choices of the poor could direct the economy to a pro-poor or poverty-reducing economy.

The review of the past seems to suggest the need for some dramatic reversal of the current theories of where the engine of growth lies, if the interest is in poverty eradication. This is difficult to do—to go against such powerful reasoning—but a start can be made by rewriting definitions, perceptions, developing new measures of poverty and new measures of progress. Diane Elson, in dialoguing with the women who met in Casablanca,[39] said:

> Perhaps one of the things that women's knowledge can do is contribute to an alternative vision of modernity and progress to those which have dominated the last two hundred years. Those visions have always been made in man's image, leaving out the domestic, the non-market, the realm of unpaid care; prioritising the large scale, the far-reaching, the expanding. But at the same time, they have contained elements of liberation, from, for instance, the drudgery of collecting fuel and water, by investment in infrastructure; from the petty-mindedness of localities cut off from wider communication; from the subjugation of some groups of people (especially women) in the name of collective 'traditions' of all kinds. Maybe women can create an alternative vision of modernity which avoids false polarities between local and global, paid and unpaid, market and non-market, sustainability and growth; individual and collective; and between the moral and the economic; and instead rests on innovative syntheses.

Others like Solita Collas-Monsod emphasise the importance of including women's unpaid work in the gross national product. Collas-Monsod was appalled that at the World Conference on Women held in Beijing, the women's movement, especially the negotiators of the final document, had proposed and got agreement on 'satellite accounts', but not on a full interpretation of their significance. 'Satellite accounts' are accounts that are drawn up in parallel to the accounts that are prepared to measure the gross national product and the related gross national income, but that bring in non-monetary work.

Collas-Monsod shared an illustration from the Philippines, which has enhanced GDP by including data which bring in what is called women's 'invisible work', i.e., work which is not paid (Figure 11.3). We can see the enhanced GDP by inclusions. In the figure below, the lower graph marked by squares is the result of GDP numbers calculated in the normal way. The graph marked by triangles is when unpaid work is included. The figure shows the drastic difference when unpaid work is included in GDP. The figure at the bottom shows GDP as usually calculated (graph marked by squares), whereas the graph marked with triangles shows GDP as adjusted to include unpaid work. This shows how much value is not included in the conventional mode of calculating GDP.

The meeting at Casablanca that drew together women from varied backgrounds and different countries revolved around the broad theme of women, peace and globalisation. The women thinkers engaged with a rethinking of the development framework itself. The group narrowed its focus to the theme 'Getting the Fundamentals Right: Women, Water and Wealth'.[40] This transliterates to the agency of women as changemakers, or as a domain (allowing for re-examining the women's movement, women's struggles and women's machineries, women's spaces). Water was taken as symbolic of a basic or fundamental issue that has political, social, economic, health, cultural and environmental ramifications, especially for poor women. The issue of wealth brought the basic macro-economic paradigms into focus along with the issues of poverty and inequality. The underlying argument in foregrounding all these issues was a need to unpack the fundamentals—the constructs and concepts that inform policies and actions—from the basis of knowledge that women have provided.

We are also thinking of introducing new measures for poverty, such as water poverty, food poverty. The UNDP human poverty index only summarises the measure as follows: 'a composite index measuring deprivations in the three basic dimensions captured in the human development index—a long and healthy life, knowledge and a decent standard of living'. We need to evolve other measures. Measures are an important instrument for turning around flawed directions. Feminists have used this approach for decades. We need to work further on this.

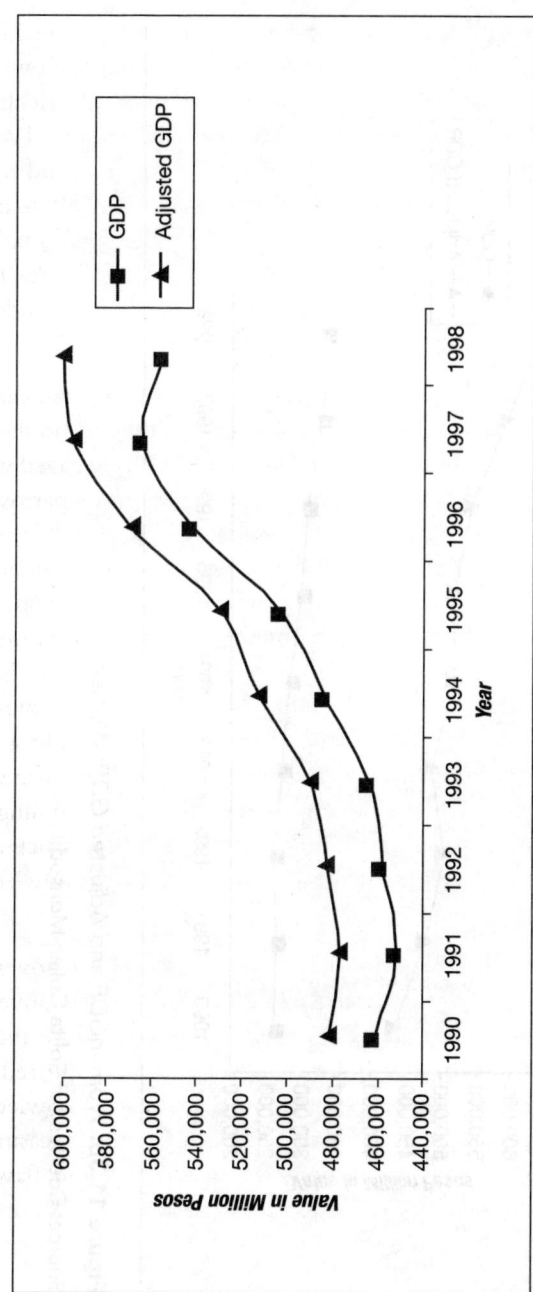

Figure 11.3a: *GDP and Adjusted GDP:Men*

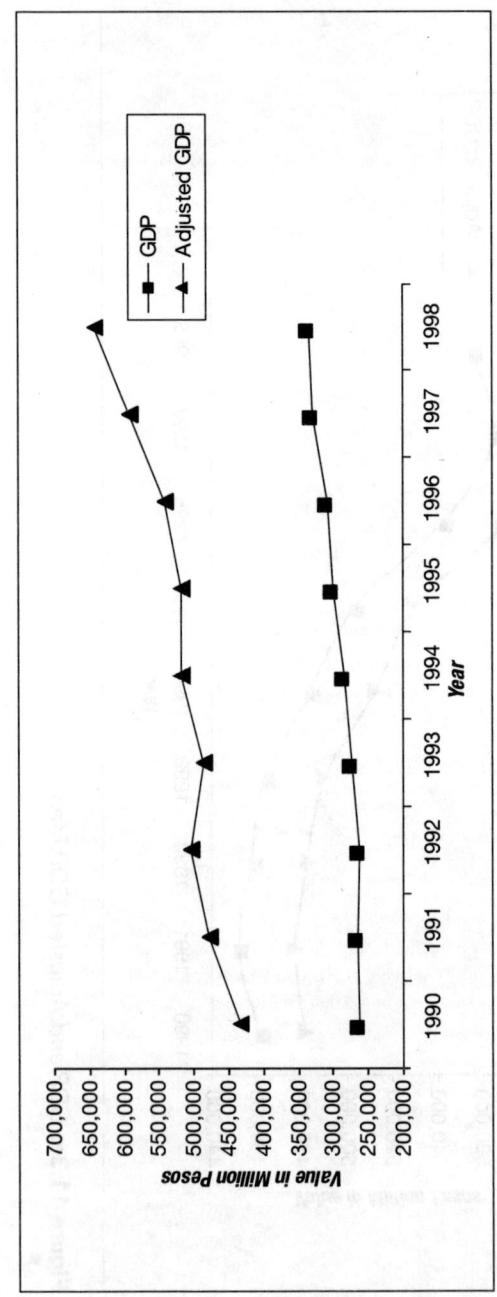

Figure 11.3b: *WomenGDP and Adjusted GDP: Women*

Source: Courtesy of Solita Collas-Monsod.

To summarise:

- There is need to take note of the new groupings of countries in the world, such as BRICS (Brazil, Russia, India, China and South Africa), and not limit knowledge to only the UN, or the G-8 which consists of only the wealthy countries.
- Women's organisations are now networked in many arenas—national, regional and global—and have an increased knowledge of development. They need to be included in the planning and design of macro-economic and social policies.
- Given the scenario in India both in terms of the macro-economic dilemmas as well as scope for change from local governments, new architectures like the feminist economic group have emerged. The UNDP gender team could, as Hope Chigudu and Diane Elson suggest in different ways, initiate a 'rethinking' process:

  - on concepts and definitions
  - on measures
  - on 'who' the movers and shakers of change are
  - on challenging inequality
  - on supporting South formations like the NAM initiative
  - on the prevailing gender architecture
  - on moving away from gender bureaus to advisories like the feminist economist group.

NOTES

1   Jain, *Women, Development, and the UN.*
2   I would like to acknowledge the work of the team at the Singamma Sreenivasan Foundation led by Ms Ahalya Bhatt and research assistant Shubha Chacko.
3   Planning Commission, *Report of the Page: Special Group on Targeting Ten Million Employment Opportunities Per Year over the Tenth Plan Period* (New Delhi: Government of India, May 2002), p. 24, http://planningcommission.gov.in/aboutus/committee/tsk_sg10m.pdf (accessed 10 April 2018).
4   1 crore = 10 million.
5   NSSO, *Household Consumer Expenditure and Employment Situation in India*, NSS 52nd Round, 1995–96, NSSO, Department of Statistics, Government of India, New Delhi, June 1998.

6   NSSO, *Household Consumer Expenditure and Employment Situation in India*, NSS 54th Round, January–June 1998, NSSO, Department of Statistics, Government of India, New Delhi, June 1999.

7   1 lakh = 100,000.

8   *Hindu Business Line*, 3 June 1999.

9   '"Jobless Growth" in Asia Fails to Tackle Poverty—UN Report', February 2007, http://www.ilo.org/asia/media-centre/news/WCMS_BK_PR_171_EN/lang–en/index.htm (accessed 21 January 2018).

10 UNDP and ILO, 'Asian Experience on Growth, Employment and Poverty', UNDP Regional Centre, Colombo, 2007, http://www.ilo.org/wcmsp5/groups/public/—asia/—ro-bangkok/documents/publication/wcms_bk_pb_142_en.pdf (accessed 21 January 2018).

11 James B. Davies, Antony Shorrocks, Susanna Sandstrom et al., 'The World Distribution of Household Wealth', 2007, https://escholarship.org/content/qt3jv048hx/qt3jv048hx.pdf?nosplash=75a51704d5844f26f6f450a2d5909af3 (accessed 11 April 2018).

12 Jayati Ghosh, 'Changes in the World of Work', December 2003, http://www.networkideas.org/feathm/sep2006/pdf/isle_changes_in_world_of_work.pdf (accessed 11 April 2018).

13 Carmen Diane Deere and Cheryl R. Doss, 'Gender and the Distribution of Wealth in Developing Countries', Research Paper no. 2006/115, UNU-WIDER, 2 October 2006.

14 Aseema Sinha, 'Globalisation, Rising Inequality, and New Insecurities in India', paper presented at the conference 'Difference and Inequality in Developing Societies', University of Virginia, Charlottesville, April 2005.

15 Ibid.

16 Raghbendra Jha, 'Reducing Poverty and Inequality in India: Has Liberalization Helped?', Working Paper no. 2004, UNU-WIDER, November 2000.

17 Sujata Patel, 'Urbanization, Development and Communalization of Society in Gujarat', in Takashi Shinoda (ed.), *The Other Gujarat* (Mumbai: Popular Prakashan, 2002).

18 Arundhati Roy, 'Intellectual Terrorist', *Deccan Herald*, 3 June 2007.

19 Human Development Network, *Philippine Human Development Report 2005: Peace, Human Security and Human Development in the Philippines*, http://hdr.undp.org/sites/default/files/philippines_2005_en.pdf (accessed 21 January 2018). See also International Humanist and Ethical Union, 'Human Rights Day—10 December 2006', http://iheu.org/human-rights-day-10-december-2006/ (accessed 11 April 2018).

20 Prabhat Patnaik, 'A Model of Growth of the Contemporary Indian Economy', *Economic & Political Weekly*, vol. 42, no. 22 (2007), pp. 2077–81.

21 D. Ravi Kanth, 'G-5: The Davids Took On the Goliaths', *Deccan Herald*, 14 June 2007.

22 Personal communication.

23 Thabo Mbeki, State of the Nation Address, 9 February 2007, http://www. sahistory.org.za/archive/2007-president-mbeki-state-nation-address-9-february-2007 (accessed 11 April 2018).

24 Manmohan Singh, Speech to the Confederation of Indian Industry, 29 May 2007.

25 Planning Commission, *Towards Faster and More Inclusive Growth: An Approach to the 11th Five Year Plan* (New Delhi: Government of India, November 2006).

26 'We Believe in Inclusive Growth: Manmohan Singh', 22 May 2007, http:// twocircles.net/2007may22/we-believe-inclusive-growth-manmohan-singh. html (accessed 11 April 2018).

27 DavaoToday.com, 'Stronger Regional Cooperation Can Promote Inclusive Growth, Says ADB President', 7 May 2007, http://davaotoday.com/main/ inbox/asia-stronger-regional-cooperation-can-promote-inclusive-growth-says-adb-president/ (accessed 21 January 2018).

28 World Bank, *World Development Report 2006: Equity and Development* (Washington, D.C.: World Bank, 2005), http://documents.worldbank.org/ curated/en/435331468127174418/pdf/322040World0Development0Rep ort02006.pdf (accessed 21 January 2018).

29 *World of Work*, 'ILO, UNDP Join Forces to Promote Growth for Decent Jobs', no. 59, April 2007, p. 41.

30 Ifzal Ali, 'Pro-poor to Inclusive Growth: Asian Prescriptions', ERD Policy Brief no. 48, May 2007.

31 *Economic & Political Weekly*, 'Promoting "Inclusive Growth"?', Editorial, vol. 42, no. 22 (2007), pp. 2031–32.

32 Sen, 'The Ends and Means of Sustainability'.

33 Devaki Jain, 'Interpreting "Inclusiveness": Report on a First Step' (unpublished).

34 A gram panchayat is a village-level elected council in India, covering an average population of 5,000 to 7,000 spread across an area of about 2,000 to 12,000 hectares.

35 Planning Commission, 'Planning at the Grassroots Level: An Action Programme for the Eleventh Five Year Plan', Report of the Expert Group, Government of India, New Delhi, March 2006.

36 V. K. Natraj, Kamlesh Mishra and Neeru Kapoor (eds), *Gandhian Alternative*, vol. 4 of *Economics Where People Matter*, Gandhian Studies and Peace Research Series no. 26, p. 318.

37 Caren Grown, Chandrika Bahadur, Jessie Handbury and Diane Elson, 'The Financial Requirements of Achieving Gender Equality and Women's Empowerment', paper prepared for the World Bank, 26 April 2006.

38 Ibid.

39 Casablanca Dream Group, 'Getting the Fundamentals Right: Women, Water and Wealth', Casablanca, 2007.

40 Ibid.

Chapter 12

Walking Together
The Journey of the Non-Aligned Movement and the Women's Movement
(with Shubha Chacko)

The Non-Aligned Movement had largely been forgotten by the women's movements both in the South and in the North. It had faded away by the end of the 20th century, if not earlier, with the passing of the great leaders of the South, such as Nehru, Nasser, Sukarno and Tito. But non-alignment was actually a parallel journey for these oppressed nations, parallel to the journey of women to liberate themselves from oppression. Women found the framework of NAM and its ideas suitable for their own quest. Since many women from the NAM countries had themselves been leaders in the freedom struggles of their countries, there was a very strong partnership between women and these political formations.

'Most women in Afghanistan don't get a chance to grow old,' Massouda Jalal, minister for women's affairs in Afghanistan, declared at the inaugural NAM Ministerial Meeting on Women and Empowerment in Cuba in 2005.[1] 'Many of them are dead before they reach old age,' she added.[2]

This revelation, while scandalous and shocking in itself, is also particularly interesting in that the minister shared this with NAM, and that NAM as a multilateral forum was seen as a place to which women could turn, where they would be heard and responded to. Another noteworthy development is that in its search for new relevance, NAM chose to engage with the theme of 'Empowering Women in Facing the Challenges of Globalisation'. 'Women', as a constituency or political subject, are back on the NAM radar.

Starting with an exploration of the idea of NAM in the context in which it was born, this article recalls its basic, rather radical tenets— tenets that find resonance with the women's movement. The following section seeks to understand NAM as a space for women by recalling some of the historical NAM women's conferences and their contribution to the international agenda on women. The paper concludes by sketching out some of the challenges and possible ways forward. We argue that NAM, and its engagement with women, has the historical and strategic potential to be the platform from which to launch an inclusive growth paradigm, a 'world' that Southern leaders are also supposedly seeking.

THE NON-ALIGNED MOVEMENT AS AN IDEA AND AS A SPECIAL SPACE

The Non-Aligned Movement was a bold and somewhat impertinent formation which challenged notions of expected behaviour by a 'motley' group of newly independent and 'young' nations. American writer Richard Wright, who was present at the 1955 Bandung Conference (attended by African and Asian states, and hosted by President Sukarno of Indonesia) where NAM's aspirations were unfurled, had this to say about the meeting: 'The scorned, insulted, offended, dispossessed, in short, the destitute people of the human race were meeting.... That meeting of the rejected was in itself like bringing the western world to trial!'[3]

In 1955, as the USA and the USSR were busy carving up the world and creating blocs and puppet regimes, a group of intrepid leaders decided to refuse to align themselves with either superpower. The Cold War was not the sole critical issue on the agenda of NAM, however. Many Western countries were so preoccupied with the Cold War that they gave scant attention to other North–South issues that underlay much of the debate that concerned NAM.[4] A cursory glance at the history of NAM reveals that the basic elements that informed its approach to international issues included the right of independent judgement, the struggle against imperialism and neo-colonialism, and moderation in relations with all big powers. Rather than a passive neutrality or an isolationist policy of non-involvement in all conflicts, it was an assertion of agency on the part of Third World nations that was considered the hallmark of being 'sovereign' and 'independent'.

Ahmad Sukarno, the then president of Indonesia, clearly enunciated this stand at the Bandung Conference: 'We are united... by a common detestation of colonialism... a common detestation of racialism... and... a common determination to preserve and stabilise peace.' He continued, 'Colonialism has its modern dress... economic control, intellectual control, actual physical control'[5]—a statement as valid today as it was more than 50 years ago. The Non-Aligned Movement invoked an imagined community and sought to create 'a poetics of a new kind of transnational, third world identity'.[6] The movement constructed a concept of the 'Third World' as a positive identity that would bind nations and people together and provoke a 'we' feeling across countries and other divides.[7]

This attempt to forge a community of this sort was markedly different from the idea of a clan, a tribe, or even a nation—all of which were considered more 'natural'. Nor was it a regional entity marked by geographical boundaries, as is the European Union; or an open non-discriminating space that admitted practically all nations, like the more powerful United Nations. The grouping was formulated on clear political and ideological lines, and in this respect NAM was a pioneer.

The demands of newly liberated countries for agency and voice in dealing with the mainstream are similar to those that women around the world have made at various times—that is, not to be treated as passive patients but to have their agency and its persistence recognised, even under circumstances of oppression, together with the roles that such agency plays in facilitating resistance. The idea of self-determination of those considered less capable and often incapable of making such decisions has informed feminist discourse and practice, as it has the NAM conferences and declarations. When India's prime minister Manmohan

Singh said at the NAM conference in Havana, 'We account for over half of humanity... yet we do not have commensurate voice in the international institutions of the world,'[8] he could very well have been speaking of the women of the world.

The basic values on which NAM was premised were solidarity, justice, equality and peace. A song that became popular in the late 1980s in Belgrade (where the first NAM summit was held in 1961, while Yugoslavia continued to play a key role in NAM) was an attempt to capture and popularise its spirit. One verse goes like this:

> When they [the leaders of NAM] built the movement of the
> Non-Aligned
> In making us believe in the right things
> They gave us a song which the world sings
> Wisdom listens, violence is blind.
> The only promise is that of the Non-Aligned.[9]

This Third World solidarity that NAM underlined appeared as early as 1964: 'At UNCTAD, which was the biggest, the longest, and the most frustrating international conference, the developed countries were caught unawares by the unprecedented unity shown by the Group of 77.'[10] The conference passed unanimous resolutions by what Harry Johnson called the 'sheer moral shock power' exercised by the developing countries'.[11] Even before this, in 1952, US Secretary of State Dean Acheson had declared that the outstanding fact of the General Assembly was its dominance by the Arab-Asian bloc.[12] By 1964, the non-aligned countries had succeeded in placing *their* economic problems forcefully on the international agenda. The women's movement too has time and again banded together across the usual divides to flag up one issue and move its agenda forward—right from the inception of the UN, when the small group of women who were present met together, although they came from different countries, were of varied backgrounds, and held a range of positions within and outside the official government delegations.[13]

Besides being a platform on which to hammer out a common cause, NAM has been a source of new ideas, of varied scope and intent.

For example, the new international economic order challenged the economic arrangements that privileged the already privileged. The NAM-sponsored 'non-aligned news agency pool'[14] aimed to counter the fact that Western media ignored large tracts of the world, or covered them only when some disaster struck or when Western interests were in some way affected. These ideas sprang from the needs, experiences and politics of the South, and were attempts to correct some of the world's gross imbalances.

Similarly, women's knowledge has challenged mainstream assumptions, supposed facts, and most classificatory systems in every discipline—from questioning notions of what constitutes 'productive' and 'unproductive' to seemingly natural dichotomies of private and public, secure or insecure, and so on.

A SPACE FOR WOMEN: TRACING THE JOURNEY OF WOMEN AND NAM

The establishment of NAM as a political entity held out much hope for many social movements. For example, it was the spirit of the Bandung Conference that was evoked by the Indonesian feminist Sukina Kusima when she visited Egypt in 1959 to promote a stronger bond between the women in Africa and Asia.[15] Pearl S. Buck, the Nobel laureate, publicly expressed her wish for the triumph of the 1955 Bandung Conference of non-aligned nations, arguing that it was valuable for the world and for women.[16]

Non-alignment provides the ideological foundation for developing a paradigm of international interaction, which allows nations to work towards peace and prosperity in co-operation while maintaining their national identity, spirit and character—and it is these same values of equality, non-discrimination and social justice that are the bedrock of the women's movement. The Non-Aligned Movement clearly saw women's role in development as an international and political issue. In contrast to the conceptualisation of issues relating to women's status as social or cultural phenomena that predominated in other bodies in the early 1960s, NAM's analysis of women in development was sharper and reflected a more complex understanding of the interconnection between trends in women's roles and status in their societies and the nature and pattern of development processes, including the latter's dependence on international, economic and political relations.[17]

The Non-Aligned Movement's idea of the path to women's equality departed from UN strategies. The UN system at this time saw 'women's status' largely as a social development issue and did not strongly connect it to the larger context of international development. Within the UN, women were still viewed as resources whose potential could be tapped. But the NAM gatherings offered a space where women from former colonies could reassert the standpoint that they were active agents in their nations, contributors to their country's progress, and not mere consumers *of social services.*

The Non-Aligned Movement also brought early news about the impact of global economic trends on women. The 1981 Ministerial Conference in New Delhi reported the impact of harmful practices of MNCs on women in both developing and developed countries: 'By exploiting the cheap labour force multinational companies find new sources of extra profits in developing countries. At the same time they fire workers and lower the wage of female workers in the developing countries'.[18] Modern technology was not serving women workers well, in NAM's analysis. It saw the self-reliance model as the antidote: 'What is particularly important to understand is that [the] self-reliant develop-ment pattern has the welfare of the people and not growth of GDP as its principal objective.'[19] The model of development advocated by NAM was to draw policy from the reality on the ground and change policies when those realities changed. The ideal that it represented was a co-operative sharing of resources between men and women, com-munity members, and states.

The NAM consultations introduced a more nuanced understanding of concepts that had seemed fairly straightforward and well understood, for example the idea of discrimination. Delegates from developing countries expanded the notion of discrimination, saying that it was 'part of a system of exploitation in every country as well as within the international economic and political order'.[20] In contrast, delegates from developed countries at many UN forums had limited the context to one of male dominance. Vida Tomsic, the Yugoslav leader and president of the People's Assembly, was enthused about the role that NAM could play vis-à-vis women's development. Developing countries, she said, have drawn attention to the circumstances which cause their nations to experience extreme poverty, and the increasing gap between developed and developing countries. 'A dramatic reflection of this general situation is the difficult social and economic situation of women in these countries.'[21] She went on to add that in such conditions, 'actions of the international community in individual social fields... have had limited effect. The consequences cannot be eliminated unless the action goes to the causes; to its roots in anachronistic and unjust international economic and political relations'[22]—a theme which needs to be urgently revisited in today's globalised era.

The president of the 38th General Assembly in July 1984, Jorge Illueca of Panama, suggested that the movement and the policy of non-alignment was 'the most dynamic and constructive force to promote the objectives of the Charter of the United Nations, as the only valid formula for achieving a new world order based on equality, justice and peace'.[23] The contribution made by NAM to the UN therefore was to strengthen it and to explore it as a space that could reflect the concerns of the Third World, rather than one entirely dominated by the powerful nations. The manner in which NAM members grouped together to use the UN space underlines their ability to strategise and band together, as well as their faith in the UN as an organisation. This resonates with what the women's movement has done. Similarly, the self-identity as a 'third bloc' constituted an important unifying strategy for these nations and enabled them to resist to some degree the UN's idea of all nations being equal—in that this was a way of going beyond formal equality to a more substantive type of equality. The achievement of women's equality is an elusive goal, since too often the ideal of realising women's rights is tied to formal and legalistic declarations about treating men and women alike.

The Non-Aligned Movement also proved to be an exciting learning ground. Along with the Afro-Asian People's Society Movement, NAM had promoted numerous related conferences, such as the Afro-Asian Youth Movement and the Afro-Asian Writers' Movement and educational exchanges, and the July 1962 Cairo Economic Conference.[24]

The resulting exchanges and networks were part of what made possible the sorts of imagining that overflowed the boundaries of the nation-state. Women participated in these conferences and meetings and thus deepened their knowledge of international relations and honed their negotiating skills and abilities. Similarly, for new states and states that are not very strong, NAM provides experience and also offers a protective umbrella for dealing with other multilateral bodies such as the UN.

The Non-Aligned Movement opened up an alternative political and organisational setting for formerly colonised women. While not denying the universalism of 'sisterhood', NAM became a space for expressing an 'imagined community of third world oppositional struggles... [that] women with divergent histories and social locations have woven together by the political threads of opposition to forms of domination that are not only pervasive but systematic'.[25] Therefore, what bound Third World women together was not merely a common suffering but also a struggle for similar political ends.

CHALLENGES TO THE WOMEN OF NAM

The Changed Scenario

A fundamental difference between the conditions when NAM was established and those that prevail at present is the configuration of global politics. The dynamics of globalisation and the current economic turbulence have produced a whole set of new problems and issues which the movement must address.

In the new age of globalisation, governments around the world have adopted policies that favour the openness of trade and financial flows, with less regulation of industry and the privatisation of state-owned enterprises. Liberalisation policies, coupled with technological advances in communications, have accelerated the impact of economic integration, eroding conventional national boundaries. These developments have also resulted in many new phenomena on the ground. For example, there has been a significant shift in the economy. For the first time in human history, more people work in services and trades than in food production.[26] The relationship between globalisation and poverty is complex: it depends not just on trade or financial globalisation, but on the interaction of globalisation with many other variables.[27] While there are widely varying conclusions on the impact of globalisation on poverty, what is clear is that poverty and deprivation affect vast populations today, even while there is unprecedented wealth.[28] The huge rise in inequalities is also a cause of concern. There has also been an increase in regional inequality, especially in the incidence of rural poverty, leading to a sluggishness in poverty reduction.[29] Other relevant trends include the fact that the globalisation process has coincided with the intensification of women's labour participation in the non-agricultural sectors. Migration too has acquired a female face. About half of today's migrants are women.[30]

The era is also marked by a rash of regional and bilateral trade agreements. The WTO has recorded more than 170 currently in force. What is also worth noting is that South–South trade has grown rapidly since the 1990s and is higher than the growth rate for world trade. Therefore, there are suggestions of creating regional monetary agreements, including flexible regional bloc exchange rate regimes and the creation of regional currencies to help the South to reduce the artificial need for dollars in the regional trade. Along with new trade agreements, other new political formations have emerged. The recent developing country blocs with a sectoral focus, such as the G-20 and G-33 on agriculture, NAMA-11 on industrial products, and G-24 on services, could be cited in this context. There are other broader formulations, such as the India–Brazil–South Africa forum, which now seeks to include China and maybe Mexico. However, there are fears that these formations would break South–South solidarity, and there are concerns about the potential for 'developing country identity' to come into conflict with the 'aspiring great power identity'.[31]

The nature of violence has also changed substantially since the early days of NAM. There has been an increase in violent conflict, especially intra-state armed conflicts, with non-state actors often the main players. These are often underpinned 'by political transition, economic dislocation, weak civil society and a weakening of the State, leading to virtual anarchy'.[32] The shift to intra-state armed conflicts and wars has witnessed a frightening increase in gender-based violence. Other grave issues include the almost devastating proportions of the environmental crisis.

Challenge of Keeping the Movement Intact

Along with these challenges, shifts and tensions that the changed scenario has thrown up, the countries of the South also face the rapid erosion of their national policy space. Debates in the non-aligned conferences began to reflect increasing divergence in the international goals of the movement and the national interests of its members. These contrary pulls are evident in that it is precisely to protect national interests that this transnational forum becomes important; and yet being part of an international group requires nations to downplay their own national identity. The long-winded declarations emerging from these conferences are often patchwork-like compromises which indicate only limited agreement on essential matters.

During the long years of the Cold War, Third World solidarity was threatened and often fragmented due to various pressures, including the fact that so many countries of the South were dependent on the West for aid, trade and investment. Tensions also persisted on the growth path that countries wanted to adopt—between those seeking economic integration and those following economic self-reliance.[33] However, as Cuba's deputy foreign minister Abelardo Moreno candidly remarked, 'We understand perfectly well that there are differences among member-countries. Not everybody has a similar stand on international affairs. Nevertheless, there are more things that unite us than those that divide us.'[34]

The women's movement is grappling with similar questions. The need to build political unity and a sense of community, even while threatened by various new concerns, questions and identities, is counterbalanced by the corresponding fear that the movement may end up relishing, enjoying, celebrating diversity—in effect splintering the movement. However, the movement also recognises the need to stay and work together, even while keeping alive its plurality.

The other issue that haunts the women's movement, rather like NAM, is that it has lost its relevance. It is argued that the agenda has been 'mainstreamed', or that women have achieved equality in most countries, and also that women have grown disenchanted with the movement. Others claim that while the women's movement had its merits, it has failed to reflect women's changing experiences and expectations.

Despite this, strong positive forward motion has been achieved over the years, and one reflection of this is the fact that international norms, standards, covenants and institutions for the protection of human rights are more developed today than at any point in history; and that the culture of human rights is gaining a new and more shared universalism. The women's movement, along with other struggles of the disenfranchised, has found fresh vibrancy and new ways of working, of strategising and moving forward. There is a lesson here for NAM: choosing to support and further these struggles may offer it a way to reinvent itself so that it remains a significant player in these changing times.

RESPONSES TO THESE CHALLENGES

While seeking to unravel the hidden dimensions of the current processes and phenomena, it is essential to apply women's knowledge[35] to development thought, design and action in order to address the crises that the world is facing today and to move towards achieving a more equitable, sustainable and just development paradigm—development for all.

The Beijing Platform for Action and the Millennium Development Goals have been valuable in focusing world attention on issues of poverty and inequality; as potentially powerful tools for progress on development, including gender; and providing frameworks and targets by which to translate the idea of the eradication of poverty and inequality into achievable realities. However, they have been overtaken by new emerging trends and have therefore lost the currency that they once had.

It seems that bureaucratic structures, like the national 'women's machineries' set up in the 1970s, have to an extent been overtaken by the overall thrust of the global political economy. They are still engaged in protective welfare legislation, while their constituency, namely women, have moved on from being the objects of welfare (although that still persists) into becoming major economic agents, albeit vulnerable ones. There is a need to reconstruct the spaces providing support for women, with more emphasis on a self-generated collective voice—as has been done for instance by SAWID (South African Women in Dialogue)—to provide an unencumbered, non-institutional space for local women's groups to engage with each other in dialogue across difference, in order to propose coherent advice to national governments.[36] The institutionalisation of civil society into registered NGOs, the role of international NGOs, and the concept of the NGO as an actor merit critical examination. Dialogue across difference, the creation of spaces for grassroots women to engage with others and create a solidarity front where consensus emerges through dialogue, was seen as one more shift away from the traditional separation of institutions into government and non-government. This shift would make way for the 'women's movement' to be involved in the NAM conferences, critically, on behalf of their less privileged sisters, whether trapped in poverty or in situations of conflict.

The allegation that the Bandung spirit has evaporated and that there is no longer a co-ordinated decision-making body of the global South for multilateral and other purposes is not without substance. Often countries react to their immediate problems with scant regard for the norms of a consensus-building body such as NAM. Or they have solutions handed out to them by the global power blocs. The need of the hour, however, is to recall that NAM stood for something significant: the 'collective actions of the global South' with 'an unmistakable desire to expunge colonialism from international relations and to eradicate the bases of inequity and injustice in the international system'[37]—aims that the feminist movement too has embraced. To pursue this trajectory we need new forms of knowledge and a reconfiguration of the field. The need is to uncover the working of the systems that undermine many nations, as well as huge sections of the population; and to develop a more reflexive assessment of the movements themselves.

The emergence of regional co-operation arrangements represents an effort to shape a more effective response to challenges now faced by the South. A blueprint for fostering newer partnership arrangements should be created to allow the factoring in of the interests and opinions of the global South, enhance their visibility, and facilitate these countries to have a greater say in the shape of the 'progress' being pursued. The growing and serious financial crisis has forced all experts and governments to call into question the neoliberal agenda that had been touted as the mantra for moving out of poverty after the 'Washington consensus'; this is an opportune moment for bold steps. The Non-Aligned Movement and other organisations have to adapt quickly to this changed scenario. The fact that Third World governments continue to use NAM and that there have been five post–Cold War summits shows the resilience of the forum—a trait that will now be tested yet again.

The Non-Aligned Movement can keep alive the Southern consciousness and provide the overarching framework and vision to create partnerships, which ultimately need to be forged at the regional and country-specific levels. It therefore needs to define a new programme of work, which should be guided by the underlying concerns of the South to retain their own national policy space in order to make decisions that are in the interest of their citizens. This will provide a robust defence against the erosion of national policy making, which is inevitable as the neoliberal agenda spreads beyond the economic sphere into social and political realms. The inherent values of multilateralism and the rule of international law lie in the fact that solutions that are reached by consensus have a better chance of delivering long-term peace and stability.

Multilateralism has brought huge positive changes for women—from the spread of the women's movement to efforts to implement programmes for women's access to material resources and the incorporation of women's rights into international law. Multilateral institutions also play a significant role in standard setting. Therefore, a reversal of this trend has serious implications for women.

Thus, women's mobilisation and activism at the local and national levels are the crucial link that will enable the effective translation of both human rights provisions and national commitments into concrete results in the lives of poor women. This connection between the local and global also gives legitimacy to global movements for gender justice.

It is critical for the women's movement to understand the dialectical links between local and global realities, in the process of identifying the main targets to grapple with and in devising adequate strategies for change. Feminists' engagement with NAM, therefore, must be conscious, critical, and refined by constant assessments of strategies and positions in order to avoid being co-opted and to stay focused on the ultimate goals.

There is therefore the need for sound analyses based on increased collaboration between feminist researchers and activists to formulate a clear conceptual framework for the feminist agenda and to draw the links between the current parameters of the global economy and the resurgence of patriarchal and fundamentalist values. 'Comparative work across the South has the potential of displacing the hegemony of the West as our default frame of reference.'[38] We need to respond to the phenomena on the ground. For example, the conditions under which women work and their location in the political economy need to be made into a visible picture; and countries, especially those in NAM, need to engage with these phenomena as an area for justice, just as they would engage with other forms of international law and networking so as to inform public policy forums, whether the UN, NAM, or national or local governments. Similarly, on the issue of migration we could envisage a self-governing covenant between the countries of the South, NAM, which would offer a certain kind of protection to women and girls who are migrating from one Southern country to another.

Taking the bold step of institutionalising a women's advisory check, rather like the environmental clearance that is now mandatory for major projects, would be a breakthrough worthy of NAM. However, such a mechanism must be very specifically designed from the perspective of women living in deprivation. In other words, the social category has to be identified, since women do not constitute a homogeneous category. Instead of looking for, or expecting to find, 'homogeneity in Third World places, feminist engagements can help lift the largely subterranean histories of lateral connections and influences above the threshold of visibility'.[39]

These issues indicate the urgent need for a more transformative agenda and a more radical rethinking of current priorities. Secure and sustainable livelihoods for less powerful groups, women and men, who form the world's majority, should become a more central concern, as should the public regulation of the power and profits of the few.[40]

To conclude, we recall the inspiring words of Jawaharlal Nehru in spelling out the objectives of NAM:

> The main objectives of that policy are: the pursuit of peace, not through alignment with any major power or group of powers but through an independent approach to each controversial or disputed issue, the liberation of subject peoples, the maintenance of freedom, both national and individual, the elimination of racial discrimination and the elimination of want, disease and ignorance, which afflict the greater part of the world's population.[41]

It is to this ideal that we implore NAM to return.

NOTES

1 The NAM Ministerial Conference was held in Putrajaya, Malaysia, from 7 to 10 May, prior to the NAM Summit in Cuba held in December 2005.

2 Baradan Kuppusamy, 'Non-Aligned Movement Takes On New Social Role', InterPress News Service, 10 May 2005, http://www.ipsnews.net/2005/05/development-asia-non-aligned-movement-takes-on-new-social-role/ (accessed 3 March 2018).

3 Richard Wright, *The Color Curtain*, quoted in Matthew Quest, 'The Lessons of the Bandung Conference: Reviewing Richard Wright's *The Color Curtain* 40 Years Later', http://www.spunk.org/texts/pubs/lr/sp001716/bandung.html (accessed 4 March 2018).

4 Siba N. Grogui, 'Postcoloniality in Global South Foreign Policy', in Jacqueline Anne Braveboy-Wagner (ed.), *The Foreign Policies of the Global South: Rethinking Conceptual Frameworks* (Boulder, CO: Lynne Rienner, 2003).

5 Mario Loyola, 'The New Cold War: Hugo Chávez and the Non-Aligned Movement', *National Review*, 28 September 2006, https://www.national-review.com/2006/09/new-cold-war-mario-loyola/ (accessed 4 March 2018).

6 Akhil Gupta, 'The Song of the Nonaligned World: Transnational Identities and the Reinscription of Space in Late Capitalism', Special Issue on Space, Identity, and the Politics of Difference, *Cultural Anthropology*, vol. 7, no. 1 (1992), pp. 63–67; see p. 67.

7 I am aware that the notion 'Third World' is often used in the West to homogenise what are in fact quite distinctive histories, cultures, and places—and to

create the 'Other'—as pointed out by Chandra Talpade Mohanty and others. Nevertheless it has also served a constructive purpose in the post-colonial world system.

8 Cited in Thomas Abraham, 'Reviving an Old Dream of Afro-Asian Cooperation', *Yale Global Online*, 24 May 2005, https://yaleglobal.yale.edu/ content/reviving-old-dream-afro-asian-cooperation (accessed 4 March 2018).

9 Gupta, 'The Song of the Nonaligned World', p. 64.

10 Satish Kumar, 'Nonalignment: International Goals and National Interests', *Asian Survey*, vol. 23, no. 4 (1983), see pp. 447–48.

11 Quoted in S. S. Mehta, 'Non-Alignment and the New International Economic Order', in K. P. Misra and K. R. Narayanan (eds), *Non-Alignment in Contemporary International Relations* (New Delhi: Vikas, 1981), pp. 174–75.

12 Edward C. Luck, *Mixed Messages: American Politics and International Organization, 1919–1999* (Washington, D.C.: Brookings Institution Press, 1999), p. 107.

13 Jain, *Women, Development and the UN*.

14 Pero Ivacic, 'The Non-aligned Countries Pool Their News—News Agency Network', *UNESCO Courier*, May–June 1986, http://findarticles.com/p/ articles/mi_m1310/is_1986_May–June/ai_4375051 (accessed 28 April 2009).

15 Laura Bier, 'Our Sisters in Struggle: Non-Alignment, Afro-Asian Solidarity and National Identity in the Egyptian Women's Press: 1952–1967', Working Paper no. 4, New York University, New York, 2002.

16 Robert Shaffer, 'Women and International Relations: Pearl S. Buck's Critique of the Cold War', *Journal of Women's History*, vol. 11, no. 3 (1999), pp. 151–75; see p. 164.

17 Veena Mazumdar, 'The Non-Aligned Movement and the International Women's Decade', monograph, n.d.

18 Vida Tomsic, cited in Breda Pavlic and Cees J. Hamelink, *The New International Economic Order: Links between Economics and Communications* (Paris: UNESCO, 1985).

19 Ibid.

20 Jain, *Women, Development, and the UN*.

21 Ibid.

22 Ibid.

23 *UN Chronicle*, 'Anniversary of Non-aligned Movement', 1984, http://findar-ticles.com/p/articles/mi_ m1309/is_v21/ai_3332143 (accessed 2 November 2007).

24 Bier, 'Our Sisters in Struggle'.

25 Ibid.

26 Mark Trumbull, 'Great Global Shift to Service Jobs: Move Over Agriculture', 4 September 2007, http://www.csmonitor.com/2007/0904/p01s02-wogi.html (accessed 4 March 2018).

27 Ann Harrison (ed.), *Globalization and Poverty*, National Bureau of Economic Research Conference Report (Chicago: University of Chicago Press, 2006).

28 For example, Kofi Annan, former UN secretary general, in a speech on the International Day for the Eradication of Poverty delivered on 17 October 2000, said: 'Almost half the world's population lives on less than two dollars a day, yet even this statistic fails to capture the humiliation, powerlessness and brutal hardship that is the daily lot of the world's poor.' See UN Press Releases, 'Secretary-General Stresses Global Responsibility to Work for More Equitable World Economy', 13 October 2000, http://www.unis.unvienna.org/unis/en/pressrels/2000/sg2691.html (accessed 12 April 2018).

29 Raghbendra Jha, 'Reducing Poverty and Inequality in India: Has Liberalization Helped?', paper prepared for the WIDER project 'Rising Income Inequality and Poverty Reduction: Are they Compatible?, 2002, https://crawford.anu.edu.au/acde/publications/publish/papers/wp2002/wp-econ-2002-04.pdf (accessed 7 March 2018).

30 Hania Zlotnik, 'The Global Dimensions of Female Migration', *Migration Information Source*, 1 March 2003, https://www.migrationpolicy.org/article/global-dimensions-female-migration/ (accessed 7 March 2018).

31 Debashis Chakraborty and Dipankar Sengupta, 'IBSAC (India Brazil, South Africa, China): A Potential Developing Country Coalition in WTO Negotiations', Occasional Paper no. 18, Centre de Sciences Humaines, New Delhi, 2006.

32 UN, 'Emerging Issues Containing Additional Material for Further Actions and Initiatives for the Preparation of the Outlook beyond the Year 2000', Report of the Secretary-General Commission on the Status of Women, E-CN-6-2000-PC/4, UN, New York, 7 February 2000.

33 Darryl C. Thomas (ed.), *The Theory and Practice of Third World Solidarity* (Westport, CT: Praeger, 2001).

34 Cited in John Cherian, 'The Relevance of NAM', *Frontline*, vol. 20, no. 4, 15–28 February 2003, http://www.frontline.in/static/html/fl2004/stories/20030228000706000.htm (accessed 7 March 2018).

35 Devaki Jain, 'Invoking Gyana, Women's Knowing, as a Vehicle for Rebellion', Background Paper for Casablanca Dream 'Women Weave Peace into Globalisation', 12–15 January 2007, http://www.casablancadream.net/meetings/casa_07_bg_jain.html (accessed 29 April 2009).

36 Devaki Jain and Shubha Chacko, 'Constructing New Frameworks: Women's Location in the Economies of the NAM Countries', paper presented at the launch of NAM Institute for the Empowerment of Women, Kuala Lumpur, 10 September 2007.

37 Jacqueline Anne Braveboy-Wagner (ed.), *The Foreign Policies of the Global South: Rethinking Conceptual Frameworks* (Boulder, CO: Lynne Rienner, 2003).

38 Mary E. John, 'Feminism, Internationalism and the West: Questions from the Indian Context', Occasional Paper no. 27, Centre for Women's Development Studies, New Delhi, 1998.

39 Ibid.
40 Nazneen Kanji and Kalyani Menon-Sen, 'What Does the Feminisation of Labour Mean for Sustainable Livelihoods?', International Institute for Environment and Development, London, 2001.
41 Cited in Ramachandra Guha, *India after Gandhi: The History of the World's Largest Democracy* (New Delhi: Picador, 2007).

Chapter 13

Morals in Politics
The Gandhian Touch

At the turn of the century, there was an intensity of preoccupation with conflict violence and its relationship with religion. The events of September 11, 2001 left an indelible mark on the course of civilisation. An unprecedented focus on religious identity emerged along with the discourse on terror. At a time when so much was being said about the association of terror with religion, when I was asked to contribute an article to the journal Man in India, *I put forward the argument that it was gross inequality coupled with extraordinary leaps in communication that had led to the kind of anger that was generating the violence. I turned to Gandhi who, at the very core of his thinking, had not only been preoccupied with inequality, but also built his philosophy of ahimsa and identification with the other in order to heal the wounds of inequality.*

In this paper, I suggest that it is tangible inequality, a growing monster in the world, that is breaking up all spaces into conflict-ridden arenas. I suggest that the speed and starkness with which it is exhibiting itself is the outcome of the particular form of economic globalisation in which political economies are driven by the purely hedonistic basis of economic progress, namely, the growth of the monetised domestic product. I point out that such a momentum or model of progress is on a self-destructive roll. I then suggest that in this context, Gandhi offers a doable political economy where the ethical underpinnings of progress drive the economy on a non-violent road to well-being.

THE ECONOMIC OTHER

As death and destruction—due to unexpected conflicts, violence, and improved technologies of violence—increase, there is a quest all over the world for security and, at a deeper level, for peaceful conduct of the business of living in the world. Simultaneously, there is also a seeking for solace, for building reconciliation by reinvoking spirituality, showing the common basis of all religions, drawing on common consciousness. I was also party to such attempts, as can be seen in the book *Speaking of Faith*,[1] where we argued that a feminist perspective and ethic affirmed that all religions had a common purpose and thus unity could be forged. The recent research on the human genome, showing that we all come from a few cells, is another reference point for claiming oneness. There is a trend then to argue that we are one, that we need to build unity within diversity, to tolerate; these are the words of advice, of hope giving, that we hear today.

In this paper, I would argue, however, that this is not enough, nor wise. I think it would feed into the enemy's armoury—if I may use military language—to trace religion, the various ethical and spiritual streams flowing out of it, and ethnicity as the basis of conflict. Invoking the spiritual and the moral, linking it erroneously with religion and tradition, is also the ammunition which is bringing out the affirmation of old identities to handle the new consumer-based disparities,[2] foregrounding the contradiction between ostensible opportunities provided by the hype on globalisation, and the reality on the ground, where the goodies are available only to the few. Today, the 'other' is being postulated as Muslim or Hindu or Christian, but the hostility and violence we see, the intolerance, I suggest, come from the economic 'other'.

As the demarcation of society and politics shifts from social and economic categories to religious and cultural categories, there is an anxiety amongst people like myself and Amartya Sen at this reinvocation of old categories. Amartya Sen, referring to the issue of identities and our freedom to choose our affiliations and associations, says:

> This issue has become particularly important in the context of the present political crisis and confrontation, with its ramifications becoming clearer since September 11, though the roots of the problem go back

much further.... By categorising the population of the world into those belonging to 'the Islamic world', 'the Christian world', 'the Hindu world', 'the Buddhist world', etc., the divisive power of classificatory priority is implicitly used to place people firmly inside a unique set of rigid boxes. Other divisions (say, between the rich and the poor, between members of different classes and occupations, between people of different politics, between distinct nationalities and residential locations, between language groups, etc.) are all submerged by this allegedly pre-eminent way of seeing the differences between people.[3]

Such pigeonholing takes the world back to the days of the crusaders of medieval times. It takes us back to the dark ages, when bigotry constituted the limits of the human imagination. Since then, not only the Enlightenment in the West but the intellectual expression of societies in the 'South' and the 'East' has extended the boundaries of our imagination to apprehend other categories of stratification and division, such as class, ethnicity, caste, gender, occupation. Nations have identified themselves not as Christian or pagan but as newly liberated or colonial. The role of religion as conqueror was eroded in the 20th century, and there was a sharp fall in attendance in churches, temples and mosques worldwide.

Philosophies were born which made any form of narrow definition of the 'moral' and the 'good', like the Ten Commandments or sacred texts, look absurd. Linguistic philosophy à la Wittgenstein, the existentialism of Jean Paul Sartre, and not least, Marxism, and then the 'universal consciousness' philosophies of the various forms of religion from Asia, literary and artistic expressions from so many sources which celebrate human existence, and 'civilisations' built around the culture of human beings and not theologies, held the space in the 20th century. Religion actually was transforming itself, e.g., the liberation theology emerging from Christianity, and many other Reformist shoots of orthodoxy were sprouting.

But recent events seem to have set the clock back, and today the term 'civilisation' or 'world' is being defined or notified in terms of religious identity—the 'Islamic world', 'Islamic civilisation', as juxtaposed with the 'Christian', 'Hindu', etc. This has led to a dangerous grouping of people 'within this new unitary system by turning to the most immediate, familiar collectively shared instrument at hand to mobilise: inherited culture. In many countries there has been a convulsive ingathering, a return to past traditions and a resurgent assertion of peoples and their leaders.'[4]

I propose that it is concentration of political power coupled with economic disparities that needs to be dismantled or redressed for healing to take place. Exclusion from power to redress injustices and the perpetuation of disparities in access to the necessities of life are firing the conflict, the hate, the militancy, the violence. Thus one can argue that persistent poverty, especially the lack of opportunities for what is called 'work with dignity', inequality, and the visible lifestyle of high-end consumerism, all perpetuated and enlarged by the effect of the visual media, has created the 'economic other'. It is this intensification of anger at inequality, injustice and invasive persecution, accompanied by the carelessness about loss of lives in spaces where 'losing life' is not such a unique happening, i.e., amongst the very poor, that can explain the increasing occurrence of human bombs.[5]

INEQUALITY INTENSIFIES: CREATING THE ECONOMIC OTHER

To support my argument that the economic divide is the real perpetrator of violence, I present some data on disparities. First, I turn to a brilliant paper that was presented by Dr Ismail Serageldin, director of the Alexandria Bibliotheca, Egypt.[6] The figures are very stark: the 400 highest income earners in the United States make as much money in a year as the entire population of 20 African nations—more than 300 million people. The income of the richest 10 per cent of the world's population is roughly 117 times higher than that of the poorest 10 per cent, which is a huge jump from the ratio in 1980, when it was about 79 times higher than the poorest 10 per cent.[7] There are other gaps too, besides those measured by income. The supposed 'knowledge revolution' has also served to accentuate old differences and create new inequalities. In 2004, less than 3 out of every 100 Africans use the internet, compared with an average of 1 out of every 2 inhabitants of the G-8 countries (Canada, France, Germany, Italy, Japan, Russia, the UK and the US). More internet users reside in the G-8 counties than in the whole of the rest of the world combined.[8]

This kind of picture is further supported by two other papers on the rising inequality in wealth and in incomes worldwide.[9] It is also clear that rather than traditional causes, it is 'new causes' that are linked to the excessively liberal economic policy regimes and the way in which economic reform policies have been carried out, that are responsible for this increase in inequality.[10] Country after country has experienced an upsurge in income inequality. Table 13.1 presents the number of countries in each period where the trend (of decreasing inequality) was reversed.

A recent World Bank study reveals that between 1820 and 1992, the income share of the bottom 60 per cent of the world's population halved to around 10 per cent, while the share of the top 10 per cent rose to more than 50 per cent.[11] The *Human Development Report 2006* draws attention to the growing inequality in the world's water and sanitation services. Entitled *Beyond Scarcity: Power, Poverty and the Global Water Crisis*, the report looks at water and sanitation as essential human rights, and their inadequacy as a vast economic cost and a cause of many social problems.[12]

In India too, the disparities have been growing in geometrical progression, especially since 1995 when 'economic reforms', a euphemism for neoliberal economic policies, trade and financial liberalisation, were introduced. Within India, the sharp and appalling rise in inequality is evident in the fact that while until 1993–94, the all-India Gini coefficient of per capita consumption expenditure was fairly stable, it has shown a marked increase since then. The magnitude and rate of change of inequalities are quite substantial, as very sharp contrasts are evident between the rural sectors of the slow-growing states and the urban sectors of the fast-growing states, as well as other geographical zones (Figure 13.1).

About 75,000 to 150,000 women die every year in India after giving birth, according to the World Health Organization. And if we delve deeper, again the story of inequality becomes evident. For example, one study shows that over 67 per cent of maternal deaths occurred among the oppressed castes and indigenous populations; in another district it was noted that 48 per cent of the women who had died had had no formal schooling.[13]

Table 13.1 *Increase in global income inequality, 1960–65 to 1991–97*

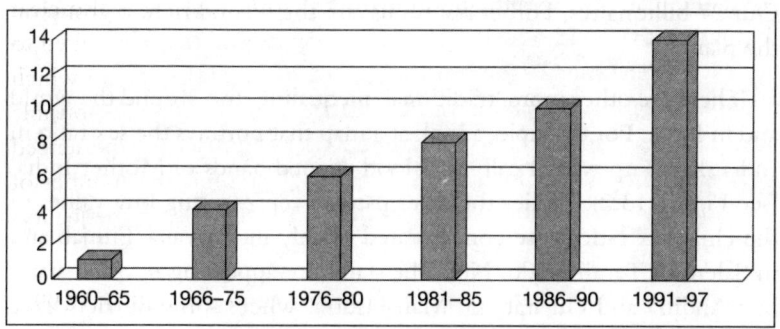

Source: Giovanni Andrea Cornia with Sampsa Kiiski, 'Trends in Income Distribution in the Post-World War II Period: Evidence and Interpretation', WIDER Discussion Paper no. 89, UNU/WIDER, Helsinki.

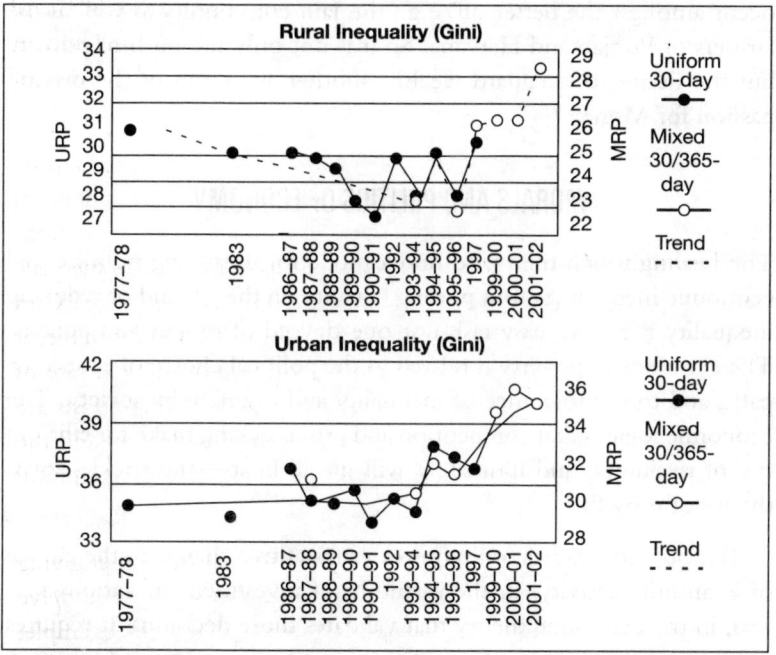

Figure 13.1 *Rising inequality in India: rural and urban*

Source: Abhijit Sen and Himanshu, 'Poverty and Inequality in India II: Widening Disparities during the 1990s', *Economic & Political Weekly*, vol. 39, no. 39 (2004), pp. 4361–75; see p. 4366.

India now ranks eighth in the world in the number of billionaires. Our 27 billionaires, Forbes assures us, are the second richest group on the planet.[14]

There are other more 'traditional' inequalities too around the world and in India. For example, a look at a map that portrays the sex ratio in India shows up what I call 'the blood-stained hands of Mother India' (see Figure 13.2). Earlier the paler patches representing low values of the child sex ratio were concentrated mainly in Haryana/Punjab and in Salem in Tamil Nadu. Now the stains are appearing in other states like Andhra and Gujarat and Maharashtra, where some districts have also shown a decrease of 50 and more points in the child sex ratio, revealing another Indic tradition—a killing field for females of the species. Detailed analysis of this phenomenon by the Registrar General as well as by the NFHS shows that the higher proportions of such killings occur amongst the better off, e.g., the Jain community as well as the farmers of Punjab and Haryana. So it is not only the push of poverty but the desire to safeguard wealth, another symptom of the driving passion for Money.[15]

MORALS AND POLITICS OF ECONOMY

The healing touch then is to find a mode for dissolving political and economic inequalities. But putting equality on the ground or reducing inequality is not an easy task nor one devoid of morals and politics. The existence of poverty is related to the political choice of economic paths and to the tolerance of inequality and injustice by society. The economic logic is that competition and profit seeking make for efficient use of resources, and ultimately will lift all boats—the trickle-down theory of growth.

But poverty eradication requires a substantive change in the choice of economic activity, in the quantum of investment in various sectors, in the economic theory that validates those decisions. It requires a shift in reasoning regarding what drives the economy and what are the indicators of progress. As the late Prof. Mahbub ul Haq lamented, 'For too long, it was assumed that development was a process that lifts all boats, that its benefits trickled down to all income classes and that it was gender-neutral in its impact. Experience teaches otherwise. Wide income disparities and gender gaps stare us in the face in all societies.' He added that growth sometimes actually immiserises and further fuels civil strife by distancing the 'haves' from the 'have nots', and that economic growth was not dealing with poverty and inequality, but actually increasing it.[16]

A person who bundled all this together, a social scientist who respected science and technology and religion, but most of all challenged us as human beings, was Mahatma Gandhi. Gandhi's ethic was actually to efface difference through absorption of the other. This idea of human existence is one of the basic tenets of Jainism, to absorb the other into oneself and thus eliminate difference and distance. This is ahimsa, a concept that was birthed by Jainism, which Gandhi says he learnt from his mother who was a practising Jain.

There was a wisdom in the thought of both Karl Marx and Mahatma Gandhi in addressing inequality as the crux of the matter, in addressing the rich, the 'haves', even though there is a crucial difference in their analysis as well as in their advice. Marx and his analysis are well known. But Gandhi's can be restated. While Marx dealt with inequality through restructuring the economic system and making the state all-powerful, Gandhi sought political solutions based on social negotiations and a 'low-profile' state.[17]

Gandhi, like Marx and Hobbes before him, saw the human being as a limited creature, capable of cruelty, narrow-mindedness, greed and violence and requiring strong medicine to be socially manageable. Indeed, when we see starving people, especially women and children marching in the thousands across national boundaries trying to escape from violence; when we hear that when child refugees cross the border, security personnel pick up girl children to sell them into the flesh trade; when we turn away from the expropriation of earth, water and mountains for 'growth'—then their perceptions seem correct.

While orthodox socialism addresses itself to inequality based on ownership of the means of production, Gandhi focused on inequality in consumption. His argument or his advocacy for austerity, for simplicity of lifestyle, was based on developing in Indians a consciousness of the problems of the poor. To consume much food or own or display too many clothes when the neighbourhood was filled with those who could neither eat nor clothe themselves was a form of violence. There is a beautiful story of how a child living near the Sabarmati Ashram asked Gandhi why he only wore a dhoti and no shirt. The child offered to bring Gandhi a shirt. Gandhi is supposed to have said that he would wear a shirt when all the millions of shirtless Indians could also afford a shirt. Thus the practice of simplicity was in some sense an attempt to emulate or imitate the lives of those who did not have enough, and thereby release resources to be able to provide for them.

Gandhi not only brought in consumption as a key issue in fostering inequality or in reverse-building equality, his practice and preaching on restrained consumption were also directed towards the conservation of nature and resource sharing. He argued that visible disparity in consumption was a form of *himsa*, violence, while ahimsa would require that we transpose our lives and the lives of the poorest. Gandhi took this technique of identification with the 'deprived' into many other domains—a mode of melting down hierarchies.

In the ashrams, or collectives, that Gandhi built, in those days, roles were constantly transposed to dismantle hierarchies. For example, everyone—men, women, children—had to do manual work as well as 'meditational' work, so that the educated would not look down on those who lived by manual work. Brahmins had to lift night soil so that night soil lifting could not hold stigma or justify untouchability. Persons belonging to all the diverse religions in India had to recite the prayers of *all* religions: a Hindu would read the Quran, the Christian, Hindu prayers. This was a way of effacing distance through muting the kinds of differences that connote hierarchy.

The ethic of simplicity bordering on austerity has a special power in visibly poor, unequal societies like India. It not only provides a demonstrative identification with the poor, but also allows a more even spread of scarce resources. As Gandhi saw it, it was also a form of ahimsa, as there was less open aggression due to less aggrandisement of scarce resources by the few. The importance of this package is that masses of Indian women—those who were poor and those from traditional contexts—could also assimilate it. It sprang from values they understood.[18]

MUTING GENDER HIERARCHIES

A vivid illustration of Gandhi's particular capacity to draw the poor and the excluded into political and economic action is offered by the way he mobilised women from traditional societies into public action. One such incident is revealing, as it brought women out, and also changed their views of themselves and the outside's views on women.

There was a time in 1930 when, along with the Salt Satyagraha, picketing against foreign textiles and liquor was taken up. Gandhiji found that the movement was not gathering enough momentum. He decided then to address himself to the women. His call was answered in Delhi under the leadership of Srimathi Satyawati Vidyalankar—Delhi's first woman satyagrahi. A group of women walked down Chandni Chowk distributing bangles to men and asking them to wear the bangles and stay at home, as now the women would be taking over the movement. This incident came to be known as the *churi andolan* (revolution through bangles). The movement caught fire: women and girls left their sheltered lives and began to court arrest by picketing liquor shops.[19]

Whenever a leader in their community was arrested, the women would organise a day of mourning. They donned saffron robes—the colour of sacrifice—to show visibly that they were prepared to suffer for this cause. In twos and threes, they sat down on chairs placed before shops selling drugs, liquor or tobacco; they pleaded with men who came to buy at these shops, to give their money instead to Gandhi. When pleading was to no avail, they flung themselves across the thresholds, daring the men to walk over their bodies.

It was something never known before in India. But money was being gathered by this army of women, fighting with its own version of satyagraha. They went to prison cheerfully. There were modern women like Jawaharlal Nehru's wife Kamala Nehru and his younger sister Krishna. But there were others, wives and daughters who had lived in purdah all their lives. These were the women who formed the masses, the strength of numbers and solidarity of action without which no boycott movements could have any effect. They were women who had emerged from behind traditional doors in response to Gandhi's call.

Like millions of other conventionally brought up girls, especially from the orthodox Vaisya community, intensified in its orthodoxy by Jainism, my mother-in-law Chameli Devi had been married into another equally well-known commercial family of Delhi jewellers, where, as expected, her life had moved around rituals and the kitchen and, of course, the inevitable *ghoonghat* (veil). She was the first Jain woman to court arrest and was sent to a jail in Lahore. What did it require for an orthodox daughter-in-law to become a freedom fighter? A khadi saree, a blouse and a pair of chappals. And a call from a saintly person.[20]

Once women were drawn out of their homes into the arena of struggle, once men got used to women working with them on important and risky tasks, women were emancipated from the greatest source of enslavement, i.e., attitudes—the attitude of men about what women can and ought to do; the attitude of women towards themselves, their own roles and their adequacy; the attitude of the *samaj*, the society, to what is right and what is wrong.

INTERPRETING GANDHI AS A GROWTH THEORIST

As a matter of doctrinal importance, the Gandhian system of economic thought runs at a tangent to conventional economic canons. While the engines of the normal theories of growth involve processes of production and investment stimulated by finance and driven by profit seeking, Gandhi's engine is buying power, the 'economic votes', as he called it, of the poor. He offered a talisman:

> Whenever you are in doubt, or when the self becomes too much with you, apply the following test. Recall the face of the poorest and the weakest man or woman whom you may have seen and ask yourself if the step you contemplate is going to be of any use to him.[21]

Mahbub ul Haq, the founder of the human development movement, gives Gandhi's talisman pride of place in his *South Asia Human Development Report*.

According to this line of reasoning, the criterion by which any political choice for economic change is made is whether it improves the condition of the poorest person. If we deal with the removal of poverty first, then the rest of the economic policies follow. Gandhi, it could be suggested, would argue that poverty eradication is a dynamic and purposeful engine of growth. His view could be called the 'bubbling-up theory of growth', which counters the old 'trickle-down theory of growth'. The 'bubbling-up' theory argues that the process of removal of poverty can itself be an engine of growth, that the incomes and capabilities of those who are currently poor have the potential to generate demand, which in turn will drive production, but of goods that are immediately needed by the poor which are currently peripheral in production. This engine of growth will bubble up and fire the economy in a much more broad-based manner. Unlike export-led growth, it will not skew production and trade into the elite trap, which is accentuating disparities and creating discontent. Gandhi even designed an economic constitution for the world in 1928:

> According to me, the economic constitution of India and for that matter, the world, should be such that no one under it should suffer from want of food and clothing. In other words, everybody should be able to get sufficient work to enable him to make the two ends meet. And this ideal can be universally realized only if the means of production of the elementary necessities of life remain in the control of the masses.[22]

Gandhi's method of linking revolutionary action, which is a one-time public action or struggle, with constructive work, which involves mundane, down-to-earth, sustained social and development work, such as providing livelihoods through khadi, offered continuity. Further, his approach of working with organisations, institutions outside of the state, what in today's language are called 'self-help groups' or civil society organisations, is more important than being in government, and enables men and women to move smoothly from struggle work to development work but outside and often against the state.

Gandhi was averse to all notions of class warfare and concepts of class-based revolution, which he saw as the cause of social violence and disharmony. Gandhi's concept of egalitarianism was centred on the preservation of human dignity rather than material development. For Gandhi, the distinctiveness of others which evokes our affection is significant only in so far as it is a starting point that aids us in reaching the highest form of moral concern—a kind of agape, or unselfish love for all. This is also elaborated by Fatema Mernissi, who proposes the concept of *ulfa*, a Sufi construct.

> Ulfa requires that you invest time and brain to figure out how you can 'harmonize' with the other so that he becomes 'anis', literally sociable and friendly, which is the very root of the Arabic word for human being 'insaan'. 'Al Anasu', the human, is by definition the creature who does not live in solitude like a savage animal (wahsha).[23]

Gandhi carried these ideas forward in extraordinary ways, for example, in his design and support of khadi (handspun and handwoven cloth). He said:

> Political economists assert that social affections are to be looked upon as accidental and disturbing elements in human nature; but avarice and the desire for progress are constant elements.... it is this human element on which the entire economics of khadi rests. The human element is not accidental; on the contrary, it is intrinsic—khadi is a superior cloth because 'it has a soul in it.'[24]

He said, further: 'There are many aspects of khadi; amongst them the spiritual one is the one I hold uppermost and the economic one next.'[25] The spiritual aspect was repentance for having willingly surrendered freedom: 'The English have not taken India; we have given it to them.... It is we, the English-knowing men that have enslaved India.... Foreign cloth constitutes our slavery.... We are purifying ourselves by discarding foreign cloth which is the badge of our slavery.'[26] Khadi was not just about employment, which only served to alienate mind, body and spirit from each other, but about engagement of the mind, body and spirit in the means of livelihood and in creating the right conditions for social life. This was its human element.[27]

LESSONS FOR THE GLOBAL COMMUNITY

How then can we draw on ahimsa, on such moral and methodological ideas, in handling today's turbulent world? The central issue in the world today is the management of the global political economy. There is deep anxiety that the new millennium, while it has brought the exciting levelling made possible by information technology and the affirmative spirit of the rights movements, also brings with it planetary deterioration and conflict arising out of the persistence of poverty and the accentuation of disparities. There is a noticeable vacuum in exemplary leadership, whether at the local, national or international level. It is here that Gandhi's ideas in political economy not only seem relevant, but are being legitimised even if without attribution by the course of experience.

Gandhi is quoted as saying there is enough in the world for everybody's need but not for everybody's greed. According to a *New York Times* article, after the financial crisis, 'greed, to put it mildly, is no longer good.'[28] A new interest in 'frugal lifestyles' and 'frugal behaviour' has emerged.[29] In a survey of Indians after the crisis on what they had been deprived of due to lower incomes, they said only those things that were, in some sense, not necessities—what they could do without!

Today's vanguard in development speaks of discrimination, of disparities as threats to economic growth and political stability, of the importance of restrained consumption, even if primarily for environmental reasons. For instance, the UNDP's *Human Development Report 1998* is on the theme of consumption, following its 1997 report on poverty.[30] It argues that ever-expanding consumption puts a strain on the environment through emissions and wastes that pollute the earth and destroy ecosystems, and through the growing depletion and degradation of renewable resources, which undermines livelihoods. The world's dominant consumers are overwhelmingly concentrated among the well off, but the burden of environmental damage from the world's consumption falls most severely on the poor.

In *A Climate of Injustice*, J. Timmons Roberts and Bradley Parks analyse the role that inequality between rich and poor nations plays in the negotiation of global climate agreements.[31] They argue that global inequality dampens co-operative efforts by reinforcing 'structuralist' worldviews and causal beliefs regarding many poor nations, eroding conditions of generalised trust, and promoting particularistic notions of 'fair' solutions. The authors develop new measures of climate-related inequality, analysing fatality and homelessness rates from hydro-meteorological disasters, patterns of 'emissions inequality', and participation in international environmental regimes. Until we recognise that reaching a North–South global climate pact requires addressing larger issues of inequality and striking a global bargain on environment and development, Roberts and Parks argue, the current policy gridlock will remain unresolved.[32]

None of our theories—of the modernisation, dependency, neoliberal or Marxist varieties—seems to be working in the sense that they have all run into trouble, even if they secured initial successes.

During the 1980s and 1990s, these theories were supplanted by a hegemonic neoliberal view of development based on 'globalisation' and 'free markets' that effectively dismisses questions of ethnicity and culture and does not try to understand nationalism, fundamentalism and terrorism. It can be maintained that the whole Western model of development, the 'paradigm of modernity' of a secular, industrial nation-state, is now in question, and that a coherent and persuasive alternative model is yet to be found.[33]

Interpreting inequality as violence, finding the ethical basis for economic growth paths—these are ideas that Gandhi spelt out, and evolved appropriate practices for, in an earlier India. The package of consumption restraint, non-violence in personal relationships, levelling hierarchies by beginning with the lowest—this constitutes morals in political economy.

NOTES

1   Eck and Jain, *Speaking of Faith*.
2   Alaknanda Patel, 'Gujarat Violence: A Personal Diary', *Economic & Political Weekly*, vol. 37, no. 50 (2002), pp. 4985–87.
3   Amartya Sen, 'Exclusion and Inclusion', South Asians for Human Rights (SAHR) Convention on 'Including the Excluded', New Delhi, 11–12 November 2001.
4   Lourdes Arizpe, 'Power of Culture', speech delivered at the 'Power of Culture' conference, Amsterdam, 8–9 November 1996.

5 Jain, 'Through the Looking Glass of Poverty'.

6 Ismail Serageldin, 'The Self and the Other: Tolerance and Justice in a Globalizing World', paper presented at the North-South Round Table 'Imperatives of Tolerance and Justice in a Globalized World', Cairo, 27–28 November 2002.

7 Robert Weissman, 'Grotesque Inequality: Corporate Globalization and the Global Gap between Rich and Poor', *Multinational Monitor*, 1 July 2003.

8 World Summit on the Information Society, 'What's the State of ICT Access around the World?', http://www.itu.int/net/wsis/tunis/newsroom/stats/ (accessed 18 March 2018).

9 Peter Edwards, 'Examining Inequality: Who Really Benefits from Global Growth?', *World Development*, vol. 34, no. 10 (2006), pp. 1667–95, see p. 1684; see also James B. Davies, Susanna Sandström, Anthony Shorrocks and Edward N. Wolff, 'The Level and Distribution of Global Household Wealth', *Economic Journal*, vol. 121, no. 551 (2010), pp. 223–54.

10 Giovanni Andrea Cornia and Julius Court, 'Inequality, Growth and Poverty in the Era of Liberalization and Globalization', Policy Brief no. 4, UNU WIDER, 2001.

11 Mihir Shah, 'Cutting Off the Chain of Hate', *Hindu*, 21 October 2008.

12 UNDP, *Human Development Report 2006: Beyond Scarcity: Power, Poverty and the Global Water Crisis* (New York: UNDP, 2006).

13 *Financial Express*, 'Maternal Mortality: This India Story Is a Shame!', 7 October 2008, http://www.financialexpress.com/archive/maternal-mortality-this-india-story-is-a-shame/370599/ (accessed 18 March 2018).

14 P. Sainath, 'The Anatomy of a Tiger India High and Low', *Hindu*, 12 November 2006.

15 Scott Baldauf, 'India's "Girl Deficit" Deepest among Educated', *Christian Science Monitor*, 16 January 2006, http://www.csmonitor.com/2006/0113/p01s04-wosc.html (accessed 18 March 2018).

16 UNDP, *Human Development Report 1995*.

17 Jain, 'Minds, Not Bodies'.

18 Jain, 'Indian Women Today and Tomorrow'.

19 Devaki Jain, 'Journey of a Woman Freedom Fighter', *Mainstream*, 1981.

20 Ibid.

21 Jain, *Minds, Bodies and Exemplars*, p. 8.

22 V. K. Natraj, Kamlesh Mishra and Neeru Kapoor (eds), *Gandhian Alternative* (*Economics Where People Matter*, vol. 4), Gandhian Studies and Peace Research Series no. 26, Gandhi Smriti and Darshan Smriti, p. 318.

23 Fatema Mernissi, 'Love in Digital Islam: Why Ibn Hazm Is a Success on the Internet', Sharjah Conference on Culture (supported by UNESCO, 2008.

24 Rahul Ramagundam, *Gandhi's Khadi: A History of Contention and Conciliation* (Hyderabad: Orient Longman, 2008), p. 106.

25 Ibid., p. 12.

26 Ibid., pp. 24–27.

27 Ibid.
28 Peter Steinfels, 'Modern Market Thinking Has Devalued a Deadly Sin', *New York Times*, 27 September 2008.
29 Jan Hoffman, 'The Frugal Teenager, Ready or Not', *New York Times*, 10 October 2008.
30 UNDP, *Human Development Report 1998: Consumption for Human Development* (New York: Oxford University Press, 1998); UNDP, *Human Development Report 1997: Human Development to Eradicate Poverty* (New York: Oxford University Press, 1997).
31 J. Timmons Roberts and Bradley C. Parks, *A Climate of Injustice: Global Inequality, North-South Politics, and Climate Policy* (Cambridge: MIT Press, 2007).
32 Ibid.
33 Emmerij, 'Development Thinking, Globalization and Cultural Diversity'.

Chapter 14

Exploring Economic Inequality
From Piketty through Adiga to Gandhi

Thomas Piketty's book, Capital in the Twenty-First Century, burst upon the world in 2013, dramatising what was by then a well-known phenomenon: not only the presence of economic inequality, but also its growth by leaps and bounds. Many UN agencies and individual economists had been pointing to this outcome of the neoliberal programme, namely, the emergence of the very rich parallel to the emergence of millions of poor. In this lecture, apart from referring to the various strands of literature on economic inequality, I referred to some solutions that had been put forward in earlier eras by political economists like Gandhi, ideas later deployed by feminist economists to argue that there is a way out of this increasing inequality.

It is a very special moment for me to be at the Azim Premji University. I am grateful to S. Giridhar and Dileep Ranjekar for giving me this opportunity. My husband, L. C. Jain, had been associated with some of the stalwarts here during the years we stayed in Bangalore, i.e., from 2000 to 2010, and he used to tell me about this innovative and outstanding educational initiative. I was therefore especially pleased to be invited here. Tomorrow, i.e., 14 November, it will be exactly four years since he left us, and since our lives, his and mine, were one, and our ideologies were also of one weave, I would like to dedicate this lecture to him. Actually, I would have liked him to read it and improve it… I would like to imagine that he is listening.

The theme on which I usually feel confident to speak is how to 'gender-ise' development policy. I have done work on this not only in Karnataka earlier, when I was doing research, but also when I was a member of the State Planning Board.[1] More recently I have participated in an exercise that I initiated to undertake a different kind of gendering of the 11th and 12th Plans. I then brought this methodology to Karnataka, and I am happy to tell you that a group of us, women economists drawn only from Karnataka, were able to intervene quite strongly in gendering the draft Karnataka 12th Plan.[2] I am told that this nucleus is now a part of the planning process in Karnataka.

I wish I had shared these methodologies with you, as then the university could have built a strong space both to understand the method of gendering public policy, as well as to create a think tank which would intervene continuously in public debate with the knowledge that emerges out of women's lived experience as well as the knowledge that comes out of academic research by women.

So then you might ask, why am I engaging with the question of economic inequality and GDP growth, and not with gender inequality, which is the running theme when it comes to women's discourse? Two reasons: First, I believe that it is almost obscene for the women's movement to demand gender equality when the macro-economic space is overwhelmed with gross economic inequalities. I have spoken out on this in lectures and other writings, such as in my recent lecture at the Roosevelt Institute, New York, titled 'The Evolution of Ideas: A Feminist's Reflections on the Partnership with the UN System'.[3] Second, in the early days of the women's movement, we used to challenge the UN and others who identified the goal as gender equality with the question, do we want to eat a piece of the poisoned cake? That is to say, if the whole system is unjust, do we want to be included in it, or should we challenge it and transform it? It is in this spirit that I am now preoccupied with the tangible and growing wealth and income inequalities that we see around us and the world over.

One might ask, why now? The answer lies in the explosion of debates, discourses and literature on the global economy as it stands now, and the debates that have been triggered on inequality by Thomas Piketty's book, *Capitalism in the Twenty-First Century*.[4] The book features in the *New York Times* bestseller list in the non-fiction category. All this means that a lot of people are reading it and talking about it.[5]

And why Gandhi? Gandhi was obsessed with inequality. My limited understanding of Gandhi is that he saw violence in the presence of inequalities, whether in the form of gender, caste, religion or income and wealth disparities, or colonial domination. Gandhi tried to enable his people to overcome such violence in moral ways, which of course is not the language of today. But it is worth thinking about these ideas, especially for the younger generation who are, in my opinion, seeking a moral philosophy which is tangible.

I want to go on a journey that builds on the current discussions on economic inequality by current economic theorists; the various ideas for rectifying this phenomenon that are being discussed; and then show how we land, after all that, in Gandhian thought! But I have a further agenda, which I hope all of you will participate in and take forward. This is to raise a well-reasoned voice—one that is neither Marxist nor neoliberal, just grounded—for another kind of economic programme for India. I hope my lecture will persuade you to join in this quest.

My lecture will unfold in the following sections. In the first section, I take up the contemporary discussion and consideration of the phenomenon of economic inequality. The second section addresses the analysis that GDP growth is led by capital, investment, and their free movement, and that labour as a factor of production has lost its charm and its place in relation to economic growth and success. The third section takes up the trickle-down theory of growth and its dependence on capital-led economic policies. In the fourth section, I outline the 'bubbling-up' theory of growth and its dependence on a broad base of livelihoods, or 'wage-led growth' as it is now called. Finally I ask: are we, in India, forfeiting the unique advantage we have to build growth with equality?

THE DISCUSSION AROUND THE PHENOMENON OF ECONOMIC INEQUALITY

I am sure that many of you here have not only heard about Thomas Piketty's book but have actually read it, engaged with the hypothesis, and developed your own response to his analysis. Piketty argues that the main driver of inequality—the tendency of returns on capital to exceed the rate of economic growth—threatens to generate extreme inequalities, stir discontent and undermine democratic values. But economic trends are not acts of God, he says. Political action has curbed dangerous inequalities in the past, Piketty argues, and may do so again.[6]

The other person I shall draw into this discussion is Aravind Adiga. Many of you may have read his book, *White Tiger*.[7] If you have not, I strongly advise you to read it. In my opinion, it is the most powerful argument against the kind of inequality, the exclusion, the wretchedness in which we have left masses of our people in the hinterlands in India—and how that breeds criminals and breaks up society. If Adiga does not awaken us to the perils of inequality, to the fact that it breeds corruption, criminality and total anarchy in morals, no one can.

While Piketty might have received an extraordinary reception, growing inequality and its impact not only on economic success but on the social and political fabric have been a subject of concern and of theories and even advisories for many decades.[8] However, of late these concerns have taken centre stage, and I want to refer to five major pre-Piketty global reports by the UN and other international agencies.[9] If I may for a minute rise to the confidence levels of my good friend Amartya Sen, I would like to state that I had drawn similar links as far back as 1997 at the UNDP conference on poverty.[10]

A striking report titled *Inequality Matters: Report on the World Social Situation 2013*,[11] prepared by the UN's Department of Social and Economic Affairs, presents data on the increase in inequality within nations and globally. It argues that 'in addition to inhibiting economic growth over time, inequality can also generate greater market volatility and instability.'[12] This is through the impact of inequality on the generation of finance-driven business cycles. The report also suggests a relationship between inequality and the onset of economic recession. It provides evidence that both the Great Depression of the 1930s and the 2007–08 Great Recession were preceded by sharp increases in income and wealth inequality and rapid rise in debt-to-income ratios among lower- and middle-income households.

Now, you would think that such an analysis and the warning it provides would really make those who are promoting the kind of GDP growth that we see today (euphemistically called 'reform', but basically involving market- and capital-led growth) sit up. This report clearly tells them that this road will lead to a crash! But such warnings are not taken note of, and all our countries are following the same mantra or programme for generating GDP growth.

Humanity Divided: Confronting Inequality in Developing Countries, the title of a UNDP report from 2013,[13] comments on the current growth paradigm, showing how the sharpest increases in income inequality have occurred in those developing countries that were especially successful in pursuing vigorous growth, and managed, as a result, to graduate into higher-income brackets. 'Economic progress in these countries has not alleviated disparities, but rather exacerbated them.'[14] Further, it suggests that there is evidence to show that increases in inequality over the last two decades were mainly on account of trade and financial globalisation processes that 'weakened the bargaining position of relatively immobile labour vis-à-vis fully mobile capital'.[15] Here we see a finger pointing clearly not only at the followers of reform, but at the mix of trade- and finance-driven growth and the neglect of labour.

The ILO's contribution[16] to these discussions is the most pertinent, being unintentionally linked to Piketty's analysis. The ILO makes a strong argument that 'it is time to reconsider the validity of these pro-capital distributional policies, and to examine the possibility of an alternative path, one based on pro-labour distributional policies, accompanied by legislative changes and structural policies.'[17] The ILO puts forth a case for wage-led growth, i.e., a growth that is led through the expansion of employment and the wages that it entails.

'Working for the Few: Political Capture and Economic Inequality', an Oxfam briefing paper,[18] argues that a situation of such deep inequality where the economy is controlled by the few will lead to policies that naturally support their interests. Feminists had flagged this link between poverty and inequality earlier,[19] but until the big agencies took up this construct and Piketty blew the whistle, this was not taken note of.

The UNCTAD report *Trade and Development Report 2010: Employment, Globalization, and Development*[20] carries this argument forward into macro-economic reasoning. It extends the proposal for a wage-led growth track with the argument that wages would have to be perceived, not just as a cost of production, but as a major source of aggregate demand, such that rising wage bills can actually propel economic recovery in slumps, and generate conditions for stable growth. The inability of economic growth to create sufficient decent work to meet the requirements of the labour force is a major part of the problem.[21]

China and India offer excellent illustrations of some of these theorems. They are both following the trade and financialisation track—and both now have galloping economic inequality of wealth and incomes. Here are two slides which dramatise this increase in income inequality in India and China in the last few years (Figure 14.1).

I love the idea of Alibaba; e-commerce enterprises like these are like the 40 thieves! Alibaba, as you know, is a Chinese e-commerce enterprise, which in September 2014 raised more than $25 billion, making it the largest IPO in history and putting its founder on the list of the top 70 wealthiest men in the world.[22] In India we have Flipkart, Amazon and Snapdeal all vying with each other for the same space, also making their founders billionaires, and my guess is that Alibaba, with the expertise of the Chinese in invading markets, might overpower them all!

Another concern that has been raised is that inequality breeds unrest and civic breakdowns, and the Arab Spring and the Occupy Wall Street movements are used to illustrate this phenomenon. But I think there has also been a flip side to this argument, as these movements are being seen as driven by the middle-class, those who are educated and also IT-savvy, who see others taking more from the pie than they themselves get—not quite a working-class revolution!

It is here that I think Aravind Adiga is relevant to our concerns. Adiga goes right to the bottom of the pile, those grubby boys we see at bus stops and tea shops in the backwaters of rural and urban India, who can see how the better off move ahead by cheating and killing, yet keep on moving. It is this sharp, tangible wretchedness of the very poor, and our total insensitivity to it, that Adiga addresses. He shows the violence that it inculcates, and at the same time how compelling it is in the circumstances.

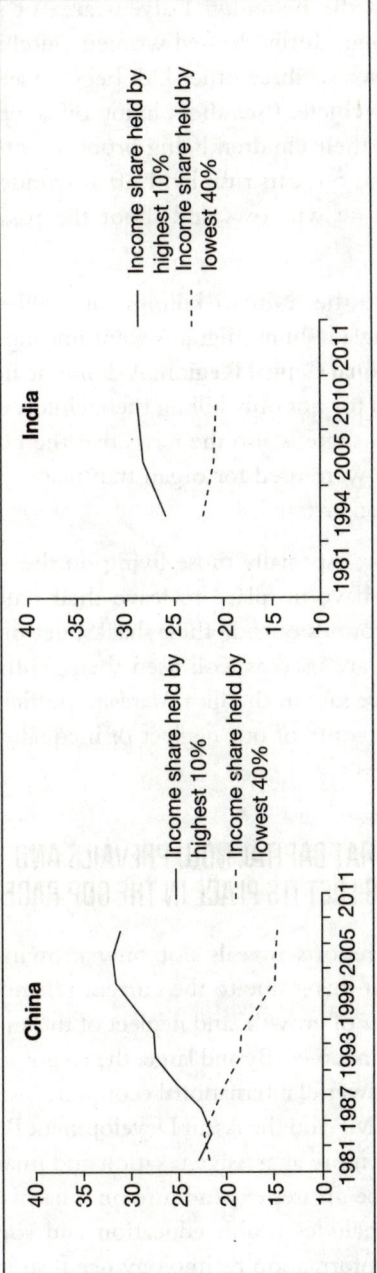

Figure 14.1 *Increasing inequality in selected middle-income countries*

Source: Fuentes-Nieva and Galasso, 'Working for the Few'.

As we drive around the better-off Lutyens area of south Delhi, we see miserable, starving, dirtily dressed women clutching babies in their arms along with two or three other kids begging at the window of our air-conditioned vehicle. I see them living on the pavements in tents made of rags, and their children being brought onto the tarmac to urinate and defecate as our cars rush by. I often wonder when they will begin to smash those windows and shoot the passengers. The inequality is so glaring.

One may recall here the 'Nithari killings' of 2005–07, when at least 38 children of Bangladeshi immigrants went missing in a wealthy housing area in the National Capital Region. A domestic help, Koli, has been sentenced to death for not only killing these children but 'eating' them. In the meantime, there is also the news that the bodies did not have torsos—the torsos were used for organ transplants, so a surgeon living next door has been arrested.

Children of the poor, especially those living on the edges, where adults go to work and have no place to leave their children except on the pavements or grounds outside their shacks, get picked up, are never found again, and are used as Koli used them, cutting them up for their organs or, as we saw in the film *Mardani*, trafficking them in brothels. This is the outcome of our neglect of inequality, of leaving the poor behind.

THE IDEA THAT CAPITAL NOW PREVAILS AND LABOUR HAS LOST ITS PLACE IN THE GDP RACE

The review of global reports reveals not only growing economic inequalities, but also that this is due to the current reliance on capital, with finance as the driver of growth, and neglect of the value of labour and the broad-basing of incomes. By and large, the response from mainstream economics and powerful international economic institutions such as the World Bank, the IMF and the Asian Development Bank has been that: (*a*) there should be more aggressive taxation and financial regulation; (*b*) there needs to be greater expenditure on what is called 'social development', which includes health education and social security; and (*c*) employment in information technology needs strengthening.[23]

There has hardly been any widely discussed critique that capital-led economic success has left labour behind, and by virtue of that has created deep and widespread unemployment in many countries, including so-called 'successful' economies such as India.[24] However, there are now reflections that resonate with what I am trying to point out. Caren Grown and Stephanie Seguino[25] set forth some general principles that can produce greater equality, premised on shifting from economies that are profit led and export oriented to those that are wage led and full-employment oriented. The framework is Kaleckian in its focus on the relationship between the distribution of income and macro-economic outcomes.

Very recently, just a week ago, K. Subramanian published a review of a book by the economist K. P. Kannan,[26] and titled his review 'On Growth without Equality'.[27] So the concern with inequality and discussions about it are catching on in India also. Capital- and inequality-led growth has other shades of impact. In Kannan's book, says Subramanian,

> there is a close scrutiny of a quarter century of growth sans employment. Data indicate that acceleration in capital intensity in the organised sector is at the expense of employment and higher growth in manufacturing has been more due to increase in labour productivity. The phenomenon of jobless growth has gone on for a quarter century. It tends to distribute more of income to capital and thus accelerate inequality.[28]

Large numbers of labourers, estimated to be around 80 per cent, are moving into the informal sector. Even the manufacturing sector is increasing the share of 'contract' labour, offering no security of employment or welfare benefits to workers. And we know that women have the predominant share in the informal sector.

In India, jobless growth has led to policy responses such as provisioning of public works schemes such as NREGA to absorb this unemployed labour. In my view, NREGA should be seen as emergency employment through public works, and not as a substitute for jobs or livelihoods that have some individual autonomy. Jobless growth is also driving men and women from rural to urban areas, pushing up distress migration. The figures of such migration in India and China are huge, and the distress thereof has also been recorded.

For example, Chang et al. in their paper on labour migration examine the striking gender-differentiated impacts of migration, such as the condition of left-behind children and the elderly.[29] In India, Nitya Rao,[30] in her paper titled 'Respect, Status and Domestic Work: Female Migrants at Home and Work', observes that inequality between regions and severe unemployment drive thousands of girls out of Jharkhand to seek insecure and often exploitative domestic work in the cities. We know of the boatloads of people from the northern tip of the African continent who tried to enter the Mediterranean or southern Europe and who were either robbed or drowned, and of several cases of human trafficking and slave trade—all because of the lack of employment opportunities in their own countries, an outcome of macro policies.

THE TRICKLE-DOWN THEORY OF GROWTH AND ITS DEPENDENCE ON THE GODDESS OF GDP

Growth rates of GDP are seen as the thermometer for testing the temperature, the well-being, of an economy. Overall, the rhetoric is that only if there is a high, steady rate of GDP growth can the state find enough funds, i.e., surpluses and finances, for spending on people's welfare, including social inputs like education, nutrition, safe drinking water, sanitation and health. The surplus available from high rates of GDP growth are widely considered a necessary base for public expenditure.[31] This argument can be summed up as the 'trickle-down theory of growth'.

The goddess of GDP has been challenged over several decades, but in my view the winner still remains the goddess. Much work has been done, and continues to be done, on alternative indicators, the most famous being the Human Development Index pioneered by Dr Mahbub ul Haq.[32] This was followed by the Commission on the Measurement of Economic Performance and Social Progress[33] set up by the former president of France, Nicolas Sarkozy, with eminent economists like Joseph Stiglitz (who chaired the commission) and Amartya Sen. Then there is the famous Bhutanese invention of gross national happiness.[34] But while all these ideas are in circulation, as we all see in the news, it is the good old GDP and its rate of growth, even in Piketty's analysis, that continues to be the main driver for measuring progress.

What is GDP, and what does it measure for us to make it the new god? As a group of mischievous indicator-wallahs, Clifford Cobb, Ted Halstead and Jonathan Rowe, wrote in their article 'If the GDP Is Up, Why Is America Down?' in the *Atlantic* in 1995,

> the GDP and its various proxies—rates of growth, expansion, and recovery—have become the very language of the nation's economic reportage and debate. We literally cannot think about economics without them. Yet these terms have increasingly become a barricade of abstraction that separates us from economic reality. They tell us next to nothing about what is actually going on.[35]

The authors further say:

> The GDP is simply a gross measure of market activity, of money changing hands. It makes no distinction whatsoever between the desirable and the undesirable, or costs and gain. On top of that, it looks only at the portion of reality that economists choose to acknowledge—the part involved in monetary transactions. The crucial economic functions performed in the household and volunteer sectors go entirely unreckoned. As a result, the GDP not only masks the breakdown of the social structure and the natural habitat upon which the economy—and life itself—ultimately depend; worse, it actually portrays such breakdown as economic gain.[36]

So the measures of progress and of economic success themselves bear the flaws, in my view. If GDP is not measuring economic well-being, as it excludes a large part of the economy and economic activity, then how can we use it as a thermometer of good health? Yet it is the growth rate of the GDP that is used as the thermometer, and also as the necessary condition for the well-being of a society.

However, the ultimate culprit in my view is not the GDP, and finding alternative measures is not the solution. The real fault, in my view, lies in the engines of growth—GDP growth which is driven by capital and the logic of free trade theory. The engines of growth, even for those who consider GDP a misleading measure such as Sen and Stiglitz, are still constituted by Capital and Trade. It is the argument of the present paper that unless this mindset is changed, growth that perpetuates so much inequality cannot be avoided.

THE 'BUBBLING-UP' THEORY OF GROWTH AND ITS DEPENDENCE ON A BROAD BASE OF LIVELIHOODS

It is time to reconsider the validity of these pro-capital distributional policies, and to examine the possibility of an alternative path, one based on pro-labour distributional policies, accompanied by legislative changes and structural policies that will make a wage-led growth regime more likely, i.e., pursue what we call a *wage-led growth strategy*, which, in our view, will generate a much more stable growth regime for the future.[37]

The wage-led growth idea is not only gaining currency in mainstream economic debates, but has been elaborated to reveal the faultlines in a capital-driven growth path. For example, Stephanie Seguino[38] argues that capital-led growth moves to high-tech manufacture or services. Capital-led growth manifests in ways that do not compromise the over-all quality of the labour force, but merely lower the cost of labour for employers, leading to the exploitation of labour in developing countries.[39]

I would like to elaborate how the wage-led growth approach or policy idea is similar, but not identical, to what Gandhi had hoped he could calibrate and set up in India. To some extent, he did it before other ideas took over. Unfortunately, the language used by Gandhi makes him look archaic, and he is often criticised for attempting to take the country back to the bullock-cart era.

During his campaign for freedom from the British, Gandhi put on the ground what he called the *charkha* (spinning wheel) programme. The British had suppressed India's textile industry by exporting raw cotton and returning manufactured cloth for sale in India. Gandhi believed this to be the greatest cause of poverty in the country.[40] The principle was to ensure that every household in India had the means to earn a wage every day. The charkha was chosen as it required nothing but hands to move it, no power or oil or water. And it could be any other activity, like handmade craft products, based on the natural skills of individuals.

Gandhi's Bania background was helpful, as he made arrangements for what are now considered essential in manufacturing, i.e., backward and forward linkages. Backward in that raw material, i.e., cotton, was provided by hundreds of units spread across India. And forward in that he opened hundreds of market outlets, the khadi shops, all over India to sell the products. We know how this system of linking the supply of raw materials to the production and then the marketing all in one chain could not be sustained, and how thus the programme has failed.

The other aspect of Gandhi's economic reasoning was that in the process, millions of such wage earners would provide the fuel for the engines of production—the demand for goods and services. A similar argument is put forward by many modern economists whom I referred to in the first section of this chapter—that a broad-based demand for goods is essential for sustainable growth. Thus, as Stephanie and others have said, wage-led growth, or Gandhi's universal livelihood–led growth, generates a demand which would ensure the supply of services and goods for the broad base of the population, and, more importantly, such growth would be steady and sustainable.

Gandhi with his usual facility of language called the purchasing power of these workers the 'economic vote'. Thus, democracy would involve not only the political vote but the economic vote of every working-age Indian citizen, made possible by ensuring that they earned their livelihood. These votes, since they come from the broader base of the population, would of course redefine what is produced in the economy. Thus, the composition of the GDP would change to suit the demand. The goddess would also be just. Diane Elson and I in the book *Harvesting Feminist Knowledge for Public Policy: Redefining Progress* have taken this further by arguing that political democracy cannot function without economic democracy. Amartya Sen offers the concept of 'public reasoning' in his book *The Idea of Justice*,[41] saying that economic decision making by the state has become so secretive that economic democracy is needed to bring more transparency and public participation.

'GDP' at Any Cost: A Satire on GDP Anonymous

GDP says what is there in life.[42]

We should worry about climate change.—GDP says, nay, it is a temporary disturbance.

Vegetables are contaminated.—GDP says, so what, there are Vegetable Washing Machines for that.

Milk is contaminated.—GDP says, so what, there are many more milk products available in the market.

Even mother's milk is contaminated.—GDP says, so what, there are enough hospitals and medicines.

GM food is threat to life.—GDP says, so what, we cannot say no to science.

Contamination of food and pollution lead to severe health problems.—GDP says, so what, people can opt for Mediclaim.

People are losing their life.—GDP says, so what, people can opt for life insurance policy.

We are missing face to face talk.—GDP says, so what, there is Facebook.

Our voices are not being heard.—GDP says, so what, there is Twitter.

There is alienation in society.—GDP says, so what, there are Internet, Twitter and Facebook for them.

Majority of working class is not paid even minimum wage.—GDP says, so what, dieting is good for health.

Ordinary people are starving.—GDP says, so what, they have two kidneys and one is saleable.

Life on earth is at risk.—GDP says so what, growth is important, what is there in just life.

Now here is the joke: India is already benefiting from the bubbling-up theory but refuses to acknowledge it.

IS INDIA FORFEITING A UNIQUE OPPORTUNITY TO HAVE GROWTH WITH EQUALITY?

A recent paper, 'Small Farmers in India: Challenges and Opportunities',[43] by S. Mahendra Dev of the Indira Gandhi Institute of Development

Research, suggests how small holdings are important for agricultural growth, food security and livelihoods in India. Small and marginal farmers account for more than 80 per cent of total farm households. According to Dev, 'The global experience of growth and poverty reduction shows that GDP growth originating in agriculture is at least twice as effective in reducing poverty as GDP growth originating outside agriculture. Small holdings play important role in raising agricultural development and poverty reduction.'[44] India still has this base of small farms, while many other countries have gone into plantation mode, which has many drawbacks.

Micro, small and medium enterprises are another huge and fertile landscape in India. In an article titled 'The Hidden Growth', Neelkanth Mishra refers to the Economic Census according to which India had 42 million enterprises in 2005, while it had fewer than a million companies.[45] Mishra writes, 'Ninety per cent of India's workforce is engaged in the informal economy (that is, not in companies). About half of India's GDP is informal (that is, not generated by incorporated enterprises.... productivity growth has been the most dramatic in the informal side of the economy.'[46] 'But if half of the GDP and 90 per cent of India's workforce are seeing such dramatic changes, why is this not reflected in GDP growth? This doesn't show up in the current GDP statistics because we don't measure it,' says Mishra.[47] While that missing economic activity can be rectified, and the 'focus on heavy infrastructure is much needed, given the challenges involved, channelling government energy into enabling the small entrepreneur to scale up may be more productive'.[48] From 1999 to 2009, 75 per cent of all new factories came up in rural India, and 70 per cent of all manufacturing jobs were created there. This should not be surprising, given that there is so little physical space available in cities: on average, rural factories deploy more capital and also employ more people. The average employee count of these 42 million enterprises was 2.4 per unit. The spread of the mobile phone and other technologies of communication has led not only to an enormous increase in small enterprises, but a matching demand by those new incomes for goods and services, often at the local level, spurring each other linking the demand to the supply. India's informal GDP, i.e., economic activity by unincorporated enterprises, is half of total GDP, among the highest ratios in the world and comparable to sub-Saharan Africa.[49]

If we look at the handicraft and handloom sectors, the figures are similarly significant. Government data reveal that the output of these sectors has been growing steadily even during the downturn. Further, they have been the steadiest contributors to India's exports and employment. The *Handloom Census of India* (2009–10)[50] shows that the handloom sector provides employment to about 4 million persons who are engaged in weaving and allied activities, of whom 78 per cent are women; 11 per cent belong to the Scheduled Castes, 19 per cent belong to the Scheduled Tribes, and 45 per cent belong to Other Backward Classes (see Tables 14.1 and 14.2). Further, 87 per cent are located in rural areas and the remaining 13 per cent in urban areas.

As of 2012,[51] employment in the handicrafts sector had risen to 7 million craftspersons in 2011–12. Of the total, 48 per cent were women; 25 per cent of the craftspersons belonged to the Scheduled Castes, 5 per cent from the Scheduled Tribes, and 23 per cent belonged to minority groups (Figure 14.2). The crafts sector accounts for 15–20

Table 14.1 *Number of adult weavers by gender (in lakhs)*

	Male	Female	Total
Number of adult handloom weavers and allied workers	8.48	29.98	38.47
Percentage of total	22.10	77.90	100

Source: National Council of Applied Economic Research, *Handloom Census of India 2009–10*, p. xvii.

Table 14.2 *Number of adult weavers by caste (in lakhs)*

	SC	ST	OBC	Others	Total
Number of adult handloom weavers and allied workers by caste	3.90	6.97	17.38	10.22	38.47
Percentage of total	10.13	18.12	45.18	26.57	100.00

Source: National Council of Applied Economic Research, *Handloom Census of India 2009–10*, p. xvii.

per cent of the country's manufacturing workforce, and contributes 8 per cent of GDP in manufacturing.

In the khadi and village industries sector,[52] the total cumulative employment was estimated to have increased to 14 million persons in 2013–14 as against 12.5 million persons in the previous year (Table 14.3).

As we go down to the state level in Bihar and Odisha, the generation of what can be called 'manufactures' comes mainly from the small-scale sector, handmade products, and then what is called 'home-based

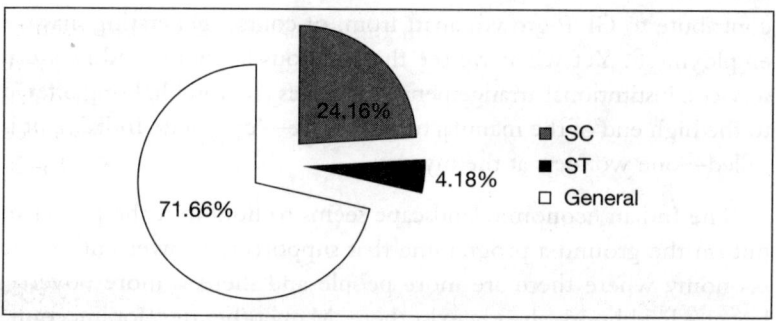

Figure 14.2 The handicrafts census (2009–10) by caste

Source: Planning Commission, Report of the Steering Committee on Handlooms and Handicrafts, p. 50.

Table 14.3 Performance of the khadi and village industries sector (2010–14) (in lakhs/crores)

Year	Production (in Crores INR)	Sales (in Crores INR)	Cumulative Employment (in Lakhs)
2010–11	673.01	917.26	10.15
2011–12	716.98	967.87	10.45
2012–13	761.93	1021.56	10.71
2013–14	809.70	1079.24	10.98

Source: Government of India, Ministry of Micro, Small and Medium Enterprises, Annual Report 2012–13, p. 79, http://www.dcmsme.gov.in/ANNUALREPORT-MSME-2012-13P.pdf (accessed 13 April 2018).

put-out work', which then builds up to the final products. The manufacturing sector in rural areas has women working in diverse small-scale enterprises and as home-based workers in *agarbatti* (incense stick) making, beedi rolling, bangle making, handicrafts, textiles, and local food processing such as papad making and pickle making, predominantly for local consumption. These are avenues of rural non-farm employment.[53]

Strengthening this supply chain in the manufacturing sector would contribute enormously to revitalising the Indian economy, generating higher and steadier demand, reducing the dependence on international finances, and insulating us from financial crises. In addition, it would contribute to GDP growth apart from, of course, generating massive employment. Yet when we see the generous handouts and financial services, institutional arrangements, tax reliefs and torchlighting offered to the high end of the manufacturing sector—'corporate India', as it is called—one wonders at the myopia.

The Indian economic landscape seems to hold in it the power to put on the ground a programme that supports the lower end of the economy where there are more people and there is more poverty, because livelihoods already exist there. Many other developing countries, especially in Africa, also have similar economic activity at the ground level. There is need for some dramatic reversal of the current theories regarding where the engine of growth lies, and how to promote inclusive growth and engage with effective poverty eradication. Such programmes would be wage led, and growth will bubble up from these spaces, bringing greater economic equality—Gandhi's basic ideal.

Given this landscape in India, and taking note of the global reviews on the state of the world economy and the crisis that the capital-led 'liberal' economic programme has created, India can still make the change and generate a growth of the GDP that creates less inequality. Not many other countries have this potential. The global reports have sounded an important alert. It is worth taking note of these signals. Blowing energy to this tail end would not only generate employment but also stimulate broad-based demand for broad-based production of goods and services, leading to a more sustainable GDP growth for India.

Many persons in India and the world over have for decades been arguing for what I have called the 'bubbling-up theory of growth'. For example, our own champion Smt. Ela Bhatt has just completed a book titled the *Anubandh: Building 100-Mile Communities*,[54] in which she makes a case for equitable growth based on empowered data that can emerge if production and consumption are linked within every 100 miles. It is full of all that we desire—ecological and environmental safety, activities and products that are suited to the region, and so forth. It can be a model for what is called 'inclusive growth'. We can go all the way back or forward to other experts and movements including Gandhi's *Hind Swaraj*,[55] the constructive programme and so forth, but it is my view that none of these initiatives can take off in the atmosphere in which we are trapped today. With global connectivity the way it is, dropping out can also be suicidal. Therefore, my argument is that we have to influence economic reasoning, economic theory, ideas on the location of the engines of growth by looking at reality and building on that. We have to show that it works, and then and only then can we sell it.

There is a space for this now, due to the alarm bells that are ringing not only on inequality, but how it impinges on the stability of the economy, etc. We need to use that space to rectify the agony into which we have pushed the poor, especially those seeking some sense of livelihood, wanting to live a dignified life. This is a challenge that I think this generation needs to address.

I still have hope, as there is so much innovative entrepreneurship coming up in the world, and especially in India. I notice the enormous mushrooming of brilliant professionals engaging with the less privileged in rural and urban spaces. So the energy and the ideology are already there. The question is how to make it a big bang. How to make it replace what is now called 'reform', how to exit from the trap that trade-led growth and financialisation have led us into. I will let you address these questions.

As intellectuals we need to question the base theory, and put forward a theory which arises from the Indian experience. Of course it will be challenged, and we may be opting out of many domains, and flounder too. But given that the base survives, and given that the current model of growth is floundering and generating crisis and perpetuating inequality, we may strike out and others may perhaps follow.

I often think of how a fistful of salt galvanised the people of India to overthrow the coloniser. It seems to me that an idea which resonates in people's minds and hearts, if supported by a broad, popular base, can effect transformation. So here is an idea, of a bubbling-up theory of growth, drawn from a base of wage and work. The process of rebuilding economic theory—of challenging the trickle-down theory— requires wide support, and I hope to find it here, at the Azim Premji University amidst those who are engaged in educating differently.

NOTES

1 I was a member of the Karnataka State Planning Board for six years (1993–99).
2 Working Group of Feminist Economists (WGFE), *Engendering Public Policy*, Report on the Work of the WGFE during the preparation of the 11th Five Year Plan (2007–12) (New Delhi: Planning Commission, 2010); Swapna Bist Joshi, *Consultation on Engendering the 12th Five Year Plan: Karnataka*, Consultation Proceedings, State Planning Board, Karnataka, Bangalore, November 2012.
3 Reproduced as chapter 13 in Devaki Jain, *Journey of a Southern Feminist* (New Delhi: Sage/Yoda, 2018), vol. 1.
4 Thomas Piketty, *Capitalism in the Twenty-First Century* (Cambridge, MA: Harvard University Press, 2014).
5 Kumar Anand, 'The Inequality Debate: Thoughts on Piketty', *Spontaneous Order*, 7 May 2014.
6 Piketty, *Capitalism in the Twenty-First Century*.
7 Aravind Adiga, *White Tiger* (New Delhi: HarperCollins, 2010).
8 Devaki Jain and Diane Elson (eds), *Harvesting Feminist Knowledge for Public Policy* (New Delhi: Sage, 2012); Jain and Banerjee, *Tyranny of the Household*.
9 Some other major reports and sources on this issue include the World Bank series *Inequality in Focus*; see also Jonathan D. Ostry, Andrew Berg and Charalambos G. Tsangarides, 'Redistribution, Inequality, and Growth', IMF Staff Discussion Note, April 2014.
10 Special event organised by UNDP, New York, 20 May 1997.
11 UN, *Inequality Matters: Report on the World Social Situation 2013*, Department of Economic and Social Affairs (New York: United Nations, 2013), http://www.un.org/esa/socdev/documents/reports/InequalityMatters.pdf (accessed 20 March 2018).
12 Ibid., p. 64.

13 UNDP, *Humanity Divided: Confronting Inequality in Developing Countries*, Bureau for Development Policy (New York: UNDP, November 2013), http://www. undp.org/content/dam/undp/library/Poverty%20Reduction/Inclusive%20 development/Humanity%20Divided/HumanityDivided_Full-Report.pdf (accessed 21 March 2018).

14 Ibid., p. 1.

15 Ibid., p. 8.

16 M. Lavoie and E. Stockhammer, 'Wage-Led Growth: Concepts, Theories and Policies', Conditions of Work and Employment Series no. 41, ILO, Geneva, http://www.ilo.org/wcmsp5/groups/public/—ed_protect/—protrav/—tra-vail/documents/publication/wcms_192507.pdf (accessed 21 March 2018).

17 Ibid., p. 1.

18 R. Fuentes-Nieva and N. Galasso, 'Working for the Few: Political Capture and Economic Inequality', Oxfam Briefing Paper no. 178, Oxfam International, Oxford, 20 January 2014.

19 See, e.g., Devaki Jain, 'Growth, Poverty and Inequality: The Linkages and Relevance of Macroeconomic Policies', UNDP Expert Group Meeting on Gender Equality, Economic Growth and Poverty Reduction, Essex University, 21–22 June 2007 (reproduced as chapter 11, this volume); Devaki Jain, 'This Thing Called "Poverty"', paper presented at a special event organised by UNDP, New York, 20 May 1997; Devaki Jain, 'The First Challengers: The Feminists of the South', *Making It Magazine*, UNIDO, 5 February 2013, http:// www.makingitmagazine.net/?p=6349 (accessed 21 March 2018), reproduced as chapter 12 in Devaki Jain, *Journey of a Southern Feminist*, vol. 1 (New Delhi: Sage/Yoda, 2018).

20 UNCTAD, *Trade and Development Report 2010: Employment, Globalization, and Development* (New York: UN, 2010), http://unctad.org/en/docs/ tdr2010_en.pdf (accessed 21 March 2018).

21 Ibid.

22 *China Daily*, 'Alibaba: Journey of the Global Tech Giant', September 2014, http://www.chinadaily.com.cn/bizchina/tech/alibaba_ipo/alibaba_ipo.html (accessed 21 March 2018).

23 Peter deSouza, 'Lessons from Mutiny on the Bounty', *Hindu*, 21 October 2014, p. 8.

24 S. Tyagi, 'First Develop India Is Plain and Simple Economics', interview with Siddhartha Birla, *Sunday Guardian*, 4 October 2014, http://www. sunday-guardian.com/business/first-develop-india-is-plain-and-simple-economics (accessed 22 March 2018).

25 Stephanie Seguino and Caren A. Grown, 'Feminist-Kaleckian Macroeconomic Policy for Developing Countries', Economics Working Paper no. 446, Levy Economics Institute, New York, 2006.

26 K. P. Kannan, *Interrogating Inclusive Growth: Poverty and Inequality in India* (New Delhi: Routledge, 2014).

27 K. Subramanian, 'On Growth without Equality', *Hindu*, 4 November 2014, http://www.thehindu.com/todays-paper/tp-features/tp-bookreview/on-growth-without-equality/article6562332.ece (accessed 22 March 2018).

28 Ibid.

29 H. Chang, X. Dong and F. MacPhail, 'Labour Migration and Time Use Patterns of the Left-Behind Children and Elderly in Rural China', *World Development*, vol. 39, no. 12 (2011), pp. 2199–10.

30 Nitya Rao, 'Respect, Status and Domestic Work: Female Migrants at Home and Work', *European Journal of Development Research*, vol. 23, no. 5 (2011), pp. 758–73.

31 Philipe Aghion and Patrick Bolton, 'A Theory of Trickle Down Growth and Development', *Review of Economic Studies*, vol. 64, no. 219 (1997), pp. 151–72.

32 Mahbub ul Haq, *The Human Development Report* (New York: UNDP, 1990).

33 Joseph E. Stiglitz, Amartya Sen and Jean-Paul Fitoussi, *Report by the Commission on the Measurement of Economic Performance and Social Progress*, http://ec.europa.eu/eurostat/documents/118025/118123/Fitoussi+Commission+report (accessed 13 April 2018).

34 Royal Government of Bhutan, Gross National Happiness Commission, http://www.gnhc.gov.bt/ (accessed 22 March 2018).

35 Cobb et al., 'If GDP Is Up, Why Is America Down?'

36 Ibid.

37 Lavoie and Stockhammer, 'Wage-Led Growth', p. 1; emphasis in original.

38 Stephanie Seguino, '"Rebooting" Is Not an Option: Towards Equitable Social and Economic Development', in Jain and Elson, *Harvesting Feminist Knowledge for Public Policy*, pp. 21–47.

39 Stephanie Seguino, 'The Effects of Structural Change and Economic Liberalization on Gender Wage Differentials in South Korea and Taiwan', *Cambridge Journal of Economics*, vol. 24, no. 4 (2000), pp. 437–59; Stephanie Seguino, 'Accounting for Gender in Asian Economic Growth', *Feminist Economics*, vol. 6, no. 3 (2000), pp. 27–58; Stephanie Seguino, 'Gender Inequality and Economic Growth: A Cross-country Analysis', *World Development*, vol. 28, no. 7 (2000), pp. 1211–30.

40 Mark Shepard, *Gandhi Today: A Report on India's Gandhi Movement and Its Experiments in Nonviolence and Small Scale Alternatives* (Simple Productions, 2012).

41 Amartya Sen, *The Idea of Justice* (Cambridge, MA: Harvard University Press, 2009).

42 Rohit Prajapati, 17 October 2014, https://groups.google.com/forum/#!topic/justice-and-gujarat/dkJK4byukQM (accessed 10 November 2014).

43 S. Mahendra Dev, 'Small Farmers in India: Challenges and Opportunities', Working Paper, Indira Gandhi Institute of Development Research, Mumbai, June 2012, http://www.igidr.ac.in/pdf/publication/WP-2012-014.pdf (accessed 22 March 2018).

44 Ibid.

45 Neelkanth Mishra, 'The Hidden Growth', *Indian Express*, 6 August 2013, http://www.indianexpress.com/news/the-hidden-growth/1151479/ (accessed 22 March 2018).

46 Ibid.

47 Ibid.

48 Ibid.

49 Ibid.

50 National Council of Applied Economic Research, *Handloom Census of India 2009–10*, http://www.handlooms.nic.in/Writereaddata/Handloom%20 report.pdf (accessed 13 April 2018).

51 Planning Commission, *Report of the Steering Committee on Handlooms and Handicrafts Constituted for the Twelfth Five Year Plan (2012–17)* (New Delhi: Planning Commission, 2012).

52 Government of India, Ministry of Micro, Small and Medium Enterprises, *Annual Report 2013–14* (New Delhi: Khadi and Village Industries Commission, 2014).

53 Renana Jhabvala and Amrita Datta, 'Women and Work in Bihar: Challenges and Emerging Policy Paradigms', paper presented at the workshop on 'Women in Informal Economy in Bihar', Patna, 11 May 2012; Devaki Jain, 'The Household Trap: Report on a Field Survey of Female Activity Patterns', in Jain and Banerjee, *Tyranny of the Household*, pp. 215–46.

54 Ela Bhatt, *Anubandh: Building 100-Mile Communities* (Ahmedabad: Navajivan, 2015).

55 M. K. Gandhi, *Hind Swaraj or Indian Home Rule* (Ahmedabad: Navajivan Publishing House, 1909).

Chapter 15

The New World Re-order

An Opportunity to Build a Feminist Political Economy

There has been an abiding concern with how to bring forth recognition of what is happening in the economies of the South, as well as the kinds of responses that partners and policy makers in the South countries are putting forward. While a focus on feminism had arrived on the international stage with the creation of the International Association for Feminist Economics, the preoccupation of the majority of feminist economists in such associations was with gender issues generally, with particular reference to the economies of the North.

Dramatic changes in the distribution of global economic power were vividly displayed by the outcome of the 2008 global economic crisis. While the GDP growth rates of most Northern economies were at an abysmal low, India and China blazed forward with growth rates of over 8 per cent, calling attention to the changing global economic order. These economies were named 'emerging economies'. Their arrival on the world economic stage had huge implications for the rest of the world, and especially for women. What the data revealed was dramatic. It was necessary for international networks of feminist economists to engage with this new phenomenon, which offered a great opportunity to foreground the gender dimension in the fast-growing countries. This became particularly interesting as China was a clearly socialist economy, whereas India was still acutely a democratic polity where the playing fields were dominated by the private sector apart from the state. What were the gender implications of this difference? It would seem worthwhile not only to examine this but also to use this analysis to critique the current economic growth models.

In this paper, I suggest that the evolving shifts in economic 'power' or 'success' in the post-crisis world have generated a new turbulence.[1] I describe some of the features of this shift in economic energy, and argue that these evolving landscapes and negotiations point to the need for the feminist agenda, especially the feminist economists' agenda, to draw up a clearly South-tethered perspective for analyses and prescriptions.

While the GDP growth rates, current account balances and trade volumes of the 're-emerging economies' (I owe this change in language from 'emerging' to '*re*-emerging' to a friend from the progressive anti-colonial movements) of the South are revealing vigour, there are many challenging issues facing these countries. Per capita incomes are still comparatively very low, and poverty numbers still very high in these countries. The gaps between the least developed nations and the re-emerging economies are also large. Several of the international negotiating processes, such as the Doha Round or the European Union–India free trade agreements, have had a complex impact on employment generally, and on women's employment specifically.

Yet the turbulence, and the uncharted spaces it has opened, offers a valuable opportunity for feminist economist and activist lobbyists from the South to reinvoke their earlier history of engaging with larger political economy debates. They could ensure that the political economies of the South are configured in a co-operative mode, in contrast to the competitive mode. They could engage in the rebuilding of national responsibility,[2] the state's responsibility for the well-being of its citizens.

Since these economies are to some extent reconstructing themselves, alongside their display of economic energy, to face many new challenges, this would be the time to use the collective strength of feminist scholars and activist associations and networks to provide an alternative economic reasoning, and promote other strong ideas that have come out of our work, such as encouraging support to the lower end of production both in terms of scale, e.g., small farms and small firms, as well as in terms of the kind of work arrangements they entail, as this would particularly benefit women.

Such a reordering of priorities for the feminist economists' agenda would entail shrugging off the current preoccupation with the impact of 'crisis 2008–09'. Crisis and bailouts might still be a situation in the North, but that is not the menu on the table in the South. It is also important to modify or reject the set agendas coming from the UN and other international bodies such as the World Bank, which set goals such as those of gender equality or the Millennium Development Goals. It is important to plunge into the task of reorienting ideas regarding the state and economic progress while the spaces are yet open.

To buttress this view, this paper will mainly lay out the current scenario, i.e., the characteristics and politics of this turbulence, as a knowledge base for building a common cause. The paper is organised in three sections. The first section draws attention to the shifts and striking differences in various economic indicators between countries of the North, earlier known as 'advanced economies', and some of the developing countries now known as 're-emerging economies'. The second section highlights some of the initiatives that are emerging, along with the challenges and doubts around them. The third section indicates some of the gendered aspects or issues that might emerge from the point of view of women's participation in the labour force and trading sectors.

The paper goes on to build an argument for a strong, South-driven feminist economics programme which will engage with this new order—with the legal spaces and the regulatory mechanisms, as well as with the regional and inter-regional economic configurations, and finally or most essentially, with national political economy spaces.

RESPONSE TO THE 2008 CRISIS: THE STRIKING DIFFERENCE BETWEEN THE NORTH AND THE SOUTH

Information and data are pouring out of the many international and regional institutions revealing the shifts in rates of GDP growth amongst countries. Post-crisis, there has been a comparative slowdown in GDP growth rates in Europe and other 'advanced' countries, whereas good and steady upward movements are being registered in many re-emerging economies, especially China and India. Many economists engaged in global think tanks are noting this change.

It is interesting to recall that for several decades, after Second World War, we had a bi-polar world with developing countries being described as 'Third' world. After the break-up of USSR, the world was broadly divided into developed and developing, with emerging market economies being treated as a sub-set of developing economies. Currently, the world appears to be moving in the direction of a spectrum where it will be increasingly difficult to draw a rigid line between developed and developing countries.[3]

Figures 15.1, 15.2 and 15.3 describe this phenomenon in various ways. The figures show that post-crisis, although GDP growth rates declined across the board, with even negative growth rates being recorded for the 'advanced' economies, the combined GDP growth rates of the emerging market economies remained positive, and recovery was relatively faster.

Another indicator of differing economic 'power' is noted in Figure 15.4, which presents the current account balances across regions. It can be seen that China and the rest of developing Asia did well during and after the crisis compared to the 'advanced' economies.

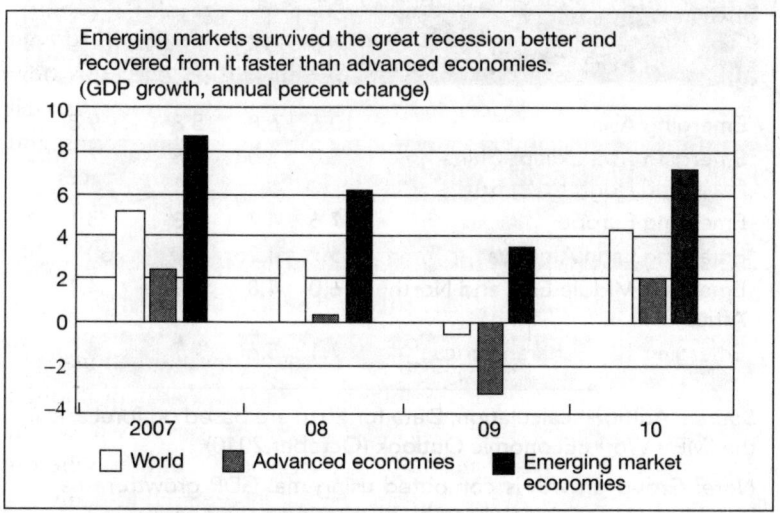

Figure 15.1 *Bouncing back*

Source: M. Ayhan Kose and Eswar S. Prasad, 'Emerging Markets Come of Age', *Finance and Development*, vol. 47, no. 4 (December 2010), pp. 7–10.

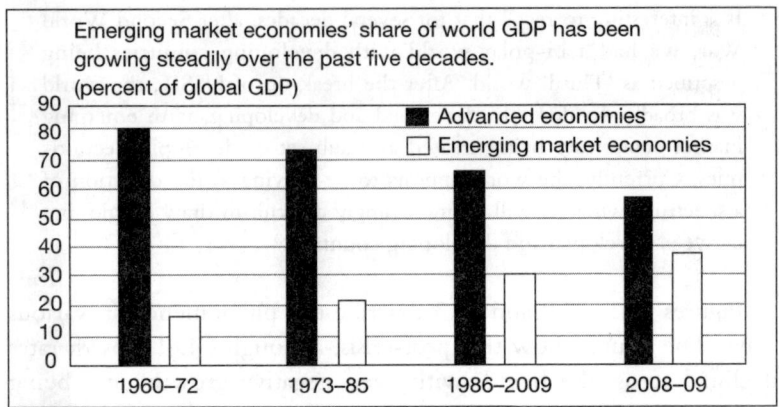

Figure 15.2 *Growing in importance*

Source: M. Ayhan Kose and Eswar S. Prasad, 'Emerging Markets Come of Age', *Finance and Development*, vol. 47, no. 4 (December 2010), pp. 7–10.

Emerging Asia experienced a mild growth slowdown during the crisis, while emerging Europe had a steep decline. (GOP growth), percent change from one year earlier)				
	2007	2008	2009	Projected 2010
Emerging Asia	10.6	6.8	5.8	9.3
Emerging Asia except China, India, and Hong Kong SAR	5.0	3.0	0.6	7.1
Emerging Europe	7.6	4.7	−6.3	3.1
Emerging Latin America	5.7	4.2	−2.0	60
Emerging Middle East and North Africa	6.0	4.8	1.9	4.1
Emerging sub-Saharan Africa	7.1	5.6	2.7	4.9

Source: Authors' calculation. Data for 2010 are based on forecasts in the IMF's World Economic Outlook (October 2010).

Note: Group growth is computed using mal GDP growth rates for individual countries weighted by purchasing power parity.

Figure 15.3 *Differing performance*

Source: M. Ayhan Kose and Eswar S. Prasad, 'Emerging Markets Come of Age', *Finance and Development*, vol. 47, no. 4 (December 2010), pp. 7–10.

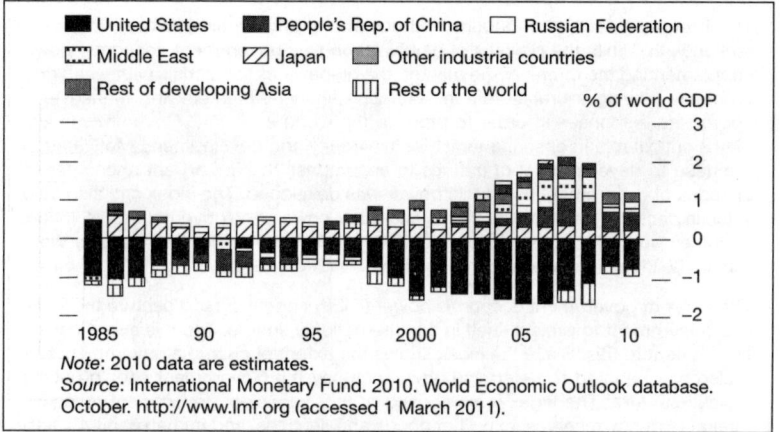

Figure 15.4 *World current account balance*
Source: Asian Development Bank, *Asian Development Outlook 2011: South-South Economic Links* (Manila: Asian Development Bank, 2011).

The 2010–11 issue of the *Economic Survey of India*[4] gives an inkling of the self-perceptions of the new emerging economies. The survey includes an annexure called the 'economic power index', which tracks changes in the ranking of the various economies. It makes the point that many who were lower in the ranking vis-à-vis the 'advanced' countries are moving up and even replacing some of those countries (see Figure 15.5).

The debates and initiatives in India and perhaps in China are focused on how to keep growth rates rising or at least at current levels, apart from competing with each other. The debates within India are geared towards maintaining its power ranking, but also respond to the fact that many countries of the South are not yet on the uptick, so that some attempts to rebuild their economies needs to be a part of the goals of countries like India.

However, the race now is more a race to the top, and many of the new power clubs are not quite enabling of their poorer cousins. On the contrary, they are moving their capital and expertise into these countries in an expansionist mode, very similar to the early colonisers. Such moves have led many scholars, for example in India, to reflect on this phenomenon as the resurrection of empire.[5]

The economic abilities of nations and governments have always been a force to reckon with. While the process of globalization saw government economic power supplementing the forces of the market, the global economic crisis witnessed governments playing a crucial role in stabilizing financial markets and managing to coordinate responses in order to prop up the world economy. Governments also play a critical role in ensuring redistributive equity and development. Motivated by the need to develop a set of metrics to encompass this import ant phenomenon, an index of government economic power was developed. The index can also be of value in deciding on the voting rights and other powers the governments of various countries ought to have in international organizations like the IMF and the World Bank. The index has been created for 10 years (2000–09) covering 112 economies.

The index of government economic power (IGEP) endeavours to capture the ability of a government to project itself in the international sphere. There is also a normative content to this. Since the index shows the extent of charge a government has, it also can be used to determine how much say the Government should have in multilateral fora. The index is composed of four variables: government revenues, foreign currency reserves, export of goods and services, and human capital. These variables broadly capture a Government's ability to raise resources, its creditworthiness and credibility in international financial markets, its influence on global economic activity, and its representational strength, that is how much of the global economy, including global manpower, it can claim to represent. In order to ensure use of standard data, the index has been constructed using three widely accepted datasets; the IFS and WEO of the IMF, and the United Nations Development Programme's (UNDP's) Human Development Index (HDI).

The 2009 results show that the top ten ranks are occupied by (1) the United States, (2) China, (3) Japan, (4) Germany, (5) India, (6) Russia, (7) Brazil, (8) France, (9) Italy, and (10) the United Kingdom. In 2000 the top ten places were held by (1) the United States, (2) Japan, (3) China, (4) Germany, (5) France, (6) the United Kingdom, (7) Italy, (8) (Republic of) Korea, (9) Canada, and (10) India. Among the top ranking economies some of the most dramatic rises in rank have been Brazil's ascent from 13th place in 2000 to 7th in 2009 and India's rise from 10th position in 2000 to 5th in 2009. Japan was replaced by China in the second spot in 2004. The United Kingdom went down from 6th place in 2000 to 10th in 2008 and continued there in 2009. Canada fell from 9th in 2000 to 15th in 2008

The changing dynamics of global economic power can be further seen, if we analyse the index values over time for some of the larger economic entities. If we compare the three top ranking countries of 2000, the US, Japan, and China, the US and Japan had a slow rise in index values, except for the slight fall in 2009. In contrast, China has risen rapidly and, after surpassing Japan in 2004, has almost reached the same level as the US in 2009 (see Figure 1).

On an analysis of the countries holding the 4th, 9th and 10th positions in 2000 (namely, Germany, Canada, and India), India moves from an index value just below Canada in 2000 to one very close to Germany by 2009 (Figure 2). Among the large economies, China and India also demonstrate remarkable robustness by not having lower index values in 2009 unlike all the other countries occupying the top ten positions in 2000.

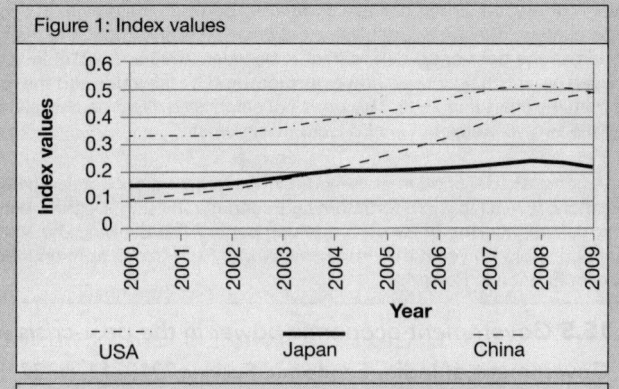

Figure 1: Index values

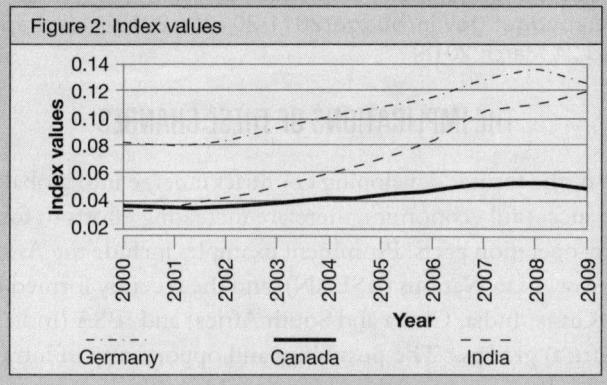

Figure 2: Index values

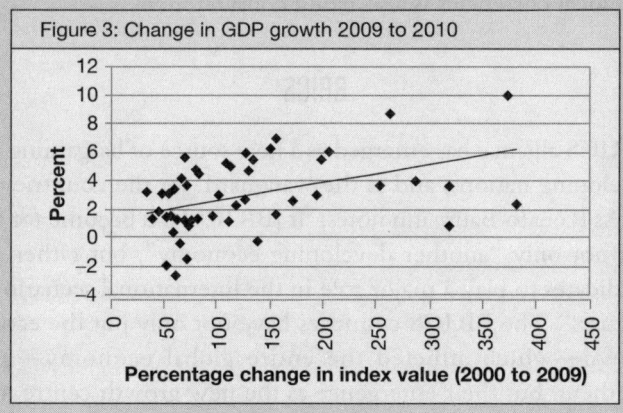

Figure 3: Change in GDP growth 2009 to 2010

Interestingly, there is a strong positive correlation between the growth in economic power (percentage change in index value between 2000 and 2009) and the change in GDP across the post-crisis period (that is between 2009 and 2010) indicating a link between growth in economic power as measured by the index and the ability to recover from the crisis (Figure 3). This does not establish a direct causal relationship between the two variables but is of descriptive interest.

Source: A complete description of the index of government economic power and its implications is available in a forthcoming Economic Division, Department of Economic Affairs, Ministry of Finance, working paper: 'The Evolving Dynamics of Global Economic Power in the Post-crisis World: Revelations from an Index of Government Economic Power'.

Figure 15.5 *Government economic power in the post-crisis world*

Source: Government of India, *Economic Survey 2010–11*, p. 27, https://www.indiabudget.gov.in/budget2011-2012/es2010-11/echap-02.pdf (accessed 24 March 2018).

THE IMPLICATIONS OF THESE CHANGES

As some of the former developing countries emerge into global promi-nence as successful economies, there are increasing efforts to form eco-nomic co-operation pacts. Prominent examples include the Association of Southeast Asian Nations (ASEAN), and the recently formed BRICS (Brazil, Russia, India, China and South Africa) and IBSA (India, Brazil, South Africa) groups.[6] The possibility and opportunity of intra-BRIC trade in local currencies is also being considered.[7]

BRICS

The BRICS alliance has emerged as a new source of bargaining power for developing nations, and as the 'vanguard' for the countries of the South. As Renato Baumann notes, 'It [BRICS] has become for several analysts not only "another developing economy", but rather one of the candidates to play a major role in the international scenario in the near future.'[8] The BRICS countries have not only put the economic meltdown—which afflicted the entire global economy—quickly behind them, but their emergence as the new growth centre has also been spectacular. The newfound confidence of the BRICS nations has seen them build new partnerships with other developing and even the least developed countries. India, China and Brazil have been at the forefront of such partnerships with a view to meeting the long-term development needs of others as well as themselves. These South–South relationships are thus seeking to redefine the context and content of economic ties.[9]

From 2000 to 2008, BRICS's share of the total world economic output rose from 16 to 22 per cent. Together, these countries accounted for 30 per cent of the increase in global output during this period. The share of China alone comprised more than half of the BRIC contribution, amounting to greater than 15 per cent of the growth in world economic output. Figure 15.6 compares key economic and development indicators for the BRIC countries, including GDP level and growth, merchandise exports, and change in the HDI.

China leads in all the key indicators among all the members of the group. What is evident is the fact that not only does China support the largest population, its GDP is roughly three times that of Brazil, Russia and India. In addition, China leads in the rate of growth in GDP, averaging at 10.2 per cent for the years 1990–2008, followed by India at 6.3 per cent. Moreover, the improvement in China's and

	Brazil	Russia	India	China
Population	194 ml.	142 ml.	1.15 bil.	1.33 bil.
GDP(2009, USS)	1.573 bil.	1.232 bil.	1.310 bil.	4.965 bil.
GDP Avg. Growth Rate (1990–2008)	2.6%	0.7%	6.3%	10.2%
GDP Projected Avg. Growth Rate (2011–14. 85 of 2009)	3.7%	4.4%	4.6%	10.3%
Merchandise Exports (2009)	153 bil.	303 bil.	162 bil.	1,201 bil.
HDI % Change (1990–2010, for brazil only 2000-2010)	7.6%	3.8%	33.3%	44.2%

Global Sharpa 2010; Data ascent World databank, UNCP Human Development Report, International Monatary Fund.

Figure 15.6 BRIC country economy and development data

India's HDIs over the past two decades has been remarkable, at about 44 per cent and 33 per cent respectively.

The countries are slowly also showing solid fronts in political forums. Four of the five BRICS countries abstained from the UN Security Council vote on the resolution authorising the use of force in Libya. South Africa, the only country to have voted in favour of the resolution, is said to have nuanced its position later, which is seen as a conscious distancing from the West.

However, there are as many critiques or doubts about the homogeneity, value and purpose of this formation as there is hope and exultation. For example, there is a view that 'all the forum's members want to build a special relationship with the United States, and wish to use the forum as a leverage to expand their political space with Washington. That is part of political jockeying in a multi-polar world.'[10] Another view is that the BRICS forum is no more than a sack of potatoes, formless and without a specific strategic orientation.[11] Further, it has been remarked that they are self-seeking, i.e., not in fact enabling of other South countries.

ASEAN

Another regional economic structure, ASEAN (made up of Brunei, Burma, Cambodia, Indonesia, Laos, Malaysia, the Philippines, Singapore, Thailand and Vietnam), has forged free trade pacts with a number of key regional economies, including China and India.[12] For example, India and ASEAN are committed to achieving a trade target of $70 billion by 2012, up 40 per cent from $50 billion in 2010. This was announced by commerce and industry minister Anand Sharma at the first India–ASEAN business fair and conclave held in New Delhi by the Ministry of Commerce and the Federation of Indian Chambers of Commerce and Industry. India and the 10-nation bloc also broadly agreed that the free trade agreement covering services and investment sectors would be in place by 2011 end. An agreement regarding the movement of natural persons means that professionals would be able to move more easily between India and ASEAN, once the pact comes into operation.

The New Focus on 'South-South' Trade

How would trade regimes change as a result of the new groupings? Will this internal trade be competitive or co-operative? Would the re-emerging economies benefit by trading with each other?

The re-emerging economies have increasingly begun to trade amongst themselves, especially over the past two decades. Figure 15.7 shows that the percentage share of emerging economy trade with the advanced nations has decreased from about 65 per cent in the 1980s to a little over 50 per cent in 2000–08, whereas the shares of the re-emerging economies in intra-regional trade has been on the rise.

Figure 15.8 displays the component-wise percentage share of emerging economies in world trade, which has been rising consistently since 1990. This rise has been sharper post-2007.

Figure 15.9 illustrates that the imports of the re-emerging economies from each other have been on a decline since the onset of the crisis. Thus, the key driver of the increase in intra-regional trade among these economies has been exports.

The volume of trade has increased by quantum leaps within BRIC countries (see Table 15.1), as mentioned earlier. Further, according to the latest data,[13] Indian exports registered the highest-ever growth rate of 37.5 per cent at $245.9 billion during 2010–11, after the government

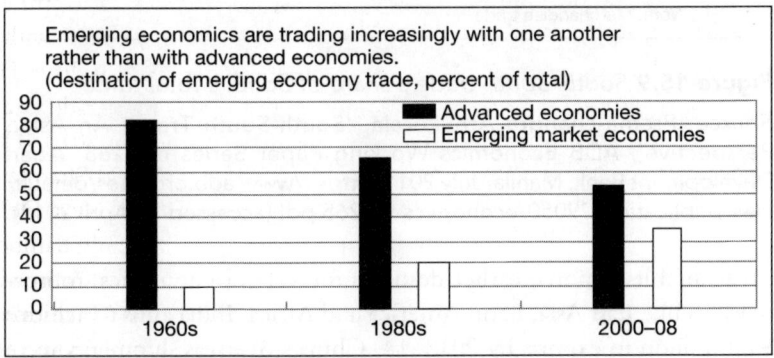

Figure 15.7 *Trading among themselves*

Source: M. Ayhan Kose and Eswar S. Prasad, 'Emerging Markets Come of Age', *Finance and Development*, vol. 47, no. 4 (December 2010), pp. 7–10.

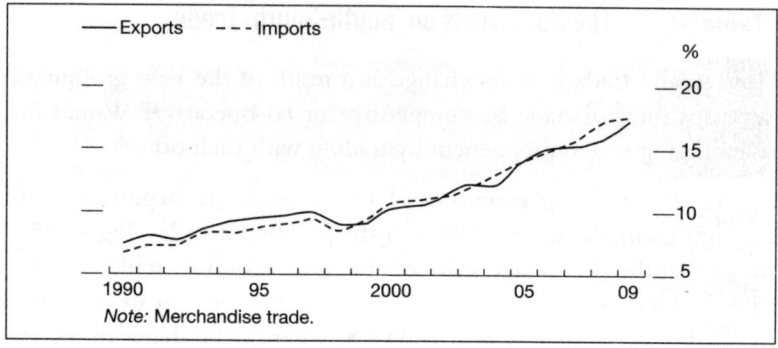

Figure 15.8 *Share of South–South trade in world trade*

Source: Prema-chandra Athukorala, 'South-South Trade: An Asian Perspective', ADB Economics Working Paper Series no. 265, Asian Development Bank, Manila, July 2011, https://www.adb.org/sites/default/files/publication/29050/economics-wp265.pdf (accessed 14 April 2018).

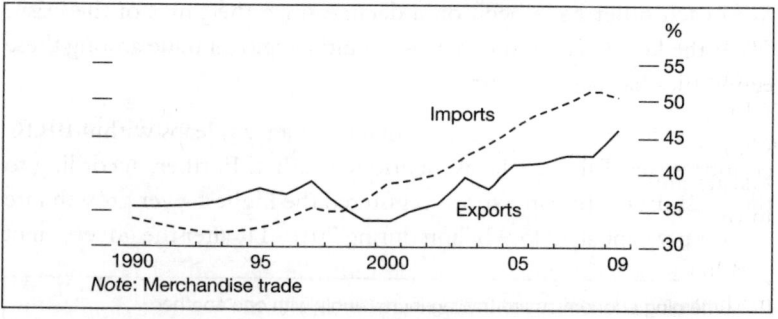

Figure 15.9 *South–South trade's share of South's total trade*

Source: Prema-chandra Athukorala, 'South-South Trade: An Asian Perspective', ADB Economics Working Paper Series no. 265, Asian Development Bank, Manila, July 2011, https://www.adb.org/sites/default/files/publication/29050/economics-wp265.pdf (accessed 14 April 2018).

diversified its exports, earlier destined for Western countries, to new markets like East Asia, Latin America and Africa. India aims to achieve $450 billion in exports by 2013–14. China's overseas shipments were more than $1.5 trillion in 2010.

There is no clear signal whether this South–South trade will be in the spirit of co-operation or in competition. Both approaches seem to

Table 15.1 *Trends in growth in trade volumes*

	(per cent change) Projections			
	2009	2010	2011	2012
World Trade Volume (goods and services) Imports	−10.7	12.0	7.1	6.8
Advanced Economies	−12.4	11.1	5.5	5.2
Emerging and Developing Economies Exports	−8.0	13.8	9.3	9.2
Advanced Economies	−11.9	11.4	6.2	5.8
Emerging and Developing Economies	−7.5	12.8	9.2	8.8

Source: IMF, World Economic Outlook, January 2011

Source: Government of India, *Economic Survey 2010–11.*

be in operation. A recent illustration of competition is the following quote from a leading government economist in India,[14] who says: 'In China's XII Plan, exports do not hold the same place. Besides, the Chinese will be vacating the lower-end of the value spectrum like textiles and leather. So who will replace them? Are we going to step in or will it be Vietnam or Turkey or Indonesia?'[15]

On the other hand, at the recent Indo–Africa Summit,[16] the officials made it clear that India's engagement with the continent would not be imperialist in nature but rather was intended to boost employment and engage in value-added types of co-operation, rather than taking resources home. However, countries like India are signing many bilateral free trade agreements with other developing countries, while simultaneously also signing trade agreements, interestingly, with the European Union! Hence, there is no set pattern or combined programme of the South.

There are also suggestions that this shift in trading relations would augur new types of economic and political governance modes drawn from the diversity of cultures:

It is useful to note that a shift in economic importance that happened after the Second World War was from the UK and Europe to USA.

There were significant common cultural traditions between the two regions. However, as economic activity shifts in future to developing countries, especially Asia, there will be a greater diversity in the social-cultural and, perhaps, political systems among these counties, and between Europe, UK, USA and these countries. In brief, over the longer term, the world will have significant diversity in the set of countries with global economic significance.[17]

This phenomenon is already showing itself, as we see the affirmation of national and regional independence from both the earlier rulers as well as from the influence of the former big powers in the West Asian region, also called the Arab region. The people-led uprisings against traditional and long-standing leaders also points to the collusion of these leaders with the Western powers for trade in oil and arms. As they negotiate liberation from those regimes, the people also seem to want to be free from those trade arrangements, and those political partnerships and cultural influences.

Fatema Mernissi, closely watching the various affirmations from her vantage point in Rabat, Morocco, sees the beginnings of real emancipation,[18] i.e., emancipation from the intellectual and cultural power of the West. This resonates with the analysis by Y. V. Reddy cited previously, that there will emerge new forms of governance and political economies.

Financial Market Initiatives

Many other initiatives are also emerging. The announcement of the inauguration of the first Latin American office of the planned Bank of the South was one such initiative. The Bank of the South is a monetary fund and lending organisation established in September 2009 by the Latin American nations of Argentina, Brazil, Paraguay, Uruguay, Ecuador, Bolivia and Venezuela. The intention of the bank is to 'strengthen regional integration; reduce asymmetries, poverty and social exclusion; promote employment and activate a virtuous cycle of sustainable development, fundamental for the economic, social and political transformation of the region'.[19] The idea is to promote the market for development lending in the 'South', as endorsed by Joseph Stiglitz: 'One of the advantages of having a Bank of the South is that it would reflect the perspectives of those in the south'; and further, 'It is a good thing to have competition in most markets, including the market for development lending.'[20]

Currency: Emerging Issues

Amongst the many ideas floating around, the latest is that the dollar as the single reserve currency should have an alternative:

> The problem with the world having only a single reserve currency came to the fore during the crisis as many countries faced dollar liquidity problems as a consequence of swift deleveraging by foreign creditors and foreign investors. Paradoxically, even as the US economy was in a downturn, the dollar strengthened as a result of flight to safety.[21]

At a recent BRICS summit,[22] it was agreed upon 'to establish mutual lines of credit in local currencies' among the member nations. The BRICS state development banks agreed to use their own currencies instead of the dollar in issuing credit or grants to each other. They will also phase out the dollar in overall settlements and lending among each other.[23] This was considered an important step towards strengthening their mutual ties 'to protect intra-BRICS trade from foreign exchange risk. The volume of this trade is only around $230 billion at present, but as a measure of potential, it is noted that the BRICS countries together account for over 15 per cent of world trade, worth over $4.5 trillion.'[24]

Here too, there are negative comments, both on the possibility of such arrangements as well as on their value:

> The political goal of appearing united prevents these countries from being outspoken on currency issues. A proposal to settle bilateral trade in their own currencies rather than in US dollars is mostly illusory. The complaints about speculative activity in commodity markets are at odds with the fact that China has some of the world's most active and volatile commodity markets.[25]

Capital Market Controls

However, there are other spaces where these countries have been able to affirm their newly found power as well as solidarity. For example:

> Representatives of emerging nations rebuffed an International Monetary Fund plan to guide them on managing huge flows of capital into their economies, viewing it as a way to constrain their actions rather than help.... Ministers of developing economies resisted vehemently, viewing the proposal as an effort by advanced economies to hamstring their policies. Brazil, Turkey, South Korea and several other developing countries have adopted capital controls over the past year to limit surging inflows. "We oppose any guidelines, frameworks or 'codes of conduct' that attempt to constrain, directly or indirectly, policy responses of countries facing surges in volatile capital inflows," Brazil's finance minister, Guido Mantega, told the IMF's steering-committee meeting. The fight over capital controls comes amid a continuing battle over who is to blame for the flood of capital flowing primarily from sluggish advanced economies into faster-growing developing countries.[26]

Yet there are many prickly issues here which are going to affect the attempt of the South countries to use currency to rectify their trade values or competitiveness.

Due to the relative 'success' of these re-emerging economies, the volume of capital flows into their economies has grown fast, leading to currency appreciations in many of these countries. For instance, the immediate impact on the economies in the region of the deluge in foreign capital flows has been steep rises in currency values. From January 2009 to November 2010, Indonesia, the Republic of Korea, Thailand and Malaysia have seen their currencies appreciate by 22.7 per cent, 17.4 per cent, 16.5 per cent and 12.4 per cent, respectively (see Figure 15.10). A number of countries such as Indonesia, Malaysia and Singapore are witnessing exchange rates against the dollar that have already exceeded their pre-crisis values.[27] It is likely that this is already happening, and that the former advanced countries, i.e., the North, will use various forms of protectionism to counter this trend.

Governments of the developing economies have attempted to insure themselves against volatile capital flows by building up foreign

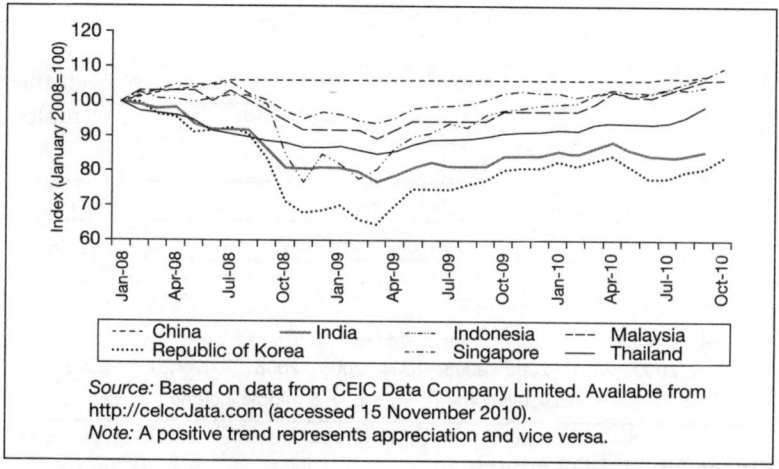

Figure 15.10 *Exchange rate movements in major developing economies, 2008–10*

Source: UN ESCAP, 'Maintaining Growth amid Global Uncertainty'.

exchange reserves. However, this may be inadequate. A vulnerability yardstick developed by ESCAP[28] indicates that the reserves of a number of countries are lower than their overall exposure to these vulnerabilities.

How Real Is This 'Power Shift'?

An important aspect of these re-emerging economies, and the assessment of their capability as well as their negotiations with the former 'economically advanced countries', comes to light by turning the lens on their relative GDP levels and per capita incomes, rather than their rate of growth of GDP. While the key re-emerging countries have higher growth rates of GDP as compared to some of the key 'developed' countries (Figure 15.11), they have much lower per capita GDP levels as well as much lower proportions of global GDP (Figure 15.12)—crucial indicators of inequality in power that are often overlooked.

Table 15.2 presents three-year averages for the past four decades of the shares of high-income countries and low- and middle-income countries in world GDP and world population. It can be seen clearly

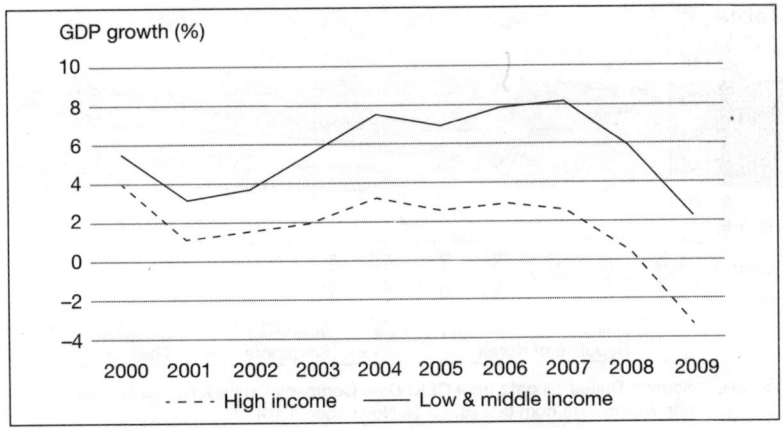

Figure 15.11 GDP growth

Source: World Bank Data, 8 July 2010.

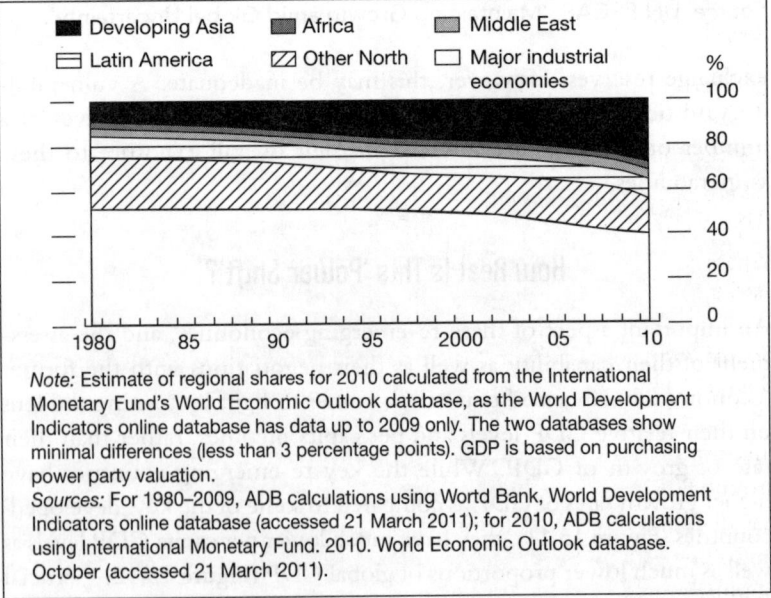

Note: Estimate of regional shares for 2010 calculated from the International Monetary Fund's World Economic Outlook database, as the World Development Indicators online database has data up to 2009 only. The two databases show minimal differences (less than 3 percentage points). GDP is based on purchasing power party valuation.
Sources: For 1980–2009, ADB calculations using Wortd Bank, World Development Indicators online database (accessed 21 March 2011); for 2010, ADB calculations using International Monetary Fund. 2010. World Economic Outlook database. October (accessed 21 March 2011).

Figure 15.12 Share of developing countries and key emerging economies in global GDP

Source: Asian Development Bank, Asian Development Outlook 2011.

Table 15.2 Country-wise shares in world GDP and population, 1970–2007 (three-year averages)

Country-wise Share in World GDP (Constant 2000$)					
	1970–72	1980–82	1990–92	2000–02	2005–07
Brazil	1.7	2.3	2.1	2	2
China	0.8	1.1	2	4	5.6
India	0.9	0.9	1.1	1.5	1.9
US	30.3	28.7	28.9	30.3	29.4
Share of Germany, Japan, US andUK	58.6	56.4	57.2	55.2	52.6
Share of Brazil, China and India	3.4	4.3	5.2	7.5	9.5
Country-wise Share in World Population					
Brazil	2.6	2.8	2.8	2.9	2.9
India	14.9	15.5	16.2	16.8	17.0
China	22.3	22.0	21.5	20.6	20.0
United States	5.5	5.1	4.7	4.6	4.6
Share of Germany, Japan, US and UK	11.9	10.7	9.6	9.0	8.7
Share of Brazil, China and India	39.8	40.3	40.4	40.3	39.9

Source: Author's calculations based on World Development Indicators, 2008
Source: UNCTAD.

that the share of developed countries in world GDP has remained at around 80 per cent in this period, while their share in world population has declined over time from 20 per cent in 1970–73 to 16 per cent in 2005–07. The burden of feeding around 84 per cent of the world population with around 20 per cent of world GDP lies on the shoulders of the developing and least developed countries.

The share of the US has remained at around 30 per cent of world GDP since the 1970s, while India's share has increased marginally from less than 1 per cent in 1970 to around 2 per cent in 2007. The highest growth in the share in world GDP has been China's, from 0.8 per cent in 1970 to 5.6 per cent in 2007. The combined share of Germany, Japan, the US and the UK in world GDP is greater than half, while the emerging economies together share less than 10 per cent of world GDP.

The GDP levels of Brazil will catch up with those of the UK, US and Japan after 46 years, 160 years and 87 years respectively. India will take another 10 years, 40 years and 25 years to attain GDP levels comparable to the UK, US and Japan respectively.

On the other hand, population shares reveal the opposite trends, drawing attention to the stark differences in per capita incomes. The combined share of Brazil, China and India in the world population is around 40 per cent, while that of Germany, Japan, the US and the UK is less than 10 per cent. Comparing the per capita income levels of high-income countries and low- and middle-income countries, we find that the gap between them has increased over time. Figure 15.13 shows that the difference between the average per capita incomes has remained high. It is interesting to note that the average per capita income in high-income countries has always been around 20 times

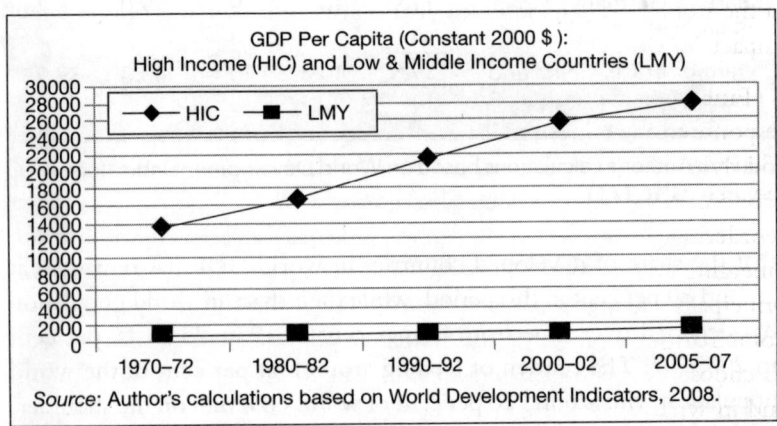

Source: Author's calculations based on World Development Indicators, 2008.

Figure 15.13 *Average per capita income in high-income countries and low- and middle-income countries, 1970–2007 (three-year averages)*

Source: UNCTAD.

higher than the average per capita income in low- and middle-income countries.

Currently in global negotiations, the higher growth rates of these countries have led to demands by developed countries for greater market access commitments from these new emerging economies. The gaps in per capita income, as well as the deeply entrenched poverty in many of these newly emerging economies, suggest the need to challenge the demand of advanced countries for a change their terms of trade with the re-emerging economies. They may be key emerging markets, but they are way behind in what is real economic capability.

FEMINIST ENGAGEMENT

Where is the entry point for engagement by women in this new scenario? One of the founding issues for feminist economics, especially in the South, was labour, work, livelihood. This was the fulcrum of feminist studies, of data critiques, of advocacy for women as workers within households, of understanding home-based work, the informal economy and so on. Another priority concern has been the goal of gender equality. In the aftermath of the financial crisis of 2008–09, most of the studies done by feminist economists and agencies reviewed the impact on women's employment and livelihoods.

Employment continues to be the major preoccupation. However, in response to the current global shift in economic power and the efforts and dynamics set in motion by the re-emerging economies, feminist economists need also to locate themselves in the bigger politics of this reordering. In this section, I first set out some initial analyses that are emerging on the impact of this general shift on conventional indicators, principally labour. Second, I describe the reality of state and market combinations in most of the world, to suggest that the issue is not to choose between state and market, but to engage with how much and in what ways to regulate economies and shape the state. Finally, reinvoking the earlier histories of women's participation in political economy debates, I argue for entering into our research and collective engagements with public policy in different ways.

Gendered Impact of the 'New' Order

Data on the gendered impact of the relative success of some economies of the South are not yet available. The 2008–09 crisis is still too recent for any changes to be observable, and the trading patterns as well as growth patterns are still to get embedded. Hence, the information we have continues to focus on the impact of the crisis, and the situation has been recorded in detail in many papers of the time.

However, Naoko Otobe of the Employment Division of the ILO, Geneva, has provided some insightful information on the gendering of employment outcomes for the last five years, bringing the data up to 2009.[29] She has tracked trends in male and female unemployment for various regions. Across most regions, the share of vulnerable employment was higher among working women than among men, except in developed economies, the European Union, Central and Southeast Europe, and the Commonwealth of Independent States (CIS) in 2008. Among the developing regions, South Asia had the highest level of vulnerable employment for both women and men, followed by Sub-Saharan Africa (Figure 15.14).[30]

Generally speaking, in high-income countries in the past, male unemployment was lower than female unemployment. However, since the global economic crisis hit, the male unemployment rate initially increased faster than female unemployment in the developed economies, showing the convergence between the two groups. As the crisis has deepened, with ripple effects across economies, it was expected that 2009 would show a higher increase in the female unemployment rate than the male unemployment rate (Figure 15.15).[31]

In Central and Southeast Europe (non-EU) and CIS, some countries have seen more severe economic downturns than others, affecting the labour market negatively. In this region, the gender gap in unemployment had been very narrow, but male unemployment was expected to rise slightly more than the female rate due to men's higher concentration in the manufacturing and construction sectors, which had been more heavily affected (Figure 15.16).[32]

In developing countries, gendered unemployment patterns vary from one region to another. In East Asia (represented by China), where

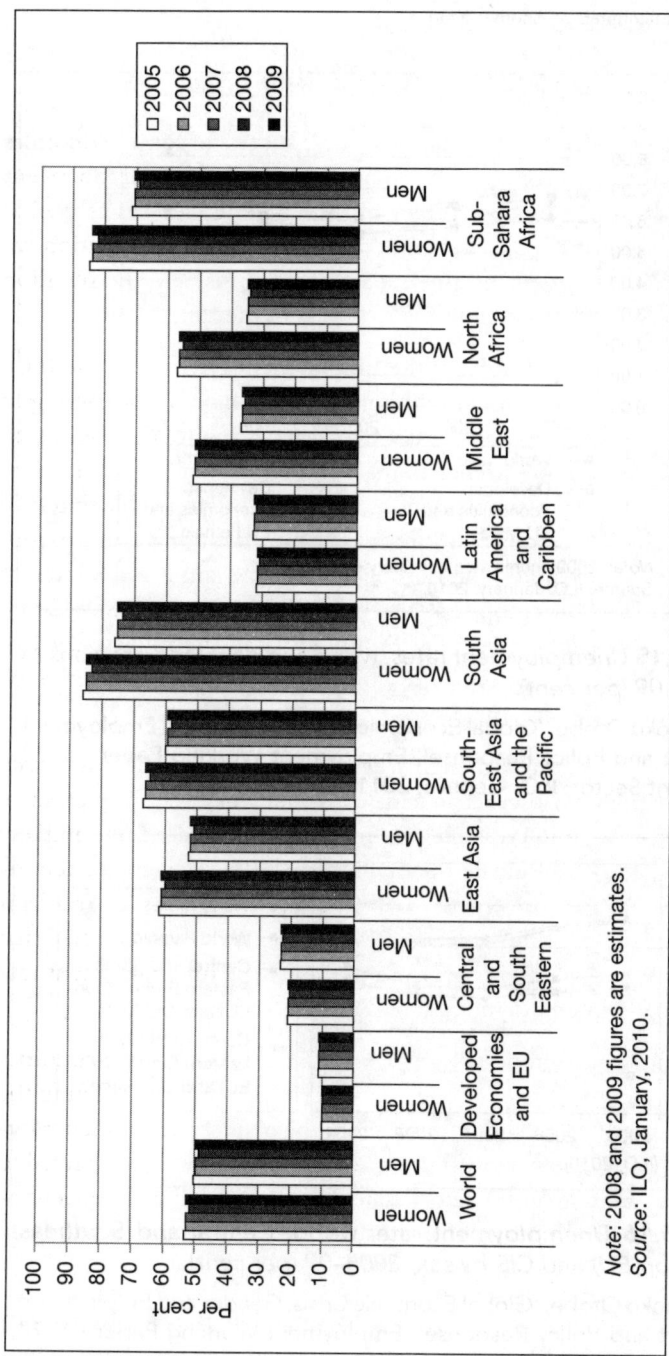

Figure 15.14 *Rate of vulnerable employment by region and sex, 2005–09 (per cent)*

Note: 2008 and 2009 figures are estimates.
Source: ILO, January, 2010.

Source: Naoko Otobe, 'Global Economic Crisis, Gender and Employment: The Impact and Policy Response', Employment Working Paper no. 74, Employment Sector, ILO, Geneva, 2011.

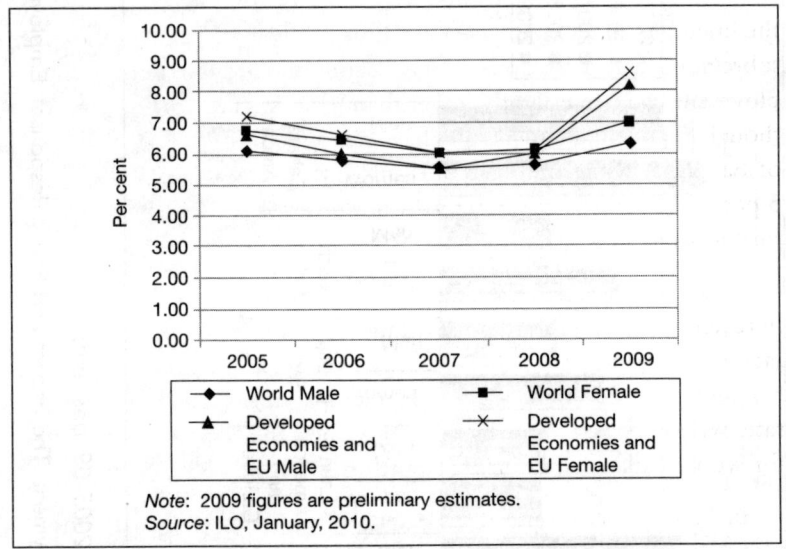

Figure 15.15 *Unemployment rates, world and developed regions by sex, 2005–09 (per cent)*

Source: Naoko Otobe, 'Global Economic Crisis, Gender and Employment: The Impact and Policy Response', Employment Working Paper no. 74, Employment Sector, ILO, Geneva, 2011.

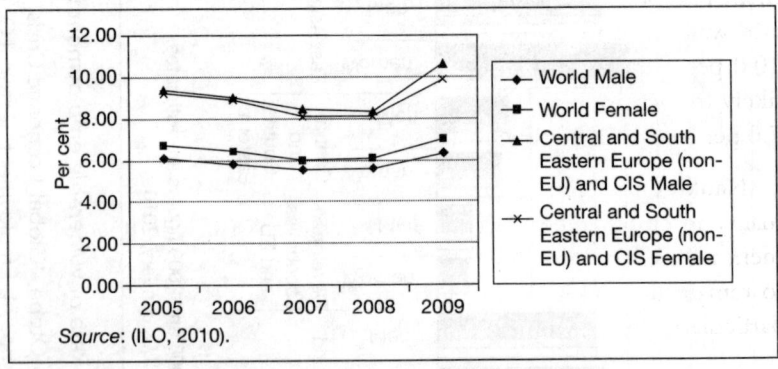

Figure 15.16 *Unemployment rate, world, Central and Southeast Europe (non-EU) and CIS by sex, 2005–09 (per cent)*

Source: Naoko Otobe, 'Global Economic Crisis, Gender and Employment: The Impact and Policy Response', Employment Working Paper no. 74, Employment Sector, ILO, Geneva, 2011.

the unemployment rates have been historically lower than in the other subregions due to continued robust economic growth, female unemployment had been slightly lower than male. Figure 15.17 shows that though the unemployment rates have increased post-crisis for the whole of East Asia, while the male unemployment rate was expected to be 5 per cent in 2009, it was below 4 per cent for the female workforce for the same year.

As for South Asia, the female unemployment rate had been higher in recent years, and this trend continued, though both female and male rates had been declining since 2005. Between 2007 and 2008, there was a slight further decline in the female unemployment rate. However, the rates were expected to rise by 1.2 and 0.6 percentage points respectively for women and men in 2009 (Figure 15.17).[33]

In Latin America and the Caribbean, on average, female unemployment rates had been historically higher than male rates by 2–3 percentage points, which constituted a bigger gender gap than in Asia. This is also one of the developing regions where, historically, women's employment-to-population ratio has been increasing during the last 10 years. Between 2007 and 2008, the female unemployment rate remained at a high 8.8 per cent compared to men's unemployment rate of 5.8 per cent in both years. The female unemployment rate was expected to rise by 1.0 to 1.9 percentage points to around 10.0 per cent, faster than the men's unemployment rate, which was likely to increase by between 0.7 to 1.2 percentage points to around 7.0 per cent in 2009 (Figure 15.18).[34]

Naoko Otobe introduces the qualifier that since the level of informality in employment is rather high in South Asia, the unemployment rate reflects those who were looking for work but could afford to remain unemployed, which is often the case for educated youth, particularly young women.

The Role of the State

Many of the emerging economies have had and continue to have strong state control, e.g., over central banks and other key sectors. Despite the

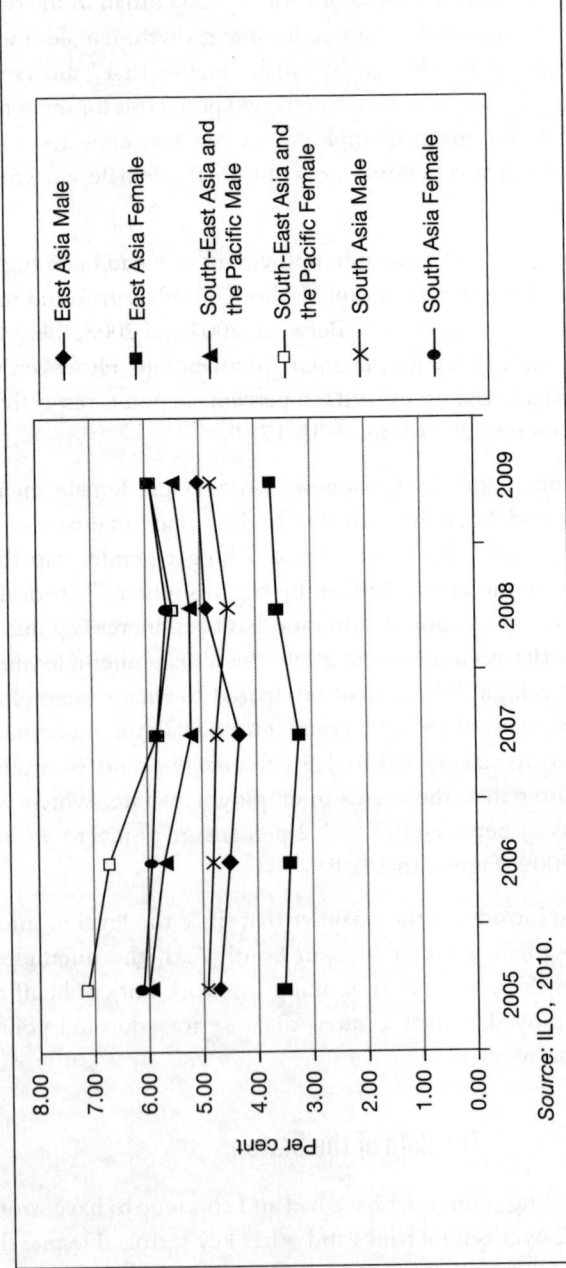

Figure 15.17 *Unemployment rate in Asia by sex, 2005–09 (per cent)*

Source: Naoko Otobe, 'Global Economic Crisis, Gender and Employment: The Impact and Policy Response', Employment Working Paper no. 74, Employment Sector, ILO, Geneva, 2011.

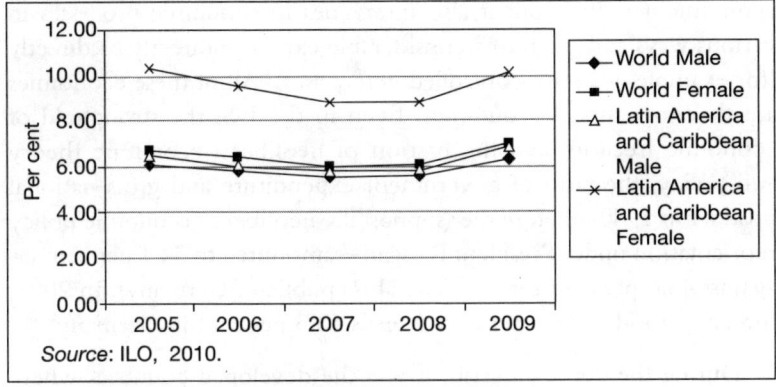

Figure 15.18 *Unemployment rate in Latin America and the Caribbean, 2005–09 by sex (per cent)*

Source: Naoko Otobe, 'Global Economic Crisis, Gender and Employment: The Impact and Policy Response', Employment Working Paper no. 74, Employment Sector, ILO, Geneva, 2011.

spread of ideas of neoliberalism and the market economy, these countries still experience the legacy of postcolonial ideas and allegiances. In the immediate aftermath of freedom, most ex-colonies veered towards what was called the 'East' in those days, i.e., the Soviet Union bloc, as this region had not been as prominent in the colonisation process. This meant inclining towards a socialist state, and as a result, towards particular forms of state control, whereby all sectors of the economy have regulatory structures which are usually handled by the bureaucracy. These regulatory processes helped some of the countries of the South, such as India and Chile,[35] navigate the financial tsunami of the 1980s.[36] Other countries, such as those in Latin America, had in the last decade elected governments which were more socialist. Thus, Chile, which had a relatively inward-looking economy and practised a regulated trade regime, was able to resist the meltdown.

All of the competing and co-operating states, whether the OECD countries, the BRIC states,[37] and now the Republic of South Africa, or other emerging countries, are 'capitalist'; they all boast economies with a strong private sector. Yet, in all of these economies, the state not only lays down the fundamental rules and regulations governing economic activities, but it also intervenes in economic processes in various ways and often to a considerable extent, indirectly or directly (for example, via state-controlled enterprises). All of these economies are therefore mixed economies. Even in the US, the stronghold of economic freedom and the bastion of neoliberal economic theory and policy, the ratio of government expenditure and gross national product in 1980—before the (supposedly neoliberal) economic policy reorientation under President Reagan—amounted to 34.1 per cent (as against 46.6 per cent for the Federal Republic of Germany). In 2008, the ratio stood at 38.8 per cent (versus 43.3 per cent in Germany).[38]

During the 2008–09 crisis, it was the developed countries where demand collapsed, so the 'trading out of crisis'[39] approach used in the past needed modification. Traditional destination markets needed to be (partially) replaced by the new markets of developing countries (within and outside the region) and by local demand. An important point is that, even in a switch from traditional to regional markets, it is still export which is relied upon by many economies in the region to sustain their recovery and growth, rather than production for the local (domestic) market.

Therefore, the question for any of these economies is not whether the state intervenes massively, but rather how it does so. This presents an opportunity for feminist economists to move on, in their advocacy, from speaking of the need for the state, to the how and what and where of the state.

Building a Strong, South-Driven Feminist Economics Programme

In the 1980s, the women's movements of the developing countries often found their best political umbrella in the spaces provided by NAM. These newly independent countries were trying to redefine themselves after decolonisation. They sought to separate themselves from the two major global warring economic powers of that time, also drawn from two opposing political ideologies—the West, liberal capitalistic; and the East, the Soviet bloc, communist and socialist. This desire gave birth to the movement or grouping called the Non-Aligned Movement.

The NAM space enabled the women's movements from the South at that time to disengage from the strong formats and frameworks that were being driven by the West via the UN. They engaged with other struggles, within which theirs was also a struggle. 'Liberation' was the keyword, and that included liberation from male domination. But gender equality was subsumed in the struggle for liberation from the legacies of domination, including intellectual domination by the 'former masters'. In many of the newly liberated countries, leaders saw struggles by women for their rights either as not of high priority, or as stimulated by Western notions, Western 'culture'. But for the women of the developing countries, acquiring space in NAM gave their concerns legitimacy in the political space of the South.[40]

This atmosphere of affirmation of a postcolonial identity by women from the former colonies was a strong part of the First UN World Conference on Women, held in Mexico in 1975.[41] The gatherings that followed continued the ethic of dissociation from Eurocentric pressures even within the women's movement. Thus, in 1985, prior to the UN World Conference on Women in Nairobi,[42] the NAM movement called its own women's conference to frame its agenda for Nairobi as a political configuration. Amongst the many networks that were formed, a network called DAWN was forged, offering a 'Third World' (as it was called then) women's perspective on development frameworks and design.

In a similar way, there is need for feminist research and mobilisation to restructure advocacy and inputs in the light of the ongoing shift in the global economic order. Questions such as whether economies should become inward looking with an emphasis on national development, and whether economies need to get back to the idea of the nation–state, involve serious issues that need to be addressed. A recent volume, *Reclaiming the Nation: The Return of the National Question in Africa, Asia and Latin America*, speaks to this rethinking. Internationalism and globalism, it suggests, have blurred and overpowered nations and national responsibilities, especially through the paradigm of illiberal liberalism. Hence, there is a return to reclaiming the nation, and to some extent the turbulence in the West Asian region also denotes that affirmation.[43]

Similarly, what kind of research and mobilisation should we undertake to ensure that the new South–South collaboration becomes co-operative and not competitive? In 1987, the South Commission was constituted by the former president of Tanzania, Julius Nyerere, with 28 economists of the South to develop a framework which would enable the South to build a just economic foundation, to pull itself out of poverty and exploitation but also to challenge the North as an economy. The commission produced many co-operative ideas such as a common currency, common grain banks, trading for benefit rather than pure profit and so on, in its seminal publication, *Challenge to the South*.[44] But at that time, the world was not ready for this change.

Now, the location of economic energy has shifted to the South, giving an opportunity for feminists to transform development based on the ideas they believe in—economic democracy, right to decent work and security for migrating persons, and so on. The need is to understand and work towards protecting those who will become vulnerable in this new context. For this, it is necessary to move away from the concern only with gender equality, to reflecting on questions of political economy and legal spaces, the value of inward-looking economies and national development as a basis for citizens to claim their rights, and engaging with the debates on regulation, i.e., the share of states and markets in economic development, and so on. The women's question needs to be located within these debates and opportunities. Feminist proposals for a just world need to participate in and engage with these ideas, and the feminist agenda needs to be designed accordingly.

NOTES

1 The contributions of Anandi Venkat, Naoko Otobe, Niha Masih, Nishtha Kochhar, Perce Bloomer, Y. V. Reddy and Muchkund Dubey are gratefully acknowledged. The views and opinions expressed here are personal. Any remaining errors and omissions are the sole responsibility of the author.

2 Samir Amin, 'Nation States: Which Way Forward?', in Sam Moyo and Paris Yeros (eds), *Reclaiming the Nation: The Return of the National Question in Africa, Asia and Latin America* (London: Pluto Press, 2011), pp. 325–44.

3 Y. V. Reddy, 'Longer-Term Consequences: Global Financial Turmoil', *Hindu Business Line*, 31 December 2010.

4 The *Economic Survey* is normally released in February, just before the presentation of the annual budget. Government of India, *Economic Survey 2010–11*, Ministry of Finance, Department of Economic Affairs, Economic Division (New Delhi: Oxford University Press, 2011).

5   Rohit Chopra, 'Resurrection and Normalisation of Empire', Reflection on Empire, *Economic & Political Weekly*, vol. 46, no. 13 (2011), pp. 42–49; Abdullahi Ahmed An-Na'im, 'Taming the Imperial Impulse: Realising a Pragmatic Moral Vision', Reflection on Empire, *Economic & Political Weekly*, vol. 46, no. 13 (2011), pp. 50–59; Manan Ahmed, 'Adam's Mirror: The Frontier in the Imperial Imagination', Reflection on Empire, *Economic & Political Weekly*, vol. 46, no. 13 (2011), pp. 60–65; Suvir Kaul, 'Indian Empire (and the Case of Kashmir)', Reflection on Empire, *Economic & Political Weekly*, vol. 46, no. 13 (2011), pp. 66–75; Chandra Talpade Mohanty, 'Imperial Democracies, Feminist Engagements', Reflection on Empire, *Economic & Political Weekly*, vol. 46, no. 13 (2011), pp. 76–84.

6   Siddharth Varadarajan, 'India Pitches for Greater IBSA, BRIC Role', *Hindu*, 16 April 2010.

7   It was agreed upon by the members of the BRIC alliance, during a summit held in Sanya, China, in April 2011, that the loans and grants made among themselves should take place in local currencies. See the discussion on currency later in this chapter.

8   Renato Baumann, 'The Geography of Brazilian External Trade: Right Option for a BRIC?', http://www.ipea.gov.br/bric/textos/100409_BRICBaumann1. pdf (accessed 24 March 2018).

9   Biswajit Dhar, 'BRICS: The Developing Giant', *Livemint*, 13 April 2011.

10 C. Raja Mohan, 'A Bag of BRICS', *Indian Express*, 12 April 2011, http://www. indianexpress.com/news/a-bag-of-brics/774808/2 (accessed 25 March 2018).

11 Ibid.

12 *Hindu*, 'India, ASEAN Set $70 b Trade Target', 3 March 2011.

13 Government of India, *Economic Survey 2010–11*.

14 Montek Singh Ahluwalia, Deputy Chairman, Planning Commission, Government of India.

15 *Hindu*, 'Textiles, Leather Exports to Gain from Chinese Policy: Montek', *Hindu*, 22 April 2011.

16 India–Africa Summit, Addis Ababa, 20–26 May 2011.

17 Y. V. Reddy, 'Recent International Financial Turmoil and Its Implications for Developing Countries', *ASCI Journal of Management*, vol. 40, no. 1 (2010), pp. 52–60.

18 Fatema Mernissi, 'Digital Scheherazade: The Rise of Women as Key Players in the Arab Gulf Communication Strategies', http://mernissi.net/books/ articles/digital_scheherazade.html (accessed 25 March 2018); Fatema Mernissi, 'Women Weave Peace into Globalisation', paper for the Casablanca Group Meeting, September 2007.

19 Technical Workshop, Bank of the South, November 2008, http://www.net-workideas.org/alt/nov2008/Quito_Workshop.pdf (accessed 25 March 2018).

20 Rory Carroll, 'Nobel Economist Endorses Chávez Regional Bank Plan', *Guardian*, 12 October 2007, http://www.guardian.co.uk/business/2007/ oct/12/venezuela.banking (accessed 26 March 2018).

21 D. Subbarao, 'Frontier Issues on the Global Agenda: Emerging Economy Perspective', Commemorative speech, 60th Anniversary Celebrations of the Central Bank of Sri Lanka, Colombo, 29 March 2011, https://www.bis.org/review/r110330d.pdf (accessed 26 March 2018).

22 Third BRICS Summit, Sanya, China, 14 April 2011.

23 David Marsh, 'BRICS Make Move to Shove Dollar Aside', Market Watch, 17 April 2011, http://www.marketwatch.com/story/brics-make-move-to-shove-dollar-aside-2011-04-17?link=home_carousel (accessed 26 March 2018).

24 Sudipto Mundle, 'Dollars, BRICS and the China Trap', Times of India, 28 April 2011.

25 Philip Bowring, 'The Big C in BRICS', Indian Express, 22 April 2011.

26 Sudeep Reddy, 'Emerging Nations Reject Capital Plan', Wall Street Journal, 18 April 2011.

27 UN ESCAP, 'Maintaining Growth amid Global Uncertainty, Economic and Social Survey of the Asia and the Pacific 2010: Year-End Update, 2010', http://www.unescap.org/sites/default/files/publications/YearendUpdate2010.pdf (accessed 26 March 2018).

28 The vulnerability yardstick is the sum of short-term debt, imports of the last quarter of the year, and stock of equity and debt portfolio capital. For more details, see ibid., pp. 21–22.

29 Naoko Otobe, 'Global Economic Crisis, Gender and Employment: The Impact and Policy Response', Employment Working Paper no. 74, Employment Sector, ILO, Geneva, 2011.

30 Ibid.

31 Ibid.

32 Ibid.

33 Ibid.

34 Ibid.

35 Heine Jorge, currently distinguished fellow, Centre for International Governance Innovation, personal communication, 2007.

36 Devaki Jain, 'Nuancing Globalisation, or Mainstreaming the Downstream, or Reforming Reform', Working Paper no. 3, Centre for Gender and Development Studies, University of the West Indies, May 2000 (reproduced as chapter 6, this volume); Devaki Jain, 'Using the Handle of Regulation to Revive the Space for Social Justice', Symposia Series 'Feminisms and Globalisation: Women 2000', NCRW, CUNY and Japan Preparatory Committee Economic Dimensions of Globalisation Panel, 7 June 2000.

37 Kin Chi Lau and Huang Ping (eds), 'China Reflected', special issue, Asia Exchange, vol. 18, no. 2 and vol. 19, no. 1 (2002–03).

38 Hanns W. Maull, 'World Politics in Turbulence', Internationale Politik und Gesellschaft (2011), pp. 11–25, http://library.fes.de/pdf-files/ipg/ipg-2011-1/2011-1__03_a_maull.pdf (accessed 26 March 2018).

39 UN ESCAP, Sustaining Dynamism and Inclusive Development: Connectivity in the Region and Productive Capacity in Least Developed Countries, Economic and Social

Survey of Asia and the Pacific 2011, http://www.unescap.org/sites/default/files/
Econimic-and-Social-Survey-2011.pdf (accessed 27 March 2018).

40 Jain, *Women, Development and the UN*, pp. 80–120.

41 First UN World Conference on Women, Mexico, 19 June–2 July 1975.

42 Third World Conference on Women, Nairobi, 15–26 July 1985.

43 Amin, 'Nation States: Which Way Forward?'

44 South Commission, *The Challenge to the South*.

Bibliography

Abeysekara, Sunila, and Marilee Karl. 'Gender Mainstreaming: An Obsolete Concept? A Conversation between Two Longtime Feminist Activists', in *Women in Action 2004-2: Examining Feminist and Social Movements* (Manila: ISIS International, 2004).

Abraham, Thomas. 'Reviving an Old Dream of Afro-Asian Cooperation', *Yale Global Online*, 24 May 2005, https://yaleglobal.yale.edu/content/reviving-old-dream-afro-asian-cooperation (accessed 4 March 2018).

Abzug, Bella. 'Women Will Change the Nature of Power', Bradford Morse Memorial Lecture, Opening Plenary, United Nations Fourth World Conference on Women, Beijing, 5 September 1995.

Adiga, Aravind. *White Tiger* (New Delhi: HarperCollins, 2010).

Agarwal, Bina. 'Work Participation of Women in Rural India: Some Data and Conceptual Biases', *Economic & Political Weekly*, vol. 20, nos 51–52 (1985), pp. A155–A164.

Agarwal, Bina, and Pradeep Panda. 'Home and the World: Revisiting Violence', *New Indian Express*, 7 August 2003.

Aghion, Philipe, and Patrick Bolton. 'A Theory of Trickle Down Growth and Development', *Review of Economic Studies*, vol. 64, no. 219 (1997), pp. 151–72.

Ahmed, Manan. 'Adam's Mirror: The Frontier in the Imperial Imagination', Reflection on Empire, *Economic & Political Weekly*, vol. 46, no. 13 (2011), pp. 60–65.

Ali, Ifzal, 'Pro-poor to Inclusive Growth: Asian Prescriptions', ERD Policy Brief no. 48, May 2007.

Amin, Samir. 'Nation States: Which Way Forward?', in Sam Moyo and Paris Yeros (eds), *Reclaiming the Nation: The Return of the National Question in Africa, Asia and Latin America* (London: Pluto Press, 2011), pp. 325–44.

Amoah, Elizabeth. 'Women, Witches and Social Change in Ghana', in Diana Eck and Devaki Jain (eds), *Speaking of Faith: Cross-Cultural Perspectives on Women, Religion and Social Change* (New Delhi: Kali for Women, 1986).

Anand, Kumar. 'The Inequality Debate: Thoughts on Piketty', *Spontaneous Order*, 7 May 2014.

An-Na'im, Abdullahi Ahmed. 'Taming the Imperial Impulse: Realising a Pragmatic Moral Vision', Reflection on Empire, *Economic & Political Weekly*, vol. 46, no. 13 (2011), pp. 50–59.

Apusigah, Agnes Atia. 'Gender Mainstreaming: The Ghana Poverty Reduction Strategy, or Is It?', in *Women in Action 2004-2: Examining Feminist and Social Movements* (Manila: ISIS International, 2004).

Arizpe, Lourdes. 'Power of Culture', speech delivered at the 'Power of Culture' conference, Amsterdam, 8–9 November 1996.

Asian Age. 'India, Pakistan on Top of Bribe-Taker List', 28 October 1999.

Athukorala, Prema-chandra. 'South-South Trade: An Asian Perspective', ADB Economics Working Paper Series no. 265, Asian Development Bank, Manila, July 2011, https://www.adb.org/sites/default/files/publication/29050/economics-wp265.pdf (accessed 14 April 2018).

Baldauf, Scott. 'India's "Girl Deficit" Deepest among Educated', *Christian Science Monitor*, 16 January 2006, http://www.csmonitor.com/2006/0113/p01s04-wosc.html (accessed 18 March 2018).

Basu, Aparna, and Bharati Ray. *Women's Struggle: A History of the All India Women's Conference, 1927–2002* (New Delhi: Manohar Books, 2003).

Baumann, Renato. 'The Geography of Brazilian External Trade: Right Option for a BRIC?', http://www.ipea.gov.br/bric/textos/100409_BRICBaumann1.pdf (accessed 24 March 2018).

Beguin, A. 'Preface', in L. Goldschmidt-Clermont, *Unpaid Work in the Household: A Review of Economic Evaluation Methods*, Women, Work and Development no. 1 (Geneva: International Labour Office, 1982).

Bhagwati, Jagdish. 'Globalization Has a Human Face', Lecture at India Habitat Centre, New Delhi, 18 October 1999.

Bhatt, Ela. *Anubandh: Building 100-Mile Communities* (Ahmedabad: Navajivan, 2015).

Bhattacharya, Sudhir. 'Women's Activities in Rural India: A Study Based on NSS 32nd Round (1977–78) Survey Results on Employment and Unemployment', NSSO, Department of Statistics, Government of India, June 1981.

Bier, Laura. 'Our Sisters in Struggle: Non-Alignment, Afro-Asian Solidarity and National Identity in the Egyptian Women's Press: 1952–1967', Working Paper no. 4, New York University, New York, 2002.

Birdsell, N., and W. McGreevey. 'The Second Sex in the Third World: Is Female Poverty a Development Issue?', paper prepared for the International Center for Research on Women Policy Roundtable, Washington, D.C., 21 June 1978.

Boserup, Ester. *My Professional Life and Publications 1929–1998* (Copenhagen: Museum Tusculanum Press, 1999).

Bowring, Philip. 'The Big C in BRICS', *Indian Express*, 22 April 2011.

Braunstein, Elissa. 'Foreign Direct Investment, Development and Gender Equity: A Review of Research and Policy', Occasional Paper 12, UNRISD, January 2006.

Braveboy-Wagner, Jacqueline Anne (ed.). *The Foreign Policies of the Global South: Rethinking Conceptual Frameworks* (Boulder, CO: Lynne Rienner, 2003).

Business Day. 'Strengthening the South through NAM: The Opportunities', 13 August 1998.

Carr, Marilyn, and Marty Chen. *Globalization and the Informal Economy: How Global Trade and Investment Impact on the Working Poor* (Geneva: ILO, 2002).

Carroll, Lewis. *Through the Looking-Glass* (London: Penguin Popular Classics, 1994 [1865]).

Carroll, Rory. 'Nobel Economist Endorses Chávez Regional Bank Plan', *Guardian*, 12 October 2007, http://www.guardian.co.uk/business/2007/oct/12/venezuela.banking (accessed 26 March 2018).

Chakraborty, Debashis, and Dipankar Sengupta. 'IBSAC (India Brazil, South Africa, China): A Potential Developing Country Coalition in WTO Negotiations', Occasional Paper no. 18, Centre de Sciences Humaines, New Delhi, 2006.

Chambers, Robert. *Notes and Reflections on a Visit to the Working Women's Forum in South India* (New Delhi: Ford Foundation, 1985).

Chandrashekhar, Rajkumari. *Aspects of Adult Education* (Madras: New Era Publication, 1982).

Chang, H., X. Dong and F. MacPhail. 'Labour Migration and Time Use Patterns of the Left-Behind Children and Elderly in Rural China', *World Development*, vol. 39, no. 12 (2011), pp. 2199–10.

Chattopadhayay, Kamaladevi. *Indian Women's Battle for Freedom* (New Delhi: Abhinav Publications, 1983).

Chen, Marty. 'Women and the Informal Sector: Realities, Statistics and Policies', paper presented at the Economic Policy Forum, International Center for Research on Women, Washington, D.C., 15 March 1996.

Chen, Shaohua, and Martin Ravallion. 'How Did the World's Poorest Fare in the 1990s?', Development Research Group, World Bank, 2000.

Cherian, John. 'The Relevance of NAM', *Frontline*, vol. 20, no. 4, 15–28 February 2003, http://www.frontline.in/static/html/fl2004/stories/20030228000706000.htm (accessed 7 March 2018).

China Daily. 'Alibaba: Journey of the Global Tech Giant', September 2014, http://www.chinadaily.com.cn/bizchina/tech/alibaba_ipo/alibaba_ipo.html (accessed 21 March 2018).

Chopra, Rohit. 'Resurrection and Normalisation of Empire', Reflection on Empire, *Economic & Political Weekly*, vol. 46, no. 13 (2011), pp. 42–49

Cobb, C., T. Halstead and J. Rowe. 'If the GDP Is Up, Why Is America Down?', *Atlantic Monthly* (October 1995), pp. 62–78.

Connolly, William. 'Democracy and Territory', in Marjorie Ringrose and Adam J. Lerner (eds), *Reimagining the Nation* (Buckingham: Open University Press, 1993), pp. 49–75.

Cornia, Giovanni Andrea, and Julius Court. 'Inequality, Growth and Poverty in the Era of Liberalization and Globalization', Policy Brief no. 4, UNU WIDER, 2001.

Cornia, Giovanni Andrea, with Sampsa Kiiski. 'Trends in Income Distribution in the Post-World War II Period: Evidence and Interpretation', WIDER Discussion Paper no. 89, UNU/WIDER, Helsinki.

Dasgupta, Shib Shankar. 'Digitising the World of Hunger', *Deccan Herald*, 17 September 2003.

DavaoToday.com. 'Stronger Regional Cooperation Can Promote Inclusive Growth, Says ADB President', 7 May 2007, http://davaotoday.com/main/inbox/asia-stronger-regional-cooperation-can-promote-inclusive-growth-says-adb-president/ (accessed 21 January 2018).

Davies, James B., Antony Shorrocks, Susanna Sandstrom et al. 'The World Distribution of Household Wealth', 2007, https://escholarship.org/content/qt3jv048hx/qt3jv048hx.pdf?nosplash=75a51704d5844f26f6f450a2d5909af3 (accessed 11 April 2018).

Davies, James B., Susanna Sandström, Anthony Shorrocks and Edward N. Wolff, 'The Level and Distribution of Global Household Wealth', *Economic Journal*, vol. 121, no. 551 (2010), pp. 223–54.

Deere, C. D. 'The Agricultural Division of Labour by Sex: Myths, Facts and Contradiction in the Northern Peruvian Sieria', Economics Department, University of Massachusetts, Amherst, 1977.

Deere, Carmen Diane, and Cheryl R. Doss. 'Gender and the Distribution of Wealth in Developing Countries', Research Paper no. 2006/115, UNU-WIDER, 2 October 2006.

Desai, Meghnad. *Development and Nationhood: Essays in the Political Economy of South Asia* (New Delhi: Oxford University Press, 2004).

DeSouza, Peter. 'Lessons from Mutiny on the Bounty', *Hindu*, 21 October 2014.

Dhar, Biswajit. 'BRICS: The Developing Giant', *Livemint*, 13 April 2011.

Dogra, Bharat. 'Protecting Forests and Livelihood: Creating Harmony, Reducing Conflict', Lovraj Kumar Memorial Lecture, SPWD, New Delhi, 1998.

Drohan, Madelaine. 'Now They Tell Us: Privatization Is No Panacea', *Globe & Mail* (Canada), 6 August 2003.

Easterly, William. 'The Lost Decades: Developing Countries' Stagnation in spite of Policy Reform, 1950–1999', World Bank, Washington, D.C., 2000.

Eck, Diana, and Devaki Jain (eds). *Speaking of Faith: Cross-Cultural Perspectives on Women, Religion and Social Change* (New Delhi, Kali for Women, 1986).

Economic & Political Weekly, 'Promoting "Inclusive Growth"?', Editorial, vol. 42, no. 22 (2007), pp. 2031–32.

Economists Interested in Women's Issues Group. 'Reports and Papers of Four Seminars', Workshop on 'Women and Poverty', Centre for Studies in Social Science, Calcutta, 1983.

Edwards, Peter. 'Examining Inequality: Who Really Benefits from Global Growth?', *World Development*, vol. 34, no. 10 (2006), pp. 1667–95

Eisenstein, Zillah. 'What's in a Name? Seeing Feminism, Universalism, and Modernity', *Wagadu*, vol. 1, no. 1 (Spring 2004).

Elson, Diane (ed.). *Male Bias in Macro-economics*;(Manchester: Manchester University Press, 1991).

Emmerij, Louis. 'Development Thinking, Globalization and Cultural Diversity', paper prepared for the North–South Round Table 'Imperative of Tolerance and Justice in a Globalised World', Cairo, 27–28 November 2002.

Financial Express. 'Maternal Mortality: This India Story Is a Shame!', 7 October 2008, http://www.financialexpress.com/archive/maternal-mortality-this-india-story-is-a-shame/370599/ (accessed 18 March 2018).

Fine, Ben. 'Globalisation and Development: The Imperative of Political Economy', paper presented at the conference 'Towards a New Political Economy of Development: Globalisation and Governance', Sheffield, July 2002.

Fong, Monica. 'Victims of Old Fashioned Statistics: Institutions and Agrarian Reform', *FAO Review on Agriculture and Development*, vol. 13, no. 3 (May–June 1980).

Food and Agriculture Organization. *Filling the Data Gap: Gender-Sensitive Statistics for Agricultural Development* (Rome: Food and Agriculture Organization, 1999), http://www.fao.org/docrep/X2785e/X2785e00.htm (accessed 22 February 2018).

Francesca, Joseph (Gigi). 'Shifting the Development Paradigm', Women 2000: Asia Pacific NGO Forum, Kasetsart University, Bangkok, 3 September 1999.

Fuentes-Nieva, R., and N. Galasso. 'Working for the Few: Political Capture and Economic Inequality', Oxfam Briefing Paper no. 178, Oxfam International, Oxford, 20 January 2014.

Fukuda-Parr, Sakiko, and A. K. Shiva Kumar (eds). *Readings in Human Development* (New Delhi: Oxford University Press, 2003).

Fukuyama, Francis. 'After Neoconservatism', *New York Times*, 19 February 2006.

Gandhi, M. K. *Hind Swaraj or Indian Home Rule* (Ahmedabad: Navajivan Publishing House, 1909).

———. 'The Better Half', in *Everyone's Gandhi* (ed. Rita Roy) (New Delhi: Gandhi Peace Foundation, 1997).

George, Susanna. 'Mainstreaming Gender as a Women's Movement Strategy: A Critique from a Reluctant Gender Advocate', in *Women in Action 2004-2: Examining Feminist and Social Movements* (Manila: ISIS International, 2004).

Ghose, Sagarika. 'E-mail Nationalism' (a review of the popular Hindi film *Kabhi Khushi Kabhi Gham*), *Indian Express*, 28 December 2001.

Ghosh, Jayati. 'Changes in the World of Work', December 2003, http://www.networkideas.org/feathm/sep2006/pdf/isle_changes_in_world_of_work.pdf (accessed 11 April 2018).

Ghosh, Shanti. 'Revaluing Women's Roles', paper presented at the conference 'Population Trends and Family Planning in South Asia', New Delhi, 14–20 March 1989.

Government of India. *Economic Survey 2010–11*. Ministry of Finance, Department of Economic Affairs, Economic Division (New Delhi: Oxford University Press, 2011).

———. *Economic Survey 2011–2012*, Chapter 2: 'Micro-foundations of Macroeconomic Development', https://www.indiabudget.gov.in/budget2011-2012/es2010-11/echap-02.pdf (accessed 8 April 2018).

————. *National Perspective Plan for Women 1988–2000 A.D.* (New Delhi: Department of Women and Child Development, Ministry of Human Resource Development, 1986).

————. *Towards Equality: Report of the Committee on Status of Women in India* (New Delhi: Department of Social Welfare, Ministry of Education and Social Welfare, 1974).

Government of India Ministry of Micro, Small and Medium Enterprises. *Annual Report 2013–14* (New Delhi: Khadi and Village Industries Commission, 2014).

Government of Karnataka. 'Panchayati Raj Law in Karnataka: A Bold Experiment in Democratic Decentralization', Department of Planning, Bangalore, 1984.

Grogui, Siba N. 'Postcoloniality in Global South Foreign Policy', in Jacqueline Anne Braveboy-Wagner (ed.), *The Foreign Policies of the Global South: Rethinking Conceptual Frameworks* (Boulder, CO: Lynne Rienner, 2003).

Grown, Caren, Chandrika Bahadur, Jessie Handbury and Diane Elson. 'The Financial Requirements of Achieving Gender Equality and Women's Empowerment', paper prepared for the World Bank, 26 April 2006.

Guha, Ramachandra. *India after Gandhi: The History of the World's Largest Democracy* (New Delhi: Picador, 2007).

Gupta, Akhil. 'The Song of the Nonaligned World: Transnational Identities and the Reinscription of Space in Late Capitalism', Special Issue on Space, Identity, and the Politics of Difference, *Cultural Anthropology*, vol. 7, no. 1 (1992), pp. 63–67.

Gupta, Shekhar. 'Welcome to Moscowashington: After September 11, the Big Boys Are Joining Hands, How Do We Play Ours?', *New Indian Express*, 19 January 2002.

Guru, Gopal. 'How Egalitarian Are the Social Sciences in India?', *Economic & Political Weekly*, vol. 37, no. 51 (2002), pp. 5003–9.

Haq, Mahbub ul. *The Human Development Report* (New York: UNDP, 1990).

Harding, Sandra (ed.). *Feminism and Methodology* (Bloomington: Indiana University Press, 1987).

————. *Is Science Multicultural? Postcolonialism, Feminisms and Epistemologies* (Bloomington: Indiana University Press, 1998).

Harrison, Ann (ed.). *Globalization and Poverty*, National Bureau of Economic Research Conference Report (Chicago: University of Chicago Press, 2006).

Harriss-White, Barbara, and S. Subramaniam (eds). *Illfare in India: Essays on India's Social Sector in Honour of S. Guhan* (New Delhi: Sage, 1999).

Hart, Gillian. 'Patterns of Household Labour Allocation in a Javanese Village', paper prepared for the A/D/C RTN Workshop on Household Studies, Singapore, August 1976.

Henderson, Hazel. *Creating Alternative Futures: The End of Economics* (Connecticut: Kumarian Press Books for a World That Works, 1996).

Hindu. 'A Loss to the World: Tribute to Mwalimu Julius Nyerere', 31 October 1999.

————. 'India, ASEAN Set $70 b Trade Target', 3 March 2011.

————. 'Somnath: Factor Population in Development Strategies', 24 April 2006.

————. 'Textiles, Leather Exports to Gain from Chinese Policy: Montek', *Hindu*, 22 April 2011.

Hirway, Indira, and Darshini Mahadevia. 'Critique of Gender Development Index: Towards an Alternative', *Economic & Political Weekly*, vol. 31, no. 43 (1996), pp. WS87–WS96.

Hoffman, Jan. 'The Frugal Teenager, Ready or Not', *New York Times*, 10 October 2008.

Human Development Network. *Philippine Human Development Report 2005: Peace, Human Security and Human Development in the Philippines*, http://hdr.undp. org/sites/default/files/philippines_2005_en.pdf (accessed 21 January 2018).

Indian Association of Women's Studies. *Reports of Three National Conferences* (Bombay, 1981).

Indian Institute of Population Sciences. *National Family Health Survey (NFHS-2), 1998–99* (Mumbai: IIPS).

International Labour Office. *Employability in the Global Economy: How Training Matters, World Employment Report 1998–99* (Geneva: International Labour Office, 1998).

ISST (Institute of Social Studies Trust). 'A Proposal on Household-Level Food Security', submitted to the FAO Nutrition Department, Rome, 1985.

————. 'Case Studies: Adult Education for Women', New Delhi, 1984.

————. *Development of Women and Children in Rural Areas: Preparation of a Plan with Focus on Women, Block Chikmagalur (Karnataka)* (New Delhi: Ministry of Rural Development, Government of India, 1985), 2 vols.

————. *Discussion Papers: Taluk-Level Conference in Gulbarga* (New Delhi: Institute of Social Studies Trust, 1982), 2 vols.

————. 'Impact on Women Workers: Maharashtra Employment Guarantee Scheme', mimeograph, New Delhi, December 1979.

————. *Integrating Women's Interest into a State Five Year Plan: Karnataka* (New Delhi: Ministry of Social Welfare, Government of India, 1984), 2 vols.

————. 'Inter-State Tasar Project: Report on a Field Survey', Chandrapur District, Maharashtra, 1982.

————. *ISST 25: Reflections* (New Delhi: Institute of Social Studies Trust, 2005).

————. *Small-Scale Forest-Based Enterprises with Special Reference to the Roles of Women* (Bangalore: ISST, 1989), vols 1 and 2, prepared for FAO, Rome.

————. 'Technical Seminar on Women's Work and Employment: Papers', ISST, New Delhi, 1982.

————. 'Women and the Planning Process: A Case Study from India', paper prepared for the conference 'Integrating Women into Development Planning', International Research and Training Institute for Advancement of Women, Santo Domingo, 1983.

Ito, Seiro. 'A Survey of Recent Economics Literature on Child Labor', in Seiro Ito (ed.), *Agricultural Production, Household Behaviour and Child Labour in Andhra Pradesh* (Chiba: Institute of Developing Economies, Japan External Trade Organization, 2005).

Ivacic, Pero. 'The Non-aligned Countries Pool Their News—News Agency Network', *UNESCO Courier*, May–June 1986, http://findarticles.com/p/articles/mi_m1310/is_1986_May–June/ai_4375051 (accessed 28 April 2009).

Jackson, Stevi, and Jackie Jones. 'Thinking for Ourselves: An Introduction to Feminist Theorising', in Stevi Jackson and Jackie Jones (eds), *Contemporary Feminist Theory* (Edinburgh: Edinburgh University Press, 1998).

Jain, Devaki. 'Advances in Feminist Theory: An Indian Perspective', paper presented at the International Sociological Association Conference, New Delhi, August 1986.

———. 'Are We Knowledge Proof? Development as Waste', Lovraj Kumar Memorial Lecture, New Delhi, 26 September 2003. [Reproduced as chapter 8, this volume.]

———. 'Are Women a Separate Issue?', *Populi*, vol. 5, no. 1 (November 1978), pp. 7–15.

———. 'Attaining Plan Objectives: The Role of New Themes in Research', paper presented at the UN Educational, Scientific and Cultural Organization Symposium on 'Methods for the Integration of Women's Issues in Development Planning', Paris, 1987.

———. 'A View from the South: A Story of Intersections', in Arvonne S. Fraser and Irene Tinker (eds), *Developing Power: How Women Transformed International Development* (New York: Feminist Press, 2004), pp. 128–37.

———. 'Close Encounters of Another Kind: Women-Led Regional Economic and Social Cooperation', Seminar on the 'Relevance of Mainstreaming the Concerns of Women in Bank Activities', Asian Development Bank, Manila, 2 March 1998.

———. 'Country Paper—India', paper prepared for the Expert Group Consultation on Women in Planning. Asian and Pacific Center for Women and Development, Tehran, 1979.

———. 'Culture of the Poor: Is Equitable Development Possible?', paper prepared for the National Conference on Culture, Bangalore, 1986.

———. 'Development as if Women Mattered: Can Women Build a New Paradigm?', lecture delivered at the pre-Nairobi consultation of the OECD Development Assistant Committee group, Paris, 1983.

———. 'Development South Style', paper prepared for a working party on development, South Commission, Geneva, 2–4 November 1988.

———. 'Development Theory and Practice: Insights Emerging from Women's Experience', *Economic & Political Weekly*, vol. 25, no. 27 (1990), pp. 1445–54.

———. 'Enabling Poverty and Inequality Reduction in South Asia', UNFPA Retreat, New York, 30 September–2 October 2002.

———. 'Five Year Plan Suggestions and Final Report: Task Force on Adult Education', ISST.

———. 'For Whom the Bell Tolls: Democracy and Development in South Asia', *Cambridge Review of International Affairs*, vol. 15, no. 2 (2002), pp. 299–310.

———. 'Globalism and Localism: Negotiating Feminist Space', paper presented at the seminar 'Rethinking Gender, Democracy and Development: Is

Decentralisation a Tool for Local Effective Political Voice?', Ferrara University and Modena University, Italy, 20–22 May 2002 (reproduced as chapter 7 in Devaki Jain, *Journey of a Southern Feminist*, vol. 1 [New Delhi: Sage/Yoda, 2018]).

————. 'Growth, Poverty and Inequality: The Linkages and Relevance of Macroeconomic Policies', UNDP Expert Group Meeting on Gender Equality, Economic Growth and Poverty Reduction, Essex University, 21–22 June 2007. [Reproduced as chapter 11, this volume.]

————. 'Home Thoughts from Abroad', University of Westville, Durban, 15 May 1999.

————. 'How Women's Leadership Can Transform the Nation: Durgabai Showed the Way', Lecture in Honour of Smt. Durgabai Deshmukh, 15 July 2004.

————. *Income Generating Activities for Women: Some Case Studies* (New Delhi: UNICEF, 1980).

————. *Indian Women* (New Delhi: Publications Division, Government of India, 1975).

————. 'Indian Women Today and Tomorrow', Padmaja Naidu Memorial Lecture, Teen Murti House, New Delhi, November 1982.

————. 'Inequality and Information Technology: Reducing Global Players' Role', *Deccan Herald*, 29 September 2000; Devaki Jain, 'Inequality and Information Technology: Caution for Karnataka, Andhra', *Deccan Herald*, 30 September 2000.

————. 'Interrogating Disciplines/Disciplining Gender: Towards a History of Women's Studies in India', 20th Anniversary Seminar, Centre for Women's Development Studies, New Delhi, 19–22 February 2001.

————. 'Invoking Gyana, Women's Knowing, as a Vehicle for Rebellion', Background Paper for Casablanca Dream 'Women Weave Peace into Globalisation', 12–15 January 2007, http://www.casablancadream.net/meetings/casa_07_bg_jain.html (accessed 29 April 2009).

————. 'Locating Ourselves in Relevance', colloquium series co-hosted by the African Gender Institute, University of Cape Town, and the Gender Equity Unit, University of Western Cape, Cape Town, 28 April 1998.

————. *Minds, Bodies and Exemplars: Reflections at Beijing and Beyond* (New Delhi: British Council Division, 1996).

————. 'Minds, Not Bodies: Expanding the Notion of Gender in Development', Bradford Morse Memorial Lecture, Opening Plenary at the Fourth World Conference on Women, Beijing, September 1995; reproduced as chapter 4 in Devaki Jain, *Journey of a Southern Feminist*, vol. 1 (New Delhi: Sage/Yoda, 2018).

————. 'Need for a Larger Vision', *Manushi*, December 1983.

————. 'Nuancing Globalisation, or Mainstreaming the Downstream, or Reforming Reform', Working Paper no. 3, Centre for Gender and Development Studies, University of the West Indies, May 2000. [Reproduced as chapter 6, this volume.]

————. 'Patterns of Female Work: Implications for Statistical Design, Economic Classification and Social Priorities', paper presented at the National Conference on Women's Studies, SNDT University, Bombay, 1981.

————. 'Perspectives on Peace', Women and Public Policy Programme, John F. Kennedy School of Government, Harvard University, 5 May 2003.

————. 'Power through the Looking Glass of Feminism', in Kathy Davis, Monique Leijenaar and Jantine Oldersma (eds), *The Gender of Power* (Leiden: Vena, 1987) (republished in *Vocabulary of Women's Politics* (New Delhi: Friedrich Ebert Stiftung, 2001).

————. 'Removing Discrimination and Poverty: The Importance of Exemplars', Convocation Address, University of Tirunelveli, October 1995.

————. 'The Culture of the Poor: Is Equitable Development Possible?', in Karuna M. Braganza and Saleem Peeradina (eds), *Cultural Forces Shaping India* (New Delhi: Macmillan, 1989).

————. 'The Empire Strikes Back: A Report on the Asian Social Forum, Hyderabad, 2–3 Jan 2003', *Economic & Political Weekly*, vol. 38, no. 1 (2003), pp. 99–101. [Later published in Jai Sen et al. (eds), *Challenging Empires* (New Delhi: Vivek Foundation, 2004), pp. 289–92.]

————. 'The First Challengers: The Feminists of the South', *Making It Magazine*, UNIDO, 5 February 2013, http://www.makingitmagazine.net/?p=6349 (accessed 21 March 2018). [Reproduced as chapter 12 in Devaki Jain, *Journey of a Southern Feminist*, vol. 1 (New Delhi: Sage/Yoda, 2018.]

————. 'The Household Trap: Report on a Field Survey of Female Activity Patterns', in Devaki Jain and and Nirmala Banerjee (eds), *Tyranny of the Household: Investigative Essays on Women's Work*, Workshop on Women in Poverty (New Delhi: Shakti Books, 1985), pp. 215–46.

————. 'The Leadership Gap: Challenge to Feminists', Presidential Address, Indian Association of Women's Studies Conference, Mysore, 1993.

————. 'The Many New Faces of Economic Development and Some Questions on How to Land Justice', North–South Round Table on 'Imperatives of Tolerance and Justice in a Globalized World', Cairo, 27–28 November 2002.

————. 'The Natural Power of Women', *Sarla Behn Granth*, 1983.

————. 'The Role of People's Movements in Economic and Social Transformation', Opening Thematic Plenary at the 1999 Seoul International Conference of NGOs, 10–16 October 1999.

————. 'The Value of the Particular to the General', paper presented at the conference 'South Asia and the United Nations', United Nations University, Tokyo, 26 May 2002.

————. 'This Thing Called "Poverty"', paper presented at a special event organised by UNDP, New York, 20 May 1997.

————. 'To Be or Not to Be? The Location of Women in Public Policy', in Gopal K. Kadekodi, S. M. Ravi Kanbur and Vijayendra Rao (eds), *Development in Karnataka: Challenges of Governance, Equity and Empowerment* (New Delhi:

Academic Foundation, 2008), pp. 107–24. [Reproduced as chapter 10 in Devaki Jain, *Journey of a Southern Feminist*, vol. 1 (New Delhi: Sage/Yoda, 2018).]

―――. 'Through the Looking Glass of Poverty', paper presented at New Hall, Cambridge, 19 October 2001.

―――. 'Tribute to Julius Nyerere', *Times of India*, 18 October 1999.

―――. 'Using the Handle of Regulation to Revive the Space for Social Justice', Symposia Series 'Feminisms and Globalisation: Women 2000', NCRW, CUNY and Japan Preparatory Committee Economic Dimensions of Globalisation Panel, 7 June 2000.

―――. 'Valuing Work: Time as a Measure', *Economic & Political Weekly*, vol. 31, no. 43 (1996), pp. WS46–WS57. [Reproduced as chapter 5 in this volume.]

―――. 'What Does It Take to Become a Citizen? Some Neglected Collective Identities in Building "Nation"', presented at the seminar 'Democracy, Communalism, Secularism and the Dilemmas of Indian Nationhood', New Delhi, January 2005.

―――. *Women, Development and the UN: A Sixty-Year Quest for Equality and Justice* (Bloomington: Indiana University Press, 2005).

―――. 'Women, Waste and Planet Safety: Proposal for North–South Alliance', Institute of Development Studies, Sussex, 9–12 July 1992.

―――. 'Women, Waste and Planet Safety: Proposal for a North–South Alliance', *Wide Bulletin*, no. 3, 1992.

―――. 'Women's Employment as Related to Rural Areas', paper presented at the Kulu Women and Development Conference, Copenhagen, 1980.

―――. 'Women's Rights between the UN Human Rights Regime and Free Trade Agreements', International Conference on 'Globalising Women's Rights: Confronting Unequal Development between the UN Rights Framework and WTO Trade Agreements', Bonn, 19–22 May 2004.

―――. 'Women's Work and Rights: An Overview', paper prepared for the National Conference on 'Engendering Macroeconomics and Macroeconomic Policies', Centre for Women's Studies, Department of Economics, Mumbai University, 29–30 September 2005.

Jain, Devaki, and Diane Elson (eds). *Harvesting Feminist Knowledge for Public Policy* (New Delhi: Sage, 2012).

Jain, Devaki, and Diane Elson, in Collaboration with the Casablanca Dreamers. 'Vision for a Better World: From Economic Crisis to Equality', UNDP, 2010, http://www.inclusivecities.org/wp-content/uploads/2012/07/Jain_Elson_UNDP_Crisis_to_equality.pdf (accessed 8 April 2018).

Jain, Devaki, and Malini Chand. 'Domestic Work: Its Implication for Enumeration on Women's Work and Employment', paper presented at the Symposium on 'Women's Work and Society', Indian Statistical Institute, New Delhi, 1982 (reproduced in K. Saradamoni, ed., *Women, Work and Society*, Calcutta: Indian Statistical Institute, 1985).

————. 'Importance of Age and Sex Specific Data Collection in Household Surveys', paper presented at the Regional Conference on Household Surveys, ESCAP, Bangkok, 1980.

————. 'Pattern of Female Work: Implication for Statistical Design, Economic Classification and Social Priorities', paper presented at the National Conference on Women's Studies, SNDT University, Bombay, 1981.

————. 'Report on a Time Allocation Study: Its Methodological Implications', paper presented at the Technical Seminar on 'Women's Work and Employment', ISST, New Delhi, 1982.

Jain, Devaki, and Mukul Mukerjee. 'Women and Their Households: The Relevance of Men and Macro Policies—An Indian Perspective', ISST, New Delhi, 1989.

Jain, Devaki, and Nirmala Banerjee (eds). *Tyranny of the Household: Investigative Essays on Women's Work*, Workshop on Women in Poverty (New Delhi: Shakti Books, 1985).

Jain, Devaki, and Pam Rajput (eds). *Narratives from the Women's Studies Family: Recreating Knowledge* (New Delhi: Sage, 2003).

Jain, Devaki, and Samia Ahmed. *Towards Just Development: Identifying Meaningful Indicators* (South Africa: UNDP, 1999).

Jain, Devaki, and Shubha Chacko. 'Constructing New Frameworks: Women's Location in the Economies of the NAM Countries', paper presented at the launch of NAM Institute for the Empowerment of Women, Kuala Lumpur, 10 September 2007.

Jain, Devaki, Nalini Singh and Malini Chand. *Women's Quest for Power: Five Case Studies* (New Delhi: Vikas, 1980).

Jain, L. C. 'Central Planning and Karnataka's Decentralized Planning', *Mainstream*, vol. 25, nos 32–33 (May 1987), pp. 15–19.

————. *Grass without Roots: Rural Development under Government Auspices* (New Delhi: Sage, 1985).

————. 'Role of Non-governmental Organizations in Development', paper prepared for the Workshop on 'Poverty in India: Research and Policy', Oxford University, 1987.

————. 'The Government's Employment Policy Disappoints', 25 September 2008, http://www.rediff.com/news/2008/sep/25guest1.htm (accessed 8 April 2018).

————. 'This Job Package Is Empty', *Hindustan Times*, 11 June 2002.

Jha, Raghbendra. 'Reducing Poverty and Inequality in India: Has Liberalization Helped?', Working Paper no. 2004, UNU–WIDER, November 2000.

Jhabvala, Renana, and Amrita Datta. 'Women and Work in Bihar: Challenges and Emerging Policy Paradigms', paper presented at the workshop on 'Women in Informal Economy in Bihar', Patna, 11 May 2012.

John, Mary E. 'Feminism, Internationalism and the West: Questions from the Indian Context', Occasional Paper no. 27, Centre for Women's Development Studies, New Delhi, 1998.

Johnson, Allan G. *The Gender Knot* (Philadelphia: Temple University Press, 1997).

Joshi, Swapna Bist. *Consultation on Engendering the 12th Five Year Plan: Karnataka*, Consultation Proceedings, State Planning Board, Karnataka, Bangalore, November 2012.

Kalpagam, U. 'Organizing Women in Informal Sector: Discourse and Practice of Politics', *Mainstream*, vol. 25, no. 13 (1986), pp. 27–33.

Kanbur, Ravi, and Lyn Squire. 'The Evolution of Thinking about Poverty: Exploring the Interactions', in Meier and Stiglitz, *Frontiers of Development Economics*, pp. 183–226.

Kanji, Nazneen, and Kalyani Menon-Sen. 'What Does the Feminisation of Labour Mean for Sustainable Livelihoods?', International Institute for Environment and Development, London, 2001.

Kannan, K. P. *Interrogating Inclusive Growth: Poverty and Inequality in India* (New Delhi: Routledge, 2014).

Kaul, Suvir. 'Indian Empire (and the Case of Kashmir)', Reflection on Empire, *Economic & Political Weekly*, vol. 46, no. 13 (2011), pp. 66–75.

Kearney, A. T. '2005 Global Retail Development Index: An Annual Study of Retail Investment', *Financial Express*, 9 July 2005.

Khare, Harish. 'Selling the United States of America in India', *Hindu*, 21 July 2005.

King-Quizon, E. 'Time Allocation and Home Production in Rural Laguna Households', paper presented at the Symposium on Household Economics, Manila, May 1977.

Kishwar, Madhu. 'Toiling without Rights: the Ho Women of Singhbhum', *Economic & Political Weekly*, vol. 22, no. 3 (January 1987), pp. 95–101.

Kose, M. Ayhan, and Eswar S. Prasad. 'Emerging Markets Come of Age', *Finance and Development*, vol. 47, no. 4 (December 2010), pp. 7–10.

Kozel, Valerie, and Barbara Parker. 'A Profile and Diagnostic of the Poverty in Uttar Pradesh', paper presented at the Poverty Monitoring and Evaluation Workshop, Planning Commission of India and the World Bank, New Delhi, 11 January 2002.

Krishnaswamy, K. S. 'On Liberalisation and Some Related Matters', *Economic & Political Weekly*, vol. 26, no. 42 (1991), pp. 2415–17, 2419–22.

Kumar, Krishna. 'Development of Women and Children in Rural Areas (DWCRA): Preparation of a Plan with Focus on Women, Block Chikmagalur (Karnataka)', proposal submitted by the ISST, New Delhi, September 1983.

Kumar, Radha. *The History of Doing: An Illustrated Account of Movements for Women's Rights and Feminism in India, 1800–1990* (London: Verso Books, 1993).

Kumar, Satish. 'Nonalignment: International Goals and National Interests', *Asian Survey*, vol. 23, no. 4 (1983).

Kuppusamy, Baradan. 'Non-Aligned Movement Takes On New Social Role', InterPress News Service, 10 May 2005, http://www.ipsnews.net/2005/05/development-asia-non-aligned-movement-takes-on-new-social-role/ (accessed 3 March 2018).

Lau, Kin Chi, and Huang Ping (eds). 'China Reflected', special issue, *Asia Exchange*, vol. 18, no. 2 and vol. 19, no. 1 (2002–03).

Lavoie, M., and E. Stockhammer. 'Wage-Led Growth: Concepts, Theories and Policies', Conditions of Work and Employment Series no. 41, ILO, Geneva, http://www.ilo.org/wcmsp5/groups/public/—ed_protect/—protrav/—travail/documents/publication/wcms_192507.pdf (accessed 21 March 2018).

Lerner, Gerda. *The Creation of Feminist Consciousness: From the Middle Ages to Eighteen-Seventy* (Oxford: Oxford University Press, 1993).

Loyola, Mario. 'The New Cold War: Hugo Chávez and the Non-Aligned Movement', *National Review*, 28 September 2006, https://www.nationalreview.com/2006/09/new-cold-war-mario-loyola/ (accessed 4 March 2018).

Luck, Edward C. *Mixed Messages: American Politics and International Organization, 1919–1999* (Washington, D.C.: Brookings Institution Press, 1999).

M. A. Singamma Sreenivasan Foundation. 'Integrating Women in Development Planning: The Role of Traditional Wisdom' (prepared for UNESCO), Bangalore, 1989.

———. 'Survival Strategies of the Poor and Traditional Wisdom: A Reflection', Round Table on Development, Bangalore, 1987, 3 vols.

Mahendra Dev, S. 'Small Farmers in India: Challenges and Opportunities', Working Paper, Indira Gandhi Institute of Development Research, Mumbai, June 2012, http://www.igidr.ac.in/pdf/publication/WP-2012-014.pdf (accessed 22 March 2018).

Mankiller, Wilma. Gwendolyn Mink, Marysa Navarro, Barbara Smith and Gloria Steinem (eds), *The Reader's Companion to U.S. Women's History* (Boston and New York: Houghton Mifflin, 1998).

Marsh, David. 'BRICS Make Move to Shove Dollar Aside', *Market Watch*, 17 April 2011, http://www.marketwatch.com/story/brics-make-move-to-shove-dollar-aside-2011-04-17?link=home_carousel (accessed 26 March 2018).

Mathaei, J. A. 'The Development of the Female Labour Force in the United States: An Historical Investigation', Department of Economics, Yale University, 1977.

Maull, Hanns W. 'World Politics in Turbulence', *Internationale Politik und Gesellschaft* (2011), pp. 11–25, http://library.fes.de/pdf-files/ipg/ipg-2011-1/2011-1__03_a_maull.pdf (accessed 26 March 2018).

Mazumdar, Vina. 'Education and Women's Equality', paper presented at the National Seminar on 'Education for Women's Equality', Vigyan Bhavan, New Delhi, 3–5 November 1985.

———. 'The Non-Aligned Movement and the International Women's Decade', monograph, n.d.

Mehra, Rekha, and Sarah Gammage. 'Trends, Countertrends and Gaps in Women's Employment', *World Development*, vol. 27, no. 3 (1999), pp. 533–50.

Mehta, Aasha Kapur. 'Recasting Indices for Developing Countries: A Gender Empowerment Measure', *Economic & Political Weekly*, vol. 31, no. 43 (1996), pp. WS80–WS86.

Mehta, S. S. 'Non-Alignment and the New International Economic Order', in K. P. Misra and K. R. Narayanan (eds), *Non-Alignment in Contemporary International Relations* (New Delhi: Vikas, 1981), pp. 174–75.

Mernissi, Fatima. 'Digital Scheherazade: The Rise of Women as Key Players in the Arab Gulf Communication Strategies', http://mernissi.net/books/articles/digital_scheherazade.html (accessed 25 March 2018).

―――. 'Femininity as Subversion: Reflections on the Muslim Concept of Nushuz', in Diana Eck and Devaki Jain (eds), *Speaking of Faith: Cross-Cultural Perspectives on Women, Religion and Social Change* (New Delhi: Kali for Women, 1986).

―――. 'Love in Digital Islam: Why Ibn Hazm Is a Success on the Internet', Sharjah Conference on Culture (supported by UNESCO0, 2008.

―――. 'Women Weave Peace into Globalisation', paper for the Casablanca Group Meeting, September 2007.

Mishra, Anupam, and Satyendra Tripathi. *Chipko Movement: Uttarakhand Women's Bid to Save Forest Wealth* (New Delhi: Peace Foundation, 1978).

Mishra, Neelkanth. 'The Hidden Growth', *Indian Express*, 6 August 2013, http://www.indianexpress.com/news/the-hidden-growth/1151479/ (accessed 22 March 2018).

Mohanty, Chandra Talpade. 'Imperial Democracies, Feminist Engagements', Reflection on Empire, *Economic & Political Weekly*, vol. 46, no. 13 (2011), pp. 76–84.

Morris, M. D., and M. B. McAlpin. *Measuring the Condition of India's Poor: The Physical Quality of Life Index* (New Delhi: Promilla and Co., 1982).

Mukherjee, M., Devaki Jain and C. P. Sujaya. 'Women, Work and Employment', paper presented at the International Workshop on Women's Studies, Trivandrum, 1989.

Mundle, Sudipto. 'Dollars, BRICS and the China Trap', *Times of India*, 28 April 2011.

Muramatsu, Yasuko. 'Gender and Economics in Japan: Japanese Women's Position in Economics and Activities of Japan Association for Feminist Economics to Advance Gender Perspective', paper presented at the Sixth Science Council of Asia Workshop, 'A Comparative Study of the Research Conditions of Women Scientists and the Present State of Women's/Gender Studies in Asian Countries: Towards Human Centered Sustainable Development', New Delhi, 17 April 2006.

Myrdal, Gunnar. *Asian Drama: An Inquiry into the Poverty of Nations* (London: Allen Lane, 1968).

Naik, Chitra. 'Making Childhood Learning Happier', *Future* (UNICEF magazine), no. 20 (1987).

Najundappa, D. M. 'Decentralized Planning Problems of Administration and Coordination', paper presented at the Seminar on Decentralization, Bangalore, 1985.

Nanavaty, Reema. 'Women Agriculture Workers', *Seminar*, no. 531 (November 2003), http://www.india-seminar.com/2003/531/531%20reema%20nanavaty.htm (accessed 22 February 2018).

National Council of Applied Economic Research. *Handloom Census of India 2009–10*, http://www.handlooms.nic.in/Writereaddata/Handloom%20report.pdf (accessed 13 April 2018).

Natraj, V. K., Kamlesh Mishra and Neeru Kapoor (eds), *Gandhian Alternative*, vol. 4 of *Economics Where People Matter*, Gandhian Studies and Peace Research Series no. 26.

New Indian Express. 'Contractors Pocket Land in the Name of IT', 24 April 2006.

Norgaard, Richard B. 'Beyond Growth and Globalization', *Economic & Political Weekly*, vol. 34, no. 36 (1999), pp. 2570–74.

Ostry, Jonathan D., Andrew Berg and Charalambos G. Tsangarides. 'Redistribution, Inequality, and Growth', IMF Staff Discussion Note, April 2014.

Otobe, Naoko. 'Global Economic Crisis, Gender and Employment: The Impact and Policy Response', Employment Working Paper no. 74, Employment Sector, ILO, Geneva, 2011.

Parikh, Kirit S. (ed.). *India Development Report 1999–2000* (New Delhi: Oxford University Press, 1999).

Parpart, Jane L., M. Patricia Connelly and V. Eudine Barriteau. *Theoretical Perspectives on Gender and Development* (Ottawa: International Development Research Centre Canada, 2000).

Parsai, Gargi. 'Medha Won't Relent Despite Soz' Plea', *Hindu*, 5 April 2006, http://www.thehindu.com/todays-paper/Medha-wont-relent-despite-Sozs-plea/article15734220.ece (accessed 16 October 2017).

Patel, Alaknanda. 'Gujarat Violence: A Personal Diary', *Economic & Political Weekly*, vol. 37, no. 50 (2002), pp. 4985–87.

Patel, Sujata. 'Urbanization, Development and Communalization of Society in Gujarat', in Takashi Shinoda (ed.), *The Other Gujarat* (Mumbai: Popular Prakashan, 2002).

Patnaik, Prabhat. 'A Model of Growth of the Contemporary Indian Economy', *Economic & Political Weekly*, vol. 42, no. 22 (2007), pp. 2077–81.

Pavlic, Breda, and Cees J. Hamelink. *The New International Economic Order: Links between Economics and Communications* (Paris: UNESCO, 1985).

Piketty, Thomas. *Capitalism in the Twenty-First Century* (Cambridge, MA: Harvard University Press, 2014).

Planning Commission. 'Approach Paper to the Tenth Five Year Plan (2002–2007), Government of India, New Delhi, 1 September 2001.

———. *Engendering Public Policy: A Report on the Work of the Working Group of Feminist Economists during the Preparation of Eleventh Five Year Plan 2007–2012* (New Delhi: Government of India, May 2010), http://planningcommission. nic.in/reports/genrep/rep_engpub.pdf (accessed 8 April 2018).

———. 'Planning at the Grassroots Level: An Action Programme for the Eleventh Five Year Plan', Report of the Expert Group, Government of India, New Delhi, March 2006.

———. *Report of the Special Group on Targeting Ten Million Employment Opportunities per Year over the Tenth Plan Period* (New Delhi: Government of India, May 2002), http://planningcommission.gov.in/aboutus/committee/tsk_sg10m.pdf (accessed 10 April 2018).

————. Report of the Steering Committee on Handlooms and Handicrafts Constituted for the Twelfth Five Year Plan (2012–17) (New Delhi: Planning Commission, 2012).

————. Towards Faster and More Inclusive Growth: An Approach to the 11th Five Year Plan (New Delhi: Government of India, November 2006).

Pritchett, Lant, and Michael Woolcock. 'Solutions When the Solution Is the Problem: Arraying the Disarray in Development', World Development, vol. 32, no. 2 (2004), pp. 191–212.

Raja Mohan, C. 'A Bag of BRICS', Indian Express, 12 April 2011, http://www.indianexpress.com/news/a-bag-of-brics/774808/2 (accessed 25 March 2018).

Rajivan, Anuradha. 'Measurement of Gender Differences Using Anthropometry', Economic & Political Weekly, vol. 31, no. 43 (1996), pp. WS58–WS62.

Ramagundam, Rahul. Gandhi's Khadi: A History of Contention and Conciliation (Hyderabad: Orient Longman, 2008).

Rao, Mohan. 'Two-Child Norm and Panchayats: Many Steps Back', Economic & Political Weekly, vol. 38, no. 33 (2003), pp. 3452–54.

Rao, Nitya. 'Respect, Status and Domestic Work: Female Migrants at Home and Work', European Journal of Development Research, vol. 23, no. 5 (2011), pp. 758–73.

Ravi Kanth, D. 'G-5: The Davids Took On the Goliaths', Deccan Herald, 14 June 2007.

Razavi, Shahra (ed.). Shifting Burdens: Gender and Agrarian Change under Neoliberalism (Bloomfield, CT: Kumarian Press, 2002).

Reddy, Sudeep. 'Emerging Nations Reject Capital Plan', Wall Street Journal, 18 April 2011.

Reddy, Y. V. 'Longer-Term Consequences: Global Financial Turmoil', Hindu Business Line, 31 December 2010.

————. 'Recent International Financial Turmoil and Its Implications for Developing Countries', ASCI Journal of Management, vol. 40, no. 1 (2010), pp. 52–60.

Rehman, Anisur. 'Some Dimensions of People's Participation in the Bhoomi Sena Movement Followed By a Discussion on the Issue', Popular Participation Programme, United Nations Research Institute for Social Development, Geneva, 1981.

Roberts, J. Timmons, and Bradley C. Parks. A Climate of Injustice: Global Inequality, North-South Politics, and Climate Policy (Cambridge: MIT Press, 2007).

Rohtagi, Jolly, et al. Moonlight in Mithila: A Feasibility Report for the Empowerment of Women Producers in Bihar (New Delhi: ISST, 1988), vols I and II.

Roy, Arundhati. 'Democracy: Who's She When She's at Home?', Outlook, 6 May 2002.

————. 'Intellectual Terrorist', Deccan Herald, 3 June 2007.

Said, Edward. Representations of the Intellectual: The 1993 Reith Lectures (New York: Vintage, 1996).

Sainath, P. 'The Anatomy of a Tiger India High and Low', Hindu, 12 November 2006.

Saxena, N. C. 'Participatory Issues in Joint Forest Management in India', Lovraj Kumar Memorial Lecture, SPWD, New Delhi, 18 September 1999.

Sebatad, Jennifer. *Struggle and Development among Self-Employed Women: A Report on the SEWA Ahmedabad India* (Ahmedabad: SEWA, 1982).

Seguino, S. 'Accounting for Gender in Asian Economic Growth', *Feminist Economics*, vol. 6, no. 3 (2000), pp. 27–58.

———. 'Gender Inequality and Economic Growth: A Cross-country Analysis', *World Development*, vol. 28, no. 7 (2000), pp. 1211–30.

———. '"Rebooting" Is Not an Option: Towards Equitable Social and Economic Development', in Jain and Elson, *Harvesting Feminist Knowledge for Public Policy*, pp. 21–47.

———. 'The Effects of Structural Change and Economic Liberalization on Gender Wage Differentials in South Korea and Taiwan', *Cambridge Journal of Economics*, vol. 24, no. 4 (2000), pp. 437–59.

———. 'The Global Economic Crisis, Its Gender Implications and Policy Responses', paper prepared for the interactive expert panel on 'The Gender Perspectives of the Financial Crisis', 53rd Session of the Commission on the Status of Women, UN, New York, 2–13 March 2009.

Seguino, Stephanie, and Caren A. Grown. 'Feminist-Kaleckian Macroeconomic Policy for Developing Countries', Economics Working Paper no. 446, Levy Economics Institute, New York, 2006.

Sen, Abhijit, and Himanshu. 'Poverty and Inequality in India: Getting Closer to the Truth', *Economic & Political Weekly*, vol. 39, no. 38 (2004), pp. 4247–63.

———. 'Poverty and Inequality in India—II: Widening Disparities during the 1990s', *Economic & Political Weekly*, vol. 39, no. 39 (2004), pp. 4361–75.

Sen, Amartya. *Development as Freedom* (New York: Anchor Books, 1999).

———. 'Exclusion and Inclusion', South Asians for Human Rights (SAHR) Convention on 'Including the Excluded', New Delhi, 11–12 November 2001.

———. 'Food Battles: Conflicts in the Access to Food', *Food and Nutrition*, vol. 10, no. 1 (1984), pp. 81–89.

———. *Identity and Violence: The Illusion of Destiny* (New Delhi: Penguin, 2006).

———. 'Population and Reasoned Agency: Food, Fertility and Economic Development', paper presented at the seminar 'Population, Environment, Development', Royal Swedish Academy of Sciences and Beijer Institute, Stockholm, October 1993.

———. 'The Ends and Means of Sustainability', Keynote Address, International Conference on 'Transition to Sustainability in the 21st Century', Inter Academy Panel on International Issues, Tokyo, May 2000.

———. *The Idea of Justice* (Cambridge, MA: Harvard University Press, 2009).

Sen, Gita, and Caren Grown. *Development, Crises, and Alternative Visions: Third World Women's Perspectives* (New York: Monthly Review Press, 1987).

Sengupta, Amit. 'Anatomy of a Satyagraha', *Tehelka*, 17 April 2006. This paper could not have been written as well as completed on time without the untiring help of M. V. Jagadeesh and Perce Bloomer.

Sengupta, Arjun. 'Delivering the Right to Development: ECSR and NGOs', *Economic & Political Weekly*, vol. 34, no. 41 (1999), pp. 2920–22.

Serageldin, Ismail. 'The Self and the Other: Tolerance and Justice in a Globalizing World', paper presented at the North-South Round Table 'Imperatives of Tolerance and Justice in a Globalized World', Cairo, 27–28 November 2002.

SEWA (Self-Employed Women's Association). *SEWA in 1988* (Ahmedabad: SEWA, 1989).

Shaffer, Robert. 'Women and International Relations: Pearl S. Buck's Critique of the Cold War', *Journal of Women's History*, vol. 11, no. 3 (1999), pp. 151–75.

Shah, Mihir. 'Cutting Off the Chain of Hate', *Hindu*, 21 October 2008.

Shepard, Mark. *Gandhi Today: A Report on India's Gandhi Movement and Its Experiments in Nonviolence and Small Scale Alternatives* (Simple Productions, 2012).

Shram Shakti. *Report of the National Commission on Self-Employed Women and Women in the Informal Sector* (New Delhi: Government of India, 1988).

Shroff, Manu. 'Globalization: A Stock-Taking', *Economic & Political Weekly*, vol. 34, no. 40 (1999), pp. 2845–49.

Singh, Nalini. 'Monitoring and Evaluation of Social Development Planning: Implications for the Women's Question', paper presented at the Consultative Meeting on 'Monitoring and Evaluation of Community-Focused Projects', Bangkok, 1979.

Sinha, Aseema. 'Globalisation, Rising Inequality, and New Insecurities in India', paper presented at the conference 'Difference and Inequality in Developing Societies', University of Virginia, Charlottesville, April 2005.

South Commission. *The Challenge to the South: The Report of the South Commission* (New York: Oxford University Press, 1990).

———. 'Towards Development: Strategy and Action Programme for the South', Objectives and Terms of Reference of the South Commission.

Sreenivasan, M. A. 'Ah! Bangalore: Turning Chellaghatta into Pourambudhi', *Deccan Herald*, 24 June 1984.

———. *Of the Raj, Maharajas and Me* (New Delhi: Ravi Dayal Publishers, 1991).

———. 'Pankajalakshmi: Energy from Sewage', *Indian Express*, 23 July 1982.

Steel, Ronald. 'Totem and Taboo', *Nation*, vol. 279, no. 8 (2004).

Steinfels, Peter. 'Modern Market Thinking Has Devalued a Deadly Sin', *New York Times*, 27 September 2008.

Stewart, Heather. 'Why Equality Is the Best Policy', *Hindu*, 26 September 2005.

Stiglitz, Joseph. *Globalization and Its Discontents* (London: Penguin, 2002).

———. 'Towards a New Paradigm for Development: Strategies, Policies and Processes', Prebisch Lecture, United Nations Conference on Trade and Development, Geneva, 1998.

Stiglitz, Joseph E., Amartya Sen and Jean-Paul Fitoussi. *Report by the Commission on the Measurement of Economic Performance and Social Progress*, http://ec.europa.eu/eurostat/documents/118025/118123/Fitoussi+Commission+report (accessed 13 April 2018).

UN Chronicle. 'Anniversary of Non-aligned Movement', 1984, http://findarticles. com/p/articles/mi_ m1309/is_v21/ai_3332143 (accessed 2 November 2007).

UNCTAD (United Nations Conference on Trade and Development). *Trade and Development Report 2010: Employment, Globalization, and Development* (New York: UN, 2010), http://unctad.org/en/docs/tdr2010_en.pdf (accessed 21 March 2018).

UNDP (United Nations Development Fund). *Human Development Report 1995: Gender and Human Development* (New York: Oxford University Press, 1995).

———. *Human Development Report 1996* (New York: Oxford University Press, 1996).

———. *Human Development Report 1997: Human Development to Eradicate Poverty* (New York: Oxford University Press, 1997).

———. *Human Development Report 1998: Consumption for Human Development* (New York: Oxford University Press, 1998).

———. *Human Development Report 1999* (New York: Oxford University Press, 1999).

———. *Human Development Report 2006: Beyond Scarcity: Power, Poverty and the Global Water Crisis* (New York: UNDP, 2006).

———. *Humanity Divided: Confronting Inequality in Developing Countries*, Bureau for Development Policy (New York: UNDP, November 2013), http://www. undp.org/content/dam/undp/library/Poverty%20Reduction/Inclusive%20 development/Humanity%20Divided/HumanityDivided_Full-Report.pdf (accessed 21 March 2018).

UNDP (United Nations Development Fund) and ILO (International Labour Organization). 'Asian Experience on Growth, Employment and Poverty', UNDP Regional Centre, Colombo, 2007, http://www.ilo.org/wcmsp5/ groups/public/—asia/—ro-bangkok/documents/publication/wcms_bk_ pb_142_en.pdf (accessed 21 January 2018).

UN ESCAP (United Nations Economic and Social Commission for Asia and the Pacific). 'Maintaining Growth amid Global Uncertainty, Economic and Social Survey of the Asia and the Pacific 2010: Year-End Update, 2010', http:// www.unescap.org/sites/default/files/publications/YearendUpdate2010.pdf (accessed 26 March 2018).

———. *Sustaining Dynamism and Inclusive Development: Connectivity in the Region and Productive Capacity in Least Developed Countries, Economic and Social Survey of Asia and the Pacific 2011*, http://www.unescap.org/sites/default/files/ Econimic-and-Social-Survey-2011.pdf (accessed 27 March 2018).

UNICEF (United Nations Children's Fund). *Adjustment with a Human Face: Protecting the Vulnerable and Promoting Growth* (Oxford: Clarendon, 1987).

UNIFEM (United Nations Development Fund for Women). *Progress of the World's Women 2005: Women, Work and Poverty* (New York: UNIFEM, 2005).

UNPF (United Nations Population Fund). 'Population, Food Production and Nutrition in India', UNFPA, New Delhi, October 1999.

UN Press Releases. 'Secretary-General Stresses Global Responsibility to Work for More Equitable World Economy', 13 October 2000, http://www.unis. unvienna.org/unis/en/pressrels/2000/sg2691.html (accessed 12 April 2018).

Subbarao, D. 'Frontier Issues on the Global Agenda: Emerging Economy Perspective', Commemorative speech, 60th Anniversary Celebrations of the Central Bank of Sri Lanka, Colombo, 29 March 2011, https://www.bis.org/review/r110330d.pdf (accessed 26 March 2018).

Subramanian, K. 'On Growth without Equality', *Hindu*, 4 November 2014, http://www.thehindu.com/todays-paper/tp-features/tp-bookreview/on-growth-without-equality/article6562332.ece (accessed 22 March 2018).

Sundar, P. 'Characteristics of Female Employment: Implications of Research and Policy', *Economic & Political Weekly*, vol. 16, no. 19 (1981), pp. 863–71.

Susskind, Ron. 'Without a Doubt', *New York Times Magazine*, 17 October 2004.

Swaminathan, M. 'A Study of Energy Use Patterns of General Background Caste', Seminar on 'Women's Work and Employment', April 1982.

———— (ed.). *Draft National Population Policy* (New Delhi: Government of India, 1994).

Sylvester, Christine. 'Homeless in International Relations? Women's Place in Canonical Texts and in Feminist Reimaginings', in Anne Phillips (ed.), *Feminism and Politics* (Oxford: Oxford University Press, 1998), pp. 44–66.

Thomas, Darryl C. (ed.). *The Theory and Practice of Third World Solidarity* (Westport, CT: Praeger, 2001).

Tickner, Ann. 'On the Frontlines or Sidelines of Knowledge and Power? Feminist Practices of Responsible Scholarship', Presidential Address at the Annual Meeting of the International Studies Association, San Diego, 23 March 2006.

Toye, John. *Dilemmas of Development* (Oxford: Blackwell, 1993).

Trumbull, Mark. 'Great Global Shift to Service Jobs: Move Over Agriculture', 4 September 2007, http://www.csmonitor.com/2007/0904/p01s02-wogi.html (accessed 4 March 2018).

Tyagi, S. 'First Develop India Is Plain and Simple Economics', interview with Siddhartha Birla, *Sunday Guardian*, 4 October 2014, http://www.sunday-guardian.com/business/first-develop-india-is-plain-and-simple-economics (accessed 22 March 2018).

UN (United Nations). 'Emerging Issues Containing Additional Material for Further Actions and Initiatives for the Preparation of the Outlook beyond the Year 2000', Report of the Secretary-General Commission on the Status of Women, E-CN-6-2000-PC/4, UN, New York, 7 February 2000.

————. 'Gender, Migration and Remittances', report of the UN International Research and Training Institute for the Advancement of Women (INSTRAW), 2004.

————. *Inequality Matters: Report on the World Social Situation 2013*, Department of Economic and Social Affairs (New York: United Nations, 2013), http://www.un.org/esa/socdev/documents/reports/InequalityMatters.pdf (accessed 20 March 2018).

————. *The World's Women: Trends and Statistics, 1970–1990* (New York: UN, 1991).

————. *World Economic Situation and Prospects 2008* (New York: UN, 2008), https://www.un.org/en/development/desa/policy/wesp/wesp_archive/2008wesp.pdf (accessed 8 April 2018).

UN Women. *1999 World Survey on the Role of Women in Development: Globalization, Gender and Work* (New York: UN Women, 1999).

Varadarajan, Siddharth. 'India Pitches for Greater IBSA, BRIC Role', *Hindu*, 16 April 2010.

Waring, Marilyn. *If Women Counted: A New Feminist Economics* (San Francisco: Harper & Row) (first published in New Zealand as *Counting for Nothing: What Men Value and What Women are Worth* [Wellington: Allen & Unwin, 1988]).

Weissman, Robert. 'Grotesque Inequality: Corporate Globalization and the Global Gap between Rich and Poor', *Multinational Monitor*, 1 July 2003.

Wignaraja, Ponna. 'Fundamentals of Poverty Eradication in South Asia: The Poor Are Not the Problem, But Are Part of the Solution', Lovraj Kumar Memorial Lecture, SPWD, New Delhi, 21 September 2001.

Woodhouse, Tom. *People and Planet* (Hartland, Devon: Green Books, 1987).

Woolf, Virginia. *A Room of One's Own* (New York: Fountain Press, and London: Hogarth Press, 1929).

Working Group of Feminist Economists (WGFE). *Engendering Public Policy*, Report on the Work of the WGFE during the preparation of the 11th Five Year Plan (2007–12) (New Delhi: Planning Commission, 2010)

World Bank. *Entering the 21st Century: World Development Report 1999/2000* (Oxford: Oxford University Press, 1999).

———. *Gender and Poverty in India*, World Bank Country Study (Washington, D.C.: World Bank).

———. *India: Poverty, Employment and Social Services*, A World Bank Country Study (Washington, D.C.: World Bank, 1989).

———. *World Development Report 2005: A Better Investment Climate for Everyone* (Washington, D.C.: World Bank, 2005).

———. *World Development Report 2006: Equity and Development* (Washington, D.C.: World Bank, 2005), http://documents.worldbank.org/curated/en/435331468127174418/pdf/322040World0Development0Report02006.pdf (accessed 21 January 2018).

World Commission on Dams. *Dams and Development: A New Framework for Development* (London: Earthscan Publications, 2000).

World of Work. 'ILO, UNDP Join Forces to Promote Growth for Decent Jobs', no. 59, April 2007.

World Summit on the Information Society. 'What's the State of ICT Access around the World?', http://www.itu.int/net/wsis/tunis/newsroom/stats/ (accessed 18 March 2018).

Wright, Richard. *The Color Curtain*, quoted in Matthew Quest, 'The Lessons of the Bandung Conference: Reviewing Richard Wright's *The Color Curtain* 40 Years Later', http://www.spunk.org/texts/pubs/lr/sp001716/bandung.html (accessed 4 March 2018).

Yamanaka, Keiko, and Nicola Piper. 'Feminized Migration in East and Southeast Asia: Polices, Actions and Empowerment', UNRISD Occasional Paper 11, December 2005.

Yimprasert, Junya Lek. 'Trade-Led Growth with Regionalism and Bilateralism: The Implications for Women's Decent Work', Opening Plenary, International Forum for Women's Rights in Development, convened by the Association for Women's Rights in Development, Bangkok, 27–30 October 2005.

Yusuf, Shahid, and Joseph Stiglitz. 'Development Issues: Settled and Open', in Gerald Meier and Joseph Stiglitz (eds), *Frontiers of Development Economics: The Future in Perspective* (New York: Oxford University Press, 2001), pp. 227–68.

Zlotnik, Hania. 'The Global Dimensions of Female Migration', *Migration Information Source*, 1 March 2003, https://www.migrationpolicy.org/article/global-dimensions-female-migration/ (accessed 7 March 2018).

Bibliography of Selected Works by Devaki Jain

BOOKS

Women's Quest For Power: Five Indian Case Studies (co-authored with Nalini Singh and Malini Chand) (New Delhi: Vikas, 1980).

The Vocabulary of Women's Politics (New Delhi: Friedrich Ebert Stiftung, 2000).

Women, Development, and the UN: A Sixty-Year Quest for Equality and Justice (Bloomington: Indiana University Press, 2005).

EDITED BOOKS

Speaking of Faith: Global Perspectives on Women, Religion & Social Change (co-edited with Diana Eck) (New Delhi: Kali for Women, 1986).

Tyranny of the Household: Investigative Essays on Women's Work (co-edited with Nirmala Banerjee) (New Delhi: Vikas, 1986).

Narratives from the Women's Studies Family: Recreating Knowledge (co-edited with Pam Rajput) (New Delhi: Sage Publications, 2003).

Harvesting Feminist Knowledge for Public Policy: Rebuilding Progress (co-edited with Diane Elson) (New Delhi: Sage Publications, 2011).

Indian Women: Contemporary Essays (co-edited with C. P. Sujaya) (New Delhi: Publications Division, Government of India, 2015).

ARTICLES

'Women's Dilemma: Sex or Class or Both?', *Voluntary Action*, 1981.

'Co-opting Women's Work into the Statistical System: Some Indian Milestones', *Sainya Shakti: A Journal of Women's Studies*, vol. 1, no. 1 (July 1983).

'Development as if Women Mattered, or Can Women Build a New Paradigm?', lecture delivered at the pre-Nairobi consultation of the OECD Development Assistant Committee group, Paris, 1983.

'Need for a Larger Vision', *Manushi*, no. 19, 1983.

'Women's Roles in Large Employment Systems', Ford Foundation, New Delhi, 1983.

'Domestic Work: Its Implications for Enumeration of Workers' (with Malini Chand Seth), in K. Saradamoni (ed.), *Women, Work and Society* (Kolkata: Indian Statistical Institute, 1985), pp. 350–65.

'Power through the Looking Glass of Feminism', in Kathy Davis, Monique Leijenaar and Jantine Oldersma (eds), *The Gender of Power* (Leiden: Vena, 1987) (republished in *Vocabulary of Women's Politics* (New Delhi: Friedrich Ebert Stiftung, 2001).

'The Culture of the Poor: Is Equitable Development Possible?', in *Cultural Forces Shaping India* (New Delhi: All India Association for Christian Higher Education, 1989).

'Development Theory and Practice: Insights Emerging from Women's Experience', *Economic & Political Weekly*, vol. 25, no. 27 (1990), pp. 1454–55.

'Can We Have a Women's Agenda for Global Development?', *Journal of the Society for International Development*, 1991.

'Gender and Poverty in India: An Overview', Institute of Social Studies Trust, Bangalore, 1991.

'Perspective Emerging from Women's Experience', in Anima Bose (ed.), *Peace and Conflict Resolution in the World Community* (New Delhi: Vikas, 1991).

'Women, Religion and Social Change', in Hem Lata Swarup and Besaria Sarojini (eds), *Women, Politics and Religion* (Etawah: AC Brothers, 1991), pp. 331–33.

'Structural Adjustment in India 1991–1992: A Gender Response', Institute of Social Studies Trust, New Delhi, August 1992.

'Sustainable Development and Environmental Changes', in Rainer Rilling et al. (eds), *Challenges: Science and Peace in a Rapidly Changing Environment* (Marburg: BdWi Verlag, 1992), vol. 1.

'Healing the Wounds of Development', in Jill Ker Conway and Susan C. Bourque (eds), *The Politics of Women's Education: Perspectives from Asia, Africa, and Latin America* (Ann Arbor: University of Michigan Press, 1993).

'Building Alliances: A Southern Perspective', *Focus on Gender*, vol. 2, no. 3 (October 1994), pp. 15–19.

'Women, Poverty and Population', Expert Group on Population Policy, Institute of Social Studies Trust, New Delhi, 18–20 January 1994.

'Future Directions for the Women's Movement: Some Post-Beijing Thoughts', in N. Rao, L. Rurup and R. Sudarshan (eds), *Sites of Change: The Structural Context for Empowering Women in India* (New Delhi: Friedrich Ebert Stiftung and UNDP, 1995).

'India: A Condition across Caste and Class', in Robin Morgan (ed.), *Sisterhood Is Global* (New York: Feminist Press, 1996).

'Valuing Work: Time as a Measure', *Economic & Political Weekly*, vol. 31, no. 43 (1996), pp. WS46–WS57.

'Women's Leadership and the Ethics of Development' (with Bella Abzug), *Gender in Development* Monograph Series no. 4 (New York: UNDP, 1996).

'Furthering the Power of the Non Aligned Movement', Non-Aligned Movement Workshop, 1998.

'Children's Rights and Women's Rights: Some Connections and Disconnections', *Development*, vol. 44, no. 2 (2001), pp. 58–62.

'Democratising Culture', in N. N. Vohra (ed.), *Culture, Democracy and Development in South Asia* (New Delhi: India International Centre, 2001).

'National Population Policy 2000: Re-examining Critical Issues' (with Mohan Rao), *Economic & Political Weekly*, vol. 36, no. 16 (2001), pp. 1299–1302.

'Participation of Women in Panchayati Raj', *India Panchayati Raj Report*, National Institute of Rural Development, New Delhi, 2001.

'Are We Knowledge Proof? Development as Waste', *Wastelands News*, vol. 19, no. 1 (August–October 2003).

'Enabling Reduction of Poverty and Inequality in South Asia', in *Population and Poverty: Achieving Equity, Equality and Sustainability* (New York: United Nations Population Fund, 2003).

'Striking Back at the Empire', in Jia Sen and Peter Waterman (eds), *World Social Forum: Challenging Empires* (New Delhi: Viveka Foundation, 2004), pp. 289–92.

'Testing the Grounds in a District in India for Its Capacity to Absorb Sen's Formula', in J. S. Sodhi (ed.), *Development as Freedom: An Indian Perspective* (New Delhi: Sri Ram Centre, 2004), pp. 124–37.

'A View From the South: A Story of Intersections', in Arvonne S. Fraser and Irene Tinker (eds), *Developing Power: How Women Transformed International Development* (New York: The Feminist Press at the City University of New York, 2004).

'Feminism and Feminist Expression: A Dialogue', in Kamala Ganesh and Usha Thakkar (eds), *Culture and the Making of Identity in Contemporary India* (New Delhi: Sage Publications, 2005).

'Feminist Networks, People's Movements and Alliances: Learning from the Ground', in Luciana Ricciutelli, Angela Miles and Margaret H. Mcfadden (eds), *Feminist Politics, Activism and Vision: Local and Global Challenges* (Toronto: Inanna Publications, 2005).

'Making Human Rights Education Inclusive: The India Experience' (with Sitharamam Kakarala), *Journal of NHRC*, vol. 4 (2005).

'The NAM Summit, Trade and Women', *South Bulletin*, no. 131 (15 September 2006).

'To Be or Not to Be: Problems in Locating Women in Public Policy', *Economic & Political Weekly*, vol. 42, no. 8 (2007), pp. 691–96.

'The Economic South: Economic Wars or Economic Peace', *Mainstream*, vol. 46, no. 6 (2008), http://www.mainstreamweekly.net/article530.html (accessed 14 April 2018).

'Unfolding Women's Engagement with Development and the UN: Pointers for the Future' (with Shubha Chacko), *Forum for Development Studies*, vol. 35, no. 1 (2008), pp. 5–36.

'Women's Engagement with Development and the UN: Pointers for the Future' (with Shubha Chacko), *Forum for Development Studies*, vol. 35, no. 1 (2008), pp. 5–36.

'On Time as a Measure of Value', Institute of Social Studies Trust, New Delhi, 2009.

'Walking Together: The Journey of the Non-Aligned Movement and the Women's Movement' (with Shubha Chacko), *Development in Practice*, vol. 19, no. 7 (2009), pp. 895–905.

'Engaging with Economic Growth: Learning from the Ground', in Christa Wichterich (ed.), *The Search for Economic Alternatives for Gender and Social Justice: Voices from India* (Brussels: WIDE, 2010), pp. 15–19.

'Morals in Politics: The Gandhian Touch', *Man in India*, vol. 90, nos 1–2 (2010), pp. 47–59.

'Yojana Bhavan and "Public Reasoning"', *Economic & Political Weekly*, vol. 55, no. 52 (2010), pp. 4–5.

'Once Were Warriors?' in Ritu Menon (ed.), *Making a Difference* (New Delhi: Women Unlimited, 2011), pp. 105–22.

'Chameli Devi Jain', in Latika Padgaonkar and Shubha Singh (eds), *Making News, Breaking News, Her Own Way* (New Delhi: Westland, 2012), pp. 1–2.

'Passion: Driving the Feminist Movement Forward', *Journal of Women's History*, vol. 24, no. 4 (2012), pp. 201–7.

'Social Income and Insecurity: A Study in Gujarat' (with Guy Standing, Jeemol Unni, Renana Jhabvala and Uma Rani), *Feminist Economics*, vol. 18, no. 3 (2012), pp. 144–45.

'Women's Participation in the History of Ideas and Restructuring of Knowledge', Working Paper WP4-2012, National Institute of Advanced Studies, Bangalore, 2012, http://eprints.nias.res.in/770/1/2012-WP4-Women%27s%20Participation%20in%20the%20History%20of%20Ideas%20and%20Reconstruction%20of%20Knowledge.pdf (accessed 16 April 2018).

'Engendering Economic Progress', in *Redistributing Care: The Policy Challenge* (UN ECLAC, 2013).

'Beyond the UN: Towards Feminist Movements' (assisted by Neha Choudhary), 2015 (unpublished).

'Understanding Leadership: Lessons from the Women's Movement', in Omita Goyal (ed.), *Interrogating Women's Leadership and Empowerment* (New Delhi: Sage Publications, 2015).

'The Evolution of Ideas: A Feminist's Reflections on the Partnership with the UN System', in Ellen Chesler and Terry McGovern (eds), *Women and Girls Rising: Progress and Resistance around the World* (New York: Routledge, 2016).

'Looking Back at the South Commission', *Economic & Political Weekly*, vol. 51, no. 9 (2016), pp. 62–66.

'Together and Apart with the Big Four: Retrospecting the Post-1975 Decades' (assisted by Neha Choudhary and Smriti Sharma), *Indian Journal of Gender Studies*, vol. 24, no. 1 (2017), pp. 73–79.

'Women of the South: Engaging with the UN as a Diplomatic Manoeuvre', in Jennifer A. Cassidy (ed.), *Gender and Diplomacy* (New York: Routledge, 2017).

'The Power of Ideas: 50 Years of Development in South Asia' (with Shubha Chacko), South Asia Society for International Development.

'Women's Contribution to Political Economy: Then and Now' (assisted by Supriya Seth) (unpublished).

PAPERS PRESENTED/KEYNOTE ADDRESSES

'Importance of Age and Sex Specific Data Collection in Household Surveys', Economic and Social Commission for Asia and Pacific, Bangkok, 1980.

'Role of Women's Organizations in Third World and ECDC: Research and Information System for the Non-aligned and Other Developing Countries', Second RIS Conference, New Delhi, 20–22 November 1985.

'Visibility of Women in Statistics and Indicators: Changing Perspective', lecture, Bombay, 1986.

'Women for a Meaningful Summit', International Assembly, Athens, 7–9 November 1986.

'Alliances and Ethics: In Retrospect', Inter-Action Forum, 'New Beginnings, New Approaches: North-South Partnership', Philadelphia, 1 May 1988.

'Alternative Development for Women', lecture, Women's Studies Seminar Programme, 1988.

'Development South Style', paper prepared for the Working Party on Development, South Commission, Geneva, 2–4 November 1988.

'Economic Programmes in National Perspective Plan for Women, 1988–2000 AD', National Conference on 'Women and Development', Jaipur, 12 February 1989.

'Implication for Women in Unorganised Sector', New Initiatives for North-East India, Shillong, 1989.

'In Search of an Identity: The Asian Woman', Role and Rights of Young Women in Asia, Asian Students Association, 1989.

'Learning from Those amongst Us: The Making of an Earth Citizen', Vigyan Bhavan, New Delhi, 16–19 January 1989.

'Revaluing Women's Roles', paper presented at the South Asia Conference on 'Population Trends and Family Planning', New Delhi, 14–20 March 1989.

'Can We Have a Women's Agenda for Global Development?', Five Years after Nairobi Conference, NOI Association, Netherlands, 3 November 1990.

'The New Balance: A View from the South', Cotonou Meetings, Foundation de France, Benin, 8–11 January 1991.

'Some Proposals for More Effective Implementation', Indian Society on Education with Special Reference to Education of the Disadvantaged Groups, Seminar on 'School Education in the 1990s: Problems and Perspectives', September 1991.

'Women in Public Life: A Case Study', India Expert Group Meeting, Vienna International Centre, 21–24 May 1991.

'Women's Economic Contributions to Families' (with Sonalde Desai), Institute of Social Studies Trust, New Delhi, 15–16 September 1991.

'"Adjusting" the Informal Sector: A Gender Development', Position Paper, UNESCO International Network for Research and Action on the Informal Sector, Bogor, Jakarta, 2–5 November 1992.

'Women: New Visions of Leadership', presentation at the Global Forum of Women, Dublin, 9–12 July 1992.

'Leadership: A Challenge to Feminists', Sixth National Conference of the Indian Association for Women's Studies, Mysore, 31 May–3 June 1993.

'Learning from the People of South Africa', National Development Conference, Cape Town, 1994.

'Necessary Conditions for Sustainable Development with Reference to North–South Relations: Is There a South?', Netherlands, 16 April 1994.

'Capitalising on Restlessness: Women's Opportunity to Transform Leadership', Inaugural Address, Commonwealth Universities Meet, SNDT Women's University, Mumbai, 15 November 1995.

'An Indian Perspective', World Conference on Women, Beijing, September 1995.

'Is There a Special Quality in Women's Leadership?', Keynote Address, National Conference of University Women's Associations, Madras, 1995.

'Minds, Not Bodies: Expanding the Notion of Gender in Development', Bradford Morse Memorial Lecture, Opening Plenary at the Fourth World Conference on Women, Beijing, September 1995.

'Removing Discrimination and Poverty: The Importance of Exemplars', Third Convocation Address, University of Tirunelveli, 18 October 1995.

'Rethinking the Indian Agenda', Keynote Address, Post-Beijing Information Seminar, British Council, New Delhi, 30 October 1995.

'Women and Trade Liberalisation: South Asia's Opportunities', UNIFEM, 30 January 1995.

'Feminist Premises for Economic Reforms', Keynote Address, *Through Women's Eyes: Gender and Economic Reforms*, exhibition and pamphlet, British Council, 1996.

'Beyond Networking: Towards Ideation' (with Supriya George), symposium on the 20th Anniversary of the National Women's Education Centre, International Forum on Women and Lifelong Learning, Saitama, Japan, 14–16 November 1997.

'Can Women Be a Political Force?' (with Vasundhara Kumar), seminar on 'Strengthening Civil Society: Voluntary Actions, Government Responses', 18–20 July 1997.

'Feminism and Feminist: A Dialogue' (with Supriya Seth), panel on 'Indigenous Feminism: Concepts, Experiments, Limitations', conference on 'Cultural Transformations in Post-colonial India', Asiatic Society of Mumbai, October 1997.

'Gender Equity and Gender Justice: Participating in India's Journey towards a Just and Peaceful Society', seminar on 'Sustainable India: Strengthening the Role of the Civil Society', New Delhi, 7–8 February 1997.

'Issues, Experiences and Initiatives in Taking Women's Agenda into the National Landscape', International Specialised Conference on 'Women and Governance: Balancing Gender Agenda with the National', 1997.

'Placing Reproductive Rights in a Framework of Overall Rights and Political Restructuring of Development', CARE India, 14 July 1997.

'Political Restructuring: Deepening Representation and Dealing with Pluralism with Reference to Women's Participation', India–South Africa Round Table, Cape Town, 15–16 May 1997.

'The Poverty Thing, or This Thing Called Poverty', UNDP, New York, 20 May 1997.

'Role of Women in the Urban Local Bodies in the Context of Constitution 74th Amendment Act', National Seminar, Ministry of Urban Affairs and Employment, Government of India, New Delhi, 1997.

'Women's Political Presence and Political Rights in India', International Development Conference, Washington, D.C., 1997.

'Close Encounters of Another Kind: Building Regional Economic Cooperation on Women's Advice and Leadership', seminar on 'Relevance of Mainstreaming the Concerns of Women in Bank Activities', Asian Development Bank, Manila, 2 March 1998.

'Special Development: Sharing of Experience', workshop with social workers from Chatsworth and surrounding areas, Durban, 18 June 1998.

'Home Thoughts from Abroad', University of Westville, Durban, 1999.

'Nuancing Globalisation or Mainstreaming the Downstream or Reforming Reform: As You Like It', Nita Barrow Memorial Lecture, Centre for Gender and Development Studies, University of the West Indies, Barbados, 12 November 1999.

'Once Were Warriors: A Retrospect on Building ISST', UGC and IAWS workshop, Chandigarh, 15–17 April 1999.

'The Role of People's Movements in Economics and Social Transformation', paper presented at the opening thematic plenary, International Conference of NGOs, 'The Role of NGOs in the 21st Century: Inspire, Empower, Act', Seoul, 10–16 October 1999.

'The Torture of Women: Some Dimensions', Lecture, 7th International Symposium on Torture, New Delhi, September 1999.

'Democratising Culture', seminar on 'Culture, Democracy and Development in South Asia', India International Centre, New Delhi, 24–25 March 2000.

Gender Advocacy Programme, Cape Town, 20–27 September 2000. Papers prepared: (a) 'Women, Economics and Development'; (b) 'Exploring Sustainable Social Development through a Gender Lens'; (c) 'International Trends and Lessons from India on Gender and Social Policy'; (d) 'Inequality and Information Technology: Report on the State of the World Forum or Alternative Millennium Summit'; (e) 'Learning from Racism to Deal with Sexism'.

'Gender and Globalisation', National Conference on Human Rights, Social Movements, Globalization and the Law, Panchgani, Maharashtra, 27 December 2000.

'How Important Is the Public Private Dichotomy: The Case of the EWRs', seminar on 'Women in Panchayat Raj', New Delhi, 27–28 April 2000.

'The Importance of Federating Women Members of Panchayat Bodies', Keynote Address, State Level Convention of Women Panchayat Presidents, Chennai, 18 October 2000.

'Inequality and Information Technology', Report on the State of the World Forum or Alternative Millennium Summit, New York, 17 September 2000.

'Journeys: What Have We Not Done? Where Have We Gone Wrong?', paper presented at CONGO Special Session, 3 June 2000.

'On Hermits and Caves: Woman Talk', Inter-Generational Round Table, New York, 3 June 2000.

'Some Current Economic Considerations', National Institute of Advanced Studies, Bangalore, 4 March 2000.

'The South Asian Drama', State of the World Forum, Development Cooperation for Poverty Reduction in South Asia, 2000.

'Strategies for Collective Action: Focus on the Global South', Bombay, 31 July–1 August 2000.

'Using the Handle of Regulation to Revive the Space for Social Justice', Economic Dimensions of Globalization Panel, 7 June 2000.

'Women's Contribution to Human Rights and Human Development', National Symposium on Human Rights and Human Development, Panel on 'Women's Contribution to Human Rights and Human Development', National Human Rights Commission and UNDP, New Delhi, 12 September 2000.

'Through the Looking Glass of Poverty', paper presented at New Hall College, University of Cambridge, 19 October 2001.

'Valuing Women: Signals from the Ground', paper presented at a Seminar on 'Cultural Diversity and Universal Norms', University of Maryland, 1 June 2001.

'A View of Racism, Racial Discrimination, Xenophobia and Related Intolerance through the Gender Lens', paper presented at a seminar organised by the National Human Rights Commission and the National Law School of India University, Bangalore, 3 August 2001.

'Challenges to the Women's Movement', Southern Regional Conference of the National Alliance of Women, Bangalore, 2002.

'Enabling Poverty and Inequality Reduction in South Asia', UNFPA Retreat, New York, 2002.

'Globalisation and Human Development: Cross-border Enlightenment', panel discussion jointly organised by the Parliamentarians' Forum for Human Development and the UNDP at the launch of the *Report on Human Development in South Asia 2001*, February 2002.

'Globalism and Localism: Negotiating Feminist Space', conference on 'Rethinking Gender, Democracy and Development: Is Decentralisation a Tool for Local Effective Political Voice?', Ferrara University and Modena University, Italy, 20–22 May 2002.

'Many New Faces of Economic Development and Some Questions on How to Land Justice', paper prepared for the North-South Round Table on 'Imperatives of Tolerance and Justice in a Globalized World', Cairo, 26–27 November 2002.

'Networks, People's Movements, and Alliances: Learning from the Ground', Know-How Conference, ISIS Women's International Cross-cultural Exchange, July 2002.

'Political Participation: A Crucial Key to Development with Justice', paper presented at Workshop IV on 'Decentralization and Institutionalizing Participatory Process: DFID, Civil Society, the Poor and Policy', 20–24 April 2002.

'Sustainable Development Is That Which Poor, Especially Poor Women, Can Sustain, Not What Sustains the Poor', paper presented at the UNFPA panel on 'Population in Sustainable Development: Reproductive Health and Gender in Poverty Reduction', South Africa, 27 August 2002.

'That We Have Not Done? Where We Have Been Mistaken?', Conference of NGOs, June 2002.

'The Value of the Particular to the General: South Asia and the United Nations', Working Group on Governance, 26 May 2002.

'Are We Knowledge Proof? Development as Waste', Lovraj Kumar Memorial Lecture, Society for Promotion of Wastelands Development, New Delhi, 25 September 2003.

'Building Budgets from Below: Women Design Fiscal Policy in Karnataka', October 2003.

'Putting Development as Freedom or the Sen Formula on the Ground', panel at the National Seminar on 'Development as Freedom: An Indian Perspective', New Delhi, 31 July–1 August 2003.

'Generating Data from Below', National Workshop on 'Experience Sharing and Capacity Building for Engendering Statistics', Thiruvananthapuram, 11–15 October 2004.

'Localizing the Global: The Double Challenge of Decentralization and Inclusion of Women', International Meeting on Local Level Gender Budgeting, India International Centre, New Delhi, 1–4 November 2004.

'Rethinking the Need for and Structure of the National Machineries for Women's Advancements', paper prepared for the UN Division for the Advancement of Women, 'The Role of National Mechanisms in Promoting Gender Equality and the Empowerment of Women: Achievements, Gaps and Challenges', Rome, 29 November 2004–2 December 2004.

'Women's Participation in the History of Ideas: The Importance of Reconstructing Knowledge', paper presented at the National Institute of Advanced Studies, Bangalore, 6 February 2004.

'Women's Rights between the UN Human Rights Framework and Free Trade Agreements: Don't Bother about the Colour', Keynote Address, WIDE's Annual Conference 'Globalising Women's Rights', Bonn, 19–22 May 2004.

'Human Rights and Development', presented at the panel on 'Human Rights and Global Economy: State and Non-State Actors', Lucerne, 10 April 2005.

'Strategies for Women's Development', Jnanabharthi, Bangalore University, 3–5 February 2005.

'To Be or Not to Be? The Location of Women in Public Policy', International Conference on 'Development in Karnataka: A Multidisciplinary Perspective', Bangalore, 2005.

'The Value of the Local', Keynote Address at the workshop on 'Gender Based Planning in Local Governance: Issues and Concerns', Centre for Development Studies, Trivandrum, 2005.

'What Does It Take to Become a Citizen? Some Neglected Collective Identities in Building "Nation"', seminar on 'Democracy, Communalism, Secularism and the Dilemmas of Indian Nationhood', New Delhi, January 2005.

'Women's Work and Rights', National Conference on 'Engendering Macroeconomics and Macroeconomic Policies', Mumbai, 29–30 September 2005.

'Lessons from History: The 60 Year Playing Out of the UN with Women and Development', Wellesley, 9 March 2006.

'Where the Outcome Document Can Be Influenced to Advance the Status of Women', NGO CSW Opening Session, New York, 6 February 2006.

'Women, Public Policy and the New World Order', lecture delivered at India Habitat Centre, New Delhi, 2 May 2006.

'Engendering MDG Based National Development Planning', Global Learning Workshop, 3–5 December 2007.

'Growth, Poverty and Inequality: The Linkage and Relevance of Macroeconomic Policies', 'Gender Equality, Economic Growth and Poverty Reduction', UNDP Expert Group Meeting, Essex University, 21–22 June 2007.

'Invoking Gyana: Women's Knowing as a Vehicle for Rebellion', background paper for the Casablanca Dreamers meeting 'Women Weave Peace into Globalisation', Morocco, 12–15 January 2007.

'The Power of Ideas: 50 Years of Development in South Asia—Shifting Our Focus from Action to Ideation', Colombo, 11–12 May 2007.

'Reversing Relationships: Changing the Terms of Reference of Women with the Official and Nonofficial Domains—from How to "Do" Development with Women to How Women "Do" Development', Oxford, April 2007.

'Shifting Our Platform in Response to Current Ground Level Phenomena' (with Shubha Chacko), Foursth World Congress of Rural Women, 'Current Developments on Issues Pertaining to Rural Women', Durban, 23–26 April 2007.

'The Value of Time Use Studies in Gendering Policy and Programme', paper presented at the International Seminar on 'Mainstreaming Time Use Survey in the National Statistical System in India', Goa, 24–25 May 2007.

'Contextualising Women's Work within the Current Macroeconomic Incentives in India' (with Reiko Tsushima), paper presented at International Labour Organization meeting, Boston, May 2008.

'Feminist Economists Engage with India's Eleventh Five Year Plan' (with Syeda Hameed, assisted by Priyanka Mukherjee and Divya Alexander), paper for the International Association for Feminist Economics conference on 'Engendering Economic Policy', Boston, 2009.

'Gendering the Macroeconomic Sky', paper presented at the UN ESCAP High-Level Intergovernmental Meeting to Review Regional Implementation of the Beijing Platform for Action and Its Regional and Global Outcomes, Bangkok, 16–18 November 2009.

'Interrogating and Rebuilding Progress', 54th Session on the Status of Women, New York, 2010.

'Unfolding the Story of Women's Journey with Development', UNDP, 14 April 2010.

'The Contribution of Women from the Lowest Income Groups to the Economy: How Time-Use Studies Can Enable an Accurate Valuation', ECLAC Conference, Santiago, 2011.

'Enabling the Aam Aurat: The Purpose of Planning Process', paper presented at the UN, New York, September 2011.

'Food Battles, or Battling for Food', UN HRC Session on 'Women: Right to Food, Food Security, Food Sovereignty', Geneva, 9 March 2011.

'The Importance of Accurate Valuation of the Contribution to Society and Economy and GDP Growth, by Women from the Lowest Income Groups: How Time Use Studies Can Enable Such an Effort', conference on 'Sexual Division of Labor', ECLAC, Chile, November 2011.

'Integrating Unpaid Work in Macroeconomics', International Workshop on 'Towards Harmonisation of Time Use Surveys at the Global Level with Special Reference to Developing Countries', New Delhi, 8 April 2011.

'The New World Reorder: An Opportunity to Build/Introduce Feminist Political Economy/Ideas', International Association for Feminist Economics, June 2011.

'Sexual Division of Labor: What Transformative Policies?', ECLAC Conference, Santiago, October 2011.

'Vision for a Better World: From Economic Crisis to Equality' (with Diane Elson, in collaboration with the Casablanca Dreamers), paper presented at the 54th Commission on the Status of Women, UNDP, New York, 2011.

'Exploring the Growth Trajectories of India and China through a Gendered Lens', Barcelona, 27 June 2012.

'Multiple Global Crises and Gender: Rethinking Alternative Paths for Development', Geneva, 25 June 2012.

'Time for a Game Shift: Multiple Global Crises and Gender—Rethinking Alternative Paths for Development', Palais des Nations, Geneva, 25 June 2012.

'Political Action for Economic Justice: A Possibility in India', panel discussion at India International Centre, New Delhi, 24 September 2013.

'Transacting Women/Gender with the "Other": Some Reflections', Nehru Centre, London, 1 July 2013.

'The Evolution of Ideas: A Feminist's Reflections on the Partnership with the UN System', conference on 'Women and Girls Rising: Historical Reflections and Future Prospects', New York, 11–12 September 2014.

'Looking Back at the South Commission', Ambedkar University Delhi, 11 February 2015.

'Thinking Together on Hierarchies and Eminence', Prof. S. Saroj Memorial Lecture, Indian Institute of Public Administration, New Delhi, 10 February 2015.

'The NAM Summit, Trade and Women', paper presented at UN ESCAP, 27 February 2016.

'Enabling Population Stabilisation through Women's Leadership in Local Self-Government: A Proposal for the Department's New Scheme' (with V. S. Elizabeth), National Institute of Health and Family Welfare, New Delhi, 18 February 2017.

'Gandhi, Inequality and the Last Girl', conference on 'Gandhi, Satyagraha and Women's Movements', ApneAap Worldwide and India International Centre, New Delhi, 30 March 2017.

REPORTS/STUDIES

'Building a Monitoring Framework for Gender Equity: Review, Analysis and Recommendations from an Exercise in 8 Districts', Karnataka Women's Information and Resource Centre (n.d.).

'Anthropological Perspective on Women's Collective Action: An Assessment of the Decade, 1975–85'.

'Methods for the Integration of Women's Issues in Development Planning: Attaining Plan Objectives', 5–9 October, Paris.

'From Dissociation to Rehabilitation: Report of an Experiment to Promote Self-Employment in an Urban Area', *Women in a Developing Economy: Report* (New Delhi: Allied Publishers, 1975).

'Employment of Women', workshop on 'Women and Development', National Institute of Public Cooperation and Child Development, New Delhi, 27–31 January 1976.

'The Experience in Implementation of the Equal Remuneration Act (ERA)', Institute of Social Studies Trust, New Delhi, 1976.

'Note for Proposal for Preparing Social Development Plans for Certain Selected States', 16 September 1976.

Draft Recommendations, Committee on Rural Employment, National Conference on Women and Development, 20 May 1979.

'Impact on Women Workers: Maharashtra Employment Guarantee Scheme', International Labour Organization, Geneva, 1979 (mimeo).

'Note for Committee on Fiscal Policy and Employment Promotion', 1979.

'Rural Children at Work: Preliminary Results of a Pilot Study' (with Malini Chand), *Indian Journal of Social Work*, vol. 2, no. 2 (1979).

'Report on Agenda Item no. 10: Household Surveys as Source of Statistics on Women, Children and Youth', 1980.

'Women's Employment as Related to Rural Areas: India', World Conference of United Nations: Mid-decade for Women, Copenhagen, 9–13 July 1980.

'HMS Employment Promotion Project: Employment Promotion with Special Reference to Women and Children', 1981.

'Patterns of Female Work: Implications for Statistical Design, Economic Classification and Social Priorities' (with Malini Chand), National Conference on Women's Studies, Bombay, 20–24 April 1981.

'Women and Planning Methodology: Comment on the Sixth Plan', 1981.

'Changing Status of Women in East Europe', Report of a Conference, *Economic & Political Weekly*, 8 February 1982.

'Report on a Time Allocation Study: Its Methodological Implications' (with Malini Chand), Institute of Social Studies Trust, New Delhi, 1982.

'Household Food Security: A Production–Consumption Link', Food and Agriculture Organization, Rome, 1983.

'Report on All-India 2-Day Workshop of the Self-Employed Women's Association', SEWA, Ahmedabad, 24–25 November 1983.

'Indian Female Households', Institute of Social Studies Trust and International Labour Organization, New Delhi, 1984.

'Women and Their Households: The Relevance of Men and Macro Policies—An Indian Perspective', paper prepared for the first ISST Study on 'Indian Female Headed Households', International Labour Organization, 1984.

'Role of Women in Development: An Intergovernmental Conference of Another Kind', *Mainstream*, 1985.

'Statistics on Women, Children and Aged in Agriculture in India: A Case Study', 1985.

'Alternative Development for Women', Institute of Social Studies Trust, New Delhi, and Mediterranean Women's Studies Institute, Kengme, July 1986.

'Notes on Alternative Development', National Conference on Women's Studies, Chandigarh, 1–4 October 1986.

'Some Issues Related to Women and Landlessness', 1986.

'Women, Religion and Social Change', IPSA workshop on 'Women, Religion and Politics', 14 August 1986.

'Perspective Emerging from Women's Experience', Peace and Conflict Resolution in the World Community, 1987.

'Building on Existing Bridges', paper prepared for Working Party on Development, South Commission, Kuwait, 22–23 October 1988.

'Empowering of Women in the Decision Making Processes in the Households, Society and Politics: Women's Political Consciousness', workshop on 'The Status of Widows, Abandoned and Destitute Women in India', 1988.

'India Arrangements for Safeguarding Women's Rights: An Area for Indo-Japanese Cooperation', 1989.

'Visibility of Women in Statistics and Indicators: Changing Perspectives', 3–7 July 1989.

'Women and Their Households: The Relevance of Men and Macro Policies, an Indian Perspective' (with Mukul Mukherjee), Institute of Social Studies Trust, 1989.

'Women, Work and Employment', Indian Council of Social Science Research, April 1989.

'Note for the Planning Commission: International Dimension of National Planning', 23 January 1990.

'The Working Girl Child', paper presented at the seminar on 'Problems of Girl Child and Remedial Measures', 9–10 June 1990.

'Women in Extreme Poverty (WEP) and the Global Political Economy: The Intersections', Institute of Social Studies Trust Seminar on Women in Extreme Poverty, Vienna, 9–12 November 1992.

'Pro-poor, Pro-environment, Pro-women', draft for the M. S. Swaminathan Committee, 12 December 1993.

'Panchayati Raj: An Institutional Platform for Women's Leadership—A Success Story from India', Panel on Women in Governance, UNDP, New York, 1995.

'Towards South Asian Solidarity: A Challenge to the Women's Movement', UNIFEM, 30 January 1995.

'The Woman Worker and Her Child Dossier', Women's Studies Resource Centre, Institute of Social Studies Trust, 1995.

'Building Closer Cooperation: Role of Women in Economy and Society', India–Japan Study Committee Meeting, Goa, 1997.

'Role of Women in Urban Local Bodies in the Context of Constitution 74th Amendment Act', 7–8 March 1997.

'Women's Studies: A Crucial Key to Feminist Purpose', International Forum on Women and Lifelong Learning, Saitama, Japan, 14–16 November 1997.

'Challenges and Opportunities: Liberia Looks Forward', Draft of a Diagnostic Analysis to Initiate a Situational Analysis, Monrovia, 1999.

'Health as a Force for Poverty', panel session on 'Health: A Force for Poverty Reduction', Social Summit +5, World Health Organization, Geneva, 2000.

'How Important Is the Private–Public Dichotomy: The Case of the EWRS', seminar on 'Women in Panchayat Raj: PRI Impact on Private Structure (Domestic Sphere)', New Delhi, 27–28 April 2000.

'Inequality and Information Technology: Report on the State of the World Forum or Alternative Millennium Summit', New York, 17 September 2000.

'Integrating LDCs in the Global Economy', UNCTAD, 2000.

'Women and the United Nations: Proposal for Collective Recall Meets', United Nations Intellectual History Project, October 2001.

'Globalization, Gender and Poverty: Sustainable Development Is That Which the Poor, Especially Poor Women Can Sustain Not What Sustains the Poor', report presented at UNFPA panel, South Africa, 27 August 2002.

'Governance and the Poor: A View from the Grassroots', Development, Governance and the Private Sector, 6 December 2002.

'Enabling Population Stabilisation through Women's Leadership in Local Self-Government: A Proposal for the Department's New Scheme' (with V. S. Elizabeth), National Institute of Health and Family Welfare, New Delhi, 17–18 February 2003.

'Gendering Public Policy: A Challenge before Data Producers and Users', Trivandrum, 11 October 2004.

'Globalizing Women's Rights: Confronting Unequal Development between the UN Rights Framework and WTO Trade Agreements', Bonn, 19–22 May 2004.

'Locating Our Work Programme in the South Asian Landscape', Fifth South Asia Regional Conference on Gender Responsive Budgeting, Bangalore, 19–20 October 2005.

'Study of Planning at the Grassroots Level: First Draft Report', December 2005.

'Engendering the Eleventh Five Year Plan from Below', Southern Regional Consultation on Engendering the Eleventh Five Year Plan from the Perspective of the Marginalized Sections of Society: Dalits, Tribals, Minorities, Urban Poor and the Unorganized Sector of Labour, Planning Commission of India, Department of Women and Child Development, UNIFEM and UNDP, 6 April 2006.

'Economic Growth and Women's Work: An Analysis' (with Shubha Chacko), RABAT (UNDP Project), December 2008.

'Influencing Planning: Constitution of Working Group on Panchayati Raj Institutions and Rural Governance for the Formulation of the Twelfth Five Year Plan (2012–2017)', Planning Commission, Government of India, New Delhi, 5 April 2011.

'The Value of Gendered Analysis of Macro-economic Policies and Programmes: Global and National', 14 September 2012.

'Co-ordinated Action to Address the Needs of Survivors of Sexual Assault: The Way Forward', Civil Society Window series of the Planning Commission, 13 February 2013 (note by Devaki Jain).

'Violence against Women: Implications for Political Economy: Report', 14 March 2013.

MONOGRAPHS

'The Leadership Gap: A Challenge to Feminists', India Association for Women's Studies, 1993.

'Minds, Bodies, and Exemplars: Reflections at Beijing and Beyond', New Delhi, 1996.

'How Women's Leadership Can Transform the Nation: Durgabai Showed the Way', Dr Durgabai Deshmukh Memorial Lecture, Hyderabad, 2004.

'What Is Wrong with Economics? Can the Aam Aurat Redefine Economic Reasoning?', Council for Social Development and India International Centre, New Delhi, 2011.

'Panchayati Raj: Women Changing Governance', *Gender in Development* series no. 5, 1996.

'Indian Women: Today and Tomorrow', Padmaja Naidu Memorial Lecture, Nehru Memorial Museum and Library, New Delhi, 1982.

'Give Girls a Chance: End Child Labour', National Commission for Protection of Child Rights, 12 June 2009.

'Role of Women in Decentralization' (with C. P. Sujaya), International Conference on Democratic Decentralisation, Thiruvananthapuram, 23–27 May 2000.

'Women, Economics and Development', seminar at University of the Western Cape, 2000, http://pmg-assets.s3-website-eu-west-1.amazonaws.com/docs/2000/appendices/000927Jain.htm (accessed 17 April 2018).

'Renaissance as Reconstruction and Other Themes', SANGOCO, South Africa, 1998.

'For Women to Lead: Ideas and Experiences from Asia—A Study on the Legal and Political Impediments to Gender Equality in Governance', Management and Governance Division, UNDP, New York, 1997.

'Minds, Not Bodies: Expanding the Notion of Gender in Development', Bradford Morse Memorial Lecture, UNDP-Beijing, 5 September 1995.

ARTICLES IN NEWSPAPERS AND MAGAZINES

'Are Women Separate Issues?', *Mainstream*, 12 August 1978.

'Subordination of Women: Analysis Needs New Categories', *Mainstream*, 26 January 1979.

'Journey of a Woman Freedom Fighter', *Mainstream*, 22 August 1981.

'Indian Women Today and Tomorrow', *Mainstream*, 9 April 1983.

'Amethi and Beyond', *Mainstream*, 9 December 1989.

'Involuntary Controls: No Place for the 79th Amendment Bill', *Indian Express*, 2 April 1994.

'World Conference on Women: An Indian Perspective', *Mainstream*, 26 August 1995.

'Women and Elections: A Lost Opportunity', *Times of India*, 1 May 1996.

'The Gender Lens: A Reconsideration of Women's Participation in Governance', *Hindu*, February 1997.

'Delhi Bores and Swadeshi', *Indian Express*, 3 April 1999, http://www.devakijain.com/pdf/jain_delhibores.pdf (accessed 17 April 2018).

'Gender Inequity as Racism', *Hindu*, 23 September 2000, http://www.devakijain.com/pdf/jain_genderinequity.pdf (accessed 17 April 2018).

'Inequality and Information Technology: Reducing Global Players' Role', *Deccan Herald*, 29 September 2000.

'For Whom the Bell Tolls', *Hindu*, 2 November 2000, http://www.devakijain. com/pdf/jain_narmada.pdf (accessed 17 April 2018).

'Sad End to a Tragic Life: Phoolan Devi Was a Woman of Intelligence Who Could Rise Above the Brutality She Had Undergone', *Deccan Herald*, 2 September 2001.

'Durban Flavours', *Deccan Herald*, 13 September 2001.

'Behind Every Woman… Lies History', *Hindu*, 30 April 2002.

'The Poor Got a Voice', *Hindu*, 5 September 2002, http://www.devakijain.com/ pdf/jain_thepoorgotavoice.pdf (accessed 17 April 2018).

'Revisiting the Development Paradigm', *Financial Express*, 20 July 2004.

'Spaces and Hopes', *Hindu*, 3 April 2005.

'A Feminist Mart' (with Seromena Asem), *Deccan Herald*, 26 October 2007.

'A Jewel in the Himalayan Crown', *Deccan Herald*, 13 January 2008.

'The Economic South: Economic Wars or Economic Peace?', *Mainstream*, vol. 46, no. 6 (26 January 2008).

'Numbers on the Half Sky', *Indian Express*, 28 February 2008.

'The Universal Didi', *Mainstream*, vol. 46, no. 23 (28 May 2008).

'Decongesting Economic Power', *Livemint*, 11 May 2009.

'Economic Crisis and Women: A Draft Review of Selected Sources of Knowledge', *Mainstream*, 20 June 2009.

'Sen and the Power of Language', *Livemint*, 20 August 2009.

'Women's Worth', *Hindustan Times*, 18 May 2010.

'Will Inclusive Growth Bring Swaraj for Hind?', *Asian Age*, 28 May 2010.

'Right Time to Decentralise Governance, Decision-Making', *The Age*, 11 May 2011.

'Her Journey into Feminism', *Hindu*, 3 July 2011.

'Women's Worlds: Interview, Devaki Jain', 27 July 2011.

'Too Many Head Cooks', *Financial Express*, 11 June 2012.

'Amul and the Woman Thing', *Financial Express*, 13 September 2012.

'The Reluctant Administrator: Remembering Anil Bordia', *Mainstream*, 15 September 2012.

'Dance of Life', *Hindu*, 20 October 2012.

'Agendas for Reforms?', *Mainstream*, 17 November 2012.

'The Rising of the Young at Jantar Mantar', *Hindu*, January 2013, http://www. thehindu.com/opinion/op-ed/the-rising-of-the-young-at-jantar-mantar/ article4328859.ece (accessed 17 April 2018).

'Remembering Gifted Architect Cyrus Jhabvala', *India Today*, 5 April 2013.

'The Quiet Champion of Human Rights', *Asian Age*, 24 April 2013.

'No Hands on the Loom', *Indian Express*, 6 June 2013.

'Tribute: Remembering K. S. Krishnaswamy, Essential Mysorean and Sensitive Economist', *Mainstream*, 20 July 2013.

'The Women behind Sirleaf', *Indian Express*, 14 September 2013.

'Manifestos Are Ignoring Real Issues' (with Deepshika Bhateja), *India Today*, 9 April 2014.

'"Lean In" to Be Taken Seriously' (with Deepshika Bhateja), *Hindustan Times*, 30 April 2014.

'Using Inequality to Engineer Growth' (with Deepshikha Bhateja), *Livemint*, 13 June 2014.

'New Reforms and Solution Commission Must Be Set Up' (with Smriti Sharma), *Asian Age*, 2 July 2014.

'Pitfalls of the Make in India Campaign', *Livemint*, 15 December 2014.

'Enabling Women, Energising Asia: The Unfinished Agenda for Gender Equality in Asian Development', *Outlook*, 2015.

'It's Time to Include Informal Economy in Measuring GDP', *Wire*, 2 February 2016.

'A Judgement for Women's Rights', *Hindu*, 15 February 2016.

'Women's Multiple Roles: The Need for Social Infrastructure', *Yojana*, September 2016.

Index

About the Author

Devaki Jain, Honorary Fellow St Anne's College, Oxford University, is Founder and former Director of the Institute of Social Studies Trust, New Delhi, India. She was previously a lecturer at the University of Delhi, a founding member of Development Alternatives with Women for a New Era (DAWN), member of the South Commission (chaired by Julius Nyerere), and of the UN eminent persons group concerned with child soldiers. She has an honorary doctorate from the University of Westville in Durban, Republic of South Africa, and has held fellowships at Harvard and Sussex Universities. She has been a member of State Planning boards and many of the Government of India's special committees related to gender and its inclusion.